A Mission to Civilize

Alice L. Conklin

A Mission
to Civilize

THE REPUBLICAN IDEA
OF EMPIRE IN FRANCE AND
WEST AFRICA, 1895–1930

STANFORD UNIVERSITY PRESS

STANFORD, CALIFORNIA

Stanford University Press
Stanford, California
© 1997 by the Board of Trustees of the
Leland Stanford Junior University

Printed in the United States of America

CIP data are at the back of the book

For Rob, Timothy, and David

Preface

It is January 1985, and I have just arrived in Dakar, Senegal, to continue research on France's *mission civilisatrice* under the Third Republic. Dakar is a sprawling and dusty African city, not as modern as Abidjan, or so I am told. The financial and governmental center remains much as it was under colonial times, when Dakar was the capital of France's West African federation. At independence, the gleaming white palace of the former governor general became, with only slight modification, the presidential palace. In this, the oldest planned part of the city dating back to the beginning of the century, streets still bear names such as Avenue Faidherbe, Avenue Roume (after French West Africa's third governor general), Rue Jules Ferry, Rue Victor Hugo, and Avenue Pasteur; outside the downtown, African names dominate: Avenue Lamine Gueye, Avenue Mohammed V. But the official city center has not bothered to divest itself of these markers of its former subjugation to republican France.

How should the modern historian read this particular postcolonial landscape? Are the French names signs of Senegalese indifference toward their former rulers, retained simply because no one has bothered to change them? Or, to the contrary, do they represent a continued "investment" on the part of the Senegalese government in a close relationship—cultural, economic, and diplomatic—with France? Do they evoke hostility? These questions are not easily answered, but they help get at issues that are at the heart of this book. At its most basic, the following study seeks to explore the illusions and justifications that lay behind the decision by French imperialists to erect republican signposts wherever they went at the end of the nineteenth century. Such an understanding may not in and of itself explain why these signposts remain in place today. On the other hand, it should at least guarantee that henceforth they will be read in one more way: as an ironic and salutory reminder of the cultural and ideological ways in which democratic France reconciled itself to overseas expansion for much of the twentieth century. Given the recent legislation in France denying automatic citizenship to children born on French soil of immigrant parents—a restriction also at odds with republican France's universalist rhetoric—this reminder seems not merely timely, but imperative.[1] France since the Revolution has claimed to extend a helping hand to the rest of the world while, in fact, pushing numerous "others" away. This trend was perhaps most pronounced in the colonies, but it continues to haunt France today.

This book began as a dissertation presented to Princeton University. During the early phases of the project, I was fortunate to work with four historians whose ideas and approaches to understanding the past have inspired many of my own. Arno Mayer first suggested that I work on the French idea of the *mission civilisatrice*, and has supported this project since its inception. It is from him that I learned to take the independent role of ideas in history—and the violence they cause—seriously. Natalie Zemon Davis posed stimulating questions about the possible similarities between an encroaching early modern state in rural France and a "civilizing" colonial state in nineteenth-century West Africa. It is a pleasure to thank her for her continuing interest in my study of the French outside of France. Robert Tignor brought to this undertaking the healthy skepticism of an Africanist dubious of any claims the French might have made to being committed "civilizers." His constant probing of what was "different" about the French in Africa helped me to rethink the relationship between metropole and colony. Finally, Philip Nord's work on French republicanism and continuing insistence that democratic politics and ideology have mattered in the past and continue to matter in France today have shaped this book at every stage.

As the project evolved, I benefited greatly from the reactions and support of a number of historians across the three different fields that this work ambitiously attempts to span: French history, colonial history, and African history. This book is much enriched by the close and critical reading the following friends and associates have given to portions of the manuscript: Vicki Caron, Steven Englund,

Sue Peabody, Rebecca Rogers, Herrick Chapman, Jeff Ravel, Tessie Liu, Rachel Fuchs, Michael Adas, Patricia Lorcin, Barbara Cooper, Odile Goerg, Jim Searing, Fred Cooper, Emmanuelle Saada, Jean Schmitz, and Emmanuelle Sibeud. My warmest thanks go to Richard Roberts, William Cohen, Julia Clancy-Smith, Len Berlanstein, Michael Osborne, and Frances Gouda, along with two anonymous readers, for wading through the entire manuscript at different stages of completion. Their collective and invariably incisive comments have made this final version that much stronger, and guided me through literature I had not completely mastered on my own. In addition, many of my colleagues in the History Department at the University of Rochester have read one or more chapters. I wish to thank Celia Applegate, Jean Pedersen, Stewart Weaver, Adrianna Bakos, Ted Brown, and Stanley Engerman for the encouragement that they have provided while constructively criticizing my project. Dan Borus went beyond the call of good citizenship and read every chapter at an early stage of revisions. His perceptive remarks helped me to clarify my arguments and point them in new directions.

I have presented portions of the manuscript at several seminars and colloquia, as well as at meetings of the American Historical Association and the Society for French Historical Studies. It is a pleasure to thank hosts and participants for the intellectual forum that they provided, and the stimulating discussions of my work to which they contributed. I am particularly grateful to members of the Princeton dissertation writers' group; Natalie Zemon Davis and the Davis Seminar; Sandria Freitag, the SSRC, the Chicago Humanities Institute, and the Committee on Southern Asian Studies at the University of Chicago, for organizing the Creating a Public: The European "Public Sphere" and Its Alternatives under Colonialism workshop; Timothy Tackett and the University of California, Irvine, Conference on Violence and the Democratic Tradition in France, 1789–1914; Celia Applegate and the Susan B. Anthony Center Colloquium; Leora Auslander and the Nineteenth- and Twentieth-Century European History workshop at the University of Chicago; Gene Lebovics and the New York Area French History seminar; Charles Becker and Saliou M'baye, conveners of the Commémoration du centenaire de la création de l'Afrique occidentale française colloquium; and Jean-Loup Amselle and Emmanuelle Sibeud, conveners of the Maurice Delafosse Table-Ronde.

Research in Paris, France, and Dakar, Senegal, was made possible by a Bourse Chateaubriand from the French government and a grad-

x
Preface

uate fellowship from Princeton University. A Junior leave from the University of Rochester and grant from the Susan B. Anthony Center allowed me to complete most of the revisions. In France and Senegal I was helped by many people. Marie-Antoinette Menier of the French National Archives, Section Outre-mer, and Saliou M'baye and Mamadou N'diaye of the National Archives of the Republic of Senegal rendered invaluable assistance. The archivists in the micro-film room of the French National Archives were always cheerful in the face of my endless demands for more and more *bobines*. Many of my revisions could not have been completed without the wonderful cooperation and efficiency of the Inter Library Loan Office of Rush Rhees Library at the University of Rochester. At Stanford University Press, I am most grateful to Norris Pope for his interest in and encouragement of this project, to Jan Spauschus Johnson for her responsive and expert shepherding of the manuscript through the editing process, and to Barbara Phillips for her careful copy-editing.

Finally I would like to thank a number of individuals for their constant personal encouragement (and forbearance) as I moved forward with this project. Harriet Jackson and Janet Horne have been close friends and intellectual *compagnons de route* for as long as I can remember. They have certainly heard most of the arguments in this book more times than they care to remember—and each time they have pushed me to think them through more clearly. Barbara Brooks and I have endlessly compared French and Japanese imperialism, when not exchanging stories about our children. In France, Laurence Gouy's companionship and hospitality have made every research trip there a pleasure. My brothers and sisters have supported this project since its inception. A lover of books, my mother inspired me to write my own. My father instilled in all of us a respect for education that has obviously borne fruit. Born at the halfway mark, Timothy is still too young to realize how much of my energy this book has absorbed. His younger brother, David, arrived just in time to delay the finishing touches. The distractions, frustrations, and sheer pleasure of raising both have helped me to keep the challenges of writing in perspective. I owe the most, however, to my husband, Rob, for his patience and humor, sharp editorial eye, and flexible and committed parenting. I cannot imagine having completed this book without him.

A.L.C.

Contents

Maps

A Note on Orthography and Translation

This book covers a wide range of African languages. Since there is still disagreement on their systematization, I have aimed first and foremost for consistency. I have followed wherever possible the *Unesco General History of Africa*, vol. 7, *Africa Under Colonial Domination 1880–1935*, edited by A. Adu Boahen. In extracts, spellings of proper names and ethnic groups are given as in the original French sources, except for the names of the colonies themselves, which have been translated into English. I have translated Soudan, which refers to the interior of French West Africa generally and to the colony so designated in 1920, as "Western Sudan" in order to distinguish it from the Democratic Republic of Sudan. All translations from the original French are my own.

A Mission to Civilize

Introduction

Civilization is a particularly French concept; the French invented the term in the eighteenth century and have celebrated the achievements of their own ever since. At no point in modern history, however, did the French make more claims for their civilization than during the "new" imperialism of the Third Republic. Of course all European powers at the end of the nineteenth century claimed to be carrying out the work of civilization in their overseas territories; but only in republican France was this claim elevated to the realm of official imperial doctrine. From about 1870, when France began to enlarge its holdings in Africa and Indochina, French publicists, and subsequently politicians, declared that their government alone among the Western states had a special mission to civilize the indigenous peoples now coming under its control—what the French called their *mission civilisatrice*.

This idea of a secular *mission civilisatrice* did not originate under the Third Republic; it nevertheless acquired a particularly strong resonance after the return of democratic institutions in France, as the new regime struggled to reconcile its aggressive imperialism with its republican ideals. The notion of a civilizing mission rested upon certain fundamental assumptions about the superiority of French culture and the perfectibility of humankind. It implied that France's colonial subjects were too primitive to rule themselves, but were capable of being uplifted. It intimated that the French were particularly suited, by temperament and by virtue of both their revolutionary past and their current industrial strength, to carry out this task. Last but not least, it assumed that the Third Republic had a duty and a right to remake "primitive" cultures along lines inspired by the cultural, political, and economic development of France.

The ideology of the civilizing mission could not but strike a responsive chord in a nation now publicly committed to institutionalizing the universal principles of 1789. At the end of the nineteenth century, few French citizens doubted that the French were materially and morally superior to—and that they lived in greater freedom than—the rest of the earth's inhabitants. Many may have scoffed at the idea that the Republic's empire was actually bestowing these blessings upon those ostensibly still oppressed. But no one questioned the premise of French superiority upon which the empire rested, or even that the civilizing mission could in fact be accomplished. Such convictions were part of what it meant to be French and republican in this period, and had a profound impact upon the way in which the French ran their colonies. Administrators—vastly outnumbered, and equipped with little more than their prejudices— relied upon the familiar categories of "civilization" and its inevitable opposite, "barbarism," to justify and maintain their hegemony overseas.[1] These categories served to structure how officials thought about themselves as rulers and the people whom they ruled, with complex and often contradictory consequences for French colonial policy—and French republican identity—in the twentieth century.

This book demonstrates just how powerful an idea the *mission civilisatrice* was under the Third Republic by examining how a particular group of colonial officials in a specific context—the governors general of French West Africa from 1895 to 1930—understood this mission. Scholars have too often dismissed the *mission civilisatrice* as window dressing. Or they have been content to label the French as racist, without bothering to explain the insidious and persistent appeal of colonial ideology, or to consider its relationship to policy making. I begin from a different set of premises. I argue that republican France invested the notion of a civilizing mission with a fairly specific set of meanings that set limits on what the government could and could not do in the colonies. By officially acting within these limits, the French managed to obscure the fundamental contradiction between democracy and the forcible acquisition of an empire. A second theme of this book is that the content of the republican *mission civilisatrice* between 1895 and 1930 was not in any sense static; rather, it evolved as the colonial situation and conditions in the metropole changed. Although always a mirror of larger trends within *l'hexagone* (as mainland France has come to be called since the retreat from Algeria in 1962), the republican idea of empire was also at times decisively shaped by circumstances in the empire itself. Last but not least, I hope to demonstrate that as a vision of what the colonies could become and a reflection of how France saw itself, civilization ideology, its evolution, and its influence provide essential insights into the history of modern French republicanism. Through the prism of the *mission civilisatrice*, the shifting ideals, conceits, and fears of the Third Republic between 1895 and 1930 are both sharply revealed and better explained.[2]

As a study of how the civilizing mission was interpreted in a specific colony, this book offers a new approach to empire studies and to the history of modern France. Both traditional imperial historiography and the newer field of African studies have underestimated the cultural and ideological dimension of modern French colonialism.[3] Most discussions of French imperialism have tended to dwell either on the economic motivations for acquiring colonies or the nationalist, political, and military reasons leading to overseas expansion.[4] And although there are numerous references to France's *mission civilisatrice* in case studies of colonial West African history, African historians have not systematically investigated its content. Modern African historiography has been more concerned with recovering the African experience of colonial rule than with analyzing French rationalizations of empire, or considering how colonial policy related to that of metropolitan France. This concern with African agency has made dramatically clear the limits of French hegemony in West Africa and given new visibility to the colonized; yet it has also had the paradoxical effect of making French rule appear more monolithic and unchanging than was actually the case.[5]

Older studies of French imperial ideology have limited themselves to investigating the theories propounded by publicists or the ideas developed exclusively in France about Africa.[6] More recently, newspapers, travel accounts, contemporary literature, geographical societies, colonial exhibitions, schoolbooks, and postcards and photographs have been mined for information about France's self-image as an imperial state and the rise (and fall) of public interest in the empire.[7] And with the development of postcolonial studies, cultural critics (in fields outside history, for the most part) are reexamining the discourse of French imperialism in an effort to better understand how representations of the "other" helped define a French "national" identity.[8] These older, more traditional histories as well as current research trends have carefully described the development and dissemination in France and the colonies of racial and cultural stereotypes regarding Africans and the evolution of competing imperialist doctrines in metropolitan circles. These studies, however, have not for the most part considered what relevance such ideas had for government officials whose task was to administer the "different" peoples within the French Empire. Nor have they adequately assessed the impact that changing political, social, and economic conditions in both the metropole and the colonies had upon the civilizing mission of the French.[9] Here postcolonial theory, despite its innovative exploration of the way knowledge and identities have been constructed through colonialism, is particularly open to criticism. Its concept of "coloniality," ironically, risks depriving Africans of any agency and French actions of any specificity, because it presents all colonizing cultures as essentially the same.

In the past few years, historical research on France has started to concentrate on the part played by the empire in the development of modern science, architecture, medicine, and technology.[10] This scholarship is beginning to take the notion of the civilizing mission more seriously; it has effectively demonstrated how the colonies could serve as either "laboratories" or outposts for policies formulated at home. Many of these studies have consciously sought to reintegrate the history of the colonies into that of the metropole—an approach that has served as a model for my own. In choosing to document the multiple facets of modern scientism or urbanism and their relationship to colonial rule, however, these "new" colonial historians have left unexamined the other ideological, political, and social influences that also made up France's *mission civilisatrice*. Michael Adas, for example, argues that the single most important component of French civilization ideology in the modern era was a belief in the scientific and technological superiority of the West. Lewis Pyenson has gone a step further and claimed that the essence of the civilizing mission was a disinterested desire by French (among other European) scholars to spread Western "exact" sciences around the globe.[11] While the material control of nature through science and technology was certainly central to French definitions of civilization, it always shared pride of place with a belief that republican

France had achieved unparalleled supremacy in the moral, cultural, and social spheres as well. And although Paul Rabinow's and Gwendolyn Wright's view of the colonies as laboratories for policies originating in the metropole has shed new light on the history of the Third Republic, their studies have suffered from a conceptual blind spot as well. In focusing on the colonies as an extension of France, they have tended to ignore the impact of the colonized upon French ideas and actions. The colonies were never just laboratories; they were sites, however unequal, of conflict and negotiation between colonizer and colonized, where French assumptions about the ability of Africans to evolve, and of France to civilize them, were contested and periodically reshaped.[12] Indeed, in the French-African encounter, ideas and cultural practices did more than simply emanate from the metropole. The empire also had an impact upon the culture of metropolitan France.

One way to address these neglected issues in the modern French experience of empire is to explore, in a particular imperial setting, what it was that a group of high-ranking republican administrators believed about themselves in relation to the "others" they encountered overseas, and how and why these beliefs evolved over time. This book proposes to do just that, through an analysis of thirty-five years of official rhetoric and decision making in French West Africa. Directly responsible to the colonial minister in Paris, yet strategically located in what the French deemed their most barbaric territory of all—sub-Saharan Africa—the office of the governor general in Dakar provides an ideal window onto the Third Republic's *mission civilisatrice* and its consequences.[13] By scrutinizing the directives and policy initiatives of this office, but also—at crucial junctures—tacking either to relevant developments in France or to African social realities on the ground, I seek to decenter the history of modern France and open new perspectives on the symbiotic relationship between empire and metropole.

What, then, were France's official civilizing ideas in West Africa between 1895 and 1930? French imperial ideology consistently identified civilization with one principle more than any other: mastery. Mastery not of other peoples—although ironically this would become one of civilization's prerogatives in the age of democracy; rather, mastery of nature, including the human body, and mastery of what can be called "social behavior." To put it another way, to be civilized was to be free from specific forms of tyranny: the tyranny of the elements over man, of disease over health, of instinct over reason, of ignorance over knowledge and of despotism over liberty. Mastery in all these realms was integral to France's self-definition under the Third Republic. It was because the French believed that they had triumphed over geography, climate, and disease to create new internal and external markets, and because they before all other nations had overcome oppression and superstition to form a democratic and rational government, that republican France deemed itself so civilized. By the same token, it was because the inhabitants of the non-European world were perceived to have failed on these same fronts—because they appeared to lack the crucial ability to master— that they were just as obviously barbarians, in need of civilizing.

A conflation of civilization with mastery was thus a defining and permanent characteristic of French rhetoric; yet the meaning of the *mission civilisatrice* also evolved as the colonial situation itself changed during the period under study. Before 1914, two tenets dominated French civilization doctrine, neither of which can be described as straightforwardly "assimilationist" or "associationist." First, confronted with the economic poverty of the indigenous populations, the French believed that civilization required that they improve their subjects' standard of living through the rational development, or what the French called the *mise en valeur*, of the colonies' natural and human resources. This objective, they thought, could best be achieved by building railroads—because railroads would link the interior to the coast and promote the exchange of peoples, currencies, commodities, and ideas—and by improving hygiene to eliminate the parasites deadly to Europeans and Africans. Second, the French insisted that civilization required that the different West African peoples had to evolve within their own cultures, to the extent that these cultures did not conflict with the republican principles of French civilization. When a conflict arose, the offending African mores were to be suppressed and replaced by French ones. After a prolonged struggle with African leaders in the Western Sudan, four African institutions were singled out for eradication: indigenous languages, slavery, barbaric customary law, and "feudal" chieftaincies. The republican virtues of a common language, freedom, social equality, and liberal justice were to take their place.

In the aftermath of World War I, this definition of France's civilizing mission began to change in subtle ways. Although the French did not renounce their belief that Africans had to evolve along their own lines, the administration no longer dwelt on the theme of eradicating institutions antithetical to French civilization. Instead, it spoke increasingly of the need to "associate" traditional West African chiefs and the first generation of French-educated Africans in policy making. "Association" meant that the members of the African elite were now supposed to be consulted in all decisions regarding them. In the postwar years French imperial authorities also rejected the formerly held opinion that railroads alone would trigger the desired increase in the African standard of living. The key to tapping the economic potential of the West African territories, these authorities now believed, was the *mise en valeur* of Africa's human resources. In theory, human *mise en valeur* meant a more intensive focus upon improving the African producer's health and farming methods compared to conditions and practices in the prewar era. In reality, the term reflected a renewed conviction that Africans would never progress unless the French made them progress, and that forcibly inculcating a hitherto absent work ethic constituted a crucial part of the Third Republic's civilizing mission in West Africa. These changes in French civilizing tenets were not arbitrary, but causally linked in part to several local factors, such as gradually improving knowledge of African cultures, and a series of colonial revolts against France's earlier imperial policies. One result of this change was that, after World War I, French civilizing tenets better served French interests than had the ones they replaced.

The changes in French ideology, however, naturally reflected—and helped reinforce—trends within *l'hexagone* as much as they did developments within colonial West Africa. Along with documenting the unstable nature of French ideology, I explore what the shifting parameters of the civilizing mission in West Africa can tell us about the evolution of the Third Republic during the crucial transition from the Belle Epoque to the 1920's. The most important metropolitan trend to shape the *mission civilisatrice* in West Africa between 1895 and 1930 was the persistence of a certain liberal republican vision among France's governing elite before World War I and its decline after the war. French republicanism was always multifaceted. Nevertheless, a core set of values animated republicans of all camps up through the war: an emancipatory and universalistic impulse that resisted tyranny; an ideal of self-help and mutualism that included a sanctioning of state assistance to the indigent when necessary; anticlericalism, and its attendant faith in reason, science, and progress;

an ardent patriotism founded on the creation of a loyal, disciplined, and enlightened citizenry; and a strong respect for the individual, private property, and morality.[14] All these ideas were embedded in the very terms *mission* and *civilisatrice* and influenced French policy making in West Africa. It was, for example, republican principles as much as the experience of the conquest itself that led the Government General in West Africa to condemn slavery and "feudalism" among African tribes. The Government General also adopted France's latest technological improvements, partly out of the traditional republican belief that science held one key to regenerating humanity. After World War I, these same values weakened as the Third Republic attempted to come to terms with the losses and traumas of the war and the growth of nationalist protest throughout the empire. Colonial discourse echoed this shift: established republican verities now surfaced in a more attenuated form in Dakar, replaced by a more conservative vision of progress—as the new respect for the African aristocracy and the greater emphasis on human *mise en valeur* attest.

Despite its importance, republicanism was not the only intellectual force determining the direction of social and political policy, in the metropole and overseas, in the first thirty years of the twentieth century. One of the most pervasive French civilizing conceits was the idea that colonial administrators had the ability and the right to transform African social milieux in order to improve society. Recent research on the origins of the welfare state in France suggests that this conviction echoed a new, more modern way of looking at society than that of mid-nineteenth-century liberalism. New scientific knowledge, the argument goes, led to the belief in France that society was a delicately balanced organism with its own laws and internal forces, which could be manipulated. This discovery resulted in a "postmoral" rethinking of the relationship between human society and its historical and natural environment, and the individual and the state. Some reformers became convinced that state intervention was required for a healthy, efficient, and productive social order; they also maintained that the best way to create this order was to alter the social milieu in which individuals functioned—rather than to act upon the individuals themselves. One consequence of such thinking was that by the century's end, there was little question that amelioration of all social milieux—whether metropolitan or colonial—"constituted the purest civilizing activity" possible.[15] Modern social planning, in short, had been born. This modern ameliorating impulse also pulled and pushed French civilizing rhetoric and policies in West Africa in a variety of ways, before but especially after World War I—although it never eclipsed France's more old-fashioned moralizing republican rhetoric.

And what, it might well be asked in the context of metropolitan influences overseas, of that other modern development—racism? Any book dealing with French imperialism must assess its role in France's *mission civilisatrice* in West Africa. That France witnessed a dramatic increase in scientific racist thinking after 1850 is beyond dispute. What is less clear is how race-thinking in the metropole affected the civilizing rhetoric and policy decisions in the empire at any given moment, and how actual colonization affected racist sentiment not only in West Africa but also in France. To the extent that racism is defined as the perception that certain groups—including Jews and various immigrant groups, as well as non-Western peoples of color—were fundamentally different from and inferior to white Europeans, then French officialdom was guilty of thinking in racialized categories and implementing oppressive measures throughout the life of the Third Republic. Both the language of the civilizing mission and French policies in West Africa, therefore, were racist.[16] Yet the official image of Africans, both at home and overseas, was not always negative in exactly the same way between 1895 and 1930. Subtle changes in French stereotypes of Africans, moreover, had important policy implications for the colonized. It is a final objective of this book, without ever denying the reality of French racism, to understand its particular course and permutations before and after World War I, as well as its ability to coexist unproblematically—at least in the eyes of contemporaries—with republican values in the first place.

There can, of course, be little doubt that colonization under the Third Republic was in large part an act of state-sanctioned violence. On the crudest level, the French forcibly "pacified" those West African groups who resisted colonization. On a more subtle level, French rule rested upon a set of coercive practices that violated their own democratic values. Africans were designated as subjects, not citizens. They had duties, but few rights. In neither case, however, did French republicans identify any contradiction between their democratic institutions and the acquisition and administration of their empire. This was because they viewed Africans as barbarians, and were continually undertaking—or claiming to undertake, as the case may be—civilizing measures on behalf of their subjects that appeared to make democracy and colonialism compatible. However misguided, self-deluding, or underfunded—indeed, because they were all these things—these claims merit our attention. As an enduring tension of French republicanism, the civilizing ideal in whose name the nation of the "rights of man" deprived so many people of their freedom deserves to be better understood. This book is a step in that direction.

CHAPTER I

The Setting

THE IDEA OF THE CIVILIZING MISSION IN 1895 AND THE CREATION OF THE GOVERNMENT GENERAL

The French nation renounces to undertake any war of conquest and will never use its force against the liberty of any people.
— National Assembly, 1790

The genie of Liberty, which has rendered the Republic—since its birth—the arbiter of all Europe, wishes to see it mistress of faraway seas and foreign lands.
— Napoleon Bonaparte, 1798

This revenge of civilization that everywhere is chasing away the barbarian seems to me to remain . . . the characteristic trait of our century.
— Alfred de Vigny, 1847[1]

By 1895, the *mission civilisatrice* had become the official ideology of the Third Republic's vast new empire. That same year, the French government decided to end the era of conquest in West Africa and inaugurate a new policy of "constructive exploitation." One result of this decision was the creation of a centralized civilian authority in Dakar, the Government General of French West Africa. Because our story is principally concerned with how the new governors general in Dakar interpreted their civilizing mandate, it is with a prehistory of the republican idea of the civilizing mission, as well a brief account of the founding of the Government General, that we will start.

The Civilizing Mission in 1895

The earliest references to France's *mission civilisatrice* under the Third Republic came not from politicians but from members of a nascent geographical movement in France. By the 1870's, the human and financial costs of conquering tropical territories had diminished significantly, thanks to certain technological advances, including the discovery of the prophylactic qualities of quinine and vastly improved weapons; at the same time, interest in new colonial expansion began to revive among a select republican elite in Paris. One measure of this renewed interest was the rather sudden growth of geographical societies, whose explicit aim was to promote the exploration of Africa and Asia as a prelude to commercial penetration and outright annexation.[2] New colonies would help compensate for the loss of Alsace-Lorraine, as well as combat French "decadence" in the wake of Sedan and the Paris Commune, by allowing the Republic to engage in the politics of grandeur. The publicists of the geographical movement were not, however, motivated by such pragmatic considerations alone. They also made it clear that colonies were desirable because they would, as one member said, "open up new fields for [France's] civilizing mission." The literature of the geographical societies repeated over and over this notion that the Third Republic had a particular obligation to colonize/civilize; regarding the colonization of central Africa, another member remarked that it was France's duty "to contribute to this work of civilization."[3] One of the many geographical journals bore the name *L'Exploration*, "journal of conquests of civilization on all points of the globe"; another was called *L'Afrique explorée et civilisée.*

Some of these publicists were optimistic enough to think that France's civilizing mission could proceed without the use of force, emphasizing instead the idea of moral conquest through the dissemination of ideas and exchange of commodities. No voice was more eloquent on this score than that of the young social economist and future member of the Institut, Paul Leroy-Beaulieu, in his classic plea for new colonies, *De la colonisation chez les peuples modernes*—first published in 1874, then reissued five times over the next thirty-four years for an ever more receptive audience. Leroy-Beaulieu hoped that new colonies would be acquired through commerce, with a minimum of violence. One of the most important goals of such colonies, along with revitalizing the mother country, was the peaceful "evolution [*acheminement*] of inferior peoples toward civilization."[4] Other propagandists, however, were not convinced that force could be so easily dispensed with in the civilizing process. Gabriel Charmes, a prominent journalist of the Third Republic, wrote a number of articles between 1877 and 1882 in the *Revue des Deux Mondes* about France's civilizing mission in the Far East; regarding Africa, he claimed:

> If France were able to establish itself permanently in North Africa, to penetrate to central Africa, to make its influence felt in the entire Sahara and to win the [Western] Sudan; if in these immense regions where only fanaticism and brigandage reign today, it were to bring—even at the price of spilled blood—peace, commerce, tolerance, who could say this was a poor use of force? . . . Having taught millions of men civilization and freedom would fill it with the pride that makes great peoples.[5]

These tracts revealed a growing receptiveness by government inner circles in the late 1870's to the idea of further colonial expansion. Between 1870 and 1878, Léon Gambetta, Charles de Freycinet, and Jules Ferry had shown only a limited interest in the geographical movement's imperial propaganda.[6] By 1878, however, the republican leadership began to accept the argument that for political and economic reasons France should begin asserting itself overseas. All three men would play a leading role in France's conquests of the 1880's and 1890's, and they would always add a moral argument when legitimating their actions. Ferry, addressing Parliament in the early 1880's, defended France's seizure of Tonkin and war with China in terms of a special French mission: "We must believe that if Providence deigned to confer upon us a mission by making us masters of the earth, this mission consists not of attempting an impossible fusion of the races but of simply spreading or awakening among the other races the superior notions of which we are the guardians." Two years later, in 1884, he added that "the superior races have a right vis-à-vis the inferior races . . . they have a right to civilize them." Although Ferry's policies did not go uncontested—both conservatives and the radical left criticized them—neither group questioned Ferry's claim that France had a unique civilizing mission. As Jacques Thobie has recently pointed out, even such critics as Henri Rochefort, Jules Vallès, and Pierre Loti objected only to the violent methods used to acquire new colonies; their hope, according to Thobie, was that these savages would agree to be civilized, thus making force unnecessary.[7]

Convinced of France's civilizing vocation, the ruling elite of the Third Republic soon made every effort to disseminate the idea as widely as possible. The textbooks of the new primary schools inculcated the message of a Republic generous to all, including benighted savages. The popular press reinforced this message and the attendant stereotypes of Africans and Asians as peoples lacking civilization.[8] An increasingly vocal colonial lobby of deputies and businessmen with colonial interests added its voice in the 1890's. The universal expositions of 1889 and 1900 imported colonial subjects to provide living examples of civilization in the making. These examples apparently worked, albeit in the crudest possible fashion. The official commentator of the 1889 fair in Paris, which included a large colonial section, wrote happily of the Africans present that they had shown themselves capable of progress. The proof was that, having arrived barefoot in a state of almost "complete savagery," the "blacks" in question had at least left France fully shod. Thanks to such innovations, the author concluded, "the moralizing role of France among these peoples still so far from our civilization" would be easier than in the past. By the time of the great 1931 Colonial Exposition, the government had a more sophisticated spokesman for its views—Hubert Lyautey, maréchal of France and former head of the Protectorate in Morocco—but the message was fundamentally the same: "In deciding to hold this Exposition, Parliament wished to show that in the aftermath of the murderous and fratricidal period that covered the earth with ruins, there remain, for our civilization, other fields of action than the battlefields."[9] That the Third Republic, then, consciously embraced the rhetoric of the civilizing mission as its official ideology of empire is hardly open to doubt. What is less apparent is where this language came from and with what meaning it was already invested when the republicans began to expand overseas in the 1880's and 1890's. To answer these questions, let us take a slight detour back to the origins of the French concept of civilization in the eighteenth century and its metamorphosis in the early nineteenth century.

It is probably impossible to determine when the term *"mission civilisatrice"* was first used in France. We do know that the noun "civilization" initially surfaced in the eighteenth century, although not before 1766.[10] By that time, French philosophes were searching for a word that would connote the triumph and development of reason, not only in the constitutional, political, and administrative domain, but in the moral, religious, and intellectual spheres as well—a word that would capture the essence of French achievements compared to the uncivilized world of savages, slaves, and barbarians. In the effort to convey this distinction, the term "civilization" was born. This concept of civilization was a unitary one. At the end of the eighteenth century, no one talked of civilizations, in the plural. Instead, the assumption was that there existed a single universal human civilization capable of winning over from savagery all peoples and nations.[11] This civilization was largely French in inspiration.

If the philosophes coined the word and idea of civilization, certain ancien régime colonial officials in the New World were among the first to insist that France actually could be civilizing the enslaved and subject peoples in its existing overseas territories.[12] Such men were necessarily shaped by the prevailing ideas in the metropole regarding the unity of humankind, the rights of the individual, and the most rational form of government. But they also had their own particular concerns that affected how they viewed the people they were governing. These concerns included maintaining order, protecting their own positions, ensuring the economic prosperity of the colony that had been entrusted to them, and considering new territories that could strengthen the existing empire and provide new posts. Indeed, because order and prosperity were beginning to break down in France's existing empire—an empire based on an increasingly problematic system of slave labor—some administrators took the eighteenth century's vague argument that savages were capable of being civilized and crystallized it into a coherent doctrine. Once articulated, this doctrine influenced metropolitan thinking, thanks to frequent contact between influential colonial administrators and certain philosophes.[13]

The colony causing administrators the most concern at the end of the eighteenth century was the lucrative sugar-producing island of Saint-Domingue. Continued expansion of the slave system had made for trouble in the racially divided Saint-Domingue society, placing the entire colonial economy at risk. This, at least, was the perception of many administrators there. One problem was the increasing incidence of slave rebellions in the form of marronage in Saint-Domingue and in neighboring colonies. Another was the many abuses committed by the white planters against their slaves, whose discontent was thereby exacerbated.[14] Under these circumstances, a few colonial administrators began to recognize that slaves were fellow human beings who, under other conditions than those maintained by their white owners, could be uplifted.[15] These officials also recommended that future settlement of other French territories be free of the stain of servitude; rather than importing servile labor, they argued, the French should have the local inhabitants produce voluntarily the raw materials essential to the French economy. Such cooperation could be secured by treating them properly and intermarrying with them. This alternative approach to colonial development was, moreover, repeatedly justified in terms of the concept of civilization. Colonization based on free labor could be successful because the native savages were able to be uplifted and the Europeans were in a position to civilize them.[16]

The crisis of slavery and the need for reform in the colonies of the New World was one context in which the notion of a mission to civilize began to emerge at the end of the eighteenth century. A similar trend was evident in the Enlightenment treatment of the non-European peoples of the Old World. Although historians are still debating just how negative the view of India, China, and the Middle East had become by the time of the French Revolution, clearly the philosophes who wrote about such places now deemed these older cultures, too, in need of civilization. The analogy with changing views of the inhabitants of the New World is not exact. Where slaves and Amerindians were upgraded from peoples devoid of civilization to peoples capable of it, Asians and Arabs in many early Enlightenment treatises had been placed on an equal footing with the Europeans, only now were downgraded to barbarians. And the categories of analysis were slightly different; while the savagery of most New World inhabitants was attributed to environmental factors, the barbarism of Asians and Arabs was defined in terms of oriental despotism and ignorance.[17] To civilize them would thus mean not only mastering nature and encouraging commercial exchange but also liberating them from political tyranny and superstition. In the end, however, these differences in no way altered the general conclusions of the French. By the time of the French Revolution, it was simply taken for granted that the entire non-Western world was in need of French civilization.[18] Such a claim conveniently dovetailed with the search for new territories outside the Americas that some colonial enthusiasts were now advocating.

The events of the French Revolution, both in the empire and at home, dramatically changed the way the French conceived of themselves as a nation and as a civilization, and therefore marked a new stage in the history of the *mission civilisatrice*. In Saint-Domingue, slaves inspired by events in the metropole rose in revolt in 1791 and freed themselves; their rebellion and its repression destroyed the island's sugar production and forced the new metropolitan government to consider an alternative colonial policy that would ensure France a supply of tropical exports and markets to replace those of the Caribbean. In France, the Revolution convinced the French that they "were the foremost people of the universe" and that *la grande nation* had an obligation to carry their revolutionary ideals beyond France's borders.[19] This loss of the old empire, combined with France's new nationalism, had dramatic implications for the future of French colonization. Among other things, it helped transform the Enlightenment belief that barbarians *could* be civilized into the imperial doctrine that France *should* be civilizing fettered and depraved peoples everywhere. This transformation was already complete by the time of France's first postrevolutionary colonial enterprise: Napoleon's expedition to Egypt in 1799.

Historians have rarely approached Napoleon's expedition as an imperial conquest. Many have examined it purely from the point of view of foreign policy, seeing it as an attempt by France to seize control of the Mediterranean and establish a base from which to threaten the British in India.[20] Others have simply included the conquest in a general history of France's revolutionary wars, thereby suggesting that the invasion of Egypt was no different from the annexation of Savoy or the establishment of republics in the Low Countries or Italy.[21] Such approaches are reasonable, insofar as Napoleon's adventure combined a variety of motives. Nevertheless, for all its importance to Napoleon's strategy for European hegemony or its affinities to the revolutionary wars of liberation, the Egyptian expedition was emphatically an act of colonial aggression—albeit one with a new outlook, compared to earlier overseas ventures.[22]

The colonial nature of the expedition can be seen most clearly when the entire enterprise is compared to the behavior of the revolutionaries in their conquests on the Continent. In the latter case, the Revolution saw its mission largely as one of liberation; in Egypt, however, in keeping with the general trends of the Enlightenment regarding non-Europeans, the mission was defined—in Napoleon's own words—as one of emancipation and "civilization."[23] This idea was manifest in Napoleon's decision to set off from France not only with troops, but with all the scientific and cultural apparatus for which the expedition is deservedly famous—an apparatus that the French had not deemed necessary for any European state they had conquered. At Napoleon's behest, a group of experts was gathered to accompany the conquest. These experts subsequently formed the famous Institut d'Egypte, founded by Napoleon in Cairo shortly after the French invasion. One purpose of the Institut was to lend its varied expertise to the conquerors, so that the French might effectively subdue the local populations and successfully exploit the land. Engineers, Islamicists, printers, natural scientists, artists, mathematicians, and astronomers were all to study conditions in Egypt, then place their knowledge at the service of the invading generals. These experts were also to bring the accumulated knowledge and skills of the West to the peoples of Egypt, while enriching that knowledge with information about the region and its celebrated past that had been lost since its descent into despotism and barbarism.[24]

The inclusion of this scientific "task force" clearly distinguished the Egyptian expedition from the plans for civilizing savages that colonial administrators had begun to elaborate before the Revolution. When an earlier generation spoke of the ability of barbarians to become civilized, they had not specifically envisaged the wholesale expatriation of French scientific, literary, and artistic culture—although this concept of acculturation was implicit in the philosophes' insistence that ignorance as well as despotic government contributed to the barbarism of the Muslim world. Napoleon transformed what was latent in Enlightenment discourse into a blueprint for cultural change. For him, the work of civilization included, in addition to encouraging trade, introducing the printing press, the French language, education, medicine, preventive hygiene, and the arts, as well as applying the principles of rational administration to fiscal, judicial, and land reform. With the help of the Institut, he proceeded on all these fronts during his short stay in Egypt.[25] Such a reworking and expansion of the definition of France's responsibilities as a colonizer was in the logic of the Revolution, which saw itself as remaking French society and, in the process, receiving a mandate to transform all humankind.

On the banks of the Nile, then, the idea, if not the term, of a special French mission to civilize had been born with the Republic. The word "civilization" also appears to have acquired many of the overtones that would be associated with the term *mission civilisatrice*—that is, the inculcation of new needs and wants, and the spread of French institutions and values deemed to be universally valid. The notion that the French had a special obligation to be generous toward those different from themselves and even to make them

French, which the Egyptian campaign first incarnated, would become a standard feature of postrevolutionary French colonial discourse. Yet, if Napoleon's language and actions were prescient of French colonial doctrine, two qualifications must be noted. First, the colonization of Egypt was short-lived and did not signify the crystallization of a new colonial ideology in France. Napoleon had no trouble reverting to the colonial status quo ante when he reintroduced slavery to Martinique and Guadeloupe after they were recaptured from the British in 1802. The second qualification involves the locus of the expedition itself. To an important degree, Napoleon's decision to bring all of French civilization to Egypt was determined by the view that he and his contemporaries held of the country as the original cradle of *les lumières*. For Napoleon to insist on the need to resurrect a past glory was not, however, to maintain that France had a mission to civilize all non-Western peoples. It was only in the next century that this particular language became pervasive. Similarly, a glance ahead indicates that Napoleon's characterization of his campaign as one designed to bring civilization back to its origins would not survive into the next century. In contrast to Napoleon's awe of Egypt's past, nineteenth-century empire builders assumed more often than not that they were introducing civilization rather than reintroducing it. This distinction would prove to be a crucial one, and it marked a third and final phase in the development of France's civilizing mission ideology between 1770 and 1870. Both the similarities and the differences between Napoleon's definition of civilization and the definition that prevailed for most of the next century were evident in the conquest of Algeria in 1830.

The conquest of Algeria is often said to have marked a new departure in French colonial policy, posing problems for which neither the doctrine nor the experience of the old empire provided ready answers.[26] Algeria differed from the surviving colonies of the Old Regime (Guadeloupe, Martinique, Ile de France, and Guyana) in that it was several times larger than any one of them, offered no sought-after and easily exploited colonial product, and had a large indigenous population who could not be ignored or intimidated. The conquest of Algeria engaged the emotions of the French people in a way the commercial ventures of the old empire never had. Finally, it was a campaign justified in the name of civilization.[27] In point of fact, the Egyptian campaign offered in all these respects a precedent for Algeria; not surprisingly, therefore, it was to the Egyptian campaign that policy makers turned when deciding how to proceed in their new North African possession. For example, with the Institut d'Egypte specifically in mind, the French chose to organize a commission in 1837 to "research and collect any information regarding the arts and the sciences" in Algeria. In addition, the government, at least initially, proceeded on the same assumption as Napoleon, that Muslim "fanaticism" was merely the result of ignorance and despotic rule. It followed that an important part of civilizing Algerians was offering them knowledge. This the July Monarchy promptly did, not through an *institut* staffed by *savants*, but rather through schools and hospitals.[28]

Yet the decision to organize a commission to study conditions in Algeria and the impulse to spread the benefits of science were not representative of all subsequent French actions in Algeria. From the beginning, there were hints that Algeria's new rulers would be even more pragmatic in their approach to colonization than Napoleon. Although its ultimate publications were impressive—running to thirty-nine volumes—the commission sent to Algeria in 1837 was only a partial reincarnation of the Institut. Whereas the Institut had had 151 members, the Algerian version had only 25, and 14 of them were military personnel. This military preponderance was an early sign of France's preeminent interest in Algeria. Notwithstanding the reference to promoting science, the commission's principal mandate appears to have been to learn about Algeria in order better to dominate and extract its resources.[29]

Another indication that the French outlook was changing in the 1830's and 1840's can be seen in the issue of intermarriage. The earliest advocates of a civilizing effort in the New World—certain colonial administrators—had accepted racial mixing as one obvious means to the behavioral changes they sought. This policy, although very different from Napoleon's plan to reintroduce all of civilization to Egypt, was at least as open-minded. Although colonial administrators had assumed that barbarians had no civilization of their own, their recommendation to remedy this situation through intermarriage meant that they were not overtly racist. How widespread this attitude was, like so much else in Enlightenment thought, remains subject to debate. What is clear is that sometime during the first thirty years of French rule, commentators on Algeria began to condemn the concept of racial mixing and, by extension, the universal assumptions that underwrote it.[30] By the 1870's, when the colonial publicist Leroy-Beaulieu first published his influential tract, *De la colonisation chez les peuples modernes*—a large portion of which was devoted to Algeria—the idea had largely disappeared.

It is true that Leroy-Beaulieu, specifically addressing himself to the proper relationship between French and Algerians, still spoke of the need for a fusion of the two peoples. But his choice of words is deceptive; he used "fusion" interchangeably with "rapprochement," and emphasized that what he meant was not a physical union of Europeans and Arabs, but a specific process of cultural change. Algerians were to become imbued with French civilization, but retain some of their own customs. They were to be placed under the same economic and social regime and follow the same general laws, although they were not to have the same political rights. The best way to accomplish this would be to grant them access to, and encourage them to use, such European institutions as schools, courts, and ministerial offices. At the same time, every effort would be made to transform living conditions and work habits and to increase agricultural productivity, through modern hygiene, road and railroad construction, and the introduction of private property. Finally, Algeria could not hope to be civilized unless France destroyed the Arab aristocracy, that "enemy of work . . . lover of luxury, of battles, of equestrian *fantasias*, and oppressor of the masses that it was supposed to protect," and whose very existence prevented the progress of colonization and the rapprochement of the two races.[31]

Leroy-Beaulieu's recommendations are worth contemplating, because they represented more than just the French abandoning the ideas of civilizing through intermarriage or the expatriation of all the arts and sciences. *De la colonisation chez les peuples modernes* also suggested a variety of other civilizing techniques not seen in the eighteenth century. This emphasis on establishing private property, increasing productivity and trade, and emancipating the masses from oppression had a long pedigree in French imperial ideology, to be sure.[32] Yet the attention paid to public works and public hygiene, along with the insistence that Algerians preserve some of their social customs, had not. If Leroy-Beaulieu is any measure, both a more limited acculturation of its subjects, and one in which the transfer of technology figured prominently, had emerged as the essence of France's civilizing mission in the first decade of the Third Republic.[33]

In fact, Leroy-Beaulieu's ideas can be taken as representative of

certain new trends in French civilization ideology in the second half
of the nineteenth century. Several painful experiences acquired in
the colonization of Algeria, along with the theory of biological racism and the onset of French industrialization at home, had predisposed the French to alter that ideology between 1830 and 1870. By
1837, when the scientific commission was formed, the army had
met fierce Algerian resistance. French soldiers were also dying from
malaria and other tropical diseases. Indeed, in the hostile Algerian
environment one of the greatest problems was not only defeating the
local populations, but identifying the proper hygienic measures and
civil engineering techniques that would make the country healthy
and profitable for future settlers. After fifteen years of educational
and health care efforts—in which metropolitan schools and medical
techniques were adopted in the colony without modification—the
French also discovered a stubborn refusal by most of their new subjects to embrace the gifts of Western culture and science so "gener-
ously" proffered.[34] These various forms of resistance made new scientific arguments about the inherent inferiority of other races that
much more believable. Meanwhile, with the help of modern technology and medicine, it became clear that the white race could adapt
to hot climates without intermarriage to acclimatized "natives."
These crosscurrents subdued any residual enthusiasm for offering all
of civilization's achievements to the colonized. Instead, French definitions of what it meant to be civilized began to shift to reflect the
latest European accomplishment: the mastery of nature through
technology and science.[35]

Leroy-Beaulieu's recommendations had already been anticipated
by administrators in Algeria in the 1850's and 1860's, and would
soon be widely shared both in France and throughout the empire.
Just how widespread the civilizing methods he advocated became
under the Third Republic will be shown in subsequent chapters.
Like Leroy-Beaulieu, the governors general of French West Africa
would not only argue for creating new needs and wants through increased trade. They would also emphasize the importance of controlled social change to be effected through the abolition of "feudalism," the introduction of justice and education "adapted" to the African environment, and the building of railroads and hospitals.
Nevertheless, specific circumstances in West Africa as well as the
emergence of a new republican regime in Paris would invest each of
these themes with a content all its own, before World War I and

again after it. Before turning to their ideas and policies, we must first meet these men, their institutions, and the West African lands and peoples that they ruled.

French West Africa in 1895

The Colonial Ministry in Paris established the Government General of French West Africa in 1895 and dissolved it only sixty-one years later, in 1956. Headed by a single colonial administrator in Dakar, the Government General federated all of France's recently conquered contiguous territories in West Africa—a vast area (nine times the size of France) extending east from France's historic base in the Senegambian basin, across the West African savanna as far as Lake Chad, and south through the Guinea highlands and forest, the forested regions of Ivory Coast, and Dahomey, to West Africa's southern littoral. The modern countries that occupy this area are Mauritania, Senegal, Ivory Coast, Guinea, Burkina Faso, Mali, Niger, and Benin.

The supercolony thus formed was named Afrique Occidentale Française (AOF) or the Federation of French West Africa. One of the primary reasons for instituting an overarching authority in West Africa was to decentralize decision making from the metropole. Only a senior official on the spot, the Paris government felt, would be sufficiently aware of events and conditions in the colony to make informed policy choices. A second reason for federating the West African territories was to facilitate what the French called their *mise en valeur*—a term best translated as "rational economic development." In France, policy priorities were shifting from continued expansion to the organization and development of the existing colonies. Most of the West African territories were poor and many were landlocked. Administered as autonomous colonies rather than a single unit, Paris argued, they would never prosper. Directly subordinate to the minister of colonies and responsible for both the administration and the development of the federation, the governors general of AOF occupied a pivotal position within the empire. Six governors general served in Dakar between 1895 and 1930: Ernest Roume, William Ponty, François Clozel, Joost Van Vollenhoven, Martial Merlin, and Jules Carde.

Despite the clear-cut motives for creating the Government General, the new institution was initially weak and incapable of per-

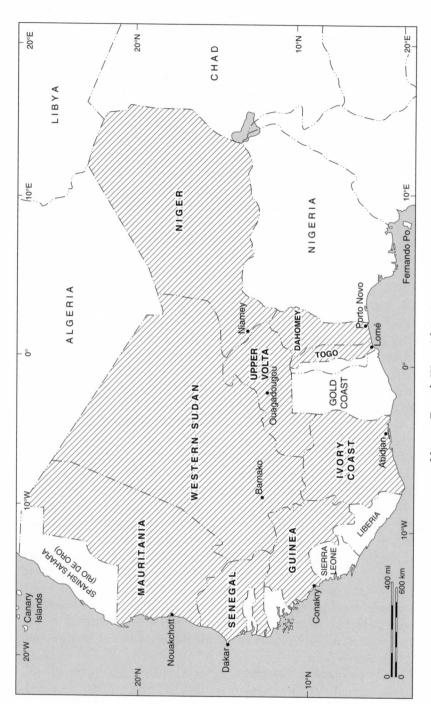

Map 1. French West Africa in 1930.

forming the economic and administrative tasks for which it had been established. The early history of the Government General was marked by repeated reforms and a rapid turnover in personnel as the government attempted to determine how to make the principle of federation work in French West Africa. This instability was partially the result of rivalry between civilian and military authorities in the colony, at a time when the conquest of West Africa was still not complete. But it was also the result of the sheer size and human diversity of the lands in question, which made the institution of any new bureaucracy problematic. Because West Africa's geography, history, and peoples are as essential as metropolitan priorities and feuding administrators to the history of the Government General and its ideology, it is with a brief overview of the physical and social landscape of West Africa that a description of the federation must start.

The dominant geographical feature of French West Africa was the savanna, a broad expanse (600 miles wide) of undulating grassland, studded with trees and bounded by the Sahara to the north and the rain forest to the south. Its soil was fertile, although its main crops, millet and sorghum, had to be grown during a short summer rainy season. A small portion of the western savanna was drained by the westward-flowing Senegal and Gambia Rivers. The Niger River and its tributaries, rising in the highlands of Guinea and flowing, first, northeast of Timbuktu, and then bending southeast, drained most of the northern and eastern portions of the savanna. The Volta River and its tributaries drained central West Africa.

The second most striking feature of West Africa was the rain forest (200 miles at its widest point). Here, in spite of two rainy seasons a year and the luxuriant foliage, the soil was poorer; ensuring a livelihood was thus more difficult. The main crops in the rain forest were rice, yams, and maize. By the time of the French conquest, much of the original forest of coastal Dahomey, but not that of either Ivory Coast or Guinea, had been cleared. The smaller rivers of Sasandra, Bandama, and Comoé drained the rain forest in Ivory Coast, and the Mono River drained Dahomey. The final geographical feature of West Africa was the desert fringe north of the savanna, where nomadic pastoralism was the norm.

Historians and ethnographers still do not have complete knowledge of the different peoples inhabiting this vast area at the end of the nineteenth century. What follows is a selective description of the best known and largest ethnic groups in those parts of West Af-

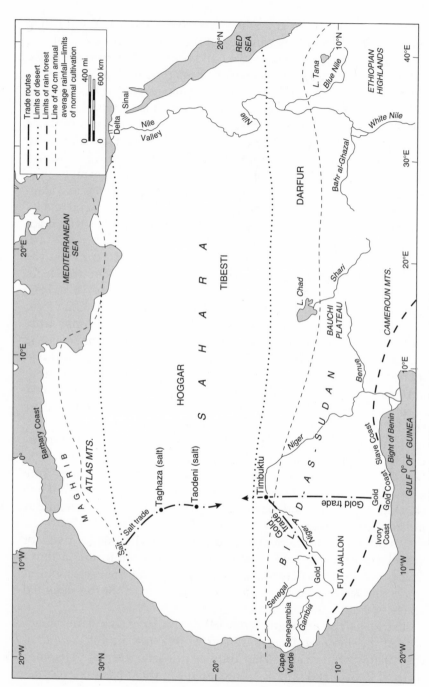

Map 2. North and West Africa: geographical features and vegetation.

rica conquered by the French. Various pastoral groups lived in the arid Saharan fringe and northern savanna known as the Sahel. These included, in the west, the Berber- and the Arabic-speaking Muslim Moors of Mauritania; farther east, particularly in the area now known as Niger, the Tuareg, a Berber people much feared as raiders; and, more to the south, the Fulani (a group that also included the Fulbe and Peuls), a predominantly Muslim people who were dispersed across the Sahel, from Senegal and Guinea to Niger and Cameroon. The Fulani, both transhumant cattle keepers and sedentary agricultural groups, were famous for the numerous jihads they launched in the nineteenth century throughout the savanna.

The southern savanna was home to a large number of sedentary farming peoples of different origin, language, and political organization. In western Senegal, the largest single group were the Wolof. The Wolof, who had been Islamicized before the arrival of the French, were farmers and traders in the coastal cities. They had traditionally been grouped in states with elaborate distinctions of hierarchy. Also in Senegambia were the animist Serer people, whose political organization varied widely, and the Tukulor, a group related to the Wolof, Serer, and Fulani, and who had been Muslim since the eleventh century. The best-known peoples of eastern Senegal and Upper Guinea, besides the Fulani, were the Mande-speaking Malinke and Soninke. Malinke and Soninke communities were also spread throughout the Western Sudan, along with two other Mande-speaking groups, the Bambara and the Dyula. The numerous Bambara, concentrated in the Middle Niger Valley, had founded two important states on the river in the seventeenth century, at Segu and Kaarta. At the end of the nineteenth century, they still retained their own cosmology and religion. The Dyula were a congeries of Mande-speaking peoples widely dispersed throughout all of West Africa as traders. They had long been Muslim.

Farther north and east of the Middle Niger, a cluster of Nilo-Saharan-speaking peoples known as the Songhay, descendants of the founders of the medieval empire of Songhay at Gao, coexisted uneasily with their Tuareg and Fulani neighbors. In the easternmost reaches of French West Africa were Chadic-speaking Hausa, most of whom had become Muslim under Fulani influence. Farther south and east of the Middle Niger, a number of Gur-speaking groups, all animist, occupied what is now Burkina Faso: the Bobo, whose political and social organization was segmentary; the Senufo, a cluster of

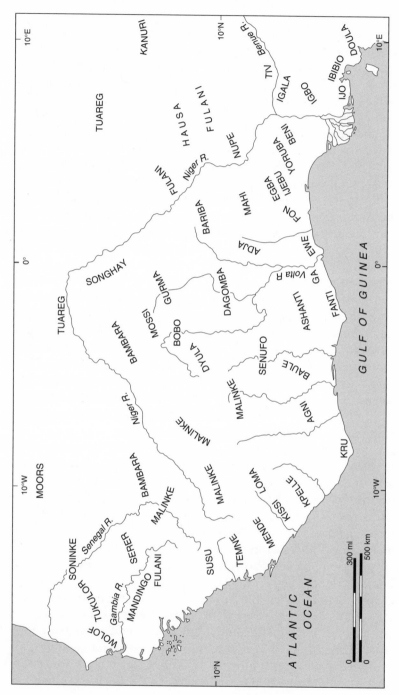

Map 3. Peoples of West Africa.

Gur-speaking peoples, who also lacked centralized forms of political authority; and the Mossi, one of the largest ethnic groups in West Africa, who were organized in four major states under a single suzerain at Ouagadougou, and in several other minor states.

Moving from the savanna to the forest zones of West Africa, the French encountered in Guinea three different groups, the Mande-speaking Kpelle, Loma, and Kissi, all of whom were "stateless." In Ivory Coast, half of which was tropical forest, the largest groups were Agni and Baule, both Akan peoples. The Akan were a cluster of Kwa-speaking peoples of the forest belt of Ivory Coast and Ghana. They comprised several kingdoms, recognized matrilineal descent, and had a long trading tradition. In what became the colony of Dahomey, the ethnic groups that figured most prominently were the Fon and the Adja of the west and central parts of the country, the Yoruba in the east, and the Bariba in the north. The Fon and the Yoruba were also Kwa-speaking peoples. The Fon lived in a centralized kingdom dating back to the eighteenth century, whereas the Yoruba were divided up among smaller autonomous kingdoms, all tracing their origin to the kingdom of Ife (in contemporary Nigeria). Islam was not an important force in the forest belt; indeed, if any outside religion was making inroads it was Christianity, thanks to the presence of missionaries and traders on the coast.

Despite their ethnic heterogeneity, the different peoples of West Africa shared certain institutions. The family was the basic unit of African social life. Most families defined themselves as either matrilineages or patrilineages. Lineage elders, usually the oldest men in the family, made decisions regarding the allocation of land, presided over marriages and funerals, and resolved disputes. Almost all societies allowed for polygyny, although the rules governing this institution varied. A second institution prevalent in West Africa—and particularly in the area that today comprises Senegal, Mali, Guinea, and Benin—was slavery. Around commercial towns and in powerful states like Segu or Dahomey, slaves were a majority of the population, where they produced food and staffed the state. In desert-side areas slaves constituted 50 percent of the population; only in what is today southern Mali and eastern Senegal were slave concentrations small, and these areas served as labor reservoirs for more centralized societies to their north. Two kinds of slavery predominated. Where large slave concentrations existed, slaves lived in separate settlements, worked under the direction of an overseer, and produced commodities for exchange. From sunrise to early afternoon they labored for their master; the rest of the day they worked their own plots, raising their own foodstuffs. The second kind of slavery obtained only where slave concentrations were low. Often described as lineage slavery, in this system the slave worked alongside his master and family, and his offspring often became free within a generation or two. The great majority of adult slaves were women.[36]

The institution of slavery in West Africa has been explained in part by the low population-to-land ratio characteristic of the region, which often resulted in a labor shortage. These shortages encouraged the expansion of slave labor, particularly once West Africa began to be drawn into commercial exchanges with the Atlantic world. The expansion of the Atlantic slave trade in the eighteenth century marked the first important increase in both forms of internal African slavery in the modern era, particularly in Lower Senegal. Slavery expanded again after 1850, when parts of West Africa began to be drawn into production of oils for the world commodity market; slave labor was used for much of this production. Finally, extensive warfare and war-induced famines in the Western Sudan in the 1880's and 1890's brought renewed slave-raiding in that region, with all its attendant miseries. Warring chiefs by tradition either enslaved those they had conquered, distributed their enemies as booty to their own soldiers, or sold them into slavery. Food shortages also led to an increase in slaves, as individuals searching for food became easy targets for raiders, and owners sold off slaves they could no longer feed. The French conquest of the Western Sudan contributed to these trends by further destabilizing the region; indeed, the French military openly tolerated the continuing trade in slaves in many of their posts for reasons of political expediency.[37]

The issue of slavery inevitably raises the question of West African economic activity and the potential of the federation for profitable *mise en valeur*. As in all preindustrial societies, agriculture was the chief occupation of most Africans. Agricultural surplus in turn made it possible to finance other types of production, the most important of which were clothing manufacture, iron working, ceramics, construction, and food processing. Exchange was widespread within West Africa before the arrival of the French; as the economic historian Anthony Hopkins has shown, most households regarded trade as a normal and integral part of their activities. Within the domestic economy, this trade was divided into two categories: local and long-distance. Local trade centered on locally produced foodstuffs and crafts. Long-distance trade specialized in luxury items such as slaves, kola nuts, and salt. External trade was of course also well established by the end of the nineteenth century; indeed, after the demise of the European and American slave markets in the 1850's, and with the onset of industrialization in Europe, a veritable "trade revolution" had taken place in West Africa. At that time, local farmers began to specialize in, and export in ever-increasing quantities, oleaginous products demanded by Europe's burgeoning industrial sector. The most important of these products were palm oil and peanuts, although gum arabic, rubber, ivory, cotton, and timber were also traded. In return, cheap manufactured goods began flowing into West Africa, principally textiles, spirits, salt, iron, tobacco, guns, and gunpowder.[38]

However impressive, this integration of West Africans into the world economy remained very regionalized in 1895, for a variety of ecological, economic, and historical reasons. Among the vast territories conquered by the French, only the Senegambian basin and the coast of Ivory Coast and Dahomey were actively engaged in the commodity export trade. Peanuts and palm kernel required a specific climate and soil. Peanuts did best in light sandy soil and a reliable long dry season. At the same time, as bulky items with a low weight-to-value ratio, they had to be grown close to the coast, where transportation costs could be controlled. Both of these conditions were met in the Senegambian basin; the Western Sudan, in contrast, although it offered the same soil and climate, was too far from the ocean to make it profitable to grow peanuts for export. Additionally—as we shall see—that part of the savanna was going through a series of political upheavals in the second half of the nineteenth century, which were hardly conducive to economic innovation. Palm oil production also suffered from a low weight-to-value ratio. Palm trees, moreover, grew naturally in only one part of West Africa, a belt along the coast stretching from Guinea to Cameroon. The greatest concentration of these trees was not in French West Africa at all, but in the British-controlled Niger delta. Only in southern Dahomey was there any notable palm oil production before the French conquest.[39]

Another important feature of French West Africa in 1895 was the unevenness of French penetration and "pacification" of the territories to which it had already laid claim. When the Government General was created, the military had successfully conquered a substantial portion—but not all—of what was soon to become the new fed-

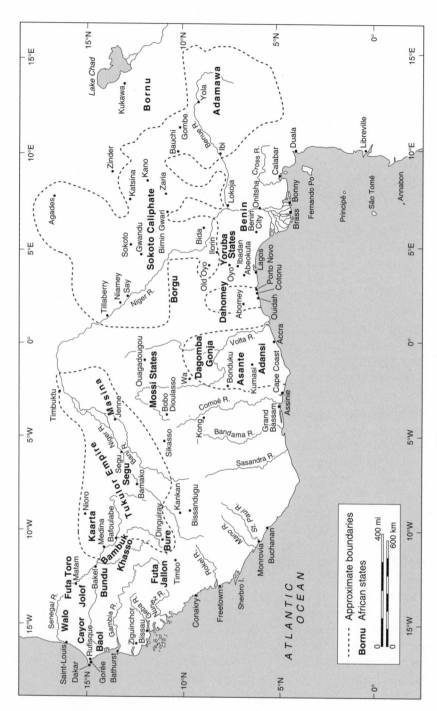

Map 4. West Africa, ca. 1870.

eration. Between the 1850's and the early 1890's, several important savanna states had posed an obstacle to French imperialist aims.[40] In the western part of the Senegambian basin, the small Wolof and Serer monarchies of Cayor, Jolof, Walo, Sine, Salum, and Baol had long competed with the French for local influence. By 1887, however, the French had established protectorates over all six of these kingdoms, thereby substantially increasing the size of France's old colony of Senegal. Farther east and south, in the Western Sudan, the army had also just defeated the formidable Tukulor Empire, founded by the Muslim cleric and jihadist al-Hajj Umar Tall. Umar's state was one of two vast, ethnically diverse empires to emerge in the Western Sudan after 1850, in part as a response to a new spirit of Islamic reform, which swept through the savanna. The second state was founded by Samori. Umar's successful conquests of peoples between 1852 and 1863 had allowed him to build up a state extending from, but not including, the city of Medina in the west, along both banks of the Niger River as far as Timbuktu. Such important formerly independent Bambara kingdoms as Dinguiray, Kaarta, Segu, and Masina had thus been brought firmly under his control. When Umar died in battle in 1863, his son Amadu inherited his empire. Amadu and the French army had clashed intermittently for thirty years in the Western Sudan, before the great Umarian leader was finally defeated in 1893. Also successfully "pacified" by 1895 were the ancient Fon kingdoms of southern Dahomey and its tributary port-kingdom of Porto Novo. In the late 1880's, the French had sought to bring these kingdoms under their influence as well, so as to ensure a link between the coast and their new possessions on the bend of the Niger River. Despite the small size of Dahomey, this conquest had proven much more difficult than the French expected. Dahomey, earlier an active participant in the Atlantic slave trade, had converted to palm oil production in the second half of the nineteenth century. Large, efficiently run plantations worked by slaves had impressed the Europeans who traded there; Dahomey boasted a superbly disciplined army as well. Not surprisingly, Dahomey's monarch, Behanzin, had refused French "protection" when first offered it in 1890. The French army finally subdued him in 1892.

In contrast to Senegal, Dahomey, and the Tukulor Empire, several other West African states had still not been brought entirely under French control in 1895, although many were on the verge of becoming protectorates. In the Western Sudan, for example, the French had not yet captured the leader of the second great state to arise out of the nineteenth-century jihads in the savanna. This leader was the Muslim reformer Samori, born in the Guinea highlands and of Dyula origin. Unlike his rivals, Umar and Amadu, for both of whom religious reform had been a sincere objective, Samori was first and foremost a soldier and conqueror, who never had time to consolidate his rule or his empire. From his home in the Guinea hinterland, he had pushed east and south of the Niger River; his most important conquests took place between 1870 and 1875. By 1890, however, Samori had lost most of them to the famous French colonial commander, Louis Archinard. For the next nine years, Samori and his cadre of *sofas* nevertheless managed to evade French colonial troops, who made it a point of honor to defeat him and in the process kept expanding France's West African empire. In 1899, Samori was finally captured. Another area, also in the Western Sudan, in which fighting was going on at the time of the founding of the Government General, was the region surrounding Lake Chad. After the conquest of Amadu, the French army turned its attention to the territory extending west of Timbuktu toward Lake Chad. Possession of this territory would guarantee the French a link between their equatorial African colonies and French West Africa. The conquest of this area had just begun in 1895. Four years later, in the year Samori was captured, the most important sultanate of the region, Zinder, capitulated.

Outside the Western Sudan, the states still opposing the French army in 1895 included the Imamate of Futa Jallon, located in the Guinea highlands. The Imamate was a theocratic state founded in the wake of Islamic reform in the nineteenth century. Although the French had signed a protectorate treaty with the Imamate before 1895, the local aristocracy was deemed insufficiently "pacified," and in 1896 the French occupied the kingdom. In the hinterland of Ivory Coast, the army confronted hostility from two additional polities, neither of which had been officially conquered in 1895. To the far north lay the great Mossi empire centered in Ouagadougou on the Upper Volta River, whose rulers, the Moro Nabas, had effectively resisted Islamicization and indeed any foreign penetration for more than two centuries. When they also refused French "protection" in the early 1890's, the French decided in 1896 to occupy Ouagadougou by force. South of Mossiland lay the loosely organized Dyula confederacy of Kong and, in the eastern half of the forest proper, the mosaic of petty chieftaincies of the Baule peoples. Both the Dyula of

Kong and the Baule proved extraordinarly hostile to the French. Since the forest terrain made "pacification" more difficult than in the open savanna, these areas, although identified as French on the map in 1895, would not truly come under France's control until World War I (see Map 4).

Despite the incomplete conquest of French West Africa, Paris had tried repeatedly since 1891 to phase out military control of the various territories and introduce civilian administration. Between 1891 and 1893, it had divided the existing French territories in West Africa, more or less arbitrarily, into five separate colonies and one military territory, Mauritania. The five colonies were Senegal, which was actually administered under two separate regimes, one for the coastal cities and one for the protectorate areas in the interior; Guinea, Ivory Coast, and Dahomey, which made up the so-called southern colonies; and the landlocked Western Sudan, the largest colony in French West Africa. Administration for each of these five colonies had been placed in the hands of a civilian governor, who determined customs tariffs, drew up the budget, and was responsible for all policy making in his colony. Despite these changes, no firm control over the French colonels still fighting Samori in the Western Sudan had been achieved. As a result, the administrative situation in French West Africa in 1895 was somewhat confused. In particular, competing interests had emerged, as the colonial army launched campaigns without consulting either the governors in whose territories it was operating, or Parliament, to whom the military was ultimately responsible. The different governors also squabbled over the boundaries of their respective colonies—boundaries that changed as more and more of the African interior was conquered.

The above description of West Africa and the state of French administration in 1895 suggests a number of reasons why a Colonial Ministry newly interested in making its colonies productive felt that the establishment of a federal framework there was necessary. Clearly, a policy of economic development was not compatible with a continuing policy of unbridled conquest, which was exactly what the new Ministry now accused the army of pursuing in the Western Sudan. West Africa was sufficiently "pacified" to wind up military operations and begin tapping the resources of the new territories already under French control. The civilian-military disputes taking place in West Africa between 1891 and 1894, coupled with the army's refusal to obey orders from Paris, had, however, already shown that such a "winding up" could not be coordinated from the metropole. What was needed instead was a civilian representative of the Third Republic on the spot, with sufficient authority to bring the military forces to heel, and to overcome the separatist sentiments of the different governors.

The relative poverty of certain West African territories was another decisive factor encouraging Paris to adopt a federal structure for West Africa. Only by pooling the resources of all their colonies could the territory as a whole, and the Western Sudan in particular, prosper and thereby justify the expenses involved in acquiring the colony in the first place.[41] This realization endowed the Government General with an economic as well as a political vocation from the outset. In addition to coordinating military and economic policy in West Africa, it would be responsible for raising sufficient revenues locally to secure loans for a modern transportation network linking the savanna to the coast, whose design and execution it was also to oversee.

Yet, if these were to be the tasks of the new Government General, it would take nine years before a truly effective federal framework for the administration and *mise en valeur* of French West Africa was worked out. This delay can be attributed principally to the continuing strength of the colonial army in West Africa, whose members still had important connections in Paris, and the weakness of the Ministry of Colonies—itself only a year old.[42] Indeed, the army showed no more inclination in 1895 to accept civilian primacy in decision making in West Africa than it had in the past. This was particularly true since Samori had still not been defeated. The minister of colonies' first reaction was thus to worry less about endowing the federal administration with fiscal autonomy than establishing its new civilian representative in Saint-Louis over the colonial army still operating in the Western Sudan.[43]

The federation created on June 16, 1895, was, from a financial point of view, very limited.[44] The governor general, who in addition to heading the entire federation, retained responsibility for the administration of Senegal, was granted little real authority over the other colonies, particularly in financial matters. Only the military powers of the lieutenant governors of Ivory Coast and Guinea were surrendered to him. Although these two colonies were to contribute to the operating costs of the Government General, they nonetheless submitted their budgets directly to the minister, rather than to the governor general. The colony of Dahomey was left out of the federation altogether. In contrast to these arrangements regarding the coastal colonies, the lieutenant governor of the Western Sudan was made subordinate in all matters to the head of the federation. Certain territories previously attached to the Western Sudan were annexed to Senegal and Guinea, in a further attempt to reduce the lieutenant governor's power. In short, the decree concentrated all military powers and responsibility for the general administration of the Western Sudan in the hands of the governor general in Saint-Louis, the seat of the new federation. It barely affected the civil administration of the other colonies.[45]

In practice, the 1895 decree was a failure on a number of fronts. The first governor general, Chaudié, found that the military authorities in the Western Sudan continued to act independently. Without control of the budgets of the individual colonies, moreover, the governor general could not deal with economic matters either. Under the existing arrangements, he could not force the member territories to contribute to the costs of the Government General; without a source of revenues, the Government General could not hope to finance the federal program of public works upon which, it was now increasingly recognized, economic growth in West Africa depended. Under Chaudié's urging, the Colonial Ministry put an end to the military-civilian conflict in 1899, by simply dismembering the Western Sudan to the advantage of the coastal colonies and giving command of all French West African forces to an officer directly responsible to the governor general.[46] The problem of how to finance the infrastructure essential to *mise en valeur*, however, remained temporarily unresolved. A solution became all the more urgent when Parliament in 1900, in keeping with the dominant economic liberalism of the era, cut off all state subsidies to the colonies. The solution would finally be provided between 1902 and 1904, thanks to the arrival of a particularly influential career administrator as governor general, Ernest Roume. More important still, with the appointment of Roume, not only was federal authority consolidated, but a clear-cut ideology of civilization began to take shape at the highest level of the West African administration. The two events, as we shall see, were not unrelated. A new era in the history of French West Africa was about to begin.

CHAPTER 2

Public Works and Public Health

CIVILIZATION, TECHNOLOGY, AND SCIENCE (1902–1914)

A dirt road [*route d'étapes*] creates a void; a railroad or steamboat brings the population back, and with it a fecund and joyous activity. This phenomenon, which was so strikingly apparent on the Dakar–Saint-Louis line, is recurring in exactly the identical fashion on the Kayes-Koulikoro line; on the finished part of the line from Conakry to the Niger, a new town, Kindia, has sprung up at the temporary terminus, and the figures confirm what a simple glance appears to reveal.

— Governor General Ernest Roume[1]

In 1902, the dynamic and experienced Ernest Roume was appointed governor general of French West Africa. Under pressure from Roume, Paris finally endowed the Government General with real fiscal autonomy and political authority. This reform allowed the new head of the federation to devote himself to the rational exploitation of West Africa's resources. At the same time, as Dakar's functions gradually increased, references to France's civilizing mission multiplied commensurately, and a clearer picture began to emerge of how the new Government General viewed its role as civilizer of the West African peoples under its control. From the outset Dakar defined its role fairly broadly to include the material and the moral improvement of Africans. Their subjects, the French insisted, would not be civilized until they simultaneously consumed more, became literate, and gave up certain barbaric social practices. This chapter investigates the theme of material improvement in the Government General's rhetoric of civilization before World War I, while Chapters 3 and 4 examine the moral dimension.

How, then, did Dakar propose to improve Africans' material existence? One civilizing idea consistently articulated by the men in Dakar was that the *mise en valeur* of the colony, upon which the federal government was now embarking, was itself part of France's mission in West Africa because it would raise the African standard of living. Such a belief was not new; what was new was the manner in which this mutually beneficial development was to take place. Railroads and modern prophylaxis against tropical diseases, Dakar insisted, were the crucial means to the desired end of a better life for Africans. This choice of means can be accounted for in a variety of ways. First, building lines of communication and making the federation healthier dovetailed with the immediate interests of the reorganized federal government, whose *raison d'être* was rational economic utilization of the colony's resources, principally through development of modern infrastructure. Indeed, so neatly did it tie in with Dakar's interests, this particular tenet blinded the French to the fact that not all development was equally beneficial to colonizer and colonized.

Second, a belief in the transformative power of the steam engine and modern hygiene reflected the Third Republic's long-standing faith in the ability of technology to promote progress, as well as a more recent struggle within the metropole to institute new public health regulations based on the latest medical findings. Industrializing Europe and the United States were the sites of two important "revolutions" in the nineteenth century: the transportation revolution at the century's beginning, and the bacteriological one, which was just gaining momentum at century's end. No one in France in the early 1900's questioned the desirability of railroads, and this confidence resurfaced in the empire. New strategies for combating invisible microbes, in contrast, were still being contested in Parliament and throughout the country—despite their proven success. Both the spectacular medical breakthroughs and the resistance they were encountering at home explain Dakar's special attachment to the civilizing potential of modern hygiene. Faced with a more hostile disease environment and greater freedom to act than in France, colonial policy makers acted boldly where republican deputies back home still hesitated to tread. The earliest governor general to expound the view that France would uplift Africans through a policy of economic development based on improved transportation and hygiene was also the man who did the most to make French *mise en valeur* of West Africa possible: Ernest Roume.

Ernest Roume and the Reorganization of the Government General, 1902–1904

Ernest Nestor Roume, a native of Marseille, was appointed governor general of French West Africa at the relatively young age of forty-four. He had entered government service through France's most prestigious school of public administration, the Ecole Polytechnique; his training as an engineer showed from the outset—as governor general, he was interested in building railroads. Since 1895, he had been attached to the Ministry of Colonies, and he had headed the Asian, African and Oceanic Section of the Bureau of Political, Economic and Administrative Affairs since 1896.[2] A prominent member of the colonial lobby, Roume had already traveled extensively on missions of inspection before he was appointed a director in the colonial service; he had participated in Indochina's recent reorganization, which he saw as an example for West Africa.[3] He was to retire from the colonial service after six years in Dakar, for health reasons. During his tenure as governor general, Roume was frequently absent from the colony for long stretches, during which he sought to raise loans in Paris for the federation. The contacts he made in government and banking circles during these trips were to be personally valuable to Roume later on.[4] An experienced financier before his appointment to head the federation, Roume remained one of the most influential agents of colonial interests in France. He eventually served as both president of the Chemin de Fer Franco-Ethiopien and administrator of the important Banque de l'Indochine. Roume would briefly rejoin the colonial service during World War I as governor general of Indochina, but after seventeen months in office he again resigned because of poor health. He remained a prominent figure in colonial circles until his death.

Roume arrived in Dakar a fervent partisan of making the federation prosper through a forward-looking policy of *mise en valeur*. His commitment to this goal was hardly surprising, given his affiliation with the colonial interest group, which included prominent economic theorists, business-oriented deputies in Parliament, industrialists, and members of the commercial bourgeoisie residing in port cities and the colonies. Beginning in the early 1890's, these men had attempted to influence policy through a variety of private organizations, the two most important of which were the Union Coloniale Française and the Comité de l'Afrique Française, and their parliamentary group, the Parti Colonial.[5] Roume's appointment represented a triumph for this lobby, which had been hoping since 1895 to transform the Government General into a more effective instrument of *mise en valeur*. How Roume thought this colonial development could best be achieved will be discussed in a moment. Given the importance of the term in French overseas development, it may be useful first to consider the general connotations of the phrase *mise en valeur* at the time Roume arrived in the colony.

The term itself is usually associated with the interwar years in France, in part because the most influential colonial minister of that period, Albert Sarraut, wrote a book entitled *La mise en valeur des colonies françaises* in 1923, and actively pursued colonial development. Although there can be no question that governmental support for a policy of *mise en valeur* increased dramatically in the 1920's, the concept first gained prominence in the 1890's, when it marked a dual shift in the "official mind" of French colonialism compared to an earlier era.[6] First, members of the colonial interest groups began to demand that the policy of continued conquest, which the Third Republic had pursued since the 1880's, now give way to a constructive phase of the *mise en valeur* of territories already acquired. In this context, the phrase was usually defined by a particular antithesis; it implied exploitation rather than more expansion.[7] Second, the term also connoted an exploitation different from what had occurred in the first half of the century. As Michael Osborne has recently put it, the end of the nineteenth century witnessed a shift in French colonial sensibility from an ethos "of unlimited exploitation to one where exploitation is married to rationality, progress and conservation."[8] The overseas territories were not to be plundered, as they might have been in the past, for whatever short-term riches they could yield. Such unlimited exploitation was inefficient and potentially undermined the long-term economic value of the colonies to the metropole. Instead, a more systematic management of French overseas resources was needed—one in which the state would have a key role. It was this more rational and progressive development that the term *mise en valeur* apparently designated.

This shift in emphasis from conquest to *mise en valeur*, and from unlimited to limited exploitation, occurred for several reasons. By the end of the nineteenth century, France had become a major industrial power and a consumer society. From the government's perspective, the development of colonial markets seemed an obvious response to the changed economic conditions that the country had been facing since the depression of the 1870's and 1880's. The colonial lobby had even more specific economic incentives for demanding a policy of exploitation led by the state. Many members of the Union Coloniale were port merchants with a stake in the smaller commercial enterprises that constituted the backbone of France's colonial economies in West Africa in the 1890s; these enterprises included, primarily, palm oil and peanut oil operations, rubber plantations, and railroad concessions.[9] These merchants were eager to expand their activities, but did not have the means to finance them alone. One of their basic tenets was that the state should become the financial partner of those private sectors of the economy desiring to undertake overseas projects but unable to raise the necessary capital on their own. This presupposed bringing the conquest to a close. The growing suspicion of the army that characterized French society and politics in the 1890's, which culminated in the Dreyfus affair (1898–1899), also dampened enthusiasm for continued expansion. In addition, the difficulties of administering the enormous and ethnically diverse tracts that the French had claimed in the African interior made consolidation increasingly necessary.

Finally, new ways of thinking about social problems in France were also part of the general push for a more rational approach to colonization. Metropolitan "experts" of all kinds, armed with improved medical and social knowledge, were reassigning blame for poverty, worker discontent, and poor health from moral depravity to hostile environments, physical fatigue, and invisible micro-organisms, and turning to the state for scientific solutions to these problems. This was the period when the bacteriological revolution seemed to prove the interdependence of all members of society—and the need for greater regulation of individual and public hygiene. The emerging discipline of sociology suggested that the breakdown of social cohesion produced by industrialization could be stemmed through the scientific study of social phenomena. Modern urban planners now emphasized the need for long-range rational planning of cities and towns, to promote maximum efficiency. Although the heyday of rationalization of the workplace would not occur until the 1920's, some were already using statistical studies at the fin-de-siècle to call for greater worker protection by the state. Colonial policy makers could not but respond to these ideas as well while they prepared to make their territories productive.[10]

By the end of the nineteeth century, then, *mise en valeur* connoted a program of rational, scientific, and progressive colonial development, in which the state would play a central role. What exactly this meant in practice can be seen in the actions of Governor General Roume. For him, inaugurating a program of *mise en valeur* required first the construction of modern communications, which all colonial propagandists supported. Roume also adapted to West Africa a host of other European technological innovations, including specialized agricultural research, scientific laboratories, and modern sanitation and health facilities; but railroads would always receive the lion's portion of available funds. Not long after his arrival, the new governor general unveiled plans for constructing a rail and telegraph network in the federation that would remain the centerpiece of his years in office. This network would link the various colonies in such a way that no part of the vast West African interior would be inaccessible from the coast. Roume's tour through the federation encouraged his early preoccupation with infrastructure. During this tour, Roume experienced firsthand the difficulties in communication and transportation created by the enormous distances that separated the various colonies under his administration; until these distances were conquered, he concluded, no real *mise en valeur* or administrative unification of French West Africa was possible.[11]

Roume nevertheless faced a large obstacle in realizing his projects. In 1902, the Government General was in no better position to embark upon so ambitious a program of *mise en valeur* than it had been in 1895. The Western Sudan had been dismembered, and the problem of military insubordination had finally been resolved. But the federal government still did not have the means to raise revenue for railroads, much less research stations and sanitation programs. Clearly, a further reorganization was necessary. It would be Ernest Roume's particular contribution to the history of French colonial rule in West Africa to oversee this reorganization from 1902 to 1904—the last reorganization until the 1920's. During those years he submitted a series of reforms to Paris that transformed the fledgling organization from a loose federation, with little authority, to one more like its recently reformed counterpart in Indochina—that is to say, a highly centralized and financially independent organ, capable of undertaking the public works program in which he so believed.

Roume submitted his first proposed reform of the Government General within a few months of his arrival in West Africa. The minister of colonies, Doumergue, immediately enacted his recommendations. The purpose of the 1902 reorganization was to increase the governor general's freedom of action in three ways. The decree relieved him of the responsibility of directly administering Senegal, provided him with the right to establish a centralized bureaucracy to supervise the territorial administrations, and authorized him to set aside a portion of each member colony's revenues; this contribution was to cover the federation's new operating costs, and help subsidize a federal program of public works designed to improve communication between the various territories. To implement these changes, the seat of the Government General was transferred from Saint-Louis to Dakar, and a new territory was created from part of Senegal and the old Western Sudan, and placed under a delegate of the governor general at Kayes. The expenses of the Government General were to be paid from a special section of the budget of this new territory, to which the other colonies would contribute. The nature of federal expenditures was determined by the Council of the Government General, which convened once a year to ratify the budgets of each territory and to discuss general administration. The lieutenant governors, the heads of the federal services, and the army and navy commanders made up this council, over which Roume presided. The council was deliberative rather than legislative. The governor general organized the different federal services and determined their responsibilities and personnel. He alone had the right to correspond directly with Paris.[12]

The reforms of 1902 considerably enhanced the authority of the governor general, and Roume planned to make the most of his new powers. In his instructions to his lieutenant governors, he made clear his intention to subordinate the territorial administrations to Dakar, by asserting full political and financial control over them.[13] Roume's primary goal, however, was to use the Government General's resources to develop the necessary modern communications network. At the first meeting of the council in December 1902, Roume announced a long-term public works program for the federation, and reported that the minister had already authorized him to draw up a bill for Parliament requesting permission to float a sixty-five-million-franc loan to finance the project. The essence of this project was, first, to dramatically extend, then link into one overarching system, the few railroads that were already under construction in the different colonies.[14] As Roume envisaged it, a grand transversal railroad would be built as the primary line of French penetration in West Africa. It would extend from the port of Dakar deep into the Sudanese interior and open the Niger Bend to French economic exploitation. Other lines penetrating inland from the French colonies on the southern littoral, Ivory Coast, Guinea, and Dahomey, would join up with this transversal. The disparate parts of West Africa would then be welded into a coherent political, administrative, and economic unit. At the same time, the port of Dakar would be significantly expanded to become the economic linchpin of the federation, since all products from the Western Sudan would be exported from there.[15] This expanded role befit Dakar as the new imperial seat of the federation, although it did not make particularly good economic sense when the ports of Guinea and Dahomey were closer. Roume's plans nevertheless met the approval of Parliament, and in July 1903 a law was passed granting the governor general the right to borrow the requested sum in French capital markets.[16] The bulk of it was to be used to carry out the first phase of Roume's ambitious public works program, and to repay earlier loans contracted by the colonies of Senegal and Guinea.

The passage of the loan bill made revision of the 1902 decree imperative.[17] Although the 1902 decree had been designed to create, in theory, a strong federal authority, it had considerably underestimated the expenses involved in both consolidating the expanded federal administration and launching a program of public works. The total revenues allocated the Government General in 1903 amounted to ten and a half million francs, generated largely from head taxes collected in the Sudanese territories.[18] This sum was clearly insufficient to secure the authorized sixty-five-million-franc loan or any future loans. What West Africa still required was an authority capable of generating greater revenues to pay for the administration in Dakar, and wealthy enough to act as a guarantor for outside capital investment. To meet this need, the Government General was reorganized for the fourth and final time in nine years.

On October 4, 1904, a decree was signed creating a fully autonomous federal budget, which French West Africa had lacked since 1895. The governor general was freed from the burden of administering Upper Senegal through an authority at Kayes; because of their potential wealth, these territories were formed into a new colony, Upper Senegal–Niger, and given their own lieutenant governor. Five colonies—Ivory Coast, Guinea, Dahomey, Senegal, and

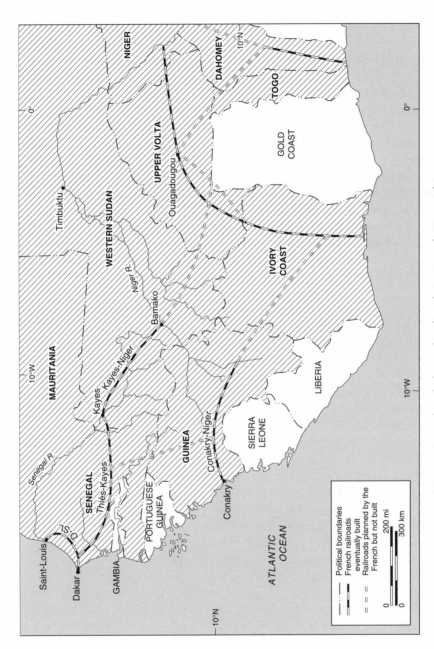

Map 5. Actual and planned railroads in French West Africa.

Upper Senegal–Niger—the military territory of the Chad-Niger region, and the territory of Mauritania placed under a commissioner responsible to Roume, now made up the federation. Most important, all trade-derived revenues from these colonies would be diverted to the budget of the Government General. Federal credits would then be allocated to individual colonies, either as part of their local budgets to defray federal personnel expenses, or as special contributions for financing public works.

In addition to railroad and port construction, Roume entrusted several other administrative tasks to the Government General to ensure that the member territories evolved as a unit. In 1903, for example, he organized a uniform federal system of education and "native" courts. He also insisted that a successful policy of resource development required the adaptation to West Africa of modern agricultural techniques and the most recent medical research. Inspectorates of Education, Agriculture, and Sanitary Services were thus organized alongside the General Inspectorate of Public Works. Each of these federal departments was supposed to have a corresponding bureau in the respective capitals of member colonies. The role of these inspectorates was not to overcentralize, but to supervise from above (*haute direction*), and to exercise overall control (*contrôle permanent*).[19] Departmental heads were regarded as inspectors in chief and technical advisers, whose opinions and recommendations Roume alone could transform into directives. To highlight the advisory nature of the different bureaus and inspectorates, Roume denied their heads the right to correspond directly with their counterparts in the colonies.

Roume's reorganization of the Government General revealed a commitment to transforming the federal government into an effective agent of *mise en valeur*, and a particular conception of how this colonial development could best take place. On the one hand, the creation of the federal budget and the contracting of the 1903 loan pointed to the primacy granted public works. On the other, the division of the federal bureaus into various inspectorates reflected a strong interest in promoting *mise en valeur* through a rational division of labor. Yet, if this reorganization provides a good indication of how Roume planned to proceed as governor general, it does not quite tell the entire story. Roume had a strong second priority for the colonial development of West Africa, after railroads and ports; this was the improvement of health conditions, or what

Roume called the *assainissement* of the colony, for both Europeans and Africans.[20]

Alongside the evidence from his own speeches, several specific initiatives indicated that Roume considered improving health conditions essential to African *mise en valeur*. He consistently allocated a small portion of the federal loans, raised primarily for infrastructure, to his Inspectorate of Sanitary Services. Twice while governor general, Roume contracted loans for infrastructure. The first time, as we have seen, was in 1903; the second, in keeping with the new possibilities that the 1904 decree had opened up, was in 1906, when the Government General felt solvent enough to request a loan of 100 million francs, to continue the construction begun in 1903. The bulk of the 1903 loan was earmarked for ports and railroads (45,000,000 fr.) and for debt repayment (14,302,717 fr.). Similarly, 88,200,000 of the 100 million francs borrowed in 1906 was to go toward rail and port construction, and an additional 2,500,000 francs was allocated for telegraph lines and 5,000,000 francs for military housing.[21] The breakdown of these budgets confirms the priority Roume granted the opening of lines of communication in West Africa. Nevertheless, in the case of each loan, Roume set aside most of the balance—5,450,000 francs in 1903 and 3,000,000 in 1906—for public health projects and medical care for Africans. No other service or inspectorate was granted a similar privilege, although some agricultural research was funded out of the federal budget.[22]

Realizing that loans by themselves would hardly suffice, Roume also took a number of legislative steps designed to improve health conditions in the federation. At the time of his arrival, West Africa still had a reputation for insalubrity, which a murderous outbreak of yellow fever in Saint-Louis in 1900 had helped dramatize. Roume was interested in stemming the spread of malaria and yellow fever in port cities, where trade stood to suffer the most from outbreaks of those diseases. Only when all member colonies were rid of these epidemics, he felt, would it be possible for West Africa to prosper. The recent discovery that these diseases were mosquito-borne led Roume to try and eliminate all possible breeding grounds for the insects.[23] To this end, he established a public health code for enforcing new sanitary regulations for the federation. A decree signed April 14, 1904, applied the provisions of the metropolitan law on public health, passed in France two years earlier (February 15, 1902) to French West Africa. This decree empowered the lieutenant governor

of each colony to enact the regulations considered necessary to prevent the spread of diseases and improve the sanitation of public and
private buildings, and required "mayors, administrators and *commandants de cercle*" to apply these regulations. It also created a
Comité Supérieur d'Hygiène et de Salubrité Publiques in Dakar to
advise the governor general.[24] As in France, water examination services were created, and new buildings were to conform to sanitary
specifications. Any case of infectious disease had to be declared, and
smallpox vaccination was made mandatory for Africans and Europeans. The decree encouraged cities and towns to equip municipal
sanitation services. One of the few additions to the 1902 law was
that administrators were also to take the necessary precautions for
destroying "the rats, mosquitoes and other insects dangerous for
public salubrity."[25] Fines were to be levied for uncovered wells and
any stagnant or standing water found on private premises. Within a
year, Roume had signed *arrêtés* creating local sanitation services in
all five colonies, with emphasis on urban areas.[26]

Last but not least, Roume turned to the problem of providing adequate medical services for the rural masses, as well as educating
them in modern hygiene. Africans, too, Roume felt, had to learn
about disease control and improve their personal hygiene, in order
for health conditions to improve generally in West Africa.[27] France
was to "spread among them [i.e., Africans] the most elementary notions of good hygiene that they completely lack, fight the terrible
rate of infant mortality that ravages their ranks, distribute the necessary medicine and cares [*soins*], isolate and treat lepers and organize the prophylactic measures against those contagious diseases
that are decimating them, particularly smallpox."[28] The following
December, Roume made good this promise and founded the Assistance médicale indigène (AMI) program, which was the charter for
African health care for the entire West African federation.[29] The AMI
rested upon two guiding principles. First, it was to provide free medical care and hygiene advice to the African populations. Twenty military and civilian doctors were recruited in 1905 to this end.[30] The
difficulty in finding colonial doctors led, a year later, to the creation
of a corps of African medical assistants to supplement their ranks.
These students were to be trained locally to work alongside French
doctors, to serve as interpreters, and, if necessary, to run a secondary
medical post. They were considered ideal propagators of modern science, who would use their newly acquired information and medical

skills to fight the influence of *marabouts* and witch doctors.[31] A special vaccination service was also organized in each colony to produce smallpox vaccine, thereby eliminating the problems of transporting it over long distances.[32] All local medical expenses, including doctors' salaries, were to be covered by the local budgets; but three million francs of the new hundred-million-franc loan, raised by the Government General in 1906, were set aside for the construction of medical posts (*groupes d'assistance indigènes*) throughout the federation. The federal administration wished each *groupe* to consist of an outpatient dispensary, an infirmary, and a house for the doctor. It recommended that additional posts be funded by each colony as it recruited more doctors. And the lieutenant governors in council agreed with Roume that Dakar be provided with a hospital for exclusive use by Africans, which the new loan would also help fund.

Dakar's new AMI had a second objective as well. The governor general's speeches and the reports of the federal sanitary services indicate that, in thinking about ways to improve the health of Africans, Dakar was envisioning nothing less than a revolution in the way their subjects lived. The AMI doctor was to be a calm and indefatigable adviser to the indigenous populations. He was also to collaborate closely with the local administrator (*commandant de cercle*) and function as a kind of public hygienist. Only the *commandant*, Roume recognized, had sufficient authority to modify the appearance of African villages. These *commandants* were now to determine how streets were to be designed, wells dug, and garbage collected. Doctor and administrator together were to persuade the Africans under their command to change their way of life, by replacing what the administration viewed as unhealthy ancestral habits with modern hygienic ones conducive to the *mise en valeur* of the federation.[33]

The years from 1902 to 1904 thus witnessed the reorganization of the Government General, the launching of a unified program of public works, and the inauguration of a public health policy for West Africa. The federal government had finally acquired fiscal autonomy, and with its new monopoly of customs receipts, port charges, and consumer taxes, Dakar could redistribute essential services and development projects more equitably among the member colonies. It could likewise finance public works requiring heavy capital investment more easily than any individual colony, as experience had shown, because of its superior ability to raise large consolidated loans. In return for appropriating these sources of revenues, the federal government paid for all colonial debts, contributions toward metropolitan expenditures, the expenses of the French judiciary, and the costs of its own administration.

These same years, however, also witnessed another development: with the consolidation of the Government General, the possibilities for articulating an ideology of civilization in Dakar increased commensurately. And, indeed, references to France's civilizing mission abound after 1902, as the expanded Dakar bureaus began to churn out directive after directive. An analysis of how the word "civilization" was used by the Government General reveals, moreover, that it encompassed a variety of themes, many of which had nothing to do with the economic vocation of the newly reorganized Government General. One theme nevertheless coincided with the material interests of the federation from the outset. This was a belief that the *mise en valeur* of African resources was itself part of France's civilizing mission in West Africa, and that railroads and improved sanitation were as essential to African progress as they were to French prosperity.

'Mise en Valeur' and the Ideology of the Civilizing Mission

Ernest Roume was certainly the consummate colonial bureaucrat and financier. From the day he arrived in Dakar in 1902, however, Roume made clear that he saw his mission overseas as something more lofty than the mere extraction of Africa's resources for the exclusive benefit of the French. As he put it, when presenting the new decree reorganizing the Government General in December 1904:

> If France were to have no other objective or ambition in West Africa than to maintain order among the native population in order to promote commerce, the need for a federal framework could be legitimately contested. But we have a higher ambition and a significantly broader intention: we wish truly to open Africa to civilization.

Roume repeated this idea over and over:

> The establishment and maintenance of order and security are the indispensable conditions for all progress, whether moral or material, and since it can now be said that this condition [in West Africa] has been met [thanks to the conquest] we are in a position to apply all our energies and available resources to the achievement of such progress.[34]

Roume's emphasis on having a higher ambition than maintaining order and allowing commerce—that of opening the colonies to civilization—confirms that the new governor general came to Dakar convinced that modern colonization should benefit France's colonial subjects as well as the metropole. It also suggests that he already had a concrete vision of what Africa could become under his direction, as well as a commitment to making this vision a reality. This is not to say that the French military administration, or the two governors general who had preceded Roume in West Africa, had failed to take France's civilizing mission seriously or had neglected to initiate measures deemed consistent with this ideology. On the contrary, the best military leaders assumed "that French rule would eventually mean the extension to Africa of the secrets of France's own prosperity and confidence: economic development, increasing wealth, education which would permit mastery of even the African environment."[35] As military conquerors, they nevertheless had even fewer resources at their disposal to effect these progressive ideals than their civilian successors. Whatever ambitions these leaders might have harbored for uplifting Africans, the day-to-day realities of maintaining control inhibited intervention in African customs, or the formulation of grandiose plans for transforming the physical and social landscape. The Government General under Roume, now organized into an autonomous organ of administration, did not feel similarly constrained. The very point of civilian rule, Roume's speeches suggested, was to ensure that the civilization that military rulers might well have dreamed of—and to which their own actions had contributed by securing peace and order in the interior—would now take place.

But what exactly did Roume mean by the term "civilization"? Clearly, he did not conflate civilization with moral progress alone. He also introduced the concept of material progress as part of France's uplifting vocation in West Africa. "We wish," he stated in 1904, "to truly open up to civilization the immense regions that the foresight of our statesmen and the bravery of our soldiers and explorers have bequeathed to us. . . . The necessary condition for achieving this goal is the creation of lines of penetration, a perfected means of transportation to make up for the absence of natural means of communication that has kept this country in poverty and barbarism."[36] This speech again hints at what subsequent statements and policy initiatives would make even more obvious: that, for

Roume, the opposite of "civilization" was not only "barbarism," but "poverty" and "isolation" as well. To be civilized, in other words, was not to be poor and marooned, but prosperous and connected—involved in a wider kind of economic activity than was currently possible in West Africa. The evidence that Roume saw progress in economic as well as moral terms is further strengthened by the reference to "the necessary condition" for achieving such civilization: "a perfected means of transportation." The notion that railroads were an indispensable first step toward civilization was also an idea to which he returned often:

> Certainly everything there is to say about the utility, the necessity of building railroads as the indispensable first step in a country's development in the modern world has been said, and we do not pretend to be adding anything new to the subject; but what characterizes the situation in West Africa in this respect is that, while most other countries have been able to attain some degree of civilization—and a quite advanced one—without railroads, here because of the [isolation and lack of natural communications] no noteworthy progress in any direction whatsoever has occurred in their absence. . . . In West Africa, outside of a very limited number of coastal zones, true economic activity cannot even be conceived without railroads. It is therefore our duty, if I may be so bold to say, as a civilized nation, to take those steps that nature itself imposes and which are the only effective ones.

The following passage reveals even more explicitly the close connection Dakar saw among modern infrastructure, commerce, and civilization:

> It is now everyone's conviction that no material or moral progress is possible in our African colonies without railroads: pacification assured, acceleration of commercial exchanges, development of agricultural production, progressive decrease in human porterage, profound modification of the current African social organization as a result of the facility with which more and more the freed laborer will have to sell his labor in the active centers of the colony, not only an instrument of administration and of material progress, but also a tool of social progress and truly a work of humanity.[37]

Yet if railroads, and modern communications generally, would be the primary instrument of a material transformation in the lives of Africans, Roume also set great store by improved health conditions. Investment in modern health services as well as in railroads in West Africa, Roume noted, was part of the debt that "as a civilized power, republican France faithful to its tradition of generosity and human fraternity owes itself to honor."[38] In his speeches, he often coupled these two programs: "The most essential [means for progress] are . . . the creation and development of a communications network and the amelioration of sanitary conditions. It is toward the realization of these two objectives that we must devote all our energies; these objectives are sought and energetically pursued in all French and foreign colonies, that is to say, those that are progressing and prospering." As Roume specified in his report on the 1906 loan, "Parallel to the work of economic penetration of West Africa by the creation and amelioration of communication routes, the government has committed itself to pursuing, with particular care, the problem of African medical assistance."[39]

These quotations prove that the federal government not only believed that it had a civilizing mission in West Africa, but also accepted that at least one part of its humanitarian mission was to bring the fruits of modern prosperity to West Africa, through a transfer of technology and Western medical practices and an increase in trade. This finding, in turn, immediately invites a second conclusion: the kind of economic activity that Roume was promoting as essential to African progress was indistinguishable from the policy of *mise en valeur* upon which the recently reorganized Government General had just embarked. The Government General had been reformed by Roume to exploit rationally African raw materials, in exchange for greater African consumption of French manufactured goods. The best means to this end, it had determined, were a communications network and the improvement of health conditions in the federation. Both policies would ensure the increase in trade upon which the federal budget depended for the bulk of its revenues. At the same time, they would directly profit Africans as well and thus constituted an aspect of France's mission overseas. The new federal administration's ideology, in short, made a virtue out of a program of economic development; the interests of the Government General and those of African producers were one and the same.

This overlap between the particular fiscal needs of the colonial state, and the doctrine of the federal government, suggests that self-interest was one powerful ingredient in determining French ideology in West Africa. Yet other influences were obviously also at work. The belief that trade would contribute to the civilizing process dated back at least as far as the Enlightenment. It had also been woven into the pro–*mise en valeur* arguments put forth by the colonial lobby in the 1880's and 1890's. French propagandists, for example, had assumed that Africans would automatically benefit from an increase in commercial activity in the French colonies, and that such benefit was itself tantamount to civilization. "Trade," Leroy-Beaulieu had argued in the 1880's, "will not spread in this part of the world except in those areas where . . . [the Europeans] open routes of communication . . . and where, through the example of their own nationals and their own initiative, they teach the natives how to have more needs by working harder and trading more. It has been said with reason that the most characteristic sign of civilization is the multiplicity of needs."[40]

The most energetic member of the Union Coloniale, Joseph Chailley-Bert, likewise believed that encouraging capitalist agriculture in North Africa and commerce in West Africa would "ultimately result in progress for all concerned." Another eloquent spokesman for the view that opening Africa to greater trade with the metropole constituted a contribution to civilization was Georges Deherme, an administrator and publicist attached to the Government General, who came to West Africa in the early 1900's and published a long and detailed account of conditions there. Deherme insisted in his preface:

> The most important result of colonization is to increase world productivity. It is at the same time a great social force for progress. The earth belongs to humanity. It belongs to those who know best how to develop it [*féconder*], increase its wealth, and in the process augment it, beautify it and elevate humanity. Colonization is the propagation of the highest form of civilization yet conceived and realized, the perpetuation of the most talented race, the progressive organization of humanity, the scientific *mise en valeur* of the planet.[41]

A few detractors did exist to what, by 1900, was fast becoming one of the unquestioned cornerstones of French ideology in West Africa and one of the great myths legitimating imperialism generally. The pioneering Africanist Maurice Delafosse cynically noted several years later:

> We proclaim ourselves the universal educator of these primitive peoples whose capacity for producing and consuming we wish to increase, out of utilitarian egoism masquerading under the name of philanthropy or social responsibility. Officially this process is called civilizing, and after all, the term is apt, since the undertaking serves to increase the degree of prosperity of our civilization.[42]

The publicist Charles Régismanset echoed these negative sentiments on the subject; he took Deherme to task for seeing colonial development in such a humanitarian light:

> European colonization a force for progress? Progress, when we have only one means for bringing blacks to our side: to stimulate artificial needs that contribute only to their unhappiness, their eternal damnation? . . . Poor black humanity. Let us at least have the frankness to admit that if we take such an interest in you, it is because you appear to us to constitute an inexhaustible reservoir of labor. . . . We intend to make the African races "yield" the maximum. . . . But what do science, justice, goodness and especially progress have to do with any of this?[43]

These rare voices of dissent, however, only confirmed the extent to which the opposite view was taken for granted.

If the belief that opening up Africa to trade was an act of civilization was widespread in nineteenth-century France, the particular means that Roume stressed to effect this end—railroads and hygiene—can nevertheless be traced to a specific combination of industrial, scientific, and social developments in France after 1850. As the Union Coloniale's man in West Africa, Roume certainly had the ear of those members with interests in the iron and steel industry. Railroad suppliers had become increasingly prominent in the Union's ranks around 1900. Their presence was directly tied to an ongoing recession in the production of rails that had started in the 1880's. These men lobbied hard for colonial railroad construction as a way out of the industry's slump, with considerable success. West Africa accounted for 11 percent of French exports of rails, 15 percent of locomotives, and 19 percent of iron and steel structures between 1900 and 1904, and these figures would hold good until the war.[44] But Roume's outlook was shaped by more than his connections to the railroad lobby. There existed a strong Saint-Simonian tradition in the metropole which placed great emphasis on transforming the African, European, and American continents through modern public works projects. Engineers in France had long believed that the steam engine could do to the African interior what had just been accomplished in the American West and France: open up new frontiers to industry and progress.[45] Such dreams had fed plans for the trans-Saharan railroad for over half a century.[46] "Civilization spreads and takes root along the paths of communication," declared the minister of public works, Charles de Freycinet, in 1880 in support of this project. "Africa, lying open before us most particularly demands our attention."[47] More modestly, these dreams had already led to the laying of French West Africa's first tracks in the 1880's and 1890's.[48] As a graduate of Polytechnique, Roume was especially conditioned to embrace this particular vision of progress.[49]

Dakar's conviction that railroads were one key to civilization also coincided with a marked infatuation by the new Third Republic with the machine and its power to promote progress. At the World Exhibition (1889) in Paris, France's governing elite sought to proclaim to the rest of the world the achievements of liberalism under the Third Republic. It did so, Deborah Silverman has shown, by building two unquestionably industrial structures of monumental scale: the Gallery of Machines, composed of wrought iron and glass panes, and the Eiffel Tower, made entirely of iron. The purpose of these structures, as their design and the materials of which they were made suggest, was to introduce to France a new public environment that conformed to the dictates of modern science. As such, the exhibition left little doubt about the Third Republic's commitment to progress through the union of industry and technology and feats of engineering prowess.[50] By the turn of the century, it is true, the government's celebration of progress through technology was more tepid. Fin-de-siècle doubts about the health and world status of French industrial civilization relative to that of Germany and the United States tempered earlier optimism.[51] Yet, at the Paris Exposition of 1900, fully half of the exhibits were devoted to industry's latest triumphs: electrification, the opening of the Paris Metropolitan, automobiles and bicycles, and wireless telegraphy.[52] Subliminally, the pride in technology remained; and in organizations with a vested interest in celebrating applied science's contributions to civilization—the Ecole Polytechnique comes immediately to mind, as well as the Third Republic's new engineering institutes—faith in the transformative power of engineering feats endured undiminished.[53] Meanwhile, there was no such pessimism overseas. West Africa, after all, was virgin territory—at least from the perspective of technology—where older verities about the creative potential of the machine and material progress still seemed entirely appropriate and were given a new outlet.

Another source for Dakar's particular attachment to railroads was the internal colonization taking place within France itself. Even before the Eiffel Tower was conceived, and long after it was completed, the Third Republic was busy promoting progress through similar means on another front: among the savage inhabitants of rural France. As Sanford Elwitt and Eugen Weber have demonstrated in different ways, Paris between 1870 and 1914 consciously sought to integrate French peasant producers into the marketplace as well as the national culture. More to the point, railroads had played a key role in the government's plans for effecting this integration, and had always been described as agents of civilization. The Freycinet Plan, hammered out between 1877 and 1883, provided state subsidies for 23,000 kilometers of railroad lines to be constructed or taken over by private companies.[54] These earlier efforts at opening up new markets and transforming the environment had not, moreover, only promised civilization. To a large extent, the construction of France's "third railway" had delivered the pledged prosperity, although the prevailing emphasis upon progress often obscured the brutal means used to achieve the desired end. In France, in keeping with this rhetoric of progress through expanded exchanges, the material life of many peasants improved as railroads and roads penetrated ever deeper into the countryside.[55] By the turn of the century, urbanites, too, were experiencing new benefits from modernized public transport, as electric trams and subways continued the revolution that railroads had inaugurated.[56] As Stephen Kern has pointed out, although railroads were not new at the turn of the century, their hold tightened on "the political, military, economic and private life" of the nation as the railroad networks themselves thickened.[57]

In West Africa as well, one of the first railroads to be built, the Dakar–Saint-Louis line, fully confirmed the belief of contemporaries that a network of rails would indeed create a "joyous activity" in its wake and benefit all humanity. Although built for strategic and political reasons as much as economic ones, this line had become lucrative shortly after its completion in the late 1880's. Senegambia was the one part of French West Africa that was exporting an African cash crop—peanuts—before the establishment of the Government General. By creating a new inland corridor along which more agricultural products and imported goods could now flow, the completion of the Dakar–Saint-Louis railroad quickly led to an expansion in Senegal's peanut production.[58] The early success of the Dakar–Saint-Louis line reinforced the impression in late-nineteenth-century France that "lines of penetration" were crucial for opening up West Africa to civilizing trade. Here was yet another factor accounting for Dakar's definition of civilization.

Roume not only privileged railroads in his civilizing rhetoric. Hygiene, too, was preeminent, and for many—but not all—of the same reasons. Like railroads, hygiene had long held a special place in the republican hierarchy of essential values, particularly as a weapon against obscurantist priests.[59] In addition, certain advances earlier in the century in the treatment of tropical diseases, such as the discovery of quinine and drainage as effective prophylaxis against malaria, had been as essential to the European penetration of North Africa as superior transport and arms technology.[60] Given the continued reputation of West Africa as the "white man's grave," it was only natural for French overseas administrators under the Third Republic to stress hygiene as part of its *mise en valeur* and, by extension, its mission to civilize. Yet tradition and precedent alone do not account for Dakar's choice. Medical knowledge had crossed a dramatic new threshold in the 1860's and 1870's, thanks to the germ theory of disease developed by, among others, Koch and Pasteur. This bacteriological revolution consisted of exposing the invisible means by which disease was spread and providing, through vaccination and improved salubrity, the means to prevent disease.[61] These discoveries affected republican society in ways that also shed light on Dakar's decision to make *assainissement* its second civilizing priority in West Africa.

In France, the work of Pasteur hardly came out of the blue; more than half a century of public health research, activity, and legislation had prepared the way for his identification of germs as vectors of disease in the 1860's. Although the implications of this discovery were initially resisted, by the 1880's a constellation of circumstances predisposed several different interest groups to act upon Pasteur's findings. Defeat in 1870 followed by the Paris Commune, continued outbreaks of cholera and typhoid, and a falling birthrate convinced many legislators that the nation was degenerating. The especially high number of doctors in republican ranks—doctors who were used to thinking of the nation (and of its decline) in medical terms—encouraged this perception.[62] Microbiology offered scientific and objective solutions to what was increasingly perceived as a problem of national security. These solutions were also compatible with solidarist notions of the state's social responsibility for its citizens emerging among republicans in the 1890's. By the end of the century, the germ theory of disease was partially responsible for several important changes occurring in the structure of France's scientific

and medical community and the Third Republic's approach to
health care generally.

One noticeable change was the emergence of a new kind of scien-
tist-physician in France (and elsewhere)—the bacteriologist—whose
new scientific method was based on field and laboratory research.
This new community dedicated itself to identifying, reproducing for
experimental purposes, and eradicating the germs and parasites responsible for the major infectious diseases throughout the industri-
alized and colonial worlds. Their preferred means of disease control
were preventive vaccinations and curative serums or the disruption
of breeding grounds.[63] Success came quickly as researchers interna-
tionally took up Koch's and Pasteur's methods. Thanks to the combined efforts of American and European researchers, the etiology of
certain killing diseases in the West—typhoid and cholera—began to
be unraveled in the 1890's. Attention then turned to the tropical climates, where the greatest challenges in this direction still lay. In
1894 the plague bacillus was isolated; in 1897–1898 the transmis-
sion of malaria by the *Anopheles* mosquito was worked out; in 1901
the vector for yellow fever, the *Aedes aegypti* mosquito, was defini-
tively identified; and in 1901–1903 the trypanosome responsible for
sleeping sickness was isolated.[64] Through these victories, the germ
theory of disease was further vindicated and the new discipline of
tropical medicine was born.[65]

As a major power with a far-flung empire, the Third Republic
committed itself both ideologically and institutionally to this new
research through one organization in particular: the Institut Pasteur.
The first opened in France in 1888, and between 1891 and 1914 no
less than seven Instituts Pasteur were founded overseas.[66] Indeed, as
Anne Marie Moulin has argued and as these figures suggest, French
bacteriological research and teaching took root more successfully
among doctors in the colonies than in the metropole. In France, academic physicians accepted Pasteur's results but failed to promote the
laboratory-based research he had pioneered. Microbiology did not become part of the medical curriculum before World War I, and the Institut Pasteur remained the only metropolitan center for medical research until World War II. In the colonies, however, military doctors,
surgeons, and veterinarians embraced Pasteurian doctrines almost
immediately.[67] After 1905, Bruno's classic textbook, *Le tour de la
France par deux enfants*, used the example of the free distribution
of serums by the Pasteur Institute in Nha Trang (Annam) to illus-

trate the notion that "France, always generous, gives to all, without counting, its benefits [*bienfaits*] and its aid." In sub-Saharan Africa—and especially the colonies of Afrique Equatoriale Française—tracking and preventing sleeping sickness became the major area of French bacteriological research after 1900.[68]

Another related change evident in France during this same period was the emergence of a reinvorgated public health movement.[69] Drawing together architects, engineers, and doctors from the highest ranks of the medical profession, here was yet another group convinced by Pasteur's findings. Brandishing the latest evidence provided by bacteriological research, they saw it as their mission to put an end to the particularism and bureaucratic chaos that characterized public health legislation and replace it with uniform up-to-date health standards throughout France. In the process they hoped to free the masses from sloth, superstition, and medical quackery, and inculcate "civilized" hygienic practices.[70] The specific reforms they sought included the spread of medical assistance to the poor, routine inspection of lodgings, the mandatory reporting of contagious disease and disinfection of lodgings, mandatory smallpox vaccination, the provision of clean water, the creation of building codes, and the formation of a new corps of state-employed public health inspectors for overseeing these regulations. The hygienists also assumed that the central government was the only agent powerful enough to enforce these measures, and so they agitated for a unified and centralized public health authority.[71] From the outset, the hygienists had a powerful base in the Chamber of Deputies and the existing public health bureaucracy; they also founded numerous private and international organizations to broadcast their message, all of which boded well for the success of their movement.[72]

Despite their growing numbers, the hygienists did not have the final say in the formulation of medical and public health policy in metropolitan France at the end of the nineteenth century. Although several new laws were passed regulating public sanitation and health care, none in the end empowered the state to the extent that the professional hygienists had hoped. As is now well documented, the great winners in the campaign for improved hygiene and health were France's equally well organized local practitioners, and property owners in general.[73] Unlike the new public health experts, these doctors were determined to keep to a strict minimum the state's involvement in the delivery of expanding medical services.[74] Their

hostility to bureaucratized forms of care and greater government intervention in citizens' lives was shared by much of the conservative
Senate, which refused to sacrifice property rights to the cause of public health. Thus, no Direction of Public Health, comparable to the
new Direction of Labor and Direction of Public Assistance, was set
up in France to coordinate and enforce health care regulations. The
national Medical Assistance Law, guaranteeing all needy citizens
free medical care at home, and a public health bill enacting many of
the hygienists' major demands, were passed in 1893 and 1902, respectively. In each case, the Senate insisted that elected mayors and
local doctors, rather than professionals working exclusively for the
state, be entrusted with the new health administration. In the case
of public health, this provision compromised the effectiveness of the
new law from the outset; mayors and doctors would have little incentive to enact the 1902 regulations, yet there would be no overarching corps of inspectors to force them to comply.[75] In the case of
medical assistance, care by state-employed physicians working in
public hospitals and dispensaries was rejected in favor, in Martha
Hildreth's words, of "liberal-market medicine on a pay for services
rendered basis."[76]

Both the new developments in domestic and colonial hygiene and
medicine, and the thwarted ambitions of policy makers in the
metropole, go a long way toward explaining not only Roume's decision to make hygiene the second key to bringing material improvement to Africans but also how he and his successors organized sanitary conditions in the colony in the name of progress and civilization. Although Dakar would not have a Pasteur Institute until the
1920's, the colony of Senegal had had a bacteriological laboratory
since 1896—well before Roume's arrival.[77] With research proceeding
under his very nose, so to speak, Roume could hardly avoid being
impressed with, as he put it, the "immortal discoveries of Pasteur."
These discoveries, he repeatedly instructed his subordinates, were
founded not on "empiricism" but on "scientific theories that were
accepted by all."[78] That they were accepted by Dakar is evident in
the policies adopted. Roume's 1904 regulation of public health was,
as we have seen, principally devoted to combating the conditions in
which the recently identified *Anopheles* and *Aedes aegypti* could
breed. William Ponty, who served as head of the federation from
1908 to 1914 and continued Roume's health policies, was equally
convinced by the new medical findings and the measures they dic-

tated. Through yearly circulars he reminded the lieutenant governors and the field administrators of the need to enforce the preventive measures against malaria and yellow fever that modern science had sanctioned; not only the elimination of standing water, but the isolation of victims in screened rooms with mosquito netting were absolutely necessary.[79] These instructions, too, emphasized the new invisible bonds linking the sick and the healthy and the social responsibilities that their presence imposed upon all members of society: "Where is the man worthy of the name, who would assume the responsibility of, through his own negligence or of that of someone for whom he is responsible, poorly defending against mosquitoes, serving as a reservoir for the virus and allowing the disease to spread?"[80]

Yet it was not only the proven effectiveness of modern *assainissement* and the success of bacteriological research overseas generally that caused Dakar to privilege modern hygiene in West Africa. In the newly conquered territories, administrators could also act with a freedom only dreamt of by the hygienists back home, and this freedom, too, made public health activism that much more appealing to the Government General. For thirty years, metropolitan officials had pushed for dramatic changes in public health legislation, with disappointing results. If Roume and Ponty were as enthusiastic as they were about the recent discoveries in colonial medicine and preventive hygiene generally, it was in part because they could simply decree the same programs into existence, complete with the means to make the new guidelines effective.[81]

Which is what they did, as a comparison of health policies in the metropole and West Africa reveals. Roume drew upon metropolitan precedents when conceptualizing his initiatives. The AMI recalled the Medical Assistance Law, and the 1902 public health bill was adopted almost *in toto* in French West Africa in 1904. Despite their similarities, these policies differed in one important way from their metropolitan counterparts. In West Africa, public health regulation was given the teeth that the 1902 law lacked in France.[82] As in France, Roume's 1904 decree made local officials—mayors, administrators, and *commandants de cercle*—responsible for applying sanitary measures. But as was not the case in France, these officials were placed under the "surveillance and technical direction" of professional "sanitary authorities"—the inspector of sanitary services in Dakar and his counterparts in each colony. Each would inspect

and control local initiatives to ensure that the provisions of the decree were being applied.[83] Roume's Inspectorate of Sanitary Services
also preceded by eighteen years the formation of a Ministère de
Santé in France. Both differences suggest that Dakar's initiatives
were shaped as much by the lack of vigorous public health legislation in France as specific conditions in West Africa.

Finally, there is one additional reason Roume stressed modern
transportation and hygiene together as the keys to the material
progress of Africans. The nineteenth century had customarily measured the march of civilization in terms of natural obstacles overcome by science and technology. The new bacteriological discoveries
may well have represented for contemporaries the most spectacular
victory over nature since the steam engine. The important point
here, however, is not which "revolution" was greater—the locomo-
tive or modern bacteriology—but rather that many contemporaries
saw them as comparable triumphs; in the end, this tendency made
more natural Roume's linking public health and railroads. Doctors
involved in colonial medicine spoke of invisible micro-organisms
and parasites as posing the same impediment to civilization as the
vast African expanses identified by Roume. "We now know," the famous tropical microbiologist and founder of the Institut Pasteur, Dr.
Albert Calmette, confidently announced in 1912,

> the various modes of propagation of the trypanosomiases that form the
> principal obstacle—one might almost say the only obstacle—to the *mise
> en valeur* of the enormous African quadrilateral that extends between
> Guinea, the Upper Nile, Rhodesia and Angola.

And in 1915 Dr. Nattan-Larrier claimed:

> It has taken thirty years for science to discover the nature and origin of
> all the great endemic diseases that seemed to have stopped civilization at
> the threshold of the tropical countries. All the problems have now been
> posed, all the solutions are in sight. The governors of our colonies think
> as men of science and act as administrators to apply the doctrines to
> which the century of Pasteur has given birth.[84]

Roume, engineer that he was, did not concede that the propagation
of any epidemic or endemic disease constituted the principal obstacle to *mise en valeur*. Indeed, as he himself admitted, "if it were absolutely necessary to assign precedence to one or the other of these
ends [railroads or health care], it would be necessary, I think, to give
preference to railroad construction, which alone allows other forms

of progress to occur."[85] In particular, railroads held the key to eradicating "the terrible specter of hunger."[86] But he was sufficiently "a man of science" to grant public health concerns second billing and to insist that railroads and modern hygiene together would open Africa to civilization.

Civilization Through Science?

Along with self-interest, then, prevailing ideologies and scientific advances in the metropole, and earlier successes in France and West Africa, encouraged the new governors general in Dakar to make certain assumptions about the best way to uplift Africans. How accurate were these assumptions, and what effect, if any, did these beliefs have upon French actions between 1895 and 1914? Did the emphasis on material progress result in any tangible gains for the colonized? Did it actually serve the interests of the new colonial state, as appears to be the case? In point of fact, the belief that France and West Africa would benefit equally from the development of raw materials and cash crops for export, and increased consumption of imports, was fallacious from the outset. It served the particular economic needs of the federation first, and those of Africans only secondarily. Such a belief was in the interests of the Government General, since its own budget depended upon the tariff revenues derived from exports and imports. Thus when trade improved, the Government General's budget expanded. An increase in commercial exchanges was not as obviously in the interest of the African producer for a simple reason. Dependent as it was upon tariff revenues for the bulk of its income, the Government General was always tempted to increase the duties it levied on African-produced export commodities and on imports. When this happened, Africans were paid less for their produce, and charged inflated prices for any manufactured products they consumed.[87] Given this built-in discrimination against the African producer and consumer, it is entirely possible that African prosperity could have been better fostered through a policy of internal and regional development, rather than through the creation of an export-dependent economy. Dakar never considered this possibility. It took for granted that material progress could best be generated by policies that satisfied its own budgetary requirements, as well as the needs of French industry and merchant capital. This assumption was reflected in its ideology of civilization.

These examples suggest that, contrary to official doctrine, there was limited overlap between French and African interests in the realm of commercial exchanges. This should not be taken to mean, however, that Dakar's conflation of trade with civilization was entirely self-serving. Part of Dakar's interpretation of the *mission civilisatrice* was the belief that railroads were the means from which all other forms of progress, including trade, would follow. Railroads, Roume repeatedly insisted, would almost single-handedly deliver Africa from the barbarism resulting from insufficient commerce with the West, and produce the market integration upon which a successful policy of civilizing *mise en valeur* ultimately depended. These same notions persisted unaltered under his successor, William Ponty. Ponty in 1911 would request, and receive approval in Paris for, Dakar's third loan, in the amount of 167 million francs, to be devoted exclusively to infrastructure.[88] Despite appearing to further the economic needs of the Government General, such an exclusive emphasis upon railroads, ironically, did little to advance the federation's economic development between 1902 and 1914.[89]

One reason for this state of affairs was that the very importance Dakar attached to infrastructure effectively blinded the administration to the variety of geographical conditions and cultural and demographic barriers, which would also have to be taken into account before a program of rapid *mise en valeur* could successfully take place. Most of West Africa did not resemble the Senegambian basin, which since the 1860's had been integrated into the world economy through peanut cultivation. By the turn of the century, indigenous elites in that area were actively encouraging cash cropping among the peasantry, and the colony boasted a well-developed rural trade network, which would facilitate further expansion.[90] There was a large difference between building a railroad in such an area, and counting on a railroad to provide a sufficient incentive to grow new crops in colonies where these same historical and cultural factors did not exist. French doctrine obscured this important reality. One result was that, in the first fifteen years of the federation, Dakar paid little attention to mobilizing or regulating the African labor necessary for its policy of colonial development, especially outside the oldest urban centers of the federation, the Four Communes of Senegal.[91] Improving African agricultural methods and compiling demographic statistics for the federation were only slightly less neglected.[92]

Only on the eve of World War I did Dakar begin to show some signs of interest in labor availability and its protection. In 1912, what appears to have been the first general circular on labor recruitment before World War I was drawn up by the interim governor general François Clozel. In his directive, Clozel suggested that individual lieutenant governors should consider submitting proposals for regulating labor contracts in their colonies. Nothing came of this suggestion; Dakar would wait until 1925 before issuing the first labor regulations in West Africa.[93] At around the same time an internal memorandum on the subject of labor in all of West Africa noted that there were no African agricultural laborers who lived exclusively by working for others. The Africans who hired themselves out did so for only part of a year, and only to a member of their extended family. This situation made it difficult for the few European farmers in West Africa, who needed steady workers to succeed. The author went on to add "that outside of the cities it is rare that there is sufficient labor to allow the complete *mise en valeur* of the federation." Whole regions would continue to remain unproductive, "because of a lack of manpower." The author nevertheless ended on an optimistic note, and his final words provide one last reminder of how much faith Dakar put, before the war, in the transforming power of technology; with the opening of new communications, with the increasing contact with Europeans, with the constant population growth, the existing labor problems "were bound to disappear."[94]

Dakar's program of *mise en valeur* in West Africa between 1902 and 1914 paid the price of a civilizing ideology forged in a different social, economic, and cultural context than the one in which it operated during the early 1900's. Railroad construction would proceed much more slowly than expected and, in the face of high costs of transportation, the lack of sufficient middlemen in the interior, low population density, and peasant resistance, would fail to elicit the anticipated results. In 1913, the total value in francs for imports and exports in the federation had not even doubled since 1903, increasing only from 155,952,303 to 277,718,152. Exports from the potentially rich coastal colonies of Guinea, Ivory Coast, and Dahomey actually decreased during the same ten-year period.[95] In Senegal alone, peanut exports continued to expand; as a result, this colony provided the federal budget with most of its revenues between 1902 and 1914.[96] In time, Dakar would change its policies and its rhetoric to emphasize other means of promoting African exports, which would result in a more favorable balance sheet for the federation.

Dakar's failure to make much headway in the *mise en valeur* of West Africa because of an exaggerated emphasis upon communications leaves one final aspect of its doctrine of material progress for us to consider: the belief that, along with railroads, a program of improved public hygiene and medical services would benefit European and African alike. Of the three material goals proclaimed by French ideology to be in the equal interest of France and Africa—increased exports, railroad construction, and more modern sanitary conditions and medical care—this one seems to be the least controversial.

Yet, even in this area, French ideology did not serve the needs of the African community as promised. As we have seen, it ranked health care considerably behind railroad construction in importance, as the tiny subsidies allotted *les services sanitaires* compared to public works indicate. And even those hygiene measures that were taken revealed several fundamental flaws. First, French health care officials subordinated individualized medical assistance available to all Africans to public health measures designed principally to eradicate the two diseases most threatening to Europeans: yellow fever and malaria. One consequence of this preoccupation was that Dakar failed to pay sufficient attention early on to one disease decimating the African populations: sleeping sickness. Unlike in the case of smallpox, a vaccination against sleeping sickness did not yet exist. Not until 1911, and then under international pressure, did Dakar take measures against sleeping sickness.[97]

This oversight highlights a second flaw of Dakar's thinking. In keeping with its greater concern for improving the health of Europeans, Roume systematically gave priority to ameliorating conditions in cities alone, at the expense of the masses in the countryside. Strictly speaking, the Government General's emphasis on eliminating yellow fever and malaria in West Africa could have benefited the colonized as well as the colonizer. But this would have been true only if the French had devoted equal energy to urban and rural *assainissement;* this was not the case under either Roume or his successor, William Ponty.[98] Practically all the circulars sent out by Ponty reminding the lieutenant governors of preventive measures against the major tropical diseases were directed toward ports and cities. Only one major directive in this same period focused specifically on controlling endemic diseases among rural Africans. This di-

rective reorganized the AMI in 1912 as part of a larger effort to recruit more European doctors to the colony; it is true that, to a
greater extent than the 1904 and 1907 AMI arrêtés, the 1912 instructions emphasized "les services de la police sanitaire, des épi-
démies, de l'hygiène et de la santé publiques" among Africans.[99] In
addition to providing free *soins médicaux* to Africans, doctors were
now to tour their sanitary districts "as frequently as possible." This
would allow them to "draw up a map of malaria and sleeping sickness . . . distribute quinine free of charge . . . show village and canton chiefs how to use this precious drug . . . and determine the *index endémique* of the localities visited."[100] These instructions anticipated a much larger program of preventive hygiene and a
campaign against infant mortality among Africans as well as Europeans that would emerge in the Third Republic after the war. In the
prewar era, however, civilization through improved hygiene and the
attenuation of endemic diseases remained a pipe dream for most of
France's subjects, despite French claims to the contrary.

And even for urban residents, the improvement was only relative.
Modern bacteriology clearly led the Government General to under-
estimate the problems of introducing Western concepts of public and
personal hygiene into a tropical environment. The colonial governments were also much too short of personnel and funds to carry out
the program of urban *assainissement* and sanitary policing that they
outlined on paper. These blind spots and structural constraints compromised what limited efforts were made to ameliorate public
health in coastal West Africa before World War I. The policy of eradicating yellow fever and malaria by destroying mosquitoes at their
source was ill-suited to rapidly growing cities of mixed population. It
was impossible to control standing water inside homes. The local
sanitary services, when they existed at all, were insufficiently
equipped, understaffed, and poorly trained. Although the 1904 decree allowed officials to enter private residences and issue fines for
health code violations, such intrusions were opposed equally by Europeans and Africans.[101] Further complicating French efforts was the
fact that Africans could carry plasmodia without displaying clinical
symptoms of malaria. Minor outbreaks of yellow fever in 1911 and
1913, and a major outbreak of the plague in Dakar in 1914, revealed
just how difficult improving health conditions along the coast was
proving to be. Through necessity, these epidemics inspired the most
ambitious—but also the most racist—sanitary project to date for Af-

ricans rather than Europeans. In 1914, the Government General announced its plan to relocate unhygienic African residents away from the European quarters, to "a model native city," complete with "roads, gutters, potable water, sewers, electric lights."[102] But this new African village, Medina, failed to realize French hopes and remained notoriously insalubrious.[103] Once again lack of funds, local resistance, and not considering urbanization from any other point of view than the sanitary one helped defeat Dakar's announced intentions.[104] Yet failure did little to encourage the French to rethink their methods. The problem, they insisted, was lax compliance with existing regulations, not the strategy endorsed by science itself.

There remain, finally, those few initiatives that Dakar did undertake to improve the health of individual Africans. The AMI, it will be recalled, had two vocations: curing the ill through dispensaries and hospitalization, and modern prophylaxis. While the impulse to cure was genuinely altruistic, in practice the French approach in this domain suffered from the same constraints as urban public health measures. Medical care was hampered early on by a shortage of doctors and provisions, and an unrealistic assessment of the task it had set for itself. Although Ponty's 1912 effort did increase medical personnel, on the eve of the war there were still only about one hundred European doctors for an estimated African population of eight to ten million (a ratio of 1:100,000).[105] The doctors who were hired continued, for the most part, to reside in town with their fellow Europeans. The African medical assistants received such superficial training, they were useless unless directly supervised by a doctor.[106] Although elaborate plans were drawn up for a model *groupe d'assistance indigène,* which could be adapted to the different colonies according to their needs, construction of an original twenty foreseen in 1906 was still going on six years later; the African hospital in Dakar took seven years to complete.[107] In the end, the greatest progress was made in the domain in which the French had had the most experience at home, and whose implementation required a single visit: smallpox vaccination. By the early 1920's the French claimed—prematurely, as it turned out—to have eliminated smallpox from most of the federation.[108]

Science and technology, Michael Adas and Daniel Headrick have argued, played a central role in creating the reality of Europe's power overseas and the myth of its superior civilization. The outlook and

policies of the Government General examined in this chapter confirm these insights, but also invite certain qualifications. As the
chief architect of Dakar's prewar *mise en valeur*, Roume articulated
a view of progress that equated economic development, and more
specifically the construction of railroads and the conquest of parasites, with the advent of civilization. However linked to the economic vocation of the Government General, these beliefs also derived from both a traditional republican faith in the uplifting potential of science and technology generally, and more recent
fin-de-siècle trends to intervene in both natural and human "milieux" in order to improve the well-being of society as a whole. In
the wake of the new medical advances in France, reformers were beginning to insist that greater urban planning and social legislation
were necessary not only for moral reasons, but for reasons of greater
productivity and rationalization. The opportunity for similar exper-
imentation in the colonies was considerably more extensive, as
Roume's initiatives prove. In the case of the Government General
of West Africa, republican faith in scientific progress and the modern
interest in improving "milieux" were mutually reinforcing.

Yet giving priority to railroads and hospitals did not translate into
immediate gains for the French, and even less so for Africans.
Roume's insistence that material progress in West Africa depended
first and foremost upon the provision of infrastructure, and secondarily upon improved hygiene, was also the product of a decided lack
of familiarity with the African continent, which excessive pride in
European science only reinforced. Just how much French power was
enhanced by Dakar's early communications and health care policies
thus remains open to debate.

Such ignorance of African conditions was perhaps not surprising
in 1904, given that West Africa had only become "French" within
the two preceding decades, and that parts of the federal territories
were not yet fully conquered. It is less easy to understand its presence ten years later, on the eve of World War I. Only in the 1920's
did Dakar widen its definition of *mise en valeur*, to emphasize more
than railroads and port construction. One important reason for this
persistence of Roume's material definition of civilization was that
only the colonial lobby in Paris had a sustained interest in overseas
development during the first decade of the twentieth century. After
the initial decisions to create and reform the Government General,
pressure from the metropolitan government for quick results in

West Africa waned. Without such pressure, Dakar was not forced to rethink its economic strategy for developing the federation's resources. In the context of this relative indifference, any delay in increasing exports could simply be attributed to the delays in building transportation and medical infrastructure.

A more local factor, however, also helps to account for the rigidity of French ideology in this domain. Before World War I, ameliorating Africans through "superior" French science constituted only one aspect of Dakar's civilizing doctrine. Of equal if not greater importance was an emphasis upon ensuring the moral progress of their subjects. Given this other preoccupation, it is hardly surprising that French ideas of *mise en valeur* did not change after the final reorganization of the Government General. How to improve Africans morally, in contrast, proved a more dynamic concept in Dakar between 1904 and 1914.

CHAPTER 3

Forging the Republican 'Sujet'

SCHOOLS, COURTS, AND THE
ATTACK ON SLAVERY (1902–1908)

We can legitimately hope to witness . . . the advancement of the
native populations to a higher state of civilization. But such a result
cannot merely be decreed; it can only be the end product of a series
of patient and converging efforts whose goal is the moral and material
improvement of the native through the maintenance of peace and
security, the opening of communications, medical assistance and
hygiene, the diffusion of elementary and professional instruction,
the development of agricultural production and, last but not least,
the guaranteed enjoyment of individual rights and of the most sacred
right of all—that of individual freedom.
— Governor General Ernest Roume[1]

 "Of ancient provenance, the vocation to a civilizing mission
took on many forms according to the possibilities and the ideology
of the moment. In the nineteenth century, the school was its preferred means."[2] Denise Bouche's opinion is echoed indirectly in the
only chapter in Eugen Weber's work on the modernization of rural
France with "civilization" in its title. This is the chapter on schools,
entitled "Civilizing in Earnest: Schools and Schooling."[3] These
statements reflect what has often been taken for granted about
France's *mission civilisatrice* in the nineteenth century: that it was
to teach non-French speakers to become French, through education.
Yet Roume's emphasis on the civilizing potential of *mise en valeur*
challenges, from the outset, the view that France had one preferred
means for uplifting Africans, and raises the general question of what
other goals besides material progress the administration in Dakar associated with the term "civilization." It also inevitably revives the
age-old debate regarding the extent to which the French conflated
civilization with not only mutually beneficial economic development, but becoming culturally French as well.
 The speeches and policies of the Government General attest to

the fact that, in addition to raising the African standard of living, the new authorities indeed believed that they had an obligation to up-lift Africans in other, more moral, ways. These sources also provide an idea of what the Government General meant by the term "moral." According to Roume, along with railroads and health care, progress required providing Africans with the security and peace of a well-policed society—a goal that military conquest had achieved. Second, the Government General had to introduce a system of mod-ern schools and courts, if it wished to advance the cause of civiliza-tion. Finally, African uplift depended upon respecting the freedom of the individual and the rights of the masses; domestic slavery and predatory aristocratic rule, which Dakar believed to be entrenched institutions in precolonial African society, had to be abolished. Hav-ing articulated this moral agenda, Roume and his successors initi-ated a variety of policies consistent with their statements.

These measures confirm that schools, while constituting one ele-ment of France's civilizing mission, in the eyes of Dakar were nei-ther the sole nor the preferred instrument for transforming African society. An assessment of these measures also, however, undermines a second assumption commonly made about French imperial ideol-ogy: that it was assimilationist—that is to say, it consciously es-poused the belief that all Africans should eventually be assimilated into French culture and society. Although a precedent for such as-similation existed in the oldest French colony of the federation, the Four Communes of Senegal, the judicial, educational, and emancipa-tionist policies enacted by Dakar make clear that the new Govern-ment General rejected the notion that part of its civilizing mission was to make Africans into Frenchmen. Instead, these policies show, the French felt they were duty-bound to respect "traditional" West African customs and to encourage the peoples of the federation to evolve within their own African cultures, with one exception. This exception was if the custom in question was deemed to conflict with the principles of civilization as defined by the Third Republic. In those cases, the Government General insisted on its obligation and its right to excise the morally reprehensible attributes and re-place them with superior French mores and institutions.

At first glance, it is tempting to attribute these civilizing ideas to the emergence in the 1890's of the colonial doctrine known as asso-ciation. Association ostensibly superseded the older concept of as-similation; reflecting the trend toward social evolutionary thinking in the social sciences, it emphasized that France respect the diversity of the colonized and their institutions. Yet the term "association" was not used in Dakar at all before World War I. Instead, much of the Government General's view of moral progress apparently derived from an older and richer French tradition still: republicanism, and, more particularly, the universal principles of 1789. The aspects of African society that the French found so objectionable, including its failure to respect the individual's right to dispose of his labor and to live free from tyranny and superstition, all reveal the impact of the ideology of the French Revolution upon the doctrine of the Government General, even after the old ideal of assimilation had been rejected; the decision to found schools for the masses was also entirely in keeping with the social agenda of the republicans now in power in Paris. In short, the Third Republic's official *mission civilisatrice* in the early 1900's was neither preeminently assimilationist nor associationist. Rather, it was profoundly republican, at a time when traditional republican values were still ascendent at home.[4]

Every Center Should Have a School

In 1903, shortly after his arrival, Roume made the education of all France's African subjects an official civilizing objective of his administration. This policy sheds light on two aspects of France's *mission civilisatrice*, as interpreted in West Africa after 1895, which French judicial policy and the attack on slavery will also illuminate. The first aspect was a belief that Africans had to evolve within their own cultures rather than that of France. In the educational realm, this belief was evident in Roume's repeated axiom that metropolitan curriculum had to be "adapted" to the special needs of the African peoples. This notion marked a conscious departure from the founding principles of the only French schools extant at the time of the creation of the Government General, those of the Four Communes in Senegal, which were based upon assimilation.[5]

The second aspect of French ideology that Dakar's educational policy highlights was the extent to which French civilization discourse in Dakar had a republican dimension. The very decision to make the education of all Africans an objective of French administration in West Africa reflected this influence. This measure can be understood only in the larger context of French educational policy in the metropole under the Third Republic. One of the Third Republic's priorities, after its consolidation in the late 1870's, was the introduction of universal, free, compulsory, lay instruction in France at the primary school level. The idea—itself inherited from the First Republic—was to create a more democratic and egalitarian society in which careers would be open to talent. It also reflected the new regime's determination to mold a loyal, patriotic, and enlightened citizenry.[6] A series of laws passed between 1881 and 1886, along with the allocation of more than 550 million francs in state subsidies and loans, ensured the success of this educational program.[7] Largely because of this commitment to primary education in the metropole, Roume automatically assumed that universal education should be a goal of the new Government General in West Africa. Other aspects of French educational policy also revealed this republican mind-set.

When the West African Federation was reorganized in 1902–1904, the coastal towns known as the Four Communes of the colony of Senegal had the most organized school service in the federation. The governors of the colonies of Guinea and Ivory Coast had proved indifferent to African education, in part because their budgets before 1902 were so insignificant. Some schools existed in southern Dahomey, thanks largely to the missionaries present there. Military officers in charge of the Western Sudan had created schools whenever possible since the early 1880's, to disseminate the principles of French civilization and train African personnel for the administration. Their efforts were, however, hampered by budgetary constraints and the difficulty of recruiting competent teachers.[8] It has been estimated that in 1903 the federation provided rudimentary education to 5,010 students, out of a total school-age population of approximately 1,200,000.[9]

The schools of the Four Communes of Senegal, which included the cities of Gorée, Saint-Louis, Dakar, and Rufisque, were the exception to the poor educational record achieved in West Africa before 1903, for a number of historical and political reasons. Unlike the territories comprising the rest of the federation, Saint-Louis and Gorée had been French since the seventeenth century. Moreover, throughout the nineteenth century they had been ruled according to assimilationist precepts.[10] As early as 1833, the local inhabitants were granted the rights of French citizens. These rights were suspended under the Second Empire but were restored by the new republican regime in 1871. In 1872, Saint-Louis and Gorée were placed under the same municipal laws as those in France, and within fifteen years Rufisque and Dakar had been granted the same status. In 1879, Senegal was permitted to send a deputy to Parliament; at the same time, its local elected assembly, the General Council, was restored. The result of these liberal reforms was to create an assimilated enclave on the coast of Senegal, where French law and educational institutions applied not only to a minority of French and mulatto Catholics, but to the more numerous Muslim inhabitants of the Four Communes as well.[11] This enclave formed an anomaly in French West Africa after 1880, when the French began to extend their conquest beyond the coastal settlements of Senegal. The territories of the interior were placed instead under special protectorate regimes, which, at least in theory, respected existing African institutions and polities.

The Four Communes also benefited from a policy of cultural assimilation, at least as far as the Catholics and mulattoes were concerned. This took the form of the early establishment of a school system based on the metropolitan model.[12] In 1903, the entire male Christian population of the Four Communes had already been educated at the primary school level. In contrast, French schools outside the Four Communes were nonexistent. The *assimilés*, as the Senegalese from the Four Communes who had successfully assimilated French culture were called, were themselves dominated by a small number of third- or fourth-generation mulatto families, who controlled local government and commerce and who considered themselves fully French.[13] Since 1847, when primary education was first officially organized in the colony, these families had insisted that the same curricula and exams used in the metropole be adopted in their schools. The same order of French missionaries, the Frères de Ploërmel, had run these schools since their founding. As far as Senegal's ruling class was concerned, the Frères de Ploërmel had served the interests of the Four Communes well. By the turn of the century, however, that was no longer true, given the realities of France's new empire.

In 1903, the new governor general of French West Africa, Ernest Roume, decided to create a federal school system that would provide free lay instruction to their African subjects. But he rejected assimilation as inappropriate and politically dangerous for a colony as vast and ethnically diverse as West Africa. Dakar made its feelings on this matter clear when it accused the Senegal secondary school of nurturing unrealistic expectations among its students and preparing a generation of drifters and *déclassés*.[14] Economic considerations re-inforced this assessment. Roume realized that the metropolitan school system, transplanted to West Africa, would not contribute to the kind of development the Government General now wished to undertake, ostensibly for everyone's benefit. This development re-quired greater African agricultural productivity and skilled workmen for infrastructure construction, not lycée graduates.

Finally, by the end of the nineteenth century assimilation had been rejected in Parisian colonial circles influenced by both racist and progressive trends in the social sciences. Physical anthropology since mid-century had emphasized Africans' racial inferiority and insisted that they were incapable of following the same trajectory as Westerners. The newer discipline of sociology also stressed the dif-ferences between human societies; but it studied cultural rather than racial differences, and did not see these differences as im-mutable. Despite their antithetical conclusions, both trends argued against a continued policy of assimilation. And social evolutionary thinking—in theory, at least—encouraged the study of each society in its own environment as a prelude to improving it. Although Afri-can cultures would not become the official object of academic re-search until the 1920's, the notion that primitive societies should evolve along their own lines was widely accepted in France by the turn of the century.[15]

For all these reasons, then, an alternative educational doctrine emerged shortly after Roume took office. What French West Africa needed, Roume reiterated, was not metropolitan education, but schools "adapted" to local conditions. The federal educational pro-gram that Dakar enacted demonstrated what this meant. On Janu-ary 22, 1903, the law separating Church and State in France was ap-plied to the colonies, and missionaries involved in running state-funded schools were summarily ejected from their institutions. The central administration promptly stepped into the breach when Roume asked the new lieutenant governor of Senegal, Camille Guy, to draw up a series of recommendations for educational reform in Africa. Guy had recently arrived in the federation, and boasted as lit-tle field experience as his superior in Dakar. An *agregé* in history (that is, one who has passed the *agrégation*, or examination for ad-mission to teaching in state secondary schools or universities), Guy had taught in a French lycée for fourteen years before joining the colonial administration in 1895.[16] He nevertheless shared Roume's interest in economic affairs; in 1900 he had published a volume entitled *Les colonies françaises: La mise en valeur de notre domaine coloniale*. His report to Roume reflected both his teaching background and his preoccupation with *mise en valeur*. He stressed the importance of vocational training, arguing that many African populations were "particularly skilled in the manual arts." He likewise suggested special commercial training, to guarantee the French trading houses the experienced African agents they needed. It would also be necessary to teach Africans how to farm, and to introduce them to new techniques and new equipment. Despite this stress on practical instruction, Guy did not rule out a more intellectual instruction in history, geography, reading and writing, and the French language. The point of education was to introduce mechanical arts and "give to these essentially malleable populations a respect for the grand principles that together constitute, so to speak, the patrimony of modern democracy."[17]

Guy's recommendations were incorporated into the 1903 arrêté establishing a federal system of free and secular—but not compulsory—schools for Africans. The arrêté, issued on November 24, envisaged four types of African education similar to those in France, but encompassing fewer grade levels: primary, professional (manual trades), higher primary (post-elementary), and commercial and teacher training.[18] Primary education was the cornerstone of the new system. Although envisioned largely for boys, the arrêté did anticipate that girls' schools should be opened wherever the demand arose. Three types of primary schools were distinguished—village, urban, and regional. Rural areas were to be divided into school regions. In each region, one-room, one-teacher village schools run by Africans trained in Dakar could be opened in any center large enough to provide them with thirty to forty pupils a year. Village schools offered a three- to six-year course of study covering one to two grade levels; their mission was primarily to teach spoken French, and secondarily hygiene, reading, writing, arithmetic, *leçons de choses* focusing on agriculture, and, in Islamicized areas, Arabic. Once these two levels had been mastered, the best students could continue at a regional school. A regional school was to be provided in the capital of each school region. It would be run by a European instructor and would offer a three-year middle course of study, comprising the next two grade levels and designed to train a new African elite. At this level, equal weight was to be given to French language, Arabic (where appropriate), reading, writing, math, geometry, drawing, French history "in its relation to the different countries of West Africa," and "notions of physical and natural science applied to hygiene, agriculture and local industry." Each regional school would also have a special section for professional training and a garden for studying agriculture. A certificate of primary study would be awarded to pupils who passed a comprehensive examination at the end of their third year.[19] In practice, students could stay on at a regional school until they completed the courses offered, and no exam was ever administered.[20]

In contrast to the adapted rural curriculum, the urban primary school was patterned on the French model, with only minor modifications. The 1903 arrêté specified that an urban primary school with a European staff and a metropolitan curriculum could be opened wherever there were sufficient numbers of French and assimilated Africans. Some adjustments of the curriculum were allowed, to meet local conditions; for example, courses in colonial history and geography were included in the Senegalese urban schools. No radical departure from the standard French course was, however, possible, because Europeans in the school had to qualify for entrance to metropolitan secondary schools and institutions of higher learning. Assimilated African students in these classes were to learn from the same textbooks used in France.

The administration's emphasis on practical training was also evident at the postprimary level. As the 1908 annual report on education insisted, "[We] are concerned above all else to ensure that the young natives who attend our schools acquire a means to earn their living honorably and to allow them to participate in the social development of the colony. After having formed the workers and the functionaries whom we may need . . . we have oriented our natives' minds toward practical things, in keeping with the program traced in 1903."[21] The arrêté anticipated three types of postprimary education—higher primary and commercial, professional, and teacher training—to be offered in two different federal institutions in Dakar. The Saint-Louis secondary school, renamed l'Ecole Faidherbe, was originally allowed to continue as a higher primary commercial school. Within four years, however, it had closed because of cost overruns. Its students were directed either to the new normal school or to the Ecole Pinet-Laprade, the federation's only professional training school. Students for Pinet-Laprade were to be recruited from all over the federation; they were to learn manual trades and to become "skilled workers."[22] The other postprimary institution foreseen by Guy was a teacher training, or normal, school.[23] In order to establish a federal school system, it was imperative to train an African teaching corps as quickly as possible. African teachers would be both cheaper and better adapted to the countryside than their French counterparts. Properly trained, they could be the ideal agents of French influence in the rural areas. They were to be recruited from throughout the federation and would undergo a three-year course of study in Dakar. The curriculum, as established in 1903 when the school was founded, was an ambitious one, combining a practical orientation with courses modeled on those offered in metropolitan schools. The point of such a combination, Dakar reaffirmed in 1912, was to "ensure that the graduates did not take themselves for mandarins once they had their piece of parchment."[24]

The school system and curriculum conceived in 1903 reflected the Government General's overall philosophy of how best to move African society along the path of civilization. The accent upon reading and writing at the regional school level was designed to guarantee the federation the literate auxiliary personnel that it needed to embark on a program of mutually beneficial *mise en valeur*. Instruction of the mass of Africans was to contribute to the same end by teaching them basic skills that would help raise their productivity. In keeping with the new trends in sociology, local history, African traditions, and Arabic were now all emphasized; this would avoid uprooting Africans from their own cultures. Instruction in French and French colonial history would also help Africans to love the motherland, to understand French motives, and to gain access to the ideas that made France civilized.

Conceived in these terms, adapted education in West Africa appeared to represent a repudiation of past assimilationism in favor of a school system founded upon respect for Africans' own traditions. Indeed, Guy's and Roume's emphasis upon teaching about indigenous cultures went—at least on paper—considerably beyond any interest that metropolitan social scientists at the turn of the century were yet displaying in African civilization. Before World War I, ethnographers in France accepted the standard division between civilized and uncivilized peoples, categorized Africans among the latter, and largely ignored them. This was true even as physical anthropology, whose racist preoccupations had prejudiced scholars against African societies for most of the nineteenth century, began to be eclipsed by sociology. Only in the late 1890's did the Ecole des Langues Orientales begin to teach a few African languages; the Ecole Coloniale also offered limited training in African customs, institutions, and history after 1905.[25] In 1903, then, the federal authorities were among the first to legitimate African cultures as objects worthy of study in France—if only for practical reasons.

However committed the Government General appeared to be to a policy of African evolution within their own cultures, it had not broken with many of the universalistic premises upon which assimilation had been based—as the described curriculum also amply attests. These premises were, after all, ones that still resonated in France under the Third Republic in the prewar years. The belief in the inherent superiority of French civilization had not disappeared from official ideology in the metropole at the end of the century. To the contrary, it underlay the early Third Republic's campaign to transform all *patois*-speaking peasants into French citizens. An equally strong desire to endow the recently enfranchised individual with the means to exercise responsibly his political rights (or her civil rights) also fueled the Republic's continuing commitment to universal education in the Belle Epoque. Given the prevalence of these ideas and motives at home, it would have been surprising had there been no trace of them overseas, particularly when the very republican decision to educate Africans had already been taken. In point of fact, republican values exercised a decisive influence on French civilizing ideas and actions in West Africa in a variety of areas, beginning with adapted education.

Several republican aspects of Dakar's new educational policy in West Africa stand out. One was the impulse to spread lay education as widely as possible at the village level, and to keep the content of that education fairly intellectual. Primary school attendance was not made mandatory in West Africa as in France, partly, of course, for practical reasons. The expense would have been prohibitive; the French Government General was in the business not of making citizens, but of civilizing its subjects. Since civilization was a slow process, and since subjects would not grow up to vote, the need for compulsion was less obvious in the colonies than in France. In addition, compulsory education might alienate unnecessarily their Mus-

lim subjects. This lack of compulsion, along with the practical curriculum and fewer grade levels taught, was what "adaptation" was
ostensibly all about. And yet, ideological considerations also played
their part. In the matter of both attendance and content, republican
habits died hard, especially with a former teacher drawing up the
blueprints. Dakar clearly desired a compulsion that it rejected on
economic and political grounds. "Education," Roume complained in
1905, "is still far from reaching the deepest reaches [*couches pro-
fondes*] of the native populations." His interim replacement in 1908
insisted, "It is possible to do more." Every center of any importance
should have a school, even if it offered only "the most rudimentary
instruction."[26]

The Government General likewise set its sights on inculcating in
all Africans the same rational outlook that permeated metropolitan
educational efforts. The guiding principles of universal primary instruction in France were that it be secular and, in the words of the
educational expert, P. Lapie, "practical and educational" (*utilitaire
et éducatif*). These principles informed Guy's and Roume's approach
to education overseas. The *école française* in West Africa was made
laïque, Roume explained, because of the religious neutrality of the
Third Republic; children, he added optimistically, would only come
more willingly when they did not have to fear proselytization.[27] Similarly, the centerpiece of the Republic's new scientific pedagogy, the
leçon des choses, was at the core of Dakar's approach to education.[28]
As in France, Africans were first to be presented with concrete objects and then, ideally, made to understand from them abstract principles. Prominently featured in Guy's organization of 1903, the *leçon
des choses* was reemphasized by Dakar in 1908:

> If we are most concerned with placing within the grasp of the natives as
> quickly as possible the *leçons de choses*, which they must know in order
> to be of real use to the European in the rational exploitation of the re-
> sources of the country, then we should consider the village school the
> most efficient instrument for achieving this result immediately. . . . The
> agents running these schools should thus be invited to make their courses
> as interesting as possible, either by varying the *leçons de choses*, or prefer-
> ably by choosing the most simple notions of hygiene or natural history
> which could.bring their students to understand the utility of these prac-
> tices introduced by civilization.[29]

Despite the limited use to which Africans were expected to put
their new ability to think "rationally," adapted education was in

this respect, too, closer to the progressive aspects of its metropolitan counterpart.[30]

Another republican influence was the decision to make French-language instruction, along with practical skills and basic literacy, an integral part of the federal educational program. French authorities themselves repeatedly presented this choice as anything but assimilationist. French was taught, they argued, not because of its inherent superiority, not because they wanted all Africans—like their metropolitan counterparts—to speak French, but because there were simply too many African dialects to master. West Africa needed a common language as badly as it needed a common railroad system, and, by default, French was the only one available.[31] This utilitarian argument was not entirely disingenuous; the provision for instruction in Arabic seemed to confirm that the French were serious about respecting local custom whenever possible. But arguments for the inherent virtues of the French language, and the importance of its dissemination for binding the colonized to the colonizer, were equally numerous. The objective of French-language instruction, according to Guy, was not to "incite Africans to renounce their country or to forget their origins," but to teach them to love their own country and France simultaneously.[32] The use of French, moreover, was crucial to making the leap from barbarism to civilization. "Even if we admit that the child who returns to his family after an elementary school education rapidly loses the use of the French language," Governor General Ponty wrote several years later, "he will not be able to erase from his memory the uplifting notions which, through the intermediary of this language, we will have caused to penetrate. The words may disappear, but the ideas will remain, and the ideas, which are our own and whose use endows us with our moral, social and economic superiority, will little by little transform these barbarians of yesterday into disciples and auxiliaries."[33]

Such arguments recalled those being made at the same time in France against regional dialects, which the governing republicans in the 1890's were increasingly identifying with obscurantism and popular religiosity, and they were seeking to eradicate more systematically than they had a generation earlier. As Caroline Ford has argued, when conservatives began winning at the polls and anticlericalism heated up again in France before and especially after the Dreyfus affair, "a common language and cultural unity had become an essential part of republican articulation of nationality."[34] In this realm also metropolitan traditions were too entrenched to be questioned even by the most sincere advocates of adapted education in Dakar.

Finally, republicanism was evident in Dakar's attitude regarding who should attend these schools. The French insisted that those who were to become the new literate auxiliary class be drawn from all social milieux, not merely from the old ruling classes. This outlook contrasted with the policy of the past, when military administrators had concentrated their educational efforts almost exclusively on the sons of chiefs, in the belief that they would remain France's natural collaborators in administering the federation.[35] The new Government General, however, had no intention of preserving the chiefs' power any more than necessary, because, as we shall see in the next chapter, it offended their republican values. This leveling emphasis was evident in the name chosen for the teacher training school in 1905: "At last," Guy announced, "rejuvenated and materially and morally regenerated, the old school for the sons of chiefs emerges from the ashes of the past under the significant and democratic name of Normal School."[36] The following passage, although written by the lieutenant governor of Guinea a year after Roume left office, also suggests the progressive democratization of African social relations which Dakar hoped to effect through education. Describing the enrollment in his village school of former slaves, alongside sons of chiefs, he noted:

> It must be recognized, to the credit of the caste called "captives," that its children rival in zeal, intelligence and work the sons of the old aristocracy. The "sons of chiefs" see them, not without jealousy, acquiring the highest marks in our classrooms. Such scholastic success is the best possible incentive for [these sons of chiefs]. This rivalry has in turn placed the schools in a positive light. Children and parents are now convinced that intelligence and knowledge alone create social superiority and that, in a future not too far away, only those who have profited from our instruction in order to learn our civilization will be able to command the authority in native society that used to be the exclusive preserve of the aristocracy.[37]

As in France, the new school system in West Africa was consciously conceived as a means for limited social mobility.

Guy's program represented Dakar's first attempt to create a unified network of rural schools throughout the federation. It was, at most, a statement of principles and a general outline of how to proceed; more detailed organization and specific curricula would only appear under the next administration. Roume, in the end, never made education a high priority while in office, and once the 1903 directive had been signed, educational initiative—to the extent that it existed at all—passed to the individual lieutenant governors.[38]

Yet even in its embryonic form, Dakar's approach to education under Roume is an important point of departure for understanding French civilizing ideology in West Africa. The tenets of adapted education confirm that, along with the practical reasons for education, Dakar felt an obligation to improve its subjects morally. Gradual evolutionism and republicanism were, moreover, essential themes of France's mission in this moral realm. Both aspects were evident in a variety of other policies that Dakar initiated in its founding years. Among the most important were the creation of a system of "native" courts and the adoption of a "native" policy designed to "liberate" Africans.[39] In these cases, however, there emerged an apparently new facet of the tenet that Africans had to evolve within their own cultures. This was the added proviso that customs antithetical to French civilization had to be suppressed. Upon closer scrutiny, this begins to look familiar; as it turned out, what Dakar defined as antithetical to civilization was determined largely by the same French republican sentiments that had played such a dominant role in its concept of African education.

Let Justice Reign

In 1903, the Government General declared that it was France's duty as civilizer to guarantee the rule of law and to institute a fair and humane system of justice throughout West Africa. Once again, political and economic considerations made such judicial control imperative. In order to endure, the colonial state had to be able to wield ultimate power to settle disputes, and to punish perceived deviant patterns of behavior—particularly crimes. Economic development also required a uniform set of laws to protect the interests of European merchants, regulate commercial relations between Africans and Europeans, and facilitate the *mise en valeur* of the territory's resources. Yet humanitarian considerations also intervened to determine the form of the new system. The new courts, Dakar stated at the outset, would respect custom insofar as it did not conflict with the principles of civilization.

When the Government General decided to organize a system of

justice throughout the federation in 1903, French courts applying French laws had already been established along the coast, where most Europeans were concentrated. However, no formal French legal system had been set up inland, where Africans continued to litigate their own disputes with little interference from the French administration. The first question to arise, therefore, when Dakar decided to unify the administration of justice, was whether French law should be extended to the interior. As had been the case with education, the Government General immediately rejected the assimilationist solution as impractical and prejudicial to the best interests of the colonized. Treaties, Roume pointed out, had been signed with African chiefs during the conquest, stipulating that African "custom" would be respected throughout the federation. As a civilized nation, France was bound to honor these agreements. A fundamental principle of the new system was thus that African "customary law" would remain the common law of the federation and that French law would only apply in the cities.[40] In keeping with this decision, "native" courts would be set up in the rural areas, while French courts were maintained in urban ones.[41]

Roume's decision confirmed what the 1903 school system had already indicated: that France had no intention of forcing its own institutions upon the colonized, as part of its civilizing mission in Africa. This did not, however, imply that France would adopt a hands-off policy toward its subjects. Complete nonintervention would have been an abdication of its important duties, as a superior civilization, to ensure that some sort of African evolution took place as a result of France's presence. A second principle of the new system therefore was that African custom would be respected only to the extent that it did not conflict with the principles of civilization. When a conflict occurred, French justice would apply.

This principle reveals, to an even greater extent than their schools, that the French felt they had a right to intervene actively in the lives and mores of their subjects. Yet, such a clause, by its very vagueness, provides no real clue to what the administration meant by the need to suppress customs that conflicted with French standards of morality. For a clearer picture of French ideology on this point, we must turn to the actual policies initiated in the name of civilization. A preliminary assessment of the legal system Roume established indicates a relative indifference by the authorities to reforming African civil custom, whose application they left almost entirely to African judges. The point was not, as a ministerial circular explained, whether civil law was simply contrary to "our European civilization." Rather, it was whether civil law was "immoral or illicit." Most of the time, the minister suggested, civil law was neither. "It is for this reason that we will under no circumstance alter especially those essential rights that result from the husband's authority over his wife, the father's authority over his children or guardianship."[42] The subordinate status of African women would, in short, receive little attention from a local administration as patriarchal overseas as the republican government was in France.[43] The only civil custom France was willing to suppress was slavery. In contrast, the French arrogated to themselves an active role in the prosecution of criminal cases. In this area of customary law, their civilizing action would eventually be most evident.

When Roume arrived in West Africa in 1902, the need to organize the administration of justice on a federation-wide basis had become pressing. The existing courts varied from colony to colony. From an ideological and a political perspective, they were deemed inadequate and dangerous. They either left Africans out of their jurisdiction altogether—a situation considered prejudicial to the preservation of French authority—or judged them according to French law, which was also at odds with the administration's outlook.[44] Traditionally, the local *commandant* had maintained order in his province through the *indigénat*, a special penal code that applied only to Africans for the punishment of specific minor offenses. It gave the French administrator the sole right to levy fines, order arrests, and issue jail sentences of up to fifteen days without appeal.[45] However useful the powers of the *indigénat* were for maintaining French authority on a day-to-day basis, they remained limited in scope and were independent of the civil and criminal laws. Throughout the 1890's, the African populations continued to adjudicate their own disputes according to their own customs, with little interference from the embryonic colonial administration. The Four Communes were the only exception. There, since the promulgation of a law on April 15, 1889, French criminal and commercial law was applied to all residents through an organized system of French courts, over which a professional magistrature presided.[46] French civil law, in contrast, applied only to non-Muslims of the Four Communes (unless they preferred French law); the French had as early as 1857 granted the Muslim elite of Saint-Louis their own courts for civil litigation, and these courts were still active when Roume arrived.[47] Technically, the law of April 15, 1889, introducing French justice, applied to all of Senegal, because it did not distinguish between the Four Communes and the protectorate areas. However, French conquest had proceeded at such a pace that, by the turn of the century, it was generally agreed that French law neither could nor should be applied wholesale to the ethnically diverse and "backward" societies in the rest of the colony. The question then arose of how best to organize a system of African justice that upheld the principles of customary law while still being controlled by the colonizer. It was this question that Roume, after first consulting the lieutenant governors, appointed a special commission in 1902 to answer.

Roume's commission first gathered in May, to consider the recommendations of the lieutenant governors and draft a decree that would harmonize the administration of native justice in the West African territories. Representatives of the French judiciary and a comparable number of colonial administrators sat on the commission. The latter, however, were assured a preponderant voice, since Roume had made his seasoned secretary general, Martial Merlin, president of the proceedings.[48] The minutes of the commission reveal that the magistrates and the administrators were most divided on the fundamental question of who should have criminal jurisdiction over Africans within the federation. Cougoul, chief of judicial services in the southern colonies, insisted that "sovereign France does not have the right to confer the responsibility of punishing felonies upon anyone other than its magistrates." African judges, he continued, were "barbaric." Africans preferred French justice, and it made sense to provide them with the system they had chosen of their own free will. He concluded, in keeping with the professional interests of the French magistrature generally, that French courts should have jurisdiction over the entire federation.[49]

Merlin riposted by pointing out that Africans did not understand French judicial procedures, and that they required a more expeditious means of settling their disputes. Assimilation, he insisted, was not the French objective: "We should try to uplift the native, but in a way appropriate to his mentality and his needs." The governor of Ivory Coast, another experienced Africa hand, had argued the same point in a letter to the colonial minister two years earlier. Clozel pointed out that the French were bound by their treaties to respect the customs in place. "These customs," he wrote, "which superficial observers regard as ridiculous, were practiced by our ancestors. I consider it both antiscientific and nefarious to try and complete in a few days an evolution for Africans which required centuries for ourselves." And he concluded that if the prescriptions of French law, which were completely unsuited to the mores of the African populations, were nonetheless applied, the French "will destroy in them all notions of morality and put nothing in their place."[50] Merlin and Clozel accepted the application of French law (or Muslim civil law) in the cities, where Europeans, *assimilés*, and a Muslim elite predominated. But they opposed extending this jurisdiction into the countryside. Their attitude reflected that of the lieutenant governors generally, who had consistently complained that French magistrates, wedded as they were to legal principles and precedents, were indifferent to the political implications of their decisions.[51]

Not surprisingly, given the logistical problems and costs associated with creating a professional magistrature, Merlin's point of view prevailed. The subsequent decree represented a triumph for the administration and, at least in theory, for the principle of respecting customary law. Under its provisions two kinds of courts were established: French and native courts. French courts, whose largely urban districts were to be determined by the governor general, had the power to adjudicate all disputes between all parties that arose within their jurisdiction, regardless of the status or nationality of those involved. They applied French law with one exception. When disputes between two Africans living within a French court's jurisdiction were matters of family or probate law, French courts applied local custom, or, in the case of Muslims, Islamic law, to the principles in the suit.[52] African or Muslim assessors were to be consulted in those cases. Alternatively, Muslim plaintiffs could continue to bring these same civil disputes before Muslim courts—for the new decree did not abolish the *tribunaux musulmans* in certain cities in 1903.

Outside the district of French courts (and Muslim courts), native courts had jurisdiction in all matters involving African subjects.[53] These courts applied customary or Muslim law to the extent that it did not conflict with the principles of French civilization. There were three degrees of native courts: village courts, province courts, and circle courts, which corresponded to the hierarchy of French administrative units. The 1903 decree gave village chiefs the power to arbitrate local civil disputes. These rulings were, however, nonbinding, and the parties could always bring their disputes before the province courts. Village chiefs were also empowered to punish minor offenses in accordance with custom; they could issue fines from one to fifteen francs, and jail sentences from one to five days, without appeal. Province courts were to be set up in the seat of each administrative subdivision. They were presided over by a canton or province chief, assisted by two notables versed in customary or Muslim law. The governor general designated these two assessors. Province courts adjudicated all disputes and misdemeanors within their district. Their sentences could be appealed before the circle court. The parties were to be informed of their right of appeal at their sentencing. The circle court served as a criminal tribunal; it tried all felonies committed by African subjects, and reviewed the decisions appealed from the province courts. The local French administrator presided over this court. Two African notables versed in customary or Muslim laws were chosen by the governor general to serve as assessors. Unlike their counterparts at the province court level, they had only a consultative voice in the proceedings. In criminal cases, the administrator acted as public prosecutor as well as judge, for it was he who, after a preliminary investigation, referred felonies to his own court for adjudication. Records were to be kept of all cases tried before the native courts. Monthly accounts of their proceedings were to be sent both to the lieutenant governor of the colony and to Dakar, where the attorney general could reopen any case. In addition, all circle court sentences exceeding five years' imprisonment were automatically reviewed by the highest court of the federation, the Chambre d'homologation.

The Chambre d'homologation was not, strictly speaking, a native court. It was described, rather, as a special chamber of the French Appeals Court, which sat in Dakar. The vice-president of the Appeals Court presided over the Chambre d'homologation. He was assisted by two legal counselors, two members of the federal administration, and two African notables (granted a consultative voice only), whose duty it was to brief the court on customary law. It was so composed to ensure that all criminal sentences of any severity had been properly and fairly rendered. The institution of the Chambre d'homologation was Roume's own contribution to the 1903 decree. It went against the recommendations of his lieutenant governors, by reintroducing an element of nonadministrative control into the native court hierarchy. Yet Roume felt that some form of supervision by professional magistrates was both politic and necessary. "We must," he wrote the minister, "provide the natives with the guarantees essential to the good distribution of justice and seek to lead them prudently and consistently to a higher level of civilization." This could best be accomplished by guaranteeing, even at this early stage in the "development" of Africans, that, where serious crimes were concerned, a judicial authority distinct from the political one would predominate.[54] In consolidating the administration's authority, Roume had adapted to West Africa at least one aspect of the separation of powers observed in France.

The institution of the Chambre d'homologation by Roume confirms that for all the governor general's concern with creating a native courts system that was inexpensive and consolidated authority in the hands of the administration, he was also interested in grafting certain metropolitan principles of justice onto customary law. Roume returned to this point in a set of instructions he issued in 1905. Besides regulating the technical administration of the new courts, these instructions explained, albeit generally, how customary law was to be applied in conformity with the dictates of French civilization. The native courts were to refer to custom primarily in civil disputes involving marriage, contracts, questions of descent, and inheritance. Administrators were to make a point of rationally classifying these customs and endowing them "with a clarity they too often lack"; this classification was the first step toward modifying African customs according "to the fundamental principles of natural law, the original source of all legislation." In the civil realm, in other words, Roume was the voice of moderation; the emphasis was less on abrupt change than on gradual and informed intervention. The one exception was slavery, which could no longer be recognized. "Native courts," Roume wrote, "cannot be permitted to rule in litigations relative to the state of captivity. . . . Furthermore, in cases submitted to them, they can no longer take account of the supposed status of captive."[55] Administrators would have to make sure that chiefs respected this innovation when they judged civil suits.

In criminal cases, in contrast, Roume was decidedly more interventionist. He specified that all corporal punishments traditionally applied now be replaced by prison terms; the use of superstitious ordeals for determining innocence or guilt was also to be eliminated. "Our civilizing action in these cases can be even more far-reaching than in civil cases." The administrators presiding over the circle courts were progressively to put French doctrines into practice and "bring the lower court judges to conform to the principles of criminal law that apply to all countries regardless of their level of civilization." These included personal accountability, equality of all before the law, and punishment proportionate to the crime.[56] Besides this general assessment of the French administrator's judicial functions, Roume had relatively little advice to offer on the daily administration of criminal justice, which was henceforth to constitute one of the *commandant's* most important and time-consuming tasks. Felonies were defined briefly as any attempt on human life or acts of slavery; misdemeanors as all other punishable attacks on either persons or property. No more precise definition, he intimated, was considered desirable; the courts were to have the greatest possible discretion both in determining what constituted an offense and in deciding its punishment.

In 1903, Roume summarized his approach to native justice:

> The population, attached as it is to its ancient customs and old traditions, thus sees with satisfaction that if we have taken it upon ourselves to bring them the principles of our civilization, we only wish to do so in a wisely progressive manner so as not to disturb their ancestral habits; [these are] themselves the reflection of a social condition that would be useful to improve but which it would be imprudent to destroy without a methodical transition.[57]

Yet it was questionable from the outset whether the achievement of such a "progressive" civilization was possible through the means envisioned by the French. The new courts were only as effective as the men who presided over them. Any success in developing African society in the manner prescribed by Roume was contingent upon first-hand knowledge of the institutions that had to be changed. Roume had recognized the need for such knowledge when he instructed his subordinates to classify the prevalent customs in their respective administrative districts. But there was no follow-up to these instructions before World War I.[58] Dakar's silence meant that the administrators had to acquaint themselves with the law that they were supposed to be respecting during this period. Although a few complied, many remained more ignorant.[59]

Contempt for these customs, moreover, was built into the very impulse to change African cultures in the first place. The 1903 decree reflected this implicit disparagement by forcing the administration of customary law into a French framework that altered its form and content. The hierarchy of courts conceived for West Africa mir-

rored the metropolitan judicial organization. The distinction between minor offenses, misdemeanors, and felonies, on the one hand,
and between civil and criminal law, on the other, was directly inspired by comparable French institutions. The decision to remove
responsibility for prosecuting crimes from chiefs, moreover, eroded
the prestige of their office. Such obvious borrowing from metropolitan institutions did not bode well for a policy of gradual evolution
within African culture. Nor was it clear, under these circumstances,
that Africans would voluntarily take advantage of the "civilized"
justice that Roume was offering.

The judicial system set up by Roume in French West Africa further confirms that an important facet of Dakar's ideology was a commitment to help Africans progress within their own cultures. Policy
makers nevertheless remained convinced that certain aspects of
French civilization were not only superior to anything that existed
in West Africa but also had universal applicability. Thanks to this
universality, France must export those aspects of its own culture
from which all humanity could benefit, despite the commitment to
respect African traditions. In the domain of education, this had
meant the French language; in the domain of justice, this meant
French criminal procedures. Both decisions reflected the hold of revolutionary and Enlightenment ideals upon policy makers under the
Third Republic. This same influence was, however, perhaps most
pervasive in a third area of French initiatives. Roume also took steps
to suppress slavery in the federation and to allow a minority of Africans to become French citizens. To a greater extent even than the
creation of schools and courts, these decisions seemed dictated by a
peculiarly republican interpretation of France's civilizing mission in
West Africa.

"Liberty is now acquired"

In addition to establishing education and "enlightened" justice,
the Government General maintained that part of its civilizing mission in Africa was to free Africans from bondage and the tyranny of
aristocratic rule. Of the two issues, slavery and anti-"feudalism," it
was the former that Roume himself addressed most directly. In so
doing, however, he was not opening a new chapter in French civilizing ideals or actions. The question of how to deal with African forms
of slavery and the internal slave trade had preoccupied certain ad-

ministrators in West Africa since 1848, when France's territories consisted of the coastal communes of Saint-Louis and Gorée and a few military posts in the Senegalese interior. At that time, the Second Republic had formally abolished the institution of slavery and all slave-trading. Any slave who touched French soil was automatically freed. Anyone who engaged in the buying and selling of slaves would be stripped of his or her citizenship. It had also established as a cardinal principle of republican ideology that France, in keeping with its liberal tradition and belief in the equality of all mankind, opposed slavery and remained at the head of the antislavery fight throughout Europe.[60]

The 1848 law—which the Second Empire did not rescind—forced the Creole elite of the French communes of Senegal to emancipate immediately the 6,000 slaves currently in their possession.[61] The provisions of the new law were nevertheless aimed primarily at the transatlantic slave trade and plantation slavery in the Antilles; they provided little guidance for dealing with indigenous slavery and the internal market in slaves in West Africa, which the army soon discovered—and which its own policy of conquest indirectly fostered—as it expanded into the Senegalese hinterland. Indeed, the newly conquered territories were made into protectorates, which ostensibly bound the French to respect local customs. One result of this vagueness was that, from the defeat of the Second Republic until the return of republican institutions in the 1870's, the French took no further action in Senegal either to suppress the domestic slave trade or to liberate runaway slaves. Even in the Four Communes, where French law was fully in force, local officials regularly returned runaway slaves from the interior to their masters, rather than liberating them as the law stipulated.[62]

With the restoration of democracy in France, however, public attention would again be drawn to the continued French tolerance of slavery and the slave trade, in coastal Senegal in particular. Much of the credit here belongs to the prominent abolitionist and ardent republican, Victor Schoelcher, the original force behind the 1848 abolition law. Now a senator, Schoelcher publicly criticized—first in Parliament and then in his polemic, *L'esclavage au Sénégal en 1880*—the government for its failure to uphold republican France's commitments in this realm. In the wake of public outcry over Schoelcher's revelations, French policy in the Four Communes began to change. After 1880, any slave who reached French territory under direct administration in Senegal was now to be freed.[63] At the same time, the emancipation of Africans from "aristocratic tyranny" and the abolition of slavery became important justifications for renewed colonial expansion in West Africa under the Third Republic.

Despite these changes on the coast and the heightened antislavery rhetoric generally, the military officers located in the African interior continued to compromise with slavery for the next two decades—with only intermittent protest from a public opinion that in the 1880's and 1890's was more concerned with applauding French victories than with monitoring policy in the new territories. In the protectorate areas of Senegal, for example, the French administration refrained from interfering directly in relations between slaves and masters, for fear of disrupting the local economy. It was during the conquest of the Western Sudan, however, that French tolerance of slavery was most marked. Here, too, necessity overcame whatever moral scruples against slavery and the slave trade might have obtained among military commanders. French troops depended on African auxiliaries and strategic alliances with African chiefs to maintain their advantage. To guarantee the loyalty of their collaborators, the French distributed captured slaves after victories, and allowed these slaves to be sold for export by their new owners. Yet even the military forces did not turn a completely blind eye to humanitarian sentiment. Slaves fleeing chiefs hostile to the French were always freed, and what were known as *villages de liberté* were set up for freed homeless slaves. The creation of such villages was popular with antislavery groups in France; the villages also provided the army with a labor supply of its own for food production, porters, and railroad construction. The colonial army also recruited slaves into the ranks of the African *tirailleurs*, giving the French needed manpower and allowing slaves to escape from their servile status.[64]

Fifty years after the formal abolition of slavery, then, the Republic's compliance in West Africa with its own law on the subject was not impressive. Political considerations on the ground and metropolitan ignorance of the compromises being made overseas account for this state of affairs. Even as fervent an abolitionist as Schoelcher claimed that treaties signed with chiefs committed France to respecting local customs, including slavery, in the new protectorates being established beyond the Four Communes. By the 1890's, how-

ever, this situation was about to change in Paris and Dakar. In West
Africa, the conquest was drawing to a close. By 1898, the army had
finally captured and defeated its most important rivals in the Western Sudan. These victories eliminated one major source of slaves—
warfare—and strengthened France's position in the African interior.
Under peacetime conditions, the slave trade began to dwindle. In addition, the decision to create the Government General signaled an
end to the protectorate era, as France's new territories were now
grouped into one supercolony. The advent of new civilian authorities in Dakar also marked the Third Republic's desire to bring its
overseas administration more in line with metropolitan values. As
the 1903 administration of justice already revealed, the new Government General was no longer willing to ignore customs repugnant
to liberal principles, just because of local treaties signed with African
chiefs. International pressure condemning all forms of slavery in Africa was now building as well. In 1890, France signed, along with
other European powers, the General Act of the Brussels International Conference, which committed all signatories to combat slavery in their territories, "in order to bring to this vast continent the
benefits of peace and civilization."[65] Parliament ratified the treaty
in December 1892. Finally, an important precedent was set in 1895
in Madagascar, when Parliament decided to abolish slavery there as
part of changing the island's status from protectorate to full-fledged
colony.[66]

In keeping with these trends, a new attitude toward slavery
emerged in French West Africa—one more consonant with the Republic's *mission civilisatrice* than the existing policy. In 1900, the
French minister of colonies instructed his subordinates in West Africa to prosecute, in French courts, the leaders of any slave caravans
that they discovered. "France," he wrote in a circular to the governors, "owes to its traditions and its principles to stay at the head of
liberal and civilizing nations, which, after having declared the abolition of slavery, now have a mission to destroy its last vestiges; the
honor of our country requires that in all the territories where our
domination is assured, the natives be brought to abandon completely the practice of slavery."[67] This call to order resonated posi-
tively among certain of West Africa's principal policy makers. For
example, the future governor general William Ponty, Dakar's delegate to the Western Sudan, wrote to his subordinates that they owed
it to the "traditions of republican France" to "take measures that

would make this ancient wound disappear." Henceforth, he no longer wished to see a category for "captives or unfree [*non-libre*]" on their censuses. This nomenclature appeared to recognize officially "a social state absolutely opposed to any idea of civilization."[68] Many other administrators in the field, however, were not so receptive to the minister's overtures. When consulted by Roume, they advised extreme caution, particularly in ending lineage slavery. The most France could do was actively seek to end the trade in slaves and declare that all children born to slaves were free at birth.[69]

Roume, to his credit, disagreed with this passive approach; like Ponty, he believed that more could be done and sooner. For him, too, slavery offended "French genius and its traditions" and contradicted "the fundamental principles of French public law." "We cannot proclaim," Roume declared, "as have certain powers with monarchist governments, which are not bound by the same doctrines as the French Republic, the theoretical freedom of the natives, only to deny it in practice." Furthermore, "individual liberty is for [France] indefeasible and inalienable. It does not recognize the individual's right to contract a personal engagement that forever deprives him of his own freedom."[70]

Roume's organization of justice in 1903 represented a first tangible antislavery measure consistent with these sentiments. As we have seen, instructions accompanying the decree made clear that masters could no longer use the courts to reclaim a slave, since such a custom was contrary to French civilization. Roume ordered an in-depth study of slavery throughout the federation as well in 1903, that the French might familiarize themselves with the institution they wished to change. That same year he also abolished the *patentes de liberté* (certificates of liberty), which the French had formerly given to liberated slaves to prove their emancipation. In the eyes of the law, all Africans were now equal. In December 1905, Roume completed his antislavery measures by abolishing the slave trade and prohibiting the alienation of any person's liberty.[71]

With these measures in place, the federal authorities did not hesitate to claim that they were now "at the forefront of the antislavery movement in Africa." French West Africa was ahead of its British neighbors in particular, whom the author of Dakar's report on slavery, Georges Deherme, accused of making France's task more difficult by harboring slavers and "enslaving" peoples "emigrating to avoid the demands of civilizing freedom." Indeed, if republican

France did not really have a civilizing mission to accomplish in West Africa, such intervention "would not be justified. There would be nothing to do but allow slavery to die out of its own consequences . . . and the evolution of African society to take place of its own accord." Instead, the administration was deliberately introducing into societies which were "following their normal course, the extraordinary factor of an external social will to precipitate and direct their evolution."[72] An essential part of this evolution, in Roume's words, was "the substitution of relations based upon contract in place of the previous order of things based upon conquest and coercion" and the inculcation of "the notion of reciprocal commitments that obligate both parties equally . . . and which are independent of the traditional status of those contracting."[73] The nonrecognition of slave status and the prohibition of the slave trade were critical steps in this civilizing direction.

It has been argued in recent years that, despite the impressive rhetoric, the French antislavery measures of 1903 and 1905 were conservative; the intention was not to free slaves overnight, but to prevent any new enslavement. This was true, and the French administration never claimed otherwise.[74] Roume shared the widespread conviction that force was necessary to get slaves to work, and that their masters would rather starve than do farm labor themselves.[75] "It would reveal," he noted, "a false knowledge of the natives to assume that they are capable of truly understanding the abstract idea of freedom . . . those [slaves] who are currently satisfied will not ask for their freedom: many of them know that once they became free, they would have to meet the necessities of a new existence exclusively through their own initiative and efforts."[76] The lieutenant governors of the colony were thus instructed to use their discretion in applying the new regulations. A circular to administrators in Upper Senegal-Niger stated that they were "to avoid propaganda that would risk provoking among the natives still living in captivity a movement of a general or collective character for which the necessary dispositions have not yet been made."[77] In May 1905, when a spontaneous slave exodus began in the Middle Niger, French troops intervened to return slaves to their masters, albeit under new conditions. In March 1906, Roume warned the administrators of Mauritania, where slavery was entrenched, to keep together those groups who were not yet "mature enough to exercise fully [the rights] of individualism." France's other social measures would gradually emancipate the laboring masses and allow them to displace their masters "whose continuing social and political influence remain an obstacle to our civilizing task." Only when a second slave exodus began in Upper Senegal-Niger in 1906 did the French finally side with the departing slaves, having discovered that freedom was neither depopulating the area nor resulting in economic disaster. To the contrary, they optimistically noted by 1909 that freed slaves in the colony were working harder than under bondage:

> Liberty is now acquired. . . . Other indications which are growing stronger daily further testify to the excellence of the task realized, and reinforce our conviction that there is a happy overlap between the immediate interests of colonization and the generous humanitarian principles whose implementation we are pursuing. It suffices, in this context, to consider the still slow but spontaneous changes that are occurring in the native *régime du travail.* Since the ancient conditions of production have been abruptly modified, the pressure of economic necessity is currently encouraging an organization of free labor; this organization is assuming a variety of interesting forms, depending on the region in question, such as labor contracts in agricultural areas. . . . Among other consequences, it is interesting to note that this latter [labor form] indicates clearly the initiative and the intelligent activity of free labor, as opposed to the proverbial apathy of the black employed in servile tasks.[78]

Elsewhere in the federation, the 1903 and 1905 decisions regarding slavery had a mixed impact, depending on the historical conditions of slavery and the attitude of local administrators. Where administrators felt strongly about slavery, and, perhaps more important, the slaves had homes to which to return, a genuine liberation took place. In areas where slaves had been part of the household for generations, the decrees of 1903 and 1905 did not change their status significantly.[79]

To emphasize only the conservative and tentative aspects of French emancipation efforts is to overlook the fact that the Government General had finally brought to an end a half-century of ambivalence regarding an institution at odds with French conceptions of humanity and natural justice. In this sense, as François Renault recognized a long time ago, Dakar's initiatives represented a major turning point in French attitudes toward slavery as part of a larger mission to civilize.[80] Although it was not Dakar's policy that "freed" slaves—they mostly freed themselves—French refusal to sanction slavery nevertheless helped some slaves leave their servile status. In this particular encounter between expediency and principle, principle had shaped the outcome. As the 1903 instructions stated, although economic and political considerations required prudence in dealing with slavery, respect for the rights of those demanding their liberty was no less important.

This principled yet cautious approach to the slavery issue was not, moreover, unique to the Government General. In its decision to act against slavery and in the way it went about attacking the institution, Dakar faithfully reflected the prevailing attitudes of France's republican elite. No formal discussion occurred in the French Chamber or Senate over whether to abolish slavery in the sub-Saharan African territories when the Government General was created. A highly revealing debate, however, did take place over Madagascar in 1896, when Parliament voted to change its status from protectorate to colony. This debate confirms that while everyone agreed that slavery had to disappear in Madagascar (and elsewhere), there was considerable disagreement over how to bring this about; and even the staunchest antislavery advocates advised that France proceed slowly in this matter. The colonial minister, and the parliamentary committee on colonies, argued against immediate emancipation in Madagascar. They pointed out that slavery there—as in West Africa—was closer to a benign system of domestic servants than to the abusive plantation system in the Caribbean. The French public, they continued, did not understand this distinction, which shed a whole different light on the "slave question." Most slaves were born into that condition, not wrenched from their homes and families by a barbaric slave trade. Rather than proclaim immediate emancipation, which would be disruptive, preliminary measures should "prepare" slaves for freedom: an interdiction on selling slaves, the opportunity for slaves to buy themselves back, the liberation of slave children at birth.[81] After ten to nineteen years of such preparation, abolition should be proclaimed.

These arguments provoked a storm of protest from the Chamber's left and center members. In rebuttal Jean Jaurès, among others, argued that, just as in the debates over abolition in 1848, "preparatory measures" were simply a means of avoiding the issue at hand: "It is on the very same day that you declare the power and the rights of France in Madagascar that you should affirm this statute of personal liberty which is today inseparable in the world from France." Once such freedom was declared, he added, the appropriate measures for implementing it could be taken. What he felt these measures should be was unclear, but he did not criticize those put forward by the colonial minister. Jaurès' eloquence carried the day. The final resolution adopted by the Chamber read, "Slavery having been abolished in Madagascar by the fact that the island is declared a French colony, the government will take measures to ensure immediate emancipation."[82]

This debate and its resolution help put in perspective Dakar's subsequent actions regarding slavery in West Africa. On the one hand, the 1896 discussion made clear that a majority of the French Chamber felt that the emancipation of slaves should be stated policy in France's new colonies. On the other hand, the final resolution revealed that even as committed a Socialist as Jaurès accepted that some transition to freedom was necessary, particularly from lineage slavery. Antislavery policy in the name of civilization in West Africa embodied both of these trends. In this context, perhaps the proper reproach against the civilian administration is not that it paid lip service to the principle of abolition while in fact preserving a servile system deeply embedded in African social mores; rather, it is that the French failed to take any responsibility for exacerbating slavery in West Africa during the conquest. By constantly describing slavery as a barbaric African practice and France as a liberating power, Dakar effectively masked the Republic's role in driving ever greater numbers of displaced Africans into involuntary servitude in the 1880's and 1890's.

Becoming French?

Abolishing slavery, like eradicating indigenous languages and customs, pestilence, poverty, and ignorance, was central to the French understanding of their mandate in West Africa. Roume's antislavery rhetoric nevertheless reveals an additional point about the French view of their *mission civilisatrice*, which Dakar's emphasis upon economic development, education, and justice did not necessarily bring out. This was the extent to which the French believed that their republican heritage imposed upon them not only a special obligation to uplift the oppressed of the earth materially, in whatever way they could, but also a specific duty to defend the individual rights of man wherever they were threatened. It was this specific commitment to the principles of freedom, the above statements imply, that set France's *mission civilisatrice* apart from other nations'

"civilizing missions," along with France's greater commitment to carrying out its humanitarian agenda. Such, at any rate, was the official view. This republican commitment to the rights of man was responsible for one additional initiative early in the life of the Government General: Roume's proposal to the Colonial Ministry to allow, for the first time, certain Africans to become citizens of the French nation.

At the time the Government General was formed, acquisition of citizenship under the Third Republic was still officially regulated by a law passed in 1889. This law had been extended to the colonies "other than Martinique, Réunion and Guadeloupe" in 1897. But its provisions applied only to nonnationals and their descendants residing in or born on French territory—colonial subjects, in other words, remained ineligible for citizenship. Indeed, the 1897 law stipulated expressly that it "changed nothing in the condition of natives in the colonies."[83] At this juncture then, French policy makers had not yet committed themselves to the principle that their new African subjects could or should become French citizens.[84] Roume, in contrast, was prepared to take the initiative in this realm. In 1907, he petitioned the minister of colonies to approve a decree for the naturalization of "meritorious" Africans. Such a decree, he informed the minister, would create a new situation in which there would be

> on the one hand, the large majority of natives who are our subjects by right of conquest, or by voluntary submission . . . on the other hand, an elite of natives who have become, by virtue of a specific legal action, French citizens, in the real and full sense of the term, justifying their ascension in the social hierarchy by their merit and by the services they have rendered, legitimately enjoying all rights that French law confers, by which they will have agreed to be bound. . . . The character of this act is, indeed, to recognize among our African subjects those most worthy and capable, those who are evolved enough to be completely bound by our laws, accept our responsibilities and be in every way our equals.

Roume's conditions for acquiring French citizenship included a West African place of birth and residence; proof of devotion to France or occupation of a position in the colonial administration salaried by the state; knowledge of French; proof of good financial standing and moral rectitude; no criminal record; and no history of bankruptcy. Without this decree, Roume concluded, "no real assimilation would be possible."[85]

[margin note: citizenship conditions]

Roume's text raised certain objections in Paris, particularly regarding the Senegalese of the Four Communes, and as a result it was not immediately accepted. Although these inhabitants could vote and were under the jurisdiction of French law, the majority had remained Muslim and continued to use Muslim courts to settle their civil suits. No law had ever been passed acknowledging their right to French citizenship, despite their privileged status—compared to the rest of the federation. Would, the minister asked, the projected decree automatically naturalize the Senegalese inhabitants—or *originaires*, as they were called—of the Four Communes? If so, would they agree to be governed by French law? Until their exact status had been determined, the minister did not feel that he could sign Roume's proposed decree into law.[86] Roume's successor would again raise the issue of citizenship, but it would be another five years before a law was finally passed stipulating the conditions under which Africans could be granted French citizenship.

Despite this delay in passing the naturalization bill, the very existence of such a *projet de décret* attests to the fact that, if Dakar believed the majority of its subjects should evolve within their own cultures, the Government General was nevertheless envisioning the selective assimilation of a small group of Africans. How frequently the privilege was extended remained to be seen. Dakar's project does not make clear how long Roume felt it would take for this assimilation to take place. Would it occur within a generation? Several generations? Nor did the project specify who would become members of this new elite or how this assimilation would occur. The new school system, for example, was manifestly targeted at denying Africans the complete education that could presumably be required for citizenship. Such vagueness notwithstanding, the premise of the decree was obvious; although it was impossible and undesirable to absorb all Africans, Dakar was asserting that, in keeping with liberal French traditions, it was accepting the principle that a West African subject could become a French citizen. Skin color alone was no barrier to naturalization, once the requisite acculturation had taken place. The only difference compared to the founding years of the Second and Third Republics was that, whereas in the nineteenth century citizenship and its attendant rights had been automatically extended en masse to the male inhabitants of France's oldest colonies, these same rights would now have to be earned individually.

This was, of course, a crucial difference, and it suggests one final conclusion: that the larger purpose of the naturalization bill was to reassure the French that they were remaining faithful to their republican principles when they were, in one very important way, betraying them. Republican imperialism should have been a contradiction in terms—a nation of *citoyens* cannot by definition possess *sujets*. One way the French reconciled themselves to this was by claiming that Africans were barbarians unfit for immediate voting rights. In this sense, their treatment recalled that of another important group denied political rights under the Third Republic: metropolitan women. Women, like Africans, were excluded from the franchise on the grounds of natural inferiority; they were not considered autonomous individuals, upon whom abstract political rights could be safely bestowed.[87] Yet, as feminist historians have shown, this was not French men's only justification of their monopoly on formal political power in the metropole. In excluding women from the vote, French legislators were also careful to assign them an alternative political role: that of constructing the nation through reproduction and domesticity.[88] This alternative role effectively prevented most women from initially questioning their exclusion, and convinced men and women alike that the Third Republic was a true democracy for all its "citizens."

In a similar spirit but a different manner, the Third Republic went beyond the description of Africans as barbarians in its attempt to legitimate—to itself and to Africans—the presence of subjects within the Republic. The government decreed a naturalization bill, through which deserving subjects could become French citizens. Although Roume explained that such a measure would only ever apply to a minority, the notion that some Africans could become French equals helped divert attention from the fact that most would remain subjects. In this case, the Republic denied the contradiction posed by the existence of "subjecthood," and the violation of rights it entailed, by regulating the conditions of its selective disappearance. No African male who deserved to be a citizen would, in theory, be denied entry into the republican brotherhood.

What was true of the naturalization bill was equally true of adapted education, the decision to suppress certain customs, and the nonrecognition of slavery during Roume's tenure. In these instances as well, the French were not content simply to qualify Africans as barbarians. They were barbarians, in each instance, capable of—and in the process of receiving—republican civilization. By inaugurating policies that were consistent with France's revolutionary heritage, Roume here too managed to normalize the presence of so many subjects in a nation of citizens. Roume's initiatives in the "moral" realm, in short, reveal that the republican *sujet* was no anomaly at all, thanks to the democratic content of Dakar's early civilizing rhetoric and actions. This specific positioning of the French as liberators—and the normalizing function it served within the Third Republic's larger political discourse—would be even more evident in Dakar under Roume's successor, William Ponty.

CHAPTER 4

"En faire des hommes"

WILLIAM PONTY AND THE
PURSUIT OF MORAL PROGRESS
(1908–1914)

In the eyes of the natives, France is *la force*, but from now
on it must be, above all else, *la justice.*
— Jules Ferry[1]

It is necessary for little black children to remember the name
[of William Ponty], for he did much to spread instruction
among them.
— Louis Sonolet[2]

In December 1907, Ernest Roume retired as governor general
of French West Africa, complaining of poor health and fatigue. William Ponty, the lieutenant governor of Upper Senegal-Niger, was appointed to replace him. Amédée William Merlaud-Ponty, a soldier-
administrator and a Freemason, could not have differed more in
background and experience from the *polytechnicien* Ernest Roume.[3]
Where the latter had first distinguished himself in the corridors of
the Finance Ministry, the former had earned high office because he
had participated in the conquest in the Western Sudan and served in
the field. Ponty was born on February 4, 1866, in Rochefort-sur-Mer.
He was awarded a law degree in 1888 and entered the colonial administration that year. In 1889, he received his first overseas posting; he served as aide-de-camp to Colonel Archinard in the Western
Sudan until 1895, thus participating in the last campaigns against
Samori. Ponty was briefly transferred to Madagascar under Gallieni,
but returned to the Western Sudan as a *commandant de cercle* in
1897. He was first promoted to the position of delegate to the governor general in the Western Sudan (1899), then in 1904 lieutenant
governor of the Western Sudan (renamed Upper Senegal-Niger),
where he remained until becoming governor general of the federa-

tion. Governor General William Ponty would die in office on the eve of World War I, having refused to leave West Africa despite years of declining health. Ponty felt that he had devoted his professional life to this part of the empire, and he had no desire to leave his post during France's moment of crisis.

Not surprisingly, given their contrasting backgrounds, Ponty arrived in Dakar with interests different from Roume's. As a veteran of the Sudanese campaigns of the 1890's, and a long-time field administrator who had risen through the ranks to head the federation, the new governor general was more experienced and interested in the day-to-day problems of ruling Africans than in the finances of railroad construction. It was to the former area of policy that he devoted most of his time and energy as governor general.[4] In so doing, he quickly revealed that his assumptions about African society and the purpose of French rule were, for all his apparent differences with Roume, consistent with the ideas articulated by his predecessor.

Ponty's conception of France's mission can best be seen in a series of linked initiatives that spanned his career. Immediately upon his arrival in Dakar, Ponty reorganized the Government General to give himself a direct role in the formulation of native policy. Shortly afterward, he drafted his famous 1909 circular introducing what he referred to as the *politique des races*, which contained the federal government's first comprehensive statement on the place chiefs should occupy in the French administrative hierarchy. At the same time, the new governor general undertook a major reform of the 1903 legal system. Both reforms occurred against the backdrop of a third priority: spreading French education among Africans. Unlike African health care, which Ponty rarely emphasized in either his speeches or his circulars, instruction was identified as the new administration's foremost social measure. Adapted education, too, was thus overhauled in this period. These various measures, which were to be applied uniformly throughout the federation, made the overall ideology of Ponty's administration perfectly clear. From his decision to involve Dakar directly in the regulation of native policy, to his attitude toward chiefs and his reform of custom and education, Ponty was driven by a conviction that it was France's responsibility to direct the emergence of a new social order in West Africa which, without becoming French, would better conform to prevailing French mores. Under his tenure the notion that democratic France had to liberate Africans from oppression and barbaric custom, and teach them French, reached its fullest expression.

The Equal Value of all People: 'La Politique des Races'

One of Ponty's first acts as governor general was to reorganize the various bureaus of the federal administration, in such a way as to give himself the preeminent say in native policy decisions that had previously been made by individual governors. In carrying out this reorganization, however, Ponty was not acting entirely on his own initiative. Between 1907 and 1908, an important mission of inspection in West Africa, under the direction of Inspector Guyho, had criticized as expensive and inefficient the hierarchy of services Roume created in 1905.[5] This mission—one of the few to arrive in West Africa before World War I—had also complained about inadequate health and educational facilities in the federation, citing several cases of mistreatment of Africans. Such missions of inspection had been part of French overseas administrative practice since 1815, when the Colonial Inspectorate was first created. The purpose of this special bureau was to provide the government in Paris with a periodic review of colonial administration in the empire.[6] In response to the Guyho inspection's criticisms, which the colonial minister seconded, Ponty abolished the office of secretary general. This eliminated all intermediaries between himself and the heads of the different services and the governor general and the lieutenant governors.[7] The governor general alone would now make all final decisions. Ponty also reserved to himself the formulation of what he called general policy—that is to say, any social, economic, or political measure affecting French relations with Africans.[8]

The purpose of Ponty's reform was ostensibly to streamline the administration and delineate the respective powers of the governor general and the lieutenant governors. Instead, it consolidated exclusive policy-making powers in the hands of the governor general and significantly broadened his functions. This reorganization signaled Dakar's new interest in regulating its subjects' political and social affairs, although it did not reveal the direction in which this policy would go. Ponty's maiden speech to the Council of the Government General, however, soon provided a clue. The French, Ponty explained, had duties toward the Africans that were like those of a tutor to his ward—"a sometimes shifty, often crude and even cruel ward, but one who needs above all to be, as I like to put it, *ap-privoisé*."[9] *Apprivoisement* would prove to be a key concept for the new governor general; it implied winning Africans over to civilization through acts of republican generosity (and also republican obligation) while never going so far as to grant them the freedoms of the French. Among the most important of such acts, it soon appeared, was curtailing the power of chiefs.

On September 22, 1909, Ponty issued a circular designed specifically to diminish further the role of all chiefs, from the lowliest village notable to heads of state, currently serving in the French administrative hierarchy. That African intermediaries of some kind were necessary, Ponty never questioned. French personnel was too scarce, and financial resources too limited, to govern directly. Ponty nevertheless was determined to reduce the prestige and independence of the traditional elite. At the same time, he insisted on the need to liberate all African groups from foreign oppressors. Ponty's motives in asserting these goals, moreover, were visibly linked to his understanding of France's civilizing mission in West Africa. As his 1909 circular would make abundantly clear, Ponty was convinced that all African chiefs were "feudal potentates" whose continued existence conflicted with the prevailing ideals of the Third Republic. To appreciate fully the originality of Ponty's 1909 circular and what this circular reveals about Dakar's ideology at the time, it is necessary to review French administrative practices and organization in West Africa since the conquest.

During the years of military expansion in West Africa, the colonial army had developed a system of administration that changed little during the entire period of French rule. It divided French territories first into colonies, then into smaller administrative units, designated as circles. Circles were further divided into subdivisions, provinces, cantons, and villages, a process that was by no means complete in 1895, when the Government General was created. A French administrator was the head of each circle and later each subdivision, but African chiefs had charge of the rest of the administrative hierarchy. Provinces, where they existed, and cantons and villages were administered by province, canton, and village chiefs, respectively.

The administrative hierarchy stayed the same, but French attitudes toward African auxiliaries or the division of territory under their control changed over time. In the early phases of territorial organization, the army had tended to recognize existing African states, once they had been defeated, as protectorates. This was particularly true when such states coincided with ethnic boundaries, appeared to be of ancient constitution, and were highly stratified. Such was the case, for example, of the six small kingdoms of Sine, Salum, Cayor, Baol, Jolof, and Walo in Senegal, the area first conquered by the French army. In return for French protection, traditional claimants were expected to collect taxes and recruit labor for the colonial state. The hierarchy of French administrative units, the circle, province, and canton, respected as much as possible comparable divisions in the precolonial political order. If any of these protected chiefs proved disloyal, as happened in Cayor, his kingdom was dismantled. The army applied the same system of indirect rule to the kingdom of Dahomey, the Fulani Almamys of the Futa Jallon, and the Mossi states of Upper Volta.[10] This system offered a pragmatic solution to the problem of governing at minimal cost recently conquered territories.

Not all parts of West Africa, however, lent themselves easily to such a system of protection. When the French began to push westward into the Sudan, they encountered a very different type of political organization and adversary. Here, recently formed empires, established by force under the banner of Islam and encompassing numerous peoples of different ethnic origins, were the norm. The best-known of these empires were the Umarian state of the Middle Niger Valley, now under the control of Umar's son Amadu, and Samori's military empire stretching along the south bank of the Niger. Because of the formidable threat that these men posed to the French, there was no question of maintaining either of their empires after their defeat. Ideology reinforced what necessity counseled. Confronted with such powerful adversaries, most colonial commanders began to see their fight as a republican crusade against "feudal" oppressors and religious tyrants with whom no compromise could be brooked—once again ignoring that their own incursions into West Africa were keeping "oppression" alive.[11] Yet in building up their own power, Samori and Umar and his son Amadu had effectively destroyed many preexisting political entities in the Western Sudan which might have offered the French an alternative political structure through which to rule. This situation posed two dilemmas for the colonial army: first, how to divide these empires and, second, where to find African auxiliaries, with sufficient authority to comply with French demands, to designate as chiefs. The stateless forest peoples of coastal Guinea and Ivory Coast posed the same problems, albeit for opposite reasons.

Faced with these dilemmas, the French colonial army developed a preference for, or had no choice but to resort to, a system of direct administration for its territories in the Western Sudan. That is to say, it subdivided all circles into cantons of more or less equal size, and made the canton the basic unit of African administration. According to this system, there were to be no collaborators between the French *commandant de cercle* and the French-appointed canton chiefs. Below these canton chiefs, village chiefs would continue to supervise affairs on the local level. Such a system was "direct" only in that it brought the French administrator into closer contact with his African subjects than was true in, say, Senegal, where an additional class of intermediaries, the province chiefs, separated the colonial administrators from the mass of Africans. In choosing its collaborators, moreover, the army was usually most concerned with finding intermediaries who would prove loyal to the French. A secondary consideration was whether they were legitimate. Finally, the army generally preferred uniformity to respect for ethnicity when it came to drawing the boundaries of each canton.[12]

The conquest of the Western Sudan would prove pivotal in determining the ideology and actions of the civilian government in West Africa until World War I. In the years immediately following Samori's defeat in 1899, several newly appointed lieutenant governors began to apply the principles of "direct" administration, worked out in the Western Sudan, to other colonies of the federation, even in areas where protectorates already existed. For example, the king of Dahomey and the Fulani Almamys saw their states subdivided into cantons of more or less uniform size, and their prerogatives considerably reduced. Independent villages among such peoples as the Kissi in Guinea were arbitrarily grouped into cantons and a canton chief appointed. Such patterns did not apply throughout the federation, since individual administrators still had considerable discretion to act as they saw fit. Thus, in parts of Senegal, Ivory Coast, Upper Volta, and Niger, local authorities who were against the dismantling of protectorates, on the grounds that they had served the French well, managed to preserve the old regime.[13] By 1902, however, this accommodation was largely a rearguard action. With the appointment of Ernest Roume and the final reorganization of the Government General, a more principled approach to indigenous authority was about to be adopted.

As governor general, Roume did not elaborate a formal declaration of principle regarding chiefs, as had been the case with slavery. But he did approve measures against several remaining precolonial rulers in different colonies. All "great native commands" and "great chiefs," he explained more than once to his subordinates, now had to be dismantled.[14] "It is best to avoid . . . granting [chiefs] commands that are too extensive, which they too often . . . abuse, and which only add . . . unjustified extra burdens to the population's normal ones."[15] Like his military predecessors, Roume accepted that these chiefs ruled by force rather than by popular consent. Such rule by force clashed with the democratic principles from which the Third Republic derived its own legitimacy, and therefore had to be attenuated. As a result of Roume's instructions, the protectorate system—or what was left of it—underwent in the early 1900's a process of further fragmentation as the rulers were either removed from power or stripped of all real authority. Former states began to be subdivided into provinces or cantons of uniform size. The administration then often appointed "new men"—from outside the families in which power had traditionally been vested—as canton chiefs to carry out the bulk of French administrative demands. With these actions in mind, Roume could with satisfaction proclaim that "the native, who knew no other regime than that of bloody conquest or of the absolute arbitrariness of chiefs, of whom he was almost always the victim, realizes that, thanks to us, the rights of the individual exist, and that a fair and firm authority is always at hand to make them respected."[16]

Roume's initiatives against chiefs indicate that another facet of French ideology in the early years of the Government General was a conviction that precolonial political power in West Africa, like slavery, was essentially barbaric and therefore conflicted with the principles of French civilization. Under Ponty, this facet of the *mission civilisatrice* developed more in the capital of the federation, thanks in part to the new governor general's direct participation in the conquest of Samori and Amadu. William Ponty had fought alongside Archinard in the bitter battles against the military aristocracy and militant Islamic movements in the Western Sudan. This experience had convinced him that the French were liberators rather than conquerors in West Africa, and taught him to view African notables—

village chiefs as well as the highest-ranking royal families—as potential enemies.[17] Ponty's subsequent years in the Western Sudan, first as delegate of the governor general, then as lieutenant governor, failed to alter either his initial negative assessment of Africa's ruling elite or his tendency to group all traditional notables as predatory tyrants. He thus came to Dakar with an even clearer sense than Roume of how African chiefs should be treated. These ideas were presented in his 1909 circular, under the rubric *la politique des races*—a term first popularized by Gallieni in Indochina.[18] Ostensibly a directive about ensuring Africans' right to progress along their own lines, this circular also endorsed an attack upon African chiefs that went considerably beyond the breakup of great commands.

Ponty's version of the *politique des races* was his contribution to Dakar's republican ideology of civilization as articulated during the first decade of the twentieth century.[19] Its main tenets clearly reflected the principles of "direct administration" the army had developed in the Western Sudan. At the same time, the *politique des races* further elaborated the civilizing notion that Africans should evolve within their own traditions. As Ponty explained it, the *politique des races* was to replace the native policy followed during the "protectorate," or conquest, era. At that time, Ponty wrote, the French had either grouped peoples of differing origins under a single ruler to simplify their administration, or accepted dealing with whatever "kinglet, warlord or mercenary" happened to be in power upon their arrival in a specific area. According to Ponty, these purely territorial commands, created by the French, had outlived their usefulness; they now posed certain dangers to French hegemony and threatened the welfare of their African subjects. The foreign chiefs were needless intermediaries between the local *commandant* and the numerous petty chiefs (*petits chefs de groupe*) under their control; these tyrants abused their power and thus discredited the French in the eyes of the local population. Under these conditions, Ponty concluded, chiefs who were currently ruling over Africans of a different ethnic group (*race*) should be replaced by individuals from the collectivity in question:

> In principle, it can only be advantageous to choose a native chief from a family of the ethnic group that he will represent; indeed, we do not have the right to sacrifice the future of one race to the future of another; each people must conserve its autonomy relative to a neighboring people; to take the side of one tribe, which was formerly dominant over that of a

conquered tribe, would be contrary to the ideas of justice and liberalism that have always presided over our action in Africa. Additionally, by allowing each ethnic group to evolve within its own particular mentality, by preserving as much as possible the particularism of the tribe, we are furthering the birth of individual effort within each group, and thus liberating the entire group from the religious or political influence of the neighboring group.[20]

The right of Africans to be governed by leaders drawn from their own people was consistent with Dakar's previously declared commitment to respect African customs, and would provide the basis for Ponty's reform of the native legal system. Ponty's concern here was again driven by the specific conditions he had encountered in the Western Sudan, where there had been a great mixing and migration of peoples in the nineteenth century, thanks to the constant warfare of rival empire-builders. Such ethnic intermingling was not as typical in the other colonies. Ponty was also manifestly inspired by French democratic principles celebrating the equality of all peoples and personal freedom, as was said by those who knew him well. "In these arbitrarily formed groups," his collaborator Paul Marty wrote, "created by the tyranny of local chiefs or the bloody madness of conquerors and *marabouts*, in these artificial groupings that we sometimes were weak enough to preserve, Ponty returned the upper hand to all the ethnic elements; he proclaimed the equal human value of all people, and their right to exist."[21]

As the very term *politique des races* suggests, the republican principle of ethnic self-determination was a dominant theme of the 1909 circular. Yet there were other themes as well. Having declared the "equal human value of all people," Ponty not surprisingly addressed another form of African oppression—one noted by his predecessor: the inequality in a society divided between "feudal oppressors" and exploited masses. Embedded within Ponty's condemnation of foreign chiefs was a more general critique of all traditional African rulers, foreign or otherwise:

> It appears that we can only gain by substituting for the policy of native territorial commands, the *politique des races*, which consists not in dividing up our authority among the mass of our subjects, but rather in rendering it more tutelary by establishing direct contact between the administrator and the subject. . . .
>
> To dissociate the parties created by the chiefs of the global territorial units is also to suppress, to make disappear, centers of resistance against us. To abolish the tyranny of one ethnic group over other ethnic groups

is better yet to destroy the hostility of the ancient aristocracy, and attract to ourselves the friendship of those collectivities which, thanks to us, acquire an independent individuality.[22]

The key phrases in this passage were "to destroy the hostility of the ancient aristocracy," "attract to ourselves the friendship of those collectivities," and the establishment of "direct contact" between the administration and its African subjects to promote "individuality." Ponty here betrayed a thinly veiled suspicion of all members of the precolonial elite; indeed, "direct contact" seemed to indicate a desire to bypass this class altogether and a preference for a more direct form of administration. What the 1909 circular hinted at in this domain, other instructions from Dakar would spell out more carefully.

Ponty's anti-aristocratic sentiment was visible, for example, in the kind of advice he routinely gave his subordinates regarding the chiefs under their command. Although the chiefs would remain, France's mission was, his directions suggested, systematically to reduce the traditional basis of their power as well as their overall numbers in the administrative hierarchy, and simultaneously increase the French presence in the lives of their subjects. Chiefs "were to be used solely to the extent that they proved useful to the the French administration and their African subjects." Africa's traditional rulers, in other words, had no intrinsic merit in Ponty's eyes. Administrators were to "dominate chiefs morally" and keep them "in check."[23] They simply could not be trusted; as Ponty put it in 1914: "My long experience in French West Africa and with the black populations has allowed me to verify absolutely that the native intermediaries between the majority of the people and the administrators of the *cercles* or their subordinates are in most cases nothing but parasites living off the population. . . . So many intermediaries, so many thieves." Meanwhile, as a counterbalance to these unsavory intermediaries, the French *commandants* were to maintain constant contact with the local population. To ensure such contact, Ponty issued a circular in 1911 directing local administrators to conduct as many *tournées* as possible within his circle.[24] The inspector of administrative affairs of each colony was also to visit every circle in his colony at least once a year. As Ponty explained it to the minister as early as 1907, pursuing France's "traditional policy of direct contact [*prise de contact*], particularly in regard to the abolition of domestic and agrarian servitude" permitted them "to envision with confidence the social progress that the application of the two primordial principles of our policy of direct contact will achieve: the suppression of the great commands [*grands commandements*] and the *politique des races.*"[25]

The distrust of all chiefs and preference for direct communication integral to the *politique des races* can be seen in one final policy decision. As time went on, Ponty was not content with simply reducing the prestige of traditional African rulers. So strong was his antipathy to what he perceived to be aristocratic vestiges in West Africa, that Ponty eventually envisaged eliminating outright all canton and province chiefs and transferring their administrative duties to village chiefs, whom the *commandant* would supervise directly. Ponty had contemplated this same policy in his capacity as lieutenant governor of Upper Senegal-Niger. At that time he had written Governor General Roume, in reference to canton chiefs, that "the administration and the natives have a common interest in getting rid of these often useless, sometimes dangerous and always onerous intermediaries."[26] A 1914 circular issued shortly before Ponty's death represented a first step in implementing this policy on a federation-wide basis. Canton chiefs, the governor general insisted, were no longer to play an active role in collecting taxes; they were merely to assist as "simple spectators." In their place, village chiefs would carry out all fiscal duties. Thus the system of administration based on the canton approached the ideal of "direct contact," since there would now be only one fiscal intermediary—the village chief— between the administration and their subjects, instead of the two that had existed previously. This system would, Ponty felt sure, win the French the loyalty of the African masses; they would face fewer oppressors in their daily lives, and come that much closer to a benevolent representative of French civilization.[27]

Ponty's circulars had a direct impact upon policy making. Throughout West Africa, the years leading up to World War I witnessed a major upheaval in the African command structure. The breakup of remaining states begun under Roume was continued. Although the lieutenant governors of certain colonies, such as Guinea and Senegal, realized that they could not abolish the offices of canton and province chiefs and still function normally, local administrators nevertheless often adopted the next best antichief measure: they deliberately excluded members of traditional ruling lineages from power, preferring to appoint new men as French administrative auxiliaries. This was more true of Guinea than of Senegal, which, for reasons that will be discussed in the next chapter, was the one colony in which Ponty's directives were not extensively applied. In other colonies, particularly the Western Sudan, where Ponty had served as lieutenant governor, an attempt was actually made to by-pass use of canton chiefs or province chiefs altogether and shift their responsibilities to village chiefs. In the colony of Niger, the Ponty years also marked an intensification in the attack upon the old regime. Finally, in Ivory Coast, years of patient collaboration with local chiefs now yielded to a brutal policy of military "pacification." Although this policy was inaugurated by a newly posted lieutenant governor to that colony, Gabriel Angoulvant, it was approved by Dakar.

However satisfying ideologically, the outcome of the policy of emancipation was not what Ponty had expected. In areas where it was taken literally, the *politique des races* created havoc for the French administration. The *commandant* of a circle suddenly found himself dealing with up to a thousand village chiefs in the place of the ten to twelve province chiefs who had been responsible for implementing French administrative demands.[28] Administration, in these circumstances, became increasingly problematic. Part of the problem was that Ponty's native policy was predicated upon a genuine misunderstanding of how African society functioned. The village chiefs, through whom Dakar now proposed to rule, were more an invention of the French than a living African reality. As an important critic, the Africanist Maurice Delafosse, would point out a few years later, the very canton and province chiefs whom the governor general was bent on eliminating usually better represented African communities than the village chiefs designated by Ponty. According to Delafosse, the only social organization common to all African populations was the family; it was extremely unusual for an African village to be administered by a "chief" as the French understood the term. By way of contrast, canton and province chiefs existed everywhere. Africans, Delafosse concluded, had already progressed beyond "primitive barbarism" to form small states. The best way to help Africans evolve within their own cultures was to accept working through these states and their traditional leaders, not destroy them or replace them with "new men." Destruction would only alienate Africans, not win them over.[29]

Dakar remained blind to this particular reality between 1902 and 1914.[30] It proceeded on the basis of its own understanding of France's mission in West Africa. This was as true in the administration of justice as in the treatment of chiefs. Like the *politique des races*, whose premises it echoed, an important reform of native justice in 1912 testified to Dakar's belief in the need to liberate Africans during Governor General William Ponty's tenure.

Reform of the Native Legal System

Ponty's interest in native justice was natural, given his strong commitment to *apprivoisement* and emancipating Africans from oppression. As the 1903 decree first organizing a system of native courts had shown, the Government General viewed the administration of justice as an important means of helping African society advance. Although Dakar had declared its intention to respect African customs, it had also stipulated that traditions contrary to "civilization" should be eradicated and Western principles of justice gradually introduced in their place. Having articulated these principles, however, the 1903 decree proved remarkably restrained in implementing them. The dominant characteristics of that law were flexibility and minimal French intervention in the lives of their subjects. So flexible, in fact, was the system that local administrators and governors freely altered—or did not alter—custom as they saw fit, with little supervision from Dakar and with little consistency among themselves.[31] Meanwhile, African society had also begun to "progress" under French rule. For both reasons, Ponty felt that the time had come for greater judicial activism on the part of the central administration. In 1912, after two years of study, Ponty passed the first reform of the 1903 decree since its inception. Like the 1909 circular inaugurating the *politique des races*, the 1912 reform reconfirmed the civilizing premises of preceding legislation, but contained two key innovations—each of which recalled a guiding principle of the *politique des races*.

First, the governor general insisted that French courts had to respect the ethnic and religious identities of the different groups living in West Africa, from the most primitive forest dweller to the most evolved *assimilé*. The court system set up by Roume did not, in Ponty's opinion, adequately conform to this principle. Urban areas had been arbitrarily placed under the jurisdiction of French courts; individual ethnic or religious groups in various parts of the federation did not benefit from courts composed exclusively of judges practicing their customs. Animist groups, in particular, were frequently being judged by courts presided over by Muslim *cadis*.

This situation was contributing to the spread of Islam and had to be remedied. Confronted with these anomalies, Ponty concluded that a more equitable system of justice could be devised—one that would return ethnic groups to their "natural" judges. This aspect of the reform reflected Ponty's belief in the right of each ethnic group to evolve freely within its own traditions, which the 1909 circular had already articulated. Such a belief derived from the Third Republic's particular commitment to respecting the voice of "the people." As Ponty put it in the introduction to his reform, in language borrowed from Rousseau: "custom, [the] natural and immediate product of social relations, is the tacit and unanimous expression of the authentic will of the population."[32]

The second novelty of the 1912 reform was a decision to expand the French role in the administration of justice in West Africa. This decision, too, stemmed from Ponty's understanding of the special role the courts could play in uplifting Africans. He felt that the original provisions of the 1903 decree did not encourage the colonial service to intervene as frequently or as uniformly as it should. The idea was not to allow diversity to persist, but to implant among the masses "the idea of a fusion, more or less complete, of custom, which will eventually give rise to a legislation reflective of both local necessities and the progress of modern civilization."[33] Greater French participation in the adjudication of disputes would also strengthen the administration's prestige. These ideas reflected that aspect of the *mission civilisatrice* that emphasized freeing Africans from principles contrary to "natural justice." It was consistent as well with the ideal of direct contact between the administration and its subjects.

Ponty's reform, promulgated on August 16, 1912, was based upon the same fundamental premise as the 1903 decree—customary law was to be respected insofar as it did not conflict with Western standards of civilization. Several changes, however, were needed to ensure that African custom really was respected. One change was to guarantee Africans access to courts composed of judges drawn from their own ethnic groups or religion. The 1903 decree had simply divided West Africa into urban areas, which automatically came under the jurisdiction of French law, and rural areas, under that of customary law. This provision violated France's promise to respect custom, because it arbitrarily imposed the formality and expensive procedure of French law upon non-French individuals who happened to be residing in cities. The 1912 decree began from the very different principle that all African *sujets*, no matter where they lived, belonged under the jurisdiction of native courts. Only Africans who had been naturalized by decree and had become French *citoyens* would continue to have access to French courts (articles 1 and 2). Before 1912, such naturalization was impossible because appropriate legislation was lacking.[34] The logical prerequisite for the 1912 reform was the signing of a naturalization decree, which received ministerial approval on May 25, 1912.[35] These new provisions had the advantage of returning urban dwellers to their natural jurisdiction, and avoiding the premature introduction of French law, while still allowing those "who are apt at understanding and using our laws" to be governed by them.[36] The only exception was the Senegalese of the Four Communes, who, without being citizens, had a historical right to use French courts, at least in Senegal.

A second measure of the new decree was also designed to ensure that African law was better respected than in the past. It derived from the principle that every ethnic and religious group had a right to be judged by a court that applied its particular custom: "Our judicial organization guarantees the natives the maintenance of their customs. The courts that apply custom, in case of disputes or punishable offenses, will be composed of judges practicing the same law as the parties who come before them, or who are referred to them." Belief in this right led Ponty to recommend the creation of a separate subdivision court for every ethnic group or religious minority of any importance in a given area. Thus, where the 1903 decree had foreseen the creation of one court per province or subdivision, article 6 of the 1912 decree anticipated the possible coexistence of several subdivision courts in a single area.[37] Jurisdiction, in short, would no longer be determined arbitrarily by place of birth, but equitably by an individual's ethnic, religious, and cultural identity.

Yet another article, or, rather, Ponty's conservative interpretation of this article, further underscored Dakar's commitment to this same principle. Article 48 stands out because it appeared at first to contradict the very premise of restricted French jurisdiction, and the strict application of custom for all African subjects (articles 1 and 6). It declared: "In civil and commercial cases, natives can, if they both agree to do so, bring their disputes before a French court."[38] This clause suggested that Dakar believed that it had an obligation to provide Africans with whatever kind of justice they preferred, regardless of their personal status, and that flexibility, not the maintenance of customary law, was the underlying principle of the new decree. Ponty, however, quickly dispelled this impression in his instructions accompanying the 1912 reform, in which he discussed Article 48 at length. He pointed out that the freedom to choose between two jurisdictions, which this article promised, raised the delicate problem of "determining to what extent natives may of their own initiative renounce their natural jurisdictions." His answer was revealing:

> It is first incontestable that a native may not, generally speaking, renounce his own customs and place himself of his own free will under French law. The maintenance of custom is not just a favor, which the natives have the right to reject. It is justified by considerations of general interest, which have to do with public order, for the regime regulating property and family are intimately correlated to African social organization.

"The status of the native," he concluded, was "indelible" and could only be erased by naturalization.[39] Having firmly stated this principle, he did, however, allow one exception. In cases involving commercial transactions, "sales, leases, etc.," he explained, custom—this did not apply in civil matters—was nonbinding. "Natives in these matters . . . can substitute different regulations, derived from a different legislation, such as French legislation."[40]

Ponty's explicit denial of an African's right to refer to French courts, except in the realm of business contracts, confirmed the provisions articulated first in the decree: that custom would henceforth constitute the common law of the federation, and that French law in its entirety would apply only to those individuals who had first proven their aptitude at using it and understanding it, by becoming naturalized French citizens. There was no question, in other words, of Africans being judged according to French law whenever they wished. This respect for customary law was dictated not only by the fact that such custom was the expression of the "authentic will" of the population. Considerations of public order reinforced what republican ideology necessarily prescribed. France, Ponty's words intimated, was not going to interfere in the traditional regulation of social relations, lest anarchy result.[41]

This said, the limitations of Ponty's restraint in the judicial realm, as in native policy, must be stressed as well. It is ironic that, in the same passage in which he warned against interfering in customary property relations upon which African social organization rested, the governor general also spoke of the exceptions that must be made when customs conflicted with civilization—not realizing, or perhaps preferring to ignore, the inconsistency of such a position. If civil law could not be changed without raising the threat of anarchy, might not the attenuation of customs contrary to civilization produce the same undesirable result? This possibility did not apparently occur to Dakar or, at any rate, affect its actions. If the first part of the 1912 reform insisted on the need to respect ethnic identities and customs, the rest of the decree revealed that, when customs were deemed contrary to civilization, Ponty was ready to graft Western principles of justice upon African law regardless of the consequences. As in 1903, this interventionist tendency was most marked in the area of criminal justice. Here, too, the continuity with the *politique des races* was striking.

The new decree introduced several innovations in the administration of criminal justice in West Africa. It abolished the right of village chiefs to punish minor offenses, on the grounds that village chiefs either abused their prerogatives or did not understand the administration's view of what constituted a minor offense.[42] In addition, the *commandant de cercle* was given the right to appeal sentences rendered at the subdivision court level in criminal cases, when he considered the punishments too lenient or too harsh. French administrators had repeatedly requested such powers of appeal, arguing that African subjects rarely dared to appeal sentences by their own chiefs, and that as the natural protectors of the masses, the French had a duty to intervene when justice had not been served. They also pointed out that rulings that were obviously flawed posed a threat to public order and likewise required official intervention.[43] Allowing administrators to challenge lower-court decisions resulted in the anomaly that the presiding judge of the circle court, the French *commandant*, tried the very case he had appealed. This rule hardly conformed to the principles of French law, but was justified on the premise that a representative of French civilization, in this case the *commandant de cercle*, was always a better informed and more benign judge than the representative of an inferior culture, the village, canton, or province chief.

These first two reforms considerably enhanced the powers of the circle administrator over those granted him by the 1903 decree. This increase in power reflected Ponty's conviction that French prestige and the well-being of France's African subjects depended upon curtailing the chiefs' traditional authority in the punishment of crimes.[44] Along with these new powers, however, went certain new responsibilities for the French. The local *commandants* were not granted an expanded role in the native legal system simply to prevent abuses by the precolonial elite; they were expected to use their influence to continue to infuse customary law with the principles and guarantees surrounding the administration of criminal justice in the West. To facilitate this task, the revised decree established more specific guidelines for when custom alone should be applied in determining and punishing criminal offenses, and under what circumstances custom had to be amended or replaced.

The 1903 decree had recognized the fundamental principle that local custom determined criminal offenses, but had then divided crimes into three categories unknown in customary law: minor offenses, which were to be referred to the village courts; misdemeanors, which were to be tried at the province court level; and felonies, which fell under the jurisdiction of the circle courts. A great deal of confusion had subsequently ensued over which offenses corresponded to which category; further and more serious questions had been raised, regarding what constituted a crime in the first place. If, for example, customary law—which, according to the 1903 decree, determined what constituted a crime—did not recognize an offense judged criminal by French standards, was such a crime to go unpunished?[45]

Given such confusion, the 1912 reform adopted a different approach to determining what constituted a punishable offense; French law was now given a dominant voice in deciding the criminality of any given action. The former distinctions of felonies, misdemeanors, and minor offenses was abolished altogether. In principle, local custom still determined what constituted a crime; in fact, Ponty wrote, "the supremacy of custom has been restricted because of the necessities of our civilizing mission."[46] This did not mean, Ponty explained, that the *commandants* were no longer to refer to custom; but they were now formally required to prosecute such acts allowed by custom that they found morally reprehensible, as well as all breaches of the administration's public ordinances, in the interest of public welfare. Included in this category were "cannibalism" and "ritual murder . . . whose legitimacy in the eyes of the natives we will not accept," and "the numerous crimes that are not punished by a penalty, inflicted in the name of society, but by compensation accorded to the victim or his family."[47] All acts of armed pillage, assault and battery or aggravated assault, arson, kidnaping, or illegal restraint, poisoning of wells, cisterns, or potable water, and mutilations were also automatically referred to the circle courts for sentencing.[48]

Finally, circle courts were now to have jurisdiction over one other group of infractions: offenses against French authority that had previously been punishable under the exceptional code of the *indigénat*. These included any crime committed by an African employed in the administration or against such an agent; offenses committed by African soldiers in complicity with civilians; usurpation of title or function; illegal wearing, with harmful intent, of uniforms belonging to agents of public authority; breach of public ordinances; any offense prejudicial to the state, colony, or public administration. Ponty did not feel that the French could abolish the *indigénat*; but he could attenuate it "to the extent that the native populations are increasingly acclimating [*s'apprivoisent*] and loyally approaching us." By now referring most of these offenses to the regular courts, Ponty was both recompensing Africans for their progress to date and guaranteeing Africans for the first time the means to defend and preserve "their rights."[49] Here again, liberal metropolitan norms were partially supplanting local prerogatives, although in this case, ironically, the prerogatives were French, not African.

Yet a third aspect of Ponty's effort to reform custom was the introduction of French justice in the prosecution and the punishment of criminals. "Our civilizing mission requires the application of the essential principles of criminal law," Ponty explained in his instructions. Thus, to prove guilt, the native courts were required by the 1912 decree to first establish that a law, ordinance or custom had been violated, then that the accused had committed the crime in question, and last that he had intended the result of his action. To punish the guilty party, the courts had to respect the following principles, also imported from France: equality of all before the law; punishment exclusive to the criminal; imposition of only the most severe sentence in cases of multiple criminality; and specificity of punishment.[50] Finally, in choosing which punishment to inflict, the courts were "to substitute appropriate penalties for those marred by needless cruelty." Custom was to be a guide as to how severe the sentence would be, but the only acceptable sentences to the French were fines, imprisonment for up to twenty years, life imprisonment, exile, or death.[51] The most revolutionary aspect of these provisions was the new emphasis on the personality of criminal offenses and the accompanying forms of punishment. In customary law as the French understood it, a village or family group could be collectively held responsible for an offense committed by one of its members. Similarly, compensation, not imprisonment, was the customary form of retribution for criminal offenses.[52]

These principles for the prosecution and the punishment of crimes were to be applied in the subdivision and the circle courts. However, because the new decree made the *commandants* primarily responsible for seeing that justice was properly rendered in criminal cases, it was questionable to what extent such principles would be upheld. Already overburdened with administrative tasks, inexperienced as judges, and concerned with maintaining order, the administrators were not likely candidates for reforming custom in keeping with the spirit of criminal law as it was practiced in the West.[53] To compensate for this lack of experience, Ponty introduced one final innovation, designed to carry to fruition his goal of civilizing Africans. He extended the accused's rights of appeal and the Chambre d'homologation's powers of review in Dakar to all judicial proceedings in West Africa.[54]

Under the provisions of the 1903 decree, only sentences in criminal cases exceeding five years' imprisonment were referred automatically for review and confirmation to the Chambre d'homologation. If the judgment were rejected, the Chambre had to send the case back to the appropriate court. Civil cases could never be reviewed beyond the circle-court level. The 1912 decree altered these provisions by empowering the prosecutor general to refer any judgment rendered by the lower courts, whose fairness he questioned, to the Chambre. In civil cases, the Chambre could either reject the appeal, or annul the decision as flawed and refer it back to the competent court. In criminal cases, the Chambre could either reject the appeal, or annul the decision and rule in the case itself, if it determined that the appropriate custom had not been applied (*application erronnée de la peine*). Its rulings were enforceable only if they benefited the accused. Although the prosecutor general alone decided which sentences could be appealed at the federal level, individuals who felt their cases deserved consideration could submit their grievances to him, in the hope that he would take appropriate action.[55] This extension of the Chambre's powers, like Ponty's other measures, marked yet another step in imposing French principles of criminal justice upon Africans; the French judges sitting on the court were now openly encouraged to apply French law over customary law when the two conflicted or when custom was silent on a point included in France's penal code. The records of the Chambre confirm, moreover, that—true to Ponty's wishes—the judges were willing to carry out their prescribed role as civilizers.

One West African custom deemed contrary to civilization, according to the new decree, was ritual murder. In 1909, the Chambre ruled in three cases involving ritual murder and explained its procedures:

> In [a] fetishist country, custom does not penalize criminal actions in which the ritual element dominates. Thus, when the religious chief or the chief of the spirits imposes the poison ordeal on an individual accused of having caused the death of an inhabitant of the village, this chief and the witch designated by him to administer the poison cannot ordinarily be prosecuted, since custom does not punish ritual murder. But if the native courts must apply local custom in all matters, this is only on the condition that it does not conflict with the principles of civilization. It is, however, against these principles to let an attack upon a human life go unpunished, even if this attack was ordered by a religious authority. It is thus proper to impose upon the offenders one of the criminal penalties provided in native justice, all the while taking into account their mentality and their social standing.[56]

Two years earlier, in 1907, the Chambre had included under the rubric ritual murder the following case, in which the ritual element lay not in the murder itself but in its punishment:

> The circle court of Bandiagara [Western Sudan] was able justly to condemn three natives to twenty years' imprisonment for murder in the first degree, regardless of a Habbé custom that spares the murderer from prosecution, if he gives one of his daughters to the parents of the victims, a sheep, tobacco and salt to the notables and a blanket to the oldest among them, and if he agrees to leave his village for three years. When this time has elapsed, he can return, but preceded by a cow whose tail he holds. The people say that it is the cow who has returned the murderer to the village. The latter is then absolved and everyone shares in the meat of the cow.

In that same year the Chambre also maintained, more generally:

> Native courts can improve upon custom, when it is contrary to French civilization, when it prescribes corporal punishments, when it does not punish actions contrary to our morality, when it does not punish actions severely enough. Thus a native court correctly refused to uphold a custom that imposed a minimum fine of a cow and a maximum fine of a slave for a certain offense, this penalty being absolutely irreconcilable with our morality.[57]

Other customs proscribed by the Chambre included the payment of blood money in cases of voluntary manslaughter (monetary transactions "affect the family or the collectivity of the offender rather than him personally. They are thus incompatible with the principles of French civilization") and the acknowledgment of the proprietary right of one person over another ("it is contrary to the principles of French civilization for an attack upon the liberty of an individual to go unpunished").[58]

Taken together with the prescriptions of the 1912 reform in matters of criminal justice, and the decision to create ethnic courts, these circle-court rulings represented a clear-cut continuation in Dakar of France's mission as first defined under Roume. They also seem to indicate that this mission was supported by everyone in the French administrative hierarchy. This impression is not entirely accurate. The response of many of Ponty's subordinates in the field to the expanded role of the prosecutor general, and of the special Chambre in Dakar, was uniformly hostile, as it had been nine years earlier when Roume first instituted the Chambre d'homologation. The new powers of review for civil law cases were "against the spirit of the 1903 decree," and custom was much too diverse to allow for a single ruling in any given case.[59] "The Chambre," Lieutenant Governor Clozel of Upper Senegal-Niger argued, "derives its legal science from the judgments rendered by the administrators, which it then aspires to turn around and review. Is there not a measure of incoherence in giving power of appeal to the least informed judge over the best informed one?" The lieutenant governor of Dahomey complained that the Chambre would be unable to judge appeals equitably, because of its unfamiliarity with custom. He also disagreed with the principle that the prosecutor general should have the right to question any sentence handed down by a native court; the centralization of such extensive powers in the hands of French magistrates, he wrote the governor general, "will allow them . . . not to apply custom, to even modify custom by precedents that will be as unattackable on legal grounds, as they will be regrettable on practical ones. A power of this kind can only be left to those who are responsible for the internal security of our colonies."[60]

The lieutenant governors' reservations did not mean they were opposed to the principle of reforming custom. To the contrary, Clozel stressed, in the same terms as Roume and Ponty, it was necessary "to encourage the native to feel and act independently of his clan.

One way of achieving this resides in the strictest application possible of the principle of punishment exclusive to the criminal. Such punishment, applied with perseverance, tact and method, will awaken in the primitive the feeling that he alone, who perpetrates the crime, must bear the consequences of his action."[61] The governors did, however, differ with Ponty on the best means to bring about the desired progress in Africans' social mores. They wished to modify the behavior of African individuals through locally determined measures. Ponty supported the professional magistrates' view that African society as a whole could and should be transformed through the introduction of judicial institutions and principles borrowed from the metropole. This difference in outlook affected the way in which the lieutenant governors and the governor general viewed the Chambre d'homologation. The former concluded that its role should be limited to noting the transformations occurring in customary law, rather than deliberately attempting to alter custom through its ruling. In contrast, Ponty felt that the Chambre's role was to apply the principles of French law every time they were more lenient than existing customs.[62] Although these contrasting points of view surely reflected a power struggle between an encroaching central bureaucracy and subordinate administrations, we should not lose sight of their ideological dimension. Dakar resolutely pursued its understanding of France's civilizing mission in the judicial realm between 1908 and 1914, even as lower-level administrators pleaded for a more pragmatic approach to introducing change.[63]

"It is the fate of every rational organization," Ponty wrote in his introduction to the 1912 reform, "to evolve from the simplicity, required at the outset, toward a certain complexity, which corresponds to the progress of civilization." This declaration of intent set the tone for what followed: a decree that aimed at recording the progress by African society, and encouraging and directing such progress in accordance with the liberal principles of the Third Republic. As the constant emphasis upon respecting custom revealed, Ponty proposed to do this in a rational, uniform, and carefully controlled manner. Indeed, when a metropolitan critic complained that Ponty was going too slowly, because he failed to transfer all judicial prerogatives from the administration to an independent judiciary that would apply French law, Dakar responded:

> Transported into a different milieu than that of France, our Civil Code would be an agent of disorder, and an architect of anarchy. Assuredly, eco-

nomic development and contact with our civilization is effecting a social revolution that is taking place before our eyes and which will be ultimately beneficial; to impose it indirectly, through judicial decisions, would be an artificial and dangerous procedure.[64]

Despite Dakar's claim to the contrary, the 1912 reform did attempt to impose "a social revolution . . . indirectly, through judicial decisions," especially in the punishment of crimes. Here, the administration felt and continued to feel an obligation to intervene. "In punishing crimes and misdemeanors," one governor general said a few years later, "native magistrates left to their own devices would render judgments that were either unnecessarily cruel or shamefully indulgent. . . . It is only by a wise and prudent jurisprudence of our courts that we will be able gradually to alter this mind-set."[65] Such intervention certainly had the potential to disrupt existing mores, if the lieutenant governors and the administrators cooperated and if Africans brought their cases to the courts. Even a carefully controlled commitment to respecting personal liberty, and elevating the dignity of the individual over that of the collectivity, was not as compatible as Dakar originally thought with its other political and economic goals in West Africa. As the few existing studies of native court records show, educated Africans in particular were quick to see in the native justice system an opportunity to challenge the authority of the French and their collaborators.[66] For the great majority of Africans the results were more mixed. "The natives tolerate easily enough the change in their traditions," a frustrated administrator wrote in 1924, "but they do not understand it and remain opposed to it in the depths of their conscience."[67]

'Une Conquête Morale': Educational Reform

The *politique des races* and the distribution of enlightened justice were two major elements of Ponty's vision for moving African society forward. During his years in office, however, Ponty let it be known that he attached the utmost importance to yet a third area of civilizing action: the spread of education and teaching of French. Like Roume before him, Ponty accepted both as essential components of France's mission in Africa. Unlike Roume's, Ponty's interest in education would be deep-seated and ongoing. After creating a uniform hierarchy of schools (village schools, regional schools, and postprimary professional schools) and generally orienting the direction

of adapted education, Roume had turned to other matters and issued
no further directives on the subject. As a result, only some of his
subordinates had applied his original instructions in their colonies.
They had had great latitude to decide exactly how and what Africans
would be taught.

Ponty was convinced that more could be done in this domain, and
done better. He therefore took several steps designed to clarify the
content and pedagogical methods of education and to increase the
number of schools available to Africans. Under his administration,
French became the official language of the federation; the first comprehensive course plan applicable to the entire federation was drawn
up, and the first manuals began to be published. These reforms in
no way challenged the principles Roume had first articulated: although instruction under Ponty would continue to be adapted to the
African environment, it would also be in French, open to all, and simultaneously practical and educational. And in one important conceptual way, Ponty's liberalism went considerably beyond that of his
predecessor. In working out the specific content of adapted education, his administration came up with a more positive definition
than Roume's of the ultimate purpose of schooling—and France's
mission civilisatrice generally—for Africans.

Ponty's special interest in education was clear from the moment
he arrived. Not a year went by without numerous circulars on the
subject, and educational accomplishments and calls to do more figured annually in Ponty's speeches before the Council of the Government General. What was needed, Ponty claimed, was not more
money, but greater effort on the part of his subordinates. The extension of education "is one of [the Government General's] essential
preoccupations"; "It appears necessary to accelerate the diffusion of
our language"; "It is necessary that native children come to our
schools in greater numbers."[68] To encourage his lieutenant governors to comply with his wishes, Ponty also explained again why education was so necessary. The same republican themes that had so
influenced the 1903 organization of education reappeared more
forcefully. Education of youth had always been "one of the essential
preoccupations of the Republic"; "in the colonies as well as in the
metropole," then, it required the "committed devotion of all."[69] Previously restricted to an elite whose collaboration was deemed necessary, it would now be extended "to all classes of society," regardless of "origin, race, caste or religion."[70] Instruction was "the most

efficient instrument of our civilizing work," since it imposed "on the natives the idea that they can and must ameliorate their living conditions," and provided them "with the means to do so." This was especially true since French primary schools, while always adapted to local conditions, were more than "schools of apprenticeship"; they also sought to awaken the African's intelligence. In addition to improving the African physically and morally, instruction was the best way to "develop the country." Education "elevates man" and "augments his appetites, that is to say, his ability to consume"; and schools trained collaborators who were badly needed.[71]

Yet in demanding more from his subordinates in the realm of French instruction, Ponty did not only develop themes from the past. He also added some new arguments in favor of education which closely related to the reform of justice and the *politique des races*. Knowledge of French was "the primordial condition of our success and its longevity," for without it "the most praiseworthy intentions" of "our administration and our justice" risked being misunderstood. Through the multiplication of schools, especially village schools—"schools of language where the children learn to understand and speak French"—French "influence will insinuate itself among the masses, penetrate and envelop them like a thin web of new affinities."[72] "All the means that we have mobilized in our *commandement* and administration of the masses must have, from the social point of view, a single objective: obtaining from our African subjects and protégés a more and more exact comprehension of the French mentality and the colonizing concepts which are the honor of the government of the Republic." This could only be done through the use of the French language. The spread of French was a means to counter Islam as well, "for experience has taught us that Muslims who know our language are less prejudiced."[73] These quotations reveal another dimension of Ponty's thinking on education. Unless Africans learned to speak French, such measures as the eradication of "feudal" vestiges and barbaric customs risked being misunderstood, and therefore remaining incomplete. Instruction by the French in French, in other words, was the glue that would make all of France's other civilizing measures stick.

Ponty followed up this verbal commitment to education with the most detailed regulations to date on African schooling. He was helped in this effort by a young and energetic new inspector of education, Georges Hardy, who arrived in 1912. An *agregé* in history,

like the architect of the 1903 arrêté, Camille Guy, and a graduate of
the Ecole Normale Supérieure, Hardy has been largely credited with
the educational reforms of the Ponty administration.[74] Yet if Hardy
wrote the later circulars to which Ponty signed his name, their inspiration was not just his. Well before Hardy's arrival, Ponty not
only expressed—as the above circulars reveal—an interest in education, but acted to renew France's educational effort in the federation.
He organized a corps of school inspectors in 1908 and created adult
courses in 1909 to spread the French language.[75] In 1910, Ponty reasserted the primacy of language instruction while promising in-
demnities to regional school directors who visited rural schools regularly. In 1911, he took the dramatic step of insisting that henceforth only French be used in native courts (even Muslim ones) and
"all administrative acts destined to be made known to the natives."[76] Until that time, Dakar had allowed Arabic to be used in the
courts as well as in official correspondence. The issues of compulsion and recruitment, and the overhaul of existing legislation, were
all discussed as well by Ponty between 1910 and 1911.[77] The ground
was therefore well prepared when Hardy arrived in the federation.
Nevertheless, it is true that the most comprehensive educational
changes by Ponty occurred on Hardy's watch and bear the unmis-
takable stamp of a lycée professor. Foremost among these changes
was Dakar's publication in 1914 of a single *plan d'études* for primary
education throughout the West African federation.[78] Most of this
plan was devoted to village and regional schools, which Ponty and
Hardy obviously felt should constitute the real heart of the French
educational effort in West Africa. Through this plan and the textbooks that accompanied it, Ponty's commitment to expanding education and a clarification of Dakar's understanding of its mission in
West Africa emerge.

Dakar's 1914 school curriculum, whose central ideas were developed again by Hardy in his book *Une conquête morale* (1917), defined for the first time at the federal level the specific content and
vocation of adapted education.[79] Village schools, in keeping with the
policy of direct contact, were to reach as many natives as possible
and establish trust so Africans would "submit to the directions that
will lead to economic and social progress." The essential means to
this contact was instruction of spoken French (five hours per week),
which would also serve as a vehicle for practical notions. Language
instruction was to proceed by a method defined as *exercises de lan-*

gage—leçons de choses. Africans would be shown an object, always from their own milieu, and be taught first its name and then its function. These lessons should cover eight topics in a school year: the school, the body, food, housing, clothing, the family, the village, and travel. Reading and writing (two and a half hours each a week) followed the same principles. At least five hours a week were to be spent in the school garden; agricultural instruction was thus to be a main focus of the village school. Another five hours were to be devoted to the simple math that future commodity producers would need to know. No specific time slot was devoted to moral education, which was to be interwoven in all lessons. Like administrators in their courts, teachers in their classrooms were to distinguish between barbaric and acceptable African morality. Examples of false African morality were vices such as vanity, laziness, and lavishness; virtues that the French were to reinforce (or introduce) included development of a conscience, duties to oneself, to one's family, to other people, to the weak and aged; respect for property and the honor of others. Where parental, community, or religious morality did not offend, schools were to reinforce it; the French did not want the African family disintegrating. When local notions offended, superior French ones were to take their place.[80]

If village schools were for the masses, regional schools were conceived to form a new elite: "quality rather than quantity." They should train competent auxiliaries and prepare students for postprimary commercial, professional, or normal courses. Sons of chiefs who might be called upon to succeed their fathers in the administration were to attend these schools, along with the brightest graduates of village schools. Here, French discipline was to be merciless, and all *mauvaises têtes*—aristocratic or not—would be expelled. Thus was the regional school yoked to Ponty's policy of "dominating chiefs morally." The regional school student should graduate convinced "that he owes the best part of his activity and loyalty to the region where he was born." To this end, the same subjects were taught as in primary schools, only at a more advanced level. Some new ones were added: the physical and natural sciences, which were to teach cause and effect; the geography of "countries the native will have occasion to visit" (the village, the region, the colony, and French West Africa) and the geography of "French power," its "economic activity . . . commercial situation . . . communication systems, wealth and power"; and history, whose primary purpose was "to make the children understand the profound difference . . . between their unstable and bloody past and the peaceful and productive present," which existed because "a powerful and generous country" had intervened. The emphasis would again be on familiarizing Africans less with French history per se than with the effects of French power in West Africa: the colonization and the administrative organization.[81] As subsequent instructions explained, the point was not, as in the metropole, to make the children love France, but rather to make them love the French. Despite this purported distinction, the regional school plan continued to replicate many aspects of metropolitan primary school education. Most of the subjects taught in West Africa were also taught in France. The chief differences were the added emphasis in West Africa on spoken French and the importance attached to the school garden. In France, the trend was toward decreasing the time devoted to manual arts (from two to three hours a week to one and a half in the 1923 curriculum reform).[82]

The same principles that guided school programs also informed the first readers for regional school students. One of the most enduring of these was Louis Sonolet's *Moussa et Gi-gla: Histoire de deux petits noirs*.[83] Modeled on Bruno's *Tour de la France par deux enfants*, *Moussa et Gi-gla* recounted the colorful adventures of two young Africans during their travels through the federation with their employer, a French merchant. All the themes of the 1914 school plan reappear: lessons of morality were interspersed among chapters on each colony, their capitals and their principal products. Additional chapters were devoted to the feats of French technology (the railroad, ports, steamboats, airplanes, modern urban hygiene), the beneficence of French administration (abolition of slavery, administration of justice, free vaccinations), the mutual advantages of French commerce ("everything that profits whites benefits blacks"),[84] examples of African loyalty to France (the capture of Samori by the *tirailleurs*), and illustrations from Africa's barbaric past and present (human sacrifices in Dahomey—now abolished; slave raiding in the Western Sudan—still going on but being fought by the French). Two chapters only were devoted to the metropole: one discussed French wealth and the industriousness of its people, and described Paris, Bordeaux, and Marseille; the other summarized the French Revolution and Napoleon, emphasizing the Republic's love of liberty and desire to spread it.[85] The book drew attention superficially to Africa's different ethnicities, but generally referred to Africans as blacks and the

French as whites. All Africans were brothers and should help each other; speaking French was one means to this end. All French and blacks belonged to the same *patrie*, and the *patrie* was a big family "in which all members must unite, love and support each other."[86] The French, "more advanced in civilization," helped the African by sharing with him the fruits of science, which was "the work of whites," but which blacks "could study and profit from." Blacks helped whites with their labor and by fighting for France.[87] In the end, Moussa grew up to be a model soldier in the colonial army, and Gi-gla returned to his natal village in Dahomey to be a model farmer.

On one level, what is most striking about these primary-school materials is how they recapitulated every civilizing theme articulated in Dakar since its founding. African children were being taught that under France's guiding hand, their home was becoming a more productive, egalitarian, and modern place. The hallmarks of civilization were technological achievements in the service of *mise en valeur*, superior morality, and the ability to speak French. To be civilized was to acquire all these attributes simultaneously. These themes, as we have seen, had emerged in a variety of other contexts between 1902 and 1914; their articulation at the heart of the school curriculum therefore only provides more proof—if any is needed—of the coherence of France's civilizing project in West Africa and the pervasiveness of its main tenets.

On another level, however, the establishment of a standardized curriculum and the publication of textbooks did lead to one important rhetorical innovation in Dakar's discussions of education and progress in West Africa. Guy's and Roume's original directive on schools had left unstated the adult African's final identity and status. Adapted education in 1903 had emphasized learning the manual arts along with reading, writing, and speaking French, and African "evolution within their own cultures." The most specific point made about Africans' future was that they would not become French and should not become *déclassés*. These negative goals were in sharp contrast to metropolitan education, which consciously sought to turn boys into patriotic citizens and girls into good *républicaines*—both deeply imbued with a sense of the French nation.

Hardy and Ponty now also endowed adapted education with a higher objective and a clearer orientation. This was not, of course, to make black children into adult French citizens. Their exposure to metropolitan history and geography, as both the school plan and

Moussa et Gi-gla suggest, was deliberately kept to a minimum because they were not destined to be naturalized en masse; rather, it was, in the words of numerous textbooks, to *en faire des hommes utiles* (to make of them useful men). The suggestion was often discreet, and the phrase never acquired any official status; it did not appear to be consciously chosen, but seemed to be spontaneous usage. Gi-gla and Moussa were repeatedly told that their destiny was to be made into *hommes utiles.*[88] "It is necessary [for the African] to rise to the *dignité d'homme*," Hardy wrote in his book *Une conquête morale*. Only "whites know themselves as men [*se connaissent en hommes*]." Schools, he reiterated to the Council of the Government General, were to make of the African child "a man and a Frenchman, in order to prepare him to become useful, and to want to become useful."[89] Georges Deherme, who wrote the federation's slavery report in 1908, used the same formula in discussing the need to eradicate human bondage. France wished to elevate Africans to a higher "humanity," to evoke in them "more human ambitions. . . . We know that in thus increasing the capacity of Africans to live, we will also increase their capacity to suffer. But it is in this way that they will truly be men."[90]

At first glance, this formula appears hardly more concrete than the silence it replaced; it is nevertheless worth noting what it does not say as well as what it actually does say. *En faire des hommes* made amply clear once again that Dakar did not believe Africans should become fully French. But the same expression suggested an alternative identity for Africans that remained consistent with the universalism of France's revolutionary heritage. Although they would not grow up to be French citizens, they would become part of something just as admirable: the fraternity of productive men. The republicanism of such a formulation is obvious, and it helps explain the rigorous intellectual content of adapted education. The obfuscating aspects of *en faire des hommes* are nevertheless equally evident. The same notion obviated the need for civic instruction; as long as the African destiny was defined in terms of utility, rather than full membership in either the French nation or some future African polity, no discussion of political responsibilities and rights was necessary. In this respect, adapted education failed the Third Republic's tradition of preparing all its children for the exercise of the *droits de l'homme*.

This was not Dakar's only failure in education. Ponty's years in office may have reaffirmed France's determination to spread instruction in West Africa, in a manner both adapted to the African environment and in keeping with republican values. Yet it is well documented that the Government General managed to achieve only one of its stated educational goals in the prewar era—creating a class of literate auxiliaries. In contrast to this success, Dakar made little headway in its second task: penetrating the masses. Between 1903 and 1913, approximately 200 schools were created, and the number of enrolled students doubled, from 5,000 to between 11,000 and 12,000—in a school-age population of 1,200,000. European personnel during the same period only increased to a total of 118 teachers, while an estimated 145 African instructors had been trained.[91] The schools that did exist were unevenly distributed throughout the federation, with the colonies of Dahomey and Senegal having more educational facilities.[92] Although the little progress that did take place occurred on Ponty's and especially Hardy's watch, the overall results were not impressive. Dakar itself constantly lamented the poor showing, but never reconsidered its overall approach to adapted education.

Even the auxiliaries that were formed did not behave as the French had expected. The majority of the new students did not become model farmers or model soldiers; instead, they went to work for the administration or for commerce, where the jobs were both more lucrative and more prestigious. "What strikes one," a post–World War I report began, "when the most capable students of the regional schools are asked what career they hope to pursue, is their desire to serve primarily in the bureaus of the government or of the circle administrators, and to thus find themselves in the entourage of those who hold authority. If a few are considering entering the teaching profession . . . no one has shown the least taste for the manual arts."[93] These clerks, moreover, would increasingly be perceived as a threat to the colonial regime; far from using their new language and knowledge of French culture to understand the French and accept their high-minded motives in colonizing West Africa, at least some members of this first generation of educated Africans would begin to challenge the exclusion of Africans from power.

A variety of reasons account for this failure to instruct African cultivators in the manner anticipated by Dakar, much less inculcate the kind of loyalty Ponty and Roume imagined. There were, of course, enormous technical difficulties in creating a network of rural schools throughout the federation: a chronic shortage of teachers, lack of funds, and inadequate textbooks and facilities. More difficult to quantify were the cultural barriers to implementing this program: understandable resistance from Africans, for whom these "adapted schools" were designed; hostility of the European community to schools in general; and apathy on the part of local administrators in the field who felt that they had more important things to do than run schools. These structural constraints would have inhibited even the most determined efforts to introduce education into the countryside.

Equally to blame, however, was the confused program of "adapted" education itself. This approach attempted to reconcile objectives that were, in the end, simply incompatible. This confusion had always been there, but Ponty's reforms brought it out with special clarity. The same school system could not by definition produce French-speaking interpreters and clerks and efficient peasant farmers; nor could it simultaneously introduce the French language and even a limited knowledge of French institutions, and prevent Africans from aspiring to equality with the colonizer.[94] Ponty and Hardy may have recognized the inherent dangers of an instruction based too closely on the metropolitan model; but they still thought in metropolitan terms when they decided to "adapt" French materials to the African environment rather than vice versa. Finally, it made little sense to promote the goal of social mobility and of keeping Africans tied to the land and "manual arts." In all these instances, Dakar's educational strategies accurately reflected contradictions in French ideology itself. This ideology embraced a paradoxical combination of practical considerations and idealistic ambitions for social change along the same lines as France. Adapted education, for better or worse, did the same.

In 1912, the Socialist deputy Maurice Viollette addressed the French Chamber of Deputies in the following terms, to much applause from the bench:

> Whatever may be said, republican France has remained profoundly idealistic and if, little by little, it has been won over by the idea of a colonial policy, if it has ratified [this idea], if it is ready to boast of it, it is because at every turn the government has explained that [such a policy] serves the cause of civilization and humanity. We have made [the country] understand the glory that there is for a nation to undertake the education of so many peoples still immersed in barbarism. We have explained that there

was cannibalism to suppress, slavery to destroy, the awful tyranny of bloody kinglets to repress. We have been told that by appearing thus as the great liberating power, we would prodigiously enhance our moral prestige as well as our economic prosperity, and that the curiosity of these peoples, awakened, would turn toward us in order to draw upon our reasoning, our methods and our tastes, and thus steeped in our genius without dreaming of an impossible assimilation, they would continue magnificently France overseas. . . . [Our] program is to bring them not in twenty-four hours, but perhaps in a century if necessary, gradually and smoothly, to that level of civilization that aging Europe through so many catastrophes and even regressions has taken thousands of centuries to reach.

To penetrate these populations with our spirit, to the point that they may produce men in the economic and moral sense of the word, capable of producing and integrating themselves through our intervention, and under our protection, in the movement of universal exchanges, this is the task that has been announced to the nation to legitimate the colonial movement.[95]

This speech, at once impassioned, universalistic, and patronizing, confirms that an entire generation of policy makers, in Paris as well as Dakar, shared Roume's and Ponty's vision of France's mission in West Africa. Much of this mission, Viollette's language reminds us yet again, was inherited from 1789. The victories of the First, Second, and Third Republics—or as many republicans imagined—could be reenacted in "feudal" Africa, producing a new democratic polity, culture, and society in the image of France.

Yet France's civilizing discourse since the founding of the Government General had always had another dimension. Fin-de-siècle science also framed Dakar's vision, whether in the guise of social evolutionary theory, improved communications technology, modern hygiene, or bacteriology. That societies change only slowly, that they are organic wholes whose parts can and should be known before the larger entity can be improved: these foundational ideas of modern sociology were current in Dakar and Paris. While hardly giving rise to any genuine French understanding of Africans, they did contribute to the decisions to adapt education and justice to the colonies. In the case of technology and the germ theory of disease, the transfer from Paris to Dakar was more direct; if anything, metropolitan trends were exaggerated overseas. Roume made the spread of railroads and preventive hygiene an integral part of the *mission civilisatrice* in West Africa.

For the most part, this scientific dimension dovetailed with Dakar's older vision of republican progress. In at least one domain, however, it introduced an ugly new form of racism, which challenged the notion that Africans and French could work together to continue magnificently France *outre-mer*. Modern medicine in particular saw the colonized less as potential disciples than as hosts to dangerous parasites that physically threatened the white race. To the intimacy of the great republican family in which Africans and French easily mixed—albeit as unequals—science juxtaposed the image of two fundamentally incompatible and different races whose trajectories could never hope to converge. The same Ponty who urged more, not less, "direct contact" with Africans knew this language as well and spoke it on occasion. When yellow fever broke out again in Dakar in 1913, he wrote that "it has been noted that the presence of natives from outside the colony in close proximity to Europeans exacerbates yellow fever and malaria"; "It is as if the *anopheles* absorbs from black blood a renewal of its strength, a new vitality"; "Black children . . . conserve and sustain the *amaryl* virus." The solution: "segregation" and "attentive surveillance" of black villages.[96]

This racist language had nevertheless remained a secondary theme in French civilization ideology under Ponty's and even Roume's administration. But with the approach of world war, both Paris and Dakar were about to shift registers. During the war, the Government General discovered that its attempts to engineer social change were not having the anticipated consequences. Instead of the expected loyalty from their subjects, France faced large-scale revolts for the first time since the conquest. In France and the world, the Great War also ushered in new actors, new ideologies, and new fears. These internal and external developments would call many of the liberal aspects of French civilizing rhetoric and policies into question, and encourage a new distancing between colonizer and colonized. In West Africa as in France, a more conservative republicanism would soon show its face.

CHAPTER 5

Revolt and Reaction

WORLD WAR I AND ITS CONSEQUENCES (1914–1930)

Our authority must above all else remain unshakable and unchallenged.
— Governor General Jules Carde[1]

From its founding until 1914, the Government General had taken for granted that African society could easily be transformed in the image of republican France. Between 1914 and 1917, this early optimism waned, and Dakar's conception of the *mission civilisatrice* began to change. Several developments help account for this shift. In West Africa, the French forcibly recruited soldiers during World War I and abruptly concluded that their earlier "emancipationist" native policies were producing unanticipated results that threatened French hegemony in West Africa. The prewar emphasis upon eradicating "feudal vestiges" was not winning over the local populations and facilitating bureaucratic rule; instead, this policy was fomenting discontent with French authority and alienating the rural masses. Conscription and its consequences also revealed that even "adapted" French education was producing a new elite of Africans, more anxious to share power equally with the colonizer than to evolve gradually within their own cultures. Throughout the 1920's, their demands continued unabated. Meanwhile in France, the devastating loss of life and property and disruption of civil society caused by *la grande guerre*, the outbreak of the Bolshevik Revolution in Russia, and the spread of Pan-Africanism abroad also contributed to a growing sense of French insecurity both at home and overseas.

The emergence of these various threats had a profound effect upon the actions and outlook of the Government General, and that of the metropole generally, in the postwar decade. Confronted with challenges to its authority, Dakar reacted by restoring order in the federation in a variety of ways. It used outright repression of rebellious chiefs and those French-educated Africans demanding equality with the colonizers; and it sought to shore up federal prestige by now distancing government in subtle and not so subtle ways from the colonized. In particular, old racisms revived and new ones took root. Both policies were symptomatic of a certain disillusionment with prewar civilizing tenets, especially those with a "liberating" dimension. These policies in turn presaged a new interpretation of the Third Republic's civilizing mission, which would emerge as well in the 1920's.

Conscription and Revolt, 1914–1918

World War I was a catalyst for dramatic change in West Africa, involving the Africans drawn into the conflict and the outlook of the Government General. As far as Dakar was concerned, the most important innovation of the war years was the metropolitan government's decision to recruit Africans, by force if necessary, to serve on Europe's battlefields. Governor General Ponty, the Colonial Ministry, and public opinion at large supported the decision to use African troops in France. These three entities all naively assumed that France's African subjects would welcome the chance to serve the country that was bringing civilization into their midst. Conscription of African soldiers and the disruption it caused helped, instead, to discredit Dakar's conception of its *mission civilisatrice* as implemented by the Government General.

The creation of a Force Noire in West Africa dated back to 1912, when, at Ponty's urging, the French government decreed that 5,000 Africans be recruited annually for the next four years. These troops were to replace the French units serving in Algeria, as well as fight in Europe in the event of war. Although enlistment was intended to be primarily voluntary, compulsory enlistment—by *voie d'appel*—was introduced, which quickly became the norm before and during World War I. Recruitment by *voie d'appel* assigned quotas to chiefs, who then had to present the necessary number of men to a *commission de recrutement* for medical inspection and enrollment.[2] When war broke out, Africans recruited by *voie d'appel* gradually rose from 4 percent to more than 10 percent of the adult male population. It is estimated that 200,000 Africans were eventually mobilized between 1912 and 1919, and that 30,000 to 31,000 lost their lives.[3]

Ponty's support for military recruitment dramatized yet another aspect of Dakar's republican ideology in West Africa as defined between 1902 and 1914. Democratic France's mission not only imposed specific duties upon the civilizing power. This mission also involved reciprocal obligations for its subjects. According to this rationale, the Third Republic was bringing to oppressed peoples everywhere the freedom and prosperity that its own citizens enjoyed to a greater extent than any other nation. In return for these gifts, France could demand—at the very minimum—the same sacrifices and devotion from its subjects that it expected from its citizenry. Before 1912, the most important obligations imposed on Africans had been taxation and free labor for building roads; nevertheless, given the Third Republic's patriotism, it was only a matter of time before defending the motherland was added to the list. The very way the Government General spoke of taxation and recruitment revealed this conflation of the duties of citizen and subject; both the head tax and conscription were described less as obligations that had to be forced upon Africans than duties willingly embraced. "For the native," Ponty stated in 1911, "taxation, far from being the sign of a humiliating servitude, is seen rather as proof that he is beginning to rise on the ladder of humanity, that he has entered upon the path of civilization. To ask him to contribute to our common expenses, is, so to speak, to elevate him in the social hierarchy." In 1914, he cabled Doumergue that the "enthusiasm would be extreme if the local populations were informed that natives would be granted the honor of fighting in France."[4]

Colonial recruitment nevertheless had its detractors. Several members of the General Staff expressed reservations about the military value of African soldiers serving in Europe. As early as 1910 the Socialists, led by Jaurès, opposed the creation of an African army, on the grounds that it could someday be used to repress the working class. The trading firms active in West Africa were particularly concerned that recruitment would deprive the rural economy of its manpower and jeopardize their profits.[5] Further criticism came from the lower echelons of the colonial administration. The lieutenant governors and the *commandants de cercle* foresaw and denounced the disruption and hatred of the French that colonial recruitment would cause. Finally, important doubts were raised by two deputies in Parliament in December 1912, when the colonial budget came up for review. Maurice Veillat, a liberal on the question of "native

rights," and François Carpot, the Creole representative from Senegal, challenged Ponty's claim that recruitment was consistent with
France's civilizing mission as practiced to date in West Africa. Veillat argued that it was fair to expect the Africans to cooperate in the
effort to "breathe life into their continent" through taxation, the *indigénat*, and labor requisitions. But he drew the line at a blood tax,
insisting that "we should not aggravate a necessary evil by asking
what they cannot give." He also objected to making chiefs responsible for recruitment. All French efforts had been directed "toward
increasing contact with the natives" and "weakening and diminishing the authority of chiefs." The government was now proposing a
complete reversal of this policy. France, he concluded, would be risk-
ing what little moral legitimacy it had acquired in the eyes of its
subjects. Chiefs would recover their power, the African masses
would suffer, and French rule would lose its prestige.[6]

Recruitment, Carpot began in an even franker speech, would be
acceptable if it were the first step toward assimilation and citizenship. But assimilation had never been the government's goal, since
there had been no serious attempt to educate Africans as Frenchmen: "Too often we have forgotten that education is the best instrument of progress and civilization, and the indispensable precon-
dition to citizenship. . . . Instead [of investing in education], under
the pretext of allowing [the African] to evolve in his own milieu, you
have always kept him apart, never consenting to raise him towards
yourself." Given this refusal of France to commit itself to the education and eventual assimilation of its subjects, Carpot declared, the
imposition of military recruitment was out of the question. Moreover, he continued, such a policy would be dangerous, because it ignored fundamental realities about the relationship between the colonizer and the colonized. West Africans, he argued, no more wanted
obligatory military service than they desired French citizenship.
Rightly or wrongly, they felt that France had dispossessed them of
the land that was theirs by birthright. It thus made no sense to ask
them to defend French national territory. Recruitment in this context could only turn them against France. "What," he asked in a direct rebuke to Ponty, "do Africans care about duty to the motherland?" France's entire approach to governing Africans, he concluded
bitterly, was to treat them as French citizens each time it was a
question of obligations and duties, and to treat them as subjects each
time it was a question of rights or privileges.[7]

Carpot's final remark brilliantly pinpointed a central ambiguity about the Third Republic's particular approach to colonizing. It was, however, a truth to which few cared to listen. Most members of Parliament, along with the colonial minister himself, did not share either Veillat's interest in or Carpot's firsthand knowledge of conditions in the West African colonies. In response to Veillat's concerns about potential abuses, the minister assured the Assembly that Ponty had been warned to supervise the chiefs involved in the mobilization effort. In the ensuing years, as the demand for military manpower mushroomed because of enormous casualties and the war's duration, the *tirailleurs'* popularity with the public grew stronger. The only remaining voice of dissent came from within West Africa, where a reduced administrative staff watched with alarm the excesses, wide-scale flights, and simmering discontent that the repeated demands for African soldiers were generating.

In 1914, on the eve of World War I, the federation had between 16,500 and 17,500 African soldiers serving in North Africa and another 14,000 scattered throughout West Africa. On July 29, two days after the Superior Command announced that the period of hostilities was now open, Ponty cabled Paris that he could send thirty-three companies, or 6,600 men, within twenty-five days to serve in France. When war broke out, Ponty promised an additional three battalions and then, in November, pledged to mobilize 20,000 men and make them available for the national defense between March and December 1915. By October 1915, Africans serving in France, North Africa, and Cameroon numbered 70,000. Of these, 32,000 had been recruited in 1915 alone, in three separate recruiting drives. Few had yet been repatriated when, on October 9, 1915, a further levy of 50,000 for 1916 was announced. Compulsory enlistment by *voie d'appel*, which had been halted before the outbreak of war, was reinstituted in 1915 to ensure that the General Command's stated goals would not only be met but repeatedly surpassed. Senegal and the sedentary populations of Upper Senegal-Niger provided proportionately more men early on, whereas the southern colonies of Ivory Coast, Dahomey, and Guinea were tapped heavily in the second and third recruiting drives in the fall of 1915. The nomadic populations in Mauritania and Niger were considered insufficiently pacified for recruitment and were spared altogether.[8]

Recruitment was unwelcome and difficult to implement from the outset. No reliable population statistics existed outside Senegal.

French administrative personnel had been drastically reduced: one-third of all *commandants*, one-half of all medical personnel, and four-fifths of communication employees had been mobilized. Understaffed and overworked, administrators usually had no choice but to rely upon their African intermediaries to round up the men demanded, and determine which villages would contribute or be spared. In general, the chiefs cooperated, though reluctantly. Where these chiefs retained some of their traditional legitimacy, recruitment took place without incident; where new men had been appointed, dependent on the French for their authority and prestige, excessive brutality in choosing recruits was often reported. According to their temperament, experience, and familiarity with their circle, individual *commandants* would attempt either to moderate the use of force or simply ignore the abuses they were powerless to stop.

African reaction to recruitment in 1914 and 1915 was the same everywhere, although most pronounced where European representation was thinnest: despair and even hysteria of the families, who were convinced their sons would never return, and who often resorted to force to release conscripts rounded up by the local authorities before these new recruits left their region of origin; passive, spontaneous, and individualized resistance in the form of flight to neighboring foreign colonies or into the bush and forests, or self-mutilation; presentation of physically unfit men, who would automatically be rejected by the army agents.[9] This last tactic hardly qualified as a form of resistance. What the decision to recruit in West Africa revealed was the deplorable state of the population after a recent famine in the Sahel, and the endemic diseases upon which French medical care had had so little impact. Given these conditions, the request for all able-bodied men three times in the same year, disrupting the cultivation and harvesting of their crops when supplies were at their lowest, antagonized not only Africans but many lieutenant governors, who feared for French authority if recruitment continued unabated. As long as Ponty was alive, these men kept silent; but when Paris announced the new goal of 50,000 recruits in October 1915, Ponty's replacement, Governor General Clozel, gave them license to speak out.[10] He then cabled the minister that the most the federation could offer was 25,000 *tirailleurs*—to no avail.[11]

The lieutenant governors' fears proved well founded. The years 1915–1916 witnessed a dramatic increase in passive resistance, and armed rebellion broke out in areas traditionally considered "pacified." These uprisings, which continued sporadically through 1917, provided the administration with its most potent argument against continued recruitment. At the same time, the rebellions brought into question past administrative policy in West Africa. Revolt did not necessarily occur where recruitment had been most intense or abusive. Indeed, it soon became clear that there was a direct correlation between rebellion and the type of native policies earlier implemented in a given circle. Wherever vestiges of former aristocracies had survived Ponty's *politique des races*, the French could count on the chiefs' loyalty and willingness to collaborate with the Government General in recruiting *tirailleurs*. For these survivors, the war seemed to offer a chance to recoup some of their declining authority by striking bargains with the administration in exchange for the men they provided. The absence of such traditional chiefs was a recurrent element in the areas where rebellion did occur, a lesson not lost on the new policy makers in Dakar.

Revolt broke out first in 1915, in the Western Sudan in the circle of Bélédougou, located to the east of Bamako in an area inhabited by the Bambara peoples.[12] Bélédougou had not borne the brunt of exactions in 1914. The new demands of 1915 thus caught the Africans by surprise. In May 1915, the canton chiefs of all the Bambara villages collectively refused to give up a single *tirailleur*. They then stopped the mails, executed the local circle guards, and retreated armed to a village, where they awaited the French. Within three weeks, they had been defeated. Subsequent analyses revealed that although hostility to recruitment was the immediate cause for the revolt, an overly zealous application of Ponty's circular on the *politique des races* in the years preceding the war accounted for the chiefs' decision to turn against the French. This circle was physically isolated; as a result, French penetration had been slow. Until Ponty's governorship, the traditional chiefs had ruled, with little interference from the local French administration. Under Ponty, the authority of these notables had deliberately been broken, leaving behind, as Clozel put it, "only the hatred of dispossessed chiefs."[13] The war had thus provided these malcontents with an opportunity to reclaim their former prestige. Their reaction fit the circumstances: unused to accommodation as a means for holding on to some of their authority, they opted for resistance in a bid to recover all of it.

The Bambara revolt was followed by a much more prolonged rebellion in western Volta, in the circles west of the Mossi regions.

This revolt lasted eight months and involved seven different ethnic groups in six neighboring circles, who nevertheless shared cultural traits. Here, too, the impetus for rebellion was a desire to return to the institutions of the past, which colonial rule had disrupted. The peoples in question were described as particularly hostile to any form of centralized government. By tradition, power was vested in councils made up of village elders. These elders, practically unknown to the French, resented the administration's appointing new canton chiefs and the concomitant decline in their own authority. Moreover, these new men freely exploited the local communities through illegal labor exactions and irregular judicial proceedings and incarcerations. In this context of generalized discontent, the demand for *tirailleurs* proved catastrophic. Recruitment in 1915 in western Volta was more intensive and abusive than at any previous point. With European personnel increasingly scarce, the moment seemed right for ousting those who had no legitimate claim to their offices. The revolt revealed how insecure the French hold on this region was and led to the area's first real conquest.[14]

Elsewhere in the federation, French authority was further put to the test. In November 1916, revolt broke out in northern Dahomey; although the excesses of recruitment were again to blame, the revolt was led by disaffected aristocrats hoping to profit individually from perceived French weakness in the area.[15] On the borders of the Sahara, in Niger, the Tuareg also rebelled.[16] An estimated 135,000 *tirailleurs* had been recruited, but at a high price to the Africans serving and future French interests in the federation. A letter written to the local administration by nomad chiefs in Upper Senegal-Niger, complaining about a wartime increase in taxation, indicates that by 1917 even chiefs who had chosen to collaborate with the French were wavering:

> Not only have we not revolted, but at the moment when the entire region was getting ready to do so, we helped suppress the rebels. . . . Because we are your friends, you profit from us to ask for *tirailleurs* and cattle, which we promptly provide. We have the French school in our encampments, while the circles of Timboctou and Gao do not have one. We have accepted to be counted and given exact information, and now we are paying the price, while those who revolted go wherever they like and pay almost no taxes. There do not have to be many more measures of this type to make our people conclude that it is better to keep a distance from the French rather than to be their friends, because only in the former case do they leave you alone.[17]

The year 1917 would nevertheless bring an improvement of sorts in the federation's fortunes, at least from Dakar's perspective. Clozel, who was ailing, was replaced by the much younger and more dynamic Joost Van Vollenhoven. Like his predecessor, Van Vollenhoven vigorously opposed continued use of the *tirailleurs*; but he also had an alternative plan to present to the Paris government. In an influential memorandum to the minister of colonies, Van Vollenhoven argued that the federation could better serve the metropole by supplying it with raw material and foodstuffs, and by not depleting its valuable human resources so essential to West Africa's *mise en valeur*. Production could be increased immediately, he insisted, if recruitment were suspended. His plan made all the more sense, since Paris had earlier that year decided on colonial *ravitaillement*. In October 1917, the General Staff was persuaded to halt recruitment temporarily, and Van Vollenhoven embarked upon a coordinated program of colonial production. The results, although they failed to meet his expectations, showed what the federation might yield after hostilities had ended.[18]

Abandonment of military recruitment proved short-lived. As the war dragged into 1918, Clemenceau determined that West Africa could provide an additional 50,000 *tirailleurs*; this time, however, he insisted that special precautions be taken to prevent the abuses that had plagued earlier recruiting drives. The coercive recruiting methods of the past were dropped in favor of a policy of persuasion, propaganda, and tangible rewards. Unlike previous mobilization efforts, recruitment in 1918 was meticulously organized from the outset. To assist its efforts, Paris appointed the recently elected deputy from the Four Communes of Senegal—and the first black African to hold that position—Blaise Diagne, to the rank of *commissaire de la République*. Diagne personally toured the federation, with a full entourage of both African and European subordinates, encouraging enlistment and advertising the benefits it could bring. He appealed directly to chiefs, assuring them that their own positions would be enhanced after the war had ended if they cooperated. He also attempted to persuade the young urban elite to join, insisting that, following his example, they could aspire to equality with the French. In addition to monetary incentives, both immediate and long-term, the French promised veterans exemption from the *indigénat*, facilitation of the naturalization process, special advantages in obtaining administrative positions, and the construction of both medical and agricultural schools.[19]

Diagne's tour was a stunning success; 63,000 *tirailleurs* enlisted—the most ever—with no further disruptions.[20] Diagne's forthright appeal convinced the old and the new African elite that it would be a mistake not to cooperate. Ironically, his very success in winning over recruits posed a new threat to French authority in West Africa—one more enduring than that of disgruntled aristocrats, and harder to contain. This threat came from the "new men" France had educated to help run the federation. Confronted during and especially after the war with growing signs of dissent from this quarter, Dakar again reacted strongly, although not as it had to the chiefs.

The Rise of Blaise Diagne, 1914–1924

The Four Communes of Senegal, alone among French possessions in West Africa, had the right to send a deputy to Parliament and enjoyed the same civil and electoral rights as municipalities in France. Most (90 percent) of the indigenous inhabitants, or *originaires*, of the Four Communes were illiterate, poor, and Muslim, and they cared little about those privileges. Two additional groups of *originaires*, however, had always taken their rights seriously and considered themselves French. These included the old, largely Catholic, *métis* or *assimilé* elite of Saint-Louis, whose links to France and French culture predated the Revolution, and a new class of French-educated, predominantly Muslim, African clerks now working in Dakar for the federal agencies or a large trading company. The administration referred to this group as *évolués*.

Under the Roume and Ponty administrations, the *assimilé* and *évolué* elements of the Four Communes received an unpleasant shock. After years of taking their French citizenship for granted, both groups suddenly learned that the new federal administration, though willing to admit that the *originaires'* special electoral privileges gave them a legal status distinct from that of the federation's other inhabitants, was not prepared automatically to recognize them as citizens of the Republic. Citizenship, according to the 1912 law on the subject, could be acquired only through an individual act of naturalization; this required, among other things, that Muslims renounce their "personal status" and accept French civil law. To add insult to injury, Dakar made clear that, despite the new rule that citizenship had to be acquired individually, it was prepared to naturalize the mulattoes and other *assimilés* of Saint-Louis, but not the *évolués*. The former group, thanks to two centuries of contact and intermarriage, shared French values, accepted the French Civil Code, and in all respects behaved as Frenchmen. Even though the *évolués* spoke French, they preferred Koranic law to French law and therefore could not be considered eligible for naturalization.[21]

Different treatment of the *originaires* reveals that the *évolués* posed a dilemma for the Government General. With their special privileges acquired at birth rather than through individual effort, their religion, and their fluent yet recently acquired French, they failed to fit neatly into either of the legal categories that Dakar was in the process of establishing for West Africans: uncivilized native subjects or assimilated French citizens. What is more, in aspiring to citizenship, they were not acting like the model "useful men" that the administration was stipulating as the proper future for educated Africans. These *hommes utiles* were by definition apolitical and subservient to the French administration. The *évolués*, in contrast, spurned farming and the army and were extremely vocal in their demands for immediate equality.

Dakar could not but feel threatened by these actions, and its first response was to deny the *évolués* many of their earlier privileges, on the grounds that these rights belonged only to authentic citizens. Whatever their aspirations, the Government General implied, the *évolués* were legally no different from France's other subjects and should be treated as such. Dakar did not go so far as to rescind their electoral privileges—a move that would have been politically unacceptable in France. But it did begin to penalize this group in other ways. For example, the same year that it passed its restrictive naturalization decree, Dakar also attacked the *évolués'* historic judicial privileges. The 1903 decree organizing justice in West Africa had respected these privileges: Europeans and Africans in the Four Communes were automatically under the jurisdiction of French courts throughout the entire federation, particularly in criminal suits.[22] In his 1912 reform, Ponty initially excluded from these same courts all *originaires* who had not been individually naturalized. His decree distinguished between citizens and "natives" and insisted that the latter had to be judged by their own magistrates whenever they left coastal Senegal. The term "native" included all individuals born in West Africa, Equatorial Africa, and foreign possessions located in those territories, who did not have "in their country of origin the status of European nationals."[23] Since the *évolués* had just been denied the status of nationals, this definition now presumably applied to them.

In preparing this decree in 1911, Ponty gave further reasons why the *assimilés* alone deserved to be considered French. As he argued before the General Council, the right of these *originaires* to French courts had been "won by two centuries of devotion to France" and could not now be reversed. They had served as France's first auxiliaries throughout the conquest; the other inhabitants of West Africa considered them to be French. But Ponty was not suggesting that the *évolués* could not aspire to the same rights as the *assimilés*. Indeed, the latter's continued use of French courts would contribute to the civilizing of all Africans:

> They will offer a propitious example for the rest of our subjects. It is to be remarked that the quality of "justiciable français" conferred upon them will have the most beneficent effect for the propagation of our law. The alacrity with which they accept the jurisdiction of French courts marks their faith in the fairness of French justice and it is thanks to their example that all natives will progressively decide to abandon their personal status in order to place themselves under the protection of French law.[24]

This quotation reflects an underlying assimilationist tendency in Ponty's thought which coexisted uneasily with his usual insistence that Africans had to evolve within their own cultures.

The legal reform of 1912, like the naturalization issue, was deeply resented by the *évolués*; they feared that they would be subject to the *indigénat*, from which they had traditionally been exempt, each time they left the Four Communes. For a variety of reasons, however, the matter of the jurisdiction to which they belonged was soon reopened. Senegalese protests and the upcoming elections in the Four Communes prompted the local administration to reconsider the issue, not of *évolué* citizenship, but of *évolué* access to French courts. Dakar had not anticipated the resentment the new measure would cause, and fear that this resentment would be exploited in the 1914 electoral campaign led the Government General to soften the impact of the 1912 decree. Ponty instructed his subordinates: "Natives registered on the electoral lists of Senegal fall, throughout that colony, under the jurisdiction of French courts. These same natives are not subject, in conformance with a long tradition, to the disciplinary powers of the administrators."[25]

Elsewhere in the federation they were to benefit from ethnic courts of Senegalese notables. These instructions were immediately contested by the lieutenant governor of Senegal, who claimed that

voter registration was a ridiculous criterion for determining jurisdiction. When prosecuting a crime, he sarcastically asked, were administrators now required to ask for a voter registration card, before
taking legal action?[26] Ponty replied that his instructions simply confirmed the traditional right of all *originaires* to use French courts—a
right, which he explained to the minister, he could not morally or
politically withdraw at this time. The *évolués*, Ponty wrote to his
superior in Paris, felt, if not humiliated, at least demeaned in their
legal and social status by the new restrictions. Legislative elections
in the Four Communes were coming up, and, he warned, the question of access to French courts could prove dangerous. Under these
conditions, Ponty concluded, his instructions were justified, even if
they did go beyond the strict letter of the decree.[27]

The question of their judicial rights thus had a partially satisfactory solution, in the eyes of the *évolués*. In other areas of policy
making, Ponty proved less sympathetic. Before 1914, the federal administration took several additional measures, all of which seemed
aimed at diminishing the status of the *évolués*. During this period, it
was ruled that only citizens could serve in the more lucrative, up-
per-level positions of the colonial service, the *cadre supérieur* or
métropolitain. This effectively barred the *évolués* from certain jobs
to which they had previously had access. Only naturalized citizens
could serve in the regular French army; other Africans had to join
the *tirailleurs*. The administration also attempted in 1914 to reform
the French school system in the Four Communes, replacing it with
one modeled on the adaptationist institutions in the rest of the
colony.[28] The *évolués* sought to reverse the impact of these measures
as well, by asserting that they were, and always had been, French
citizens, regardless of whether they accepted the Civil Code. Their
growing resentment was responsible for an event that Dakar did not
think possible, even as it warned Paris in 1913 about a possibly tur-
bulent electoral campaign: the *évolués* formed a strong enough coali-
tion to defeat the incumbent mulatto deputy from Senegal to Parliament, François Carpot, and to elect in February 1914 one of their
own, Blaise Diagne.

Diagne was a French-educated black African; he had worked in the
customs corps for almost twenty years in different parts of the empire before turning to politics in his home colony of Senegal. His
election would have marked a major deterioration in French-*évolué*
relations under any circumstances.[29] In his campaign, Diagne had

promised his *évolué* backers that, as their deputy, he would make sure that their historic rights and citizenship were acknowledged in Paris. Both Diagne and Dakar knew that Parliament, in its ignorance of conditions overseas, was more susceptible to appeals to traditional French liberalism than the Government General. Coinciding with the onset of recruitment in West Africa, Diagne's rise to power had even more disruptive implications. The outbreak of war suddenly made his political agenda that much easier to implement, by providing him with an immediate cause upon which to build the *évolués'* case: recruitment. Support for recruitment, Diagne correctly realized, could be exchanged for concessions from the metropolitan government regarding the future of French rule for the *évolués* and for all Africans. Diagne's first success was to convince Parliament to pass a law on October 19, 1915, which allowed the *originaires* of the Four Communes to serve in the French army rather than the separate colonial troops into which the rest of France's subjects were being drafted. A year later, Diagne sponsored a second law, whose purpose was ostensibly to extend the provisions of the 1915 decree to the *originaires'* descendants living outside the Four Communes. This second law included an important clause absent from the first: "The natives of the *communes de plein exercise* of Senegal and their descendants are and remain French citizens subject to the military obligations contained in the law of October 19, 1915." Parliament also passed this law, unaware of the important legal implications and political repercussions that "are and remain French citizens" would have in West Africa.[30]

Dakar was scandalized by Parliament's action, which conflicted fundamentally with its gradually carved-out position on the question of *évolué* rights. Consulted ahead of time by the Colonial Ministry on the proposed law of 1915, Clozel and his interim replacement, Gabriel Angoulvant, wrote lengthy memoranda warning of the disastrous political problems and the undesirable precedent that this privilege would create for the future administration of the federation. Such a move, they pointed out, could be attacked on legal grounds, since it made place of birth a criterion for acquiring citizenship for some subjects but not for others. This distinction was arbitrary and was bound to cause jealousy among the *évolués* of other colonies who would not enjoy the same privilege. How could French citizenship be reconciled with the preservation of the Muslim personal status, which allowed polygamy? The law said nothing about giving up this status in favor of the Civil Code.[31] Such an anomaly, Angoulvant claimed apoplectically, would be nothing less than the "negation of our social organization, of our civilization, of our genius . . . if it is not the end of France." On a more pragmatic level, returning *tirailleurs* and chiefs would be disgruntled by the privilege granted the Senegalese. Their discontent could make administration impossible.[32] Despite Dakar's dire warnings, the minister refused to change the law's wording. Diagne spent the rest of the war lobbying the government tirelessly to abandon its authoritarian recruiting methods and to improve military benefits for the West African contingents. The Clemenceau government's 1918 decision to adopt a new recruiting strategy of propaganda and material incentives, and appoint Diagne *commissaire de la République,* with rank equal to that of the Governor General, prove that his efforts were rewarded.

By the end of the war, Diagne had acquired a reputation throughout West Africa as a spokesman for the rights of all Africans against a demanding and authoritarian colonial administration. In 1919, some of Dakar's worst predictions were realized when Diagne used his hard-won visibility to sweep the municipal and General Council elections in the Four Communes. For the first time, the new indigenous elite held all of Senegal's elected offices. Diagne took advantage of his strengthened position to broaden his attack upon the federation's exclusion of most Africans from power. France, he argued, had once promised assimilation; as recently as 1916, it had recognized the citizenship of the *originaires.* Diagne now demanded that the Government General grant the *originaires* the same access to jobs as Europeans and extend the political rights of the Four Communes to the inhabitants of the rest of Senegal.[33] He also requested that the French Penal Code be extended to the federation, thus making all Africans subject to the same punishments for felonies and misdemeanors as French citizens.[34]

These new demands only further alienated the Government General, with good reason. They promised, if successful, to have the most damaging repercussions upon the federation's political and economic interests. Senegal was the federation's richest colony, thanks to its peanut crop. The profitability of this cultivation depended upon a carefully worked-out collaboration between the old ruling elite there and the French administration. By agreeing to allow the former aristocracy to stay and carry out routine administrative tasks, even when Dakar's instructions were to the contrary, the different lieutenant governors of the colony had ensured that the successful peanut crops of the precolonial era had continued under colonial rule, with minimal cost to the French. The chiefs had agreed because this system allowed them to retain their traditional access to wealth; the peasants had cooperated because it represented a continuation of what they had always known.

Diagne's demand for the enfranchisement of the rural areas posed a direct threat to this arrangement. This was nothing less than the urban *évolués'* bid for the peasants' allegiance and an attempt to discredit the collaborating chiefs in the eyes of the rural masses. If this were to happen, the local French officials would have to create a new administration in Senegal—a frightening thought indeed, since French administrative costs were skyrocketing with postwar inflation, and French personnel remained scarce.[35] A collapse of the system could only mean political chaos and economic disaster for Senegal and the entire federation.

Dakar also worried, legitimately enough (as we shall see), that Senegalese "Diagnism" was spreading to other colonies:

"Diagnism," which is all-powerful at the moment, has precipitated a movement, and it is under the influence [of this movement] that certain threats of strikes in the public services have sprung up in many colonies previously thought to be immune [from Diagnism].

We may well worry about what will happen the day our indigenous collaborators become more numerous. This day is in fact near. . . . Bitter because they cannot attain the positions, which their ambitious and disordered imaginations encourage them to strive after, they follow with passionate interest the political struggles taking place in Senegal.[36]

Such fears led Governor General Martial Merlin to act quickly to contain the threat Diagne posed. As was true of the revolts during the war years, ignoring this threat would diminish the authority of the Government General. Silencing Diagne nevertheless required greater diplomacy than putting down armed rebellion, in part because the weapons Diagne wielded to contest colonial rule were the very promises France had made in coming to West Africa in the first place. Diagne astutely couched his reformist demands in the language of the *mission civilisatrice* and interspersed his criticisms of the colonial system with declarations of loyalty to France. Sometimes Diagne's statements were practically indistinguishable from those of the administration. For example, when agitating for an extension of the French Penal Code to all Africans, he stated: "The aim of this reform . . . is to provide the populations of West Africa with new guarantees without attacking the social discipline which it is necessary for them to continue to observe. . . . It is undeniable . . . that the native mentality has much improved in AOF and has visibly evolved toward our ideas and civilization. It is time to recognize this [evolution]." These statements suggest that the deputy felt French, and that he did not believe he was doing anything more than challenging the Third Republic to remain true to its ideals.[37]

Confronted with such familiar language, Dakar determined that the best way to "prevent any attack on our authority" consisted of "respecting the historic rights of the *originaires* but nevertheless resituating them in the common law [of the rest of the federation], through a more precise text" and "cantonizing their elected representatives within narrow limits."[38] In practice, this meant reorganizing Senegal's liberal political institutions, in order to give the administration and its aristocratic allies a greater voice than that of the *originaires*. In 1920, Dakar reamalgamated the budget of the rest of the colony with that of the Four Communes. The General Council of Senegal, renamed the Colonial Council, was likewise changed to allow an equal number of chiefs and urban representatives to sit on it. Since the chiefs were dependent upon the colonial state for their positions, they could be counted on to vote with the administration.[39] These changes could be justified on the grounds that the chiefs, too, had a right to participate in the colony's representative institutions.

These actions effectively checked Diagne. Outmaneuvered by Dakar, the deputy decided in 1924 to drop his confrontational platform and come to terms with the colonial administration. Diagne's demands for political equality for all Africans would soon, however, be taken up by a new generation of nationalist leaders in the Four Communes, who felt betrayed by their deputy's apparent abdication. During the entire interwar period, Dakar was not free from pressure for political assimilation by the *évolués* in Senegal.[40] Nor was this pressure limited to that colony. Another legacy of the war years was the growth of similar ambitions among other groups of West Africans, albeit for different reasons. Africans serving as *tirailleurs* overseas often found themselves treated as equals in the trenches by French soldiers. During their stay overseas, they observed a much more stratified white society than that which existed in the colonies. A few educated Africans stationed in France came into contact for the first time with the ideas of revolutionary socialism and Pan-Africanism. "The *laisser aller* that reigned on the front," one local administrator noted, "caught the *tirailleurs'* attention. . . . [They now] are saying dangerous things. They are telling our subjects that the Europeans in the colony were very different from the Europeans in France, that the latter greeted the *tirailleurs* as brothers, opened their wallets to them, gave them food and procured for them white women, that equality existed for everyone and between everyone."[41]

Additionally, the small but growing number of *évolués* from colonies other than Senegal had heard from Diagne himself that political and economic conditions within the empire would improve after the war had ended, and they optimistically saw in Diagne's own rise to power a promise of things to come. These war-related experiences significantly broadened the intellectual horizons of West Africans everywhere, and made them increasingly combative. Throughout the 1920's, Dakar faced sporadic strikes by urban workers for better pay, particularly in Senegal; the political mobilization of the old and new elite in France's second-oldest West African colony, Dahomey; and the formation in Paris of a group of committed anticolonialists—both French and African—affiliated with the French Communist Party. These actions also formed part of the changing political circumstances in which colonial rule and ideology in West Africa had to operate after 1914.

'Evolué' Contestation and Repression, 1920–1930

In the 1920's, French officials in West Africa saw signs of unrest all around them.[42] The center for resistance to the regime remained the colony of Senegal, where the first strikes began to compound the problems caused by Diagnism. In 1919, both French and African railway workers at Thiès, an important depot for peanuts, went on strike for higher wages.[43] In April 1923, the interim governor general broke up the Senegalese section of the postal association (Comité de l'Association des PTT), for requesting the dismissal of a certain French administrator.[44] In 1925, the railway workers again went on strike in Thiès, and later that year the workers on the Senegal-Niger line also refused to go to work, because of mistreatment by their overseer. As the governor general commented in his political report of that year,

We must not hide the fact that certain elements of the population and certain milieux are not totally insensitive to the eventual agitations of . . . syndicalism. . . . In Senegal, the periodic play of electoral passions has gradually exalted in one part of the urban population, certainly not a Senegalese nationalism, the term is too strong, but particularist sentiments that clever propaganda knows how to exploit in order to achieve its own criminal ends. The syndicalist spirit has already penetrated certain worker centers.[45]

Coastal Dahomey was another thorn in the side of the Government General. This area, like the Four Communes of Senegal, had a small but important well-to-do mulatto population and a long history of trade with the West. It had also been the locus of greater missionary activity than any other French colony of the federation except Senegal. The missionaries had provided local inhabitants with greater opportunities for primary education than existed in its neighboring colonies, Guinea and Ivory Coast. As a result, even before World War I, the colony of Dahomey saw the emergence of a modern elite committed to defending its own economic interests. Without the political freedoms that existed in the Four Communes, however, this elite had no institutional means for demanding redress of their grievances—although they did have a flourishing press. During the war, several Dahomeyan *évolués* serving in France took advantage of the opportunity to establish contact with the incipient anticolonial movement. Among them was Louis Hunkanrin, whom the Government General soon came to view with as much hostility as it had for Diagne.[46]

Hunkanrin, like Diagne, was a product of the French educational system. His checkered career included stints teaching, working for a commercial trading house, and several jail terms. Hunkanrin's real passion, however, was politics. In 1913 and 1914 he participated in Diagne's electoral campaign, and metropolitan and Senegalese newspapers published his articles critical of the local administration. In 1914 he returned to Dahomey and founded a branch of the anticolonial group, the Ligue des Droits de l'Homme.[47] After the war he worked for the French in Paris, but in 1920 he returned to Dahomey, where he was imprisoned for subversive activities; this did not prevent Hunkanrin from either directing a press campaign against the new lieutenant governor of Dahomey, Fourn, or reestablishing a local branch of the Ligue des Droits de l'Homme.[48] Both during and after the war, Hunkanrin remained a staunch advocate of political assimilation for Africans. Like Diagne, he accepted the basic values and goals of French colonization; his quarrel with the Government General was therefore over means, not ends. Hunkanrin believed that the local administration was flouting the tenets of the *mission civilisatrice*, when it refused to extend French education, automatic citizenship, and the rule of French law to all West Africans. These ideas were sufficient to antagonize the Government General, not least because of Hunkanrin's influence upon his fellow *évolués*. Demands for greater political concessions did not let up from Dahomeyans in Paris throughout the 1920's.[49]

Dahomey worried Dakar for another reason as well. A major tax revolt took place in the port city of Porto Novo in 1923.[50] In that year, to compensate for postwar inflation, the head tax was suddenly raised from 2.25 francs per person to 15 per man, 10 per woman, and 5 per child. Passed in January, this increase elicited no reaction until mid-February. At that time, a delegation of leaders from the Ligue des Droits de l'Homme complained about the tax increase to Henri Michel, the representative from Dahomey to the Conseil Supérieur des Colonies in Paris, who happened to be visiting the colony. In subsequent days, clandestine meetings were held throughout the cities, port workers went on strike, and a mass meeting was organized to insist that no taxes be paid. The local governor responded by calling in the troops. The French had never promulgated the Third Republic's 1881 law on freedom of association in the federation, and it remained illegal to assemble without permission from the colonial administration. This prohibition effectively drove most political activity underground in the interwar period, making the French that much more out of touch with African discontent as it developed—and that much more ready to use force to repress it. Troops flooded into the city, at which point the movement began to spread to the countryside; resistance, which now included several chiefs, nevertheless remained passive. On February 25, Dakar authorized a state of siege and the deployment of additional troops. These measures quickly brought the revolt under control. All participating chiefs and urban leaders were arrested, although the administration held the latter more responsible. The civilization of these "intellectuals" the lieutenant governor maintained, was only "a brilliant varnish covering ignorance and fatuousness." Their demented ambitions, not excessive taxation, had caused the rioting.[51]

Dakar's postwar unease was further compounded by the emergence of new anticolonial ideologies in Europe and the United States, and the attendant fear that these doctrines would "contaminate" France's West African subjects. These doctrines included the development of Pan-Negroism and Pan-Africanism in the United States, under the leadership of Marcus Garvey, and the call for international revolution in France; their "subversiveness" was that all offered visions of progress, alternatives to the civilizing mission of the French. Between 1920 and 1935, the newly formed French Communist Party (PCF) accepted Lenin's argument that colonial wars of liberation were vital to the collapse of capitalism and the triumph of the proletarian revolution throughout the world.[52] Garvey's newspaper, the *Negro World*, which championed such concepts as Africa for the Africans, opposition to any form of European rule, and the need for nationhood and national independence, began to arrive in federal ports in 1920. In 1923, Dakar reported to the colonial minister that three representatives of the Universal Negro Improvement Association (UNIA) had arrived in Liberia; instructions were promptly given "to the effect that these undesirables, of American origin, were not to enter French territory."[53] A handful of educated West Africans, who had stayed on in Paris after the war, became active in the Pan-African movement. Many were members of the French Communist Party as well.[54] These anticolonial radicals published a succession of newspapers condemning the atrocities of French rule and advocating alternatives from political assimilation to home rule. Some of these newspapers also made their way to French West Africa.

Although there was no evidence that these newspapers were widely circulated, their very presence in port cities and in the depots along the train routes was enough to raise Dakar's worst suspicions. Its final word on the 1919 work stoppage in Senegal, for example, was that the strikers had believed foreigners' self-interested encouragement. The draft of the governor general's speech to the Council of the Government General in 1924 complained about the new elite being worked up by "the actions and propaganda of a certain press with subversive tendencies, and which is making every effort to implant the revolutionary virus in the most evolved milieux." A year earlier, the governor general had insisted that it was to Bolshevism that "we owe the existence of the Hunkanrins . . . former agents of the administration. . . . It was the agitation of these *déclassés*, stimulated by the exhortations of the communist press" that lay behind the Porto Novo revolt in February.[55] Dakar further insisted in 1926 that under the pretext of defending the right of people to self-determination, [Moscow's propagandists] have imagined that they can exploit the animosity between the races against the colonial imperialisms; thus, through an unanticipated reversal, international communism has transformed itself into nationalism. These new tendencies of revolutionary propaganda are potentially very dangerous, because they correspond to the more or less obscure aspirations of that entire category of feverish young men, who . . . wish to lead their fellow countrymen out of the primitive structures and the order that we have established.[56]

Given these "dangers," containment became the order of the day. Hunkanrin, unlike Diagne, did not have powerful friends in Paris. The tax revolts in Dahomey provided the Government General with a convenient pretext for removing this unwanted voice from his colony of origin. In 1923, despite a lack of any direct evidence that Hunkanrin had been involved, the interim governor general banished him to ten years' imprisonment in Mauritania. Governor General Jules Carde applauded this measure against "the Bolshevik of Dahomey," adding that "the chateau life that awaits him there should be adequate to set him back on the proper path."[57] Surveillance of "suspect" Africans was intensified; this group included anyone who had served in France or appeared to belong to an organization of any kind. On January 15, 1921, Dakar created a federal *service anthropométrique*, to compile dossiers on suspect Africans throughout the federation. Although compliance was sporadic at the local level, Dakar claimed to have 100,000 *fiches* in 1930.[58] Freedom of the press did not emerge unscathed. Before the war, citizens in West Africa had legally enjoyed the same freedom of press established in France by the law of 1881. In the 1920's, Dakar repeatedly and successfully petitioned Paris for permission to curb this freedom. Decrees in 1921 and 1928 prohibited the circulation of seditious material, gave Dakar the right to censor all drawings, cartoons, paintings, and emblems considered prejudicial to French authority, and allowed it to suppress the sale, circulation, or publication of any newspaper in any language in West Africa that it considered defamatory. Although the Government General could not go so far as to forbid individual Africans from receiving seditious French newspapers published in the metropole, it confidentially instructed the lieutenant governors to censor all incoming mail. The French Penal Code guaranteed the inviolability of correspondence, but considerations of public safety in West Africa, Dakar explained, allowed this principle to be ignored in practice.[59]

Confronted, then, with multiple signs of discontent, the Government General sought first to contain those deemed a danger to its own authority, which policy the Ministry of Colonies fully sanctioned. Such repression provides telling proof of a heightened vulnerability among the colonizers, but it was not the only way the French attempted to reassert their hegemony in West Africa in the postwar decade. Equally striking was a new emphasis in the rhetoric of French officials on how different Africans were from French, and how important it was now to keep the two races separate. These expressions took on a variety of forms. Most revealing, perhaps, was a reconsideration of French naturalization policy toward the colonized and in a more racialized direction; colonial officials now began to wonder whether anyone not born on metropolitan soil could become French. Greater consciousness of race, however, emerged in other ways as well. Sexual relations between French and Africans, which the administration had once encouraged, were now increasingly condemned in favor of white wives and families. And the French worried more about miscegenation and its consequences for French rule.

Revolts by disgruntled chiefs and *évolué* contestation do not alone account for this heightened consciousness of race in the 1920's; certain metropolitan developments also contributed to it. For example, there can be no doubt that the bloodbath of World War I exacerbated long-standing French fears about depopulation; the use of colonial labor in France during the war, followed by a sizable influx of North African immigrants after the war, enflamed race relations as well within France. Finally, a shift to the right in Parliament helped to bring French racism more into the open.[60] In the 1920's, the French government was concerned with regenerating the nation and restoring order at home and overseas—two preoccupations that put race at the heart of the republican agenda.

The rapid growth of three movements in France—eugenics, social hygiene, and pro-natalism—makes clear this growing preoccupation. Despite slightly different concerns, all three shared a larger agenda: the qualitative and quantitative improvement of the French race. None of these movements was new in the interwar period. France's discourse on national degeneration dated back to the beginning of the Third Republic. What was new was the governmental support that advocates of racial regeneration now received.[61] The postwar vitality of these organizations can be measured in a number of ways. In 1920, the first cabinet-level health ministry, the Ministère de l'Hygiène, de l'Assistance et de la Prévoyance Sociale, was created. That same year the government founded the national Ecole de Puériculture and passed the famous July 31 law against abortion and the advertising and sale of contraceptives. In 1922, a corps of visiting nurses was created, to go directly to the masses in their homes and teach them basic hygiene. In 1923, a course in child rearing (*puériculture*) was made mandatory for all schoolgirls. The following year the government created, with help from the Rockefeller Foundation, the National Social Hygiene Office. By 1931, the Office was a well-financed, multifaceted organ that coordinated the fight not only for a higher birthrate, but against venereal disease, tuberculosis, and alcoholism, as well as cancer, typhoid fever, diphtheria, infant mortality, and mental illness.[62] In another pro-natalist gesture, Parliament changed France's naturalization laws in 1927 (these laws deliberately excluded colonial subjects) to allow more rapid inclusion of second-generation immigrants.[63] Finally, laws on social insurance and family allowances were passed in 1930 and 1932, to combat depopulation by providing monthly allowances to parents with children and guaranteeing all women pre- and postnatal care.

As this brief listing suggests, most of these measures were not openly directed against people of color. If anything, they targeted French women more than Africans and Asians, who were now seen as so many wombs in the service of the nation. French deputies were more willing than in the prewar years to use state funds to improve and replenish France's "depleted" racial stock, at the expense of individual rights if necessary; but they did not explicitly equate Frenchness with whiteness. Nevertheless, the intense focus on the biological renewal of France, and the passing of legislation consciously cast in the language of racial degeneration and regeneration, confirms that a heightened awareness of race characterized the metropole as well as the empire for much of the interwar era. This awareness also encouraged Frenchmen overseas to think in more racialized terms about themselves and their subjects—especially once Africans began asking for the same rights as Frenchmen.

Republican Universalism Reconsidered

To argue that the 1920's witnessed an intensification of race consciousness particularly in the realm of citizenship in West Africa might at first seem surprising. The 1918 decree passed by Paris facilitating naturalization for African veterans had suggested that France would now open its doors more widely—thus revalidating the generous premises of the 1912 legislation. Preeminent among those premises, it will be recalled, was the notion that republican France should be encouraging the selective assimilation of an elite group of Africans. The criteria for acquiring such citizenship, moreover, had been relatively simple. An African subject who learned French, served the French administration loyally, and agreed to obey the precepts of French law and the Civil Code would be included in the French family of citizens with a full complement of rights—regardless of his skin color. Conversely, all those who failed to meet these criteria deserved to be excluded from this family; they would remain *sujets*, with duties instead of rights.

But statements made by both Dakar and Paris in the 1920's indicate that colonial officials were less sure that any African would ever be worthy of the rights of citizenship the Third Republic had once promised. Such doubts were a conscious response to Diagne's successful campaign in 1915 for *originaire* citizenship, and continuing demands by other *évolués* for a recognition of comparable rights. As Governor General Merlin put it in an internal memorandum in 1921,

> The failure of the policy of assimilation became flagrant the day we noticed, among those natives trained in our schools and abruptly separated from their environment, a different frame of mind and a marked tendency to elude the discipline, which an evolved society has the right to expect of its members. Undoubtedly, in West Africa, some elite subjects have avoided the normal consequences of this kind of displacement, but the aspirations of the majority are directed toward different objectives from those that the colonizer intended for them, in their own best interest, of course.

Similar reservations were voiced by the interim governor general in 1923:

> We have an ever greater interest in according naturalizations only to individuals whose absolute loyalty has been proven, and whose right to this exceptional favor has been well and truly earned. The objective of the decrees of May 25, 1912, March 25, 1915, and February 14, 1918, was not, indeed, to grant automatically naturalizations to individuals who had met the objective conditions for citizenship enumerated in these texts. In leaving it up to the competent authorities to decide if these conditions were backed up by evidence of sufficient morality and loyalty, the legislature

purposefully intended to limit to an elite access to the rights that citizenship confers.

I believe that in the future we cannot be too circumspect in considering demands for naturalization. To the contrary, current events should incite us to examine such demands with the most extreme attention.[64]

True to its words, Dakar authorized few naturalizations in the 1920's. According to Raymond Buell, who visited the colony in 1927, only eighty-eight Africans were granted citizenship between 1914 and 1925, fourteen of whom were former *tirailleurs*.[65]

In suggesting that Africans were not just less evolved than the French but perhaps too different ever to be assimilated, the Government General was not, however, acting alone. In 1925, the colonial minister asked the legal branch of the Conseil Supérieur des Colonies to study the "status of the natives in France's colonies and protectorates."[66] Like Dakar, Paris had also now discovered that too many colonial subjects, who were not yet culturally French, were aspiring to citizenship for the wrong reasons:

The point is to know to what degree it is possible to satisfy the aspirations of the indigenous populations without jeopardizing our domination. . . . Is it politic, is it in our interest to encourage naturalization? Generally speaking, no. Certainly, we must welcome those . . . of our subjects who can genuinely be assimilated, that is to say who have sincerely moved close to us by abandoning their customs, their mores and adopted ours. . . . But how many will we find who fit this category? Obviously very few. The others, those who solicit the status of citizen . . . only to obtain certain advantages will always be dangerous.

And, again like Dakar, in reviewing French naturalization policy, the Conseil revealed a growing skepticism about whether subjects could "genuinely be assimilated" at a future date—although its racism here was explicit. In its deliberations, the Conseil members repeatedly questioned an access that an earlier generation of officials had taken for granted. "A Frenchman born in France of French parents and whose ancestors always lived on French soil," one member declared, "[is] not of the same nature as a subject born . . . on recently annexed territory." The latter belonged to collectivities whose ethnic characteristics were "incompatible with our own." When one scratched the Frenchified surface of an educated African, "the old [i.e., primitive] man" always reappeared. It was therefore necessary to abandon the idea of "fusing through naturalization two such ethnically distinct populations." Only "a born European is a citizen";

to offer citizenship to an African would be not only dangerous, but "a lie."[67]

Intensifying racism in France did not, in the end, lead to a rescinding of the naturalization decrees. To its credit, the Third Republic could not—or would not—officially abandon its policy of selective assimilation. But the colonial minister and the Government General did together revise the 1912 and 1918 decrees in 1932 in order to stiffen considerably the requirements for African applicants. At first glance, their most notable innovation was that the citizenship granted would no longer be strictly personal, but would include the applicant's extended family (illegitimate children too). This apparent liberalization compared to the 1912 decree was, however, more than offset by another proviso. In order to qualify, the individual African and his wife and children now had to prove, according to rigorously defined criteria, that they *all* were culturally French.[68] A circular by Governor General Carde accompanying the local application of the decree explained that naturalization would clearly be misguided if the evolved African was "subjected to influences in his home that were directly opposed to the direction of his evolution." The applicant had to be monogamous, and he had to have availed himself of the French *état-civil* to register his marriage and the birth of his children as they occurred. Such early and continuous use of the *état-civil* would indicate "a constant tendency toward our civilization." Another requirement was that he had provided his children with a French education. Finally, he had to prove that "he had elevated himself above his original milieu," that "he had sufficiently detached himself from customary institutions to renounce them," and that "by his mentality, conduct and tendencies, he was worthy of the favor being solicited."[69]

The discussion of extending citizenship to colonial subjects in general, and West Africans in particular, is revealing. Confronted with escalating African demands for inclusion in the French polity, colonial officials imposed surveillance upon the colonized and drew clearer and more restrictive boundaries around who was French and who was African. Citizenship, moreover, was not the only area in which such racial and cultural chauvinism manifested itself in the postwar decade. When colonial officials reassessed French naturalization policies, they now openly condemned interracial unions, recommending instead that French administrators marry white women and start families. To some extent, these recommendations followed inevitably from the fact that more white women were living in the colonies in the 1920's than ever before. French colonial rule had become entrenched enough to include spouses, and the medical establishment now considered West Africa safe for women as well as men.[70] Nevertheless, larger fears about the future of French authority also determined the postwar ban on *petites épouses* (as concubines were called) and enthusiasm for white endogamy. Like the growing doubts about assimilation, both represented a distancing from the colonized in the wake of African resistance to the French.

Although French theorists in the metropole had long since abandoned the notion of assimilating their subjects through intermarriage, outright condemnation of concubinage in West Africa and endorsement of marriage to a white woman was new in the 1920's. Before the war, the Government General had openly tolerated interracial unions. "For those who lack the moral strength necessary to endure two years of continence," a manual from the 1890's for West African administrators had counseled, "only one line of conduct is possible: a temporary union with a well-chosen native woman."[71]

There was a widespread feeling, moreover, that French wives hindered the job effectiveness of field *commandants*. As the eminent African ethnographer and future governor Maurice Delafosse said in his popular account of bush life, "Any married colonial loses a third of his value and a married *broussard* [bush administrator] loses at least 3/4 of his."[72] By the end of World War I, however, a different perspective was taking hold. For example, Georges Hardy, who served as director of the Ecole Coloniale from 1926 to 1931 after a long stint in West Africa as inspector of education, did not say his administrators should marry. But to introduce more rigorous standards in selection and training for the colonial service, he did say that they could marry. His only concern was that they choose the right wife: "There exists, for women as for men, certain specifically colonial virtues. . . . Attempt to find out whether she will adapt to being isolated amongst the natives, far from dancing-teas and the idle talk of salons. Because it is with the natives above all that you will live, and not everyone can accept this." Despite the negative female stereotype that Hardy invoked here, he acknowledged that fewer administrators were currently "decivilizing themselves," thanks to the ever greater presence of European women.[73]

Other ostensible liberals in colonial circles were affected by these same ideas, as the work of René Maunier suggests. In 1932, he published the first volume of his *Sociologie coloniale*, a compilation of lectures he had delivered at the University of Paris on the subject of contact between the races throughout history. At one point, he cited approvingly an ancient author who argued that the only permanent contact between different peoples "occurred through the woman." Such "sexual union" was the superior form of contact between the races. Maunier, however, then implied that although such unions might have been encouraged in places like South America, Algeria, and South Africa with positive results, they should not continue. Concubinage was dangerous because it presented single white males with exotic mores and "decivilized" them. France itself now faced "penetration" by "thousands, hundreds of thousands of natives" arriving as immigrants, which demanded the utmost caution. From these developments, Maunier drew one major conclusion: that the exodus of white women to the colonies was a positive step, because it would end the harmful influences of *petites épouses*. Henceforth, "population [of the colony] would occur—which was really for the better—through white households."[74]

Maunier's and Hardy's views together provide evidence of new preference for marriage with white women over concubinage in West Africa—although the two men were not responding to the same phenomena. As a colonial administrator, Hardy appeared to be reacting specifically to conditions overseas, where French authority now stood threatened; Maunier's reference to the new waves of immigrants "penetrating" France suggests that what he feared was the sexual union of these male immigrants of color with white women in the metropole. Despite these differences, their specific references to "decivilization" indicate why interracial unions in general were being condemned. These unions weakened French prestige by encouraging the administrator to "go native," thus blurring the distinction between colonizer and colonized. Colonial administrators needed instead, they implied, companions of their own race and culture who would keep intact a specifically white French civilization.

Colonial manuals during the interwar years developed these same ideas. They stressed, for example, the desirability of taking a French wife overseas and assumed that her principal role would be to bring French civilization with her, to keep all things African at bay. The French woman was "to maintain our prestige" by following the "ethnic principle": separate European living quarters from those of the indigenous populations. Women were warned to keep their distance from their servants, who would invariably be male.[75] Men and women alike should preserve a certain elegance, "for elegance does not exclude strength—rather the opposite." Elegance imbues one with dignity, and "it is necessary to prove [to the natives] that *la Française* . . . is a worthy and elevated women."[76] Wives were also to decorate their homes in ways that distinguished them from the colonized. In short, it was the job of woman "to create France" wherever she went. And just to make sure that the colonial couple remained thoroughly French, they should return to the metropole every two to three years.[77]

Needless to say, there was another way in which white women could contribute decisively to the "creation of France" overseas. "It is not sufficient to possess territory, it is also necessary for the French to establish themselves there . . . in order to secure our prestige."[78] How better to establish themselves than by starting a family? All guides took for granted that motherhood was the colonial woman's first vocation, and they devoted as much attention to instructing women how to raise their children as on how to manage a household. In this emphasis on reproduction, the focus on separation from the colonized was even more apparent. On the most basic level, the exhortation for whites to reproduce among themselves condemned sexual relations between the races. Commentators repeatedly contrasted the richness of white French family life with the emptiness of concubinage; a native mistress "constantly betrayed . . . emotional poverty, intellectual insufficiency." On another level, the child-rearing techniques clearly excluded the involvement of the colonized. To ensure both the fitness and Frenchness of the children, contact with the servants would be carefully regulated; at a certain age the children would go back to France. Once they were gone, women could make themselves useful by introducing native women to basic hygiene, as well as by studying local customs. In this way she would become a true partner—her husband's intellectual as well as sexual companion.[79]

The encouragement of French families instead of *petites épouses* was another way colonial officials set new barriers between themselves and Africans in the 1920's in a bid to strengthen French dominance. Other barriers, however, also emerged in this period—closely related to the condemnation of concubinage. A variety of French legal experts, publicists, and colonial administrators began now to talk openly about the dangers miscegenation posed for their rule, and to view the offspring of mixed marriages—known as *métis*—as suspiciously as they did most educated Africans.[80] A growing literature in the interwar years assumed that the *métis*, like the *évolué*, automatically aspired to the rights of French citizenship because of the white blood in his or her veins.[81] The general feeling among colonial administrators, however, was that as a half-breed, the *métis* could not and should not become French. The new influence of eugenic thinking in this era encouraged these conclusions. In his *Sociologie coloniale*, Maunier criticized miscegenation on the grounds of the "well-known Mendelian law . . . the law of hybridization," which stated "that a return to the primitive takes place, that the native type always carries the day."[82]

Confronted with this "Mendelian law," colonial officials in the 1920's could imagine only one possible outcome of continued *métissage*. Spurned by the country he or she most identified with, the *métis* was likely to revolt against it. The long-term solution to this problem, as we have seen, was for a variety of experts to recommend an end to *métissage* altogether, through French endogamy. The short-term solution was to regulate the legal status of existing *métis*. Dakar was no stranger to the debates. In 1930, the Government General issued its first decree ever specifying when mixed-bloods of unknown parentage could become citizens. While this legislation was no more liberal than that affecting other African subjects, the mere fact that *métis* were considered worthy of a decree of their own simply because they had one white parent confirms that new barriers were being established between Africans and French, particularly as the latter began contesting French rule in a dramatically changed colonial, national, and international context.[83]

World War I marked a watershed in the history of the Government General. The decision to conscript Africans helped trigger a pattern of confrontation and reaction between colonizer and colonized that continued throughout the postwar decade. Part and parcel of this reaction was a more racialized perception of Africans in Dakar, which metropolitan concerns with national regeneration after the trauma of world war further encouraged. Yet repression and a new distancing were not the total of France's response to Africans, either at home or overseas, between 1914 and 1930. The Government General, with encouragement from Paris, also adopted a new approach to civilizing Africans. Despite its disillusionment with rebellious chiefs, ambitious *évolués*, and untrustworthy *métis*, Dakar did not doubt in the 1920's that it still had a mission to perform in West Africa. But in probing the causes of revolt it frankly admitted that many of its most cherished policies of the past had not yielded the expected dividends—and had actually hurt the interests of the Government General. As a result, an amended version of the civilizing mission would emerge, along with revolt and reaction, in France and West Africa between 1914 and 1930. In keeping with the altered climate of the postwar era, this revised civilization discourse would be considerably more conservative than the one it replaced.

CHAPTER 6

"Democracy" Reinvented

CIVILIZATION THROUGH ASSOCIATION (1914–1930)

The great majority of our West African societies are very backward, compared to our modern civilization. We should attempt to bring about intellectual and material development by means adapted to their mentality and without ever forgetting that the moral perfectibility of individuals and races does not imply immediate accession to a social level equal to that of the most evolved nations; rather, stages must be passed through, each of which requires a long initiation.
— Governor General Martial Merlin[1]

The period between 1914 and 1930 opened up a new era in the civilizing actions and assumptions of the Government General. French policy and ideology changed to reflect both transformations in the metropole and the political needs of the colonial state. These needs were starkly exposed by the revolts that had occurred during World War I and by the *évolués'* continued demand for political equality with French citizens throughout the 1920's. Such challenges made clear to federal authorities that they had made a mistake in attempting to divest chiefs of their authority and in maintaining all power in their own hands—two policies identified with France's civilizing mission in West Africa. Dakar thus began to reconsider these policies even before the war ended. In particular, it recommended reappointing customary chiefs to office, and suggested a "new deal" for the educated elite. These policy changes were given a name familiar in France and some colonies since the 1890's, but new in the Government General of West Africa in the 1920's: association.[2]

Association was accompanied by the appearance of new themes in French civilization ideology, legitimating Dakar's policy reorientation. These themes remained within a republican framework, but the emphasis was clearly different. In the postwar period, the Government General no longer maintained that France had an obligation to free Africans from "feudal bondage" by systematically removing traditional elites from power. It also quietly abandoned the view that the new elite would be ready to share in policy making only in some distant future. Dakar now argued that African society could better progress if chiefs were retained in office, where they would be regularly consulted, as well as trained, by the French. Thanks to their education, these chiefs could in turn "civilize" the rural masses under their influence, whom the chiefs would also represent. Instead of its former vagueness with respect to the new elite, the Government General proclaimed that this group could participate in a limited capacity alongside the French in their own government. In all these ways, Dakar insisted, association would begin to democratize power in West Africa.

This chapter traces the change in Dakar's policies and rhetoric, by examining the administrations of four governors general: François Clozel (1915–1917), Joost Van Vollenhoven (1917–1918), Martial Merlin (1919–1923), and Jules Carde (1923–1930).[3] Despite differing backgrounds, these men shared the same vision of how to rule Africans. This vision was based on principles quite different from those of a generation earlier. For example, through the concept of association, French colonial administrators in Dakar embraced a much more positive image of traditional West African social and political organization than had existed in the past. Federal authorities now insisted that their subjects had institutions, such as the chieftaincy, which were not nearly so exploitative as the French had once thought and therefore deserved to be respected. These images suggested that the postwar governors general were becoming genuinely interested in understanding the different cultures of West Africa, and were now prepared to preserve them for their own sake. In fact, Dakar's reassessment was motivated more by a desire to contain the *évolués* in particular, and to reestablish "discipline" among their subjects in general, than by any intrinsic interest in either African civilizations or democratization. To borrow Eric Hobsbawm's and Terence Ranger's useful concept, Dakar "reinvented" an ostensibly African form of democracy as part of its bid to reassert republican hegemony in the federation.[4]

Although not so directly relevant as local challenges to French authority, political and cultural developments in the metropole, too, encouraged the new direction emerging in West Africa in the 1920's. We have already noted the greater conservatism and xenophobia in

France after the war's devastation, and the willingness of legislators to enact pro-natalist and social hygiene measures designed to regenerate France's racial stock. A by-product was an intensified emphasis on restoring traditional morality—both veterans and policy makers sought to make sense of the war by recreating the "world they had lost" at Verdun. Gender relations, in this context, were particularly affected. Women who had worked in the munitions factories were now exhorted to return to the home and reproduce for *la patrie*; female suffrage was firmly rejected, and the virtues of patriarchy reasserted. These same concerns with restoring domestic order reverberated overseas, as Dakar's growing interest in respecting chiefs whose power was "traditional" and "familial" fully attests. In the interwar years, an intensification of racialized thinking and reassertion of neo-traditional values went hand in hand, at home and in the empire.

Background to Association, 1914–1918

In June 1915, Ponty died in Dakar and was replaced by an old Africa hand, François Clozel. François-Joseph Clozel was born on March 29, 1860, in the Ardèche. He had served in Algeria, first in the Régiment des Zouaves and then as secretary of a mixed *commune*, before entering the colonial service in 1893. From 1896 to 1907, he was posted to Ivory Coast—where no French civilian administration yet existed—and was appointed lieutenant governor of that colony in 1903. In 1907, he took Ponty's place at the head of Upper Senegal-Niger, where he remained until being named governor general on Ponty's death. As an administrator in West Africa, Clozel had a history of opposing, from the outset, Ponty's attempts to win over the African masses through divesting their leaders of power. In his capacity as a *commandant* and then as governor, he had worked out collaborative relations with chiefs in Ivory Coast from 1901 to 1907. As lieutenant governor of Upper Senegal-Niger, he had sought to mitigate the effects of the *politique des races*, fully aware of the potential disruption such an assault on the precolonial elite would cause.[5]

Clozel brought to Dakar the interests of an amateur ethnographer intimately acquainted with and genuinely interested in the peoples he administered. By the time of his appointment to Dakar, Clozel had already published two books about Ivory Coast, one on local customs and the other describing his relations with African chiefs.[6] Clozel had also encouraged his subordinates to study the customs of local peoples. Characteristically, one of his first acts as governor general was to found the Comité d'Etudes Historiques et Scientifiques de l'AOF, whose objective was to promote and publish research on the history of West African peoples and their civilizations. The Comité's bulletin was published by the Government General. An additional sign of Clozel's interest in African history was his decision to appoint, as his director of political affairs, his old friend and colleague, the Africanist Maurice Delafosse.

Delafosse was a colonial administrator who had served with Clozel in Ivory Coast and briefly in Upper Senegal-Niger. By temperament and vocation, however, Delafosse was a scholar, whose pioneering work in West African history would ultimately win him more distinction than his partially successful career in the colonial service. In the years leading up to World War I, Delafosse returned to Paris to teach African languages and history at the Ecole des Langues Orientales and the Ecole Coloniale—subjects added to the curriculum only in 1899; in 1912, at the invitation of Clozel, he published the first in what would be a series of critically acclaimed accounts of the peoples of the Western Sudan before the French conquest.[7] These books popularized the notion that Africans had civilizations that differed from those of the West but were in no way inferior. After serving in Dakar during the war, Delafosse resumed his teaching in Paris. Throughout his life, Delafosse sought repeatedly to educate policy makers in Dakar and public opinion in France on the history of Africa, and to influence policy decisions in directions that he considered compatible with France's mission to uplift morally and materially its African subjects. These directions had little to do with Ponty's stereotypes of barbarism; they emphasized instead the need to respect African institutions, which Delafosse had studied.

Specifically, Delafosse believed that the French administration had made a fundamental mistake in trying to rule Africans through "feudal emancipation" and "direct contact," and that this mistake could be corrected by first studying, then working through, indigenous political structures. Delafosse would see some of his ideas put into action, particularly when he was in Dakar as head of the bureau of native affairs under Clozel and Van Vollenhoven; and after the war he would have the satisfaction, as we shall see, of helping to found the Institut d'Ethnologie in Paris. More often than not, however, Delafosse's work suffered the fate of that of many scholars in service to the state. That is to say, the Government General and the Colonial Ministry listened selectively to his advice and tended to use only those ideas that coincided with their own economic and political interests. Clozel was the first governor general to incorporate in his political directives any of Delafosse's research. The result was a series of new governmental circulars that deviated dramatically, in content and in tone, from the federal administration's earlier policies.

When Clozel took control of the federal administration, he not only faced the daunting task of restoring administrative order to the Dakar bureaus, which, given Ponty's illness, had fallen into disarray. He was also saddled with organizing the most difficult recruitment during the war years. As a result of rebellion in the interior, first in the fall of 1915, then again in November 1916, much of the governor general's attention and energy was focused on reasserting French control in the Western Sudan. Like many local witnesses, Clozel thought these revolts were a response to long-standing grievances about the exercise of French authority, not just recruitment alone. Encouraged in this assessment by Delafosse, Clozel issued new instructions for the appointment of chiefs throughout the federation. These instructions stressed the importance of respecting customary lineages when appointing chiefs, thereby implicitly legitimating a precolonial institution that earlier administrators had dismissed as parasitic and tyrannical. Henceforth, Clozel insisted, in a revision of his predecessor's instructions, chiefs were to be chosen in conformity with local tradition after consultation with the local populations; no new men were to be appointed in recompense for services rendered to the French.[8]

Clozel's recommendations departed from Ponty's "fierce struggle against chiefs," as an official later described prewar policies. As such, they offered one clue that Dakar was reassessing tactics that had been taken for granted as part of the *mission civilisatrice* in West Africa under Ponty and Roume. Clozel's innovations did not, however, stop with reversing Dakar's instructions on chiefs. In a letter to the minister in February 1917, Clozel presented a plan for reorganizing the federation after the war. The boundaries of West Africa, he argued, should be redrawn to take into account its human and economic geography, "such as it appears to us through the historical formation of large ethnic groups and the currents determined by the nature, needs and customs of their inhabitants." As he envisioned it, the arbitrary borders dividing French, English, and German territories would disappear; certain colonies would be abolished altogether, such as Senegal and Upper Senegal-Niger. An expanded Mauritania and Senegambia would take their places. All Moors would thus be grouped for the first time under one authority. Their territory would include Saint-Louis and both banks of the Senegal River, which "historically always was and should remain the reverse of a barrier: that is to say a means of contact and communication." In this way, Mauritania would be spared from becoming a purely desert country. Senegambia, located to the south of Mauritania with Dakar as its capital, and expanded to include the circles of Kayes, Bafoulabé, Kita, and Bélédougou from Upper Senegal-Niger, as well as the Guinean circle of Koumbia, would constitute a vast territory specializing in peanut and rice production. Guinea would be enlarged by the addition of British Sierra Leone, and Dahomey would be yielded to England in exchange; Ivory Coast's boundaries would not change. All that would be left of Upper Senegal-Niger would be Niger proper, which could be divided between Upper Niger (whose territory would coincide with that of the ancient empire of Songhay) and Lower Niger (whose territory would include the Hausa-speaking peoples of eastern Ghana, Togo, and part of Nigeria).[9]

Clozel's reorganization would not be implemented. Territorial exchanges between France and England had been periodically advocated before, to no avail. The plan also ignored the vested interests of the Senegalese *originaires* of the Four Communes. In this last instance, ironically, Clozel's suggestions met constraints not dissimilar to those that had plagued Ponty's vision of African society, although Clozel's myopia lay in the opposite direction. Whereas Ponty had tended to view all precolonial African elites as "feudal" and sought to decrease their influence, Clozel idealized the past and failed to take into account the irreversible social and economic changes that had taken place since the French conquest. These included, principally, the movements of rural populations and the growth of urban centers—changes, moreover, that the war was only intensifying and that the interwar period would magnify. In the postwar reorganization of the federation, the only boundary alteration was the creation of two new colonies, Niger and Upper Volta, in the Western Sudan, although some of Clozel's ideas for developing the federation's resources according to geographic and climatic zones would be taken up by Governors General Merlin and Carde.

Recent revolts, then, coupled with Diagne's rising influence and the growing conservative climate in Paris, had only confirmed Clozel's lifelong belief that the French had to respect preexisting African institutions if they wished to avoid future rebellions, much less accomplish anything constructive in West Africa. These developments would also lead to a similar conclusion by a new generation of leadership in Dakar—a generation that, for the most part, did not share Clozel's interest in African history. This was true for Clozel's successor, the energetic Joost Van Vollenhoven, who, at the age of forty, was the youngest man ever to be appointed governor general.[10] Van Vollenhoven remains a legendary figure in the annals of French imperial history, despite his brief tenure in office (1917–1918). In January 1918, only eight months after his appointment to Dakar, and shortly after a new colonial recruiting drive was announced, he resigned and returned to the front. There he was killed during a spectacular charge on German lines. It was assumed at the time that Van Vollenhoven left office out of pique at the appointment of an African, the Senegalese deputy to Parliament, Blaise Diagne, to head the new recruiting effort. In fact, Van Vollenhoven quit his post because he did not believe that the governor general could share the powers and prerogatives of office with anyone else, white or black, within the colonial administration. This reaction was entirely in character for a man who felt that, at every level of the bureaucracy, there could only be "one who commands" and who created something of a mystique about the exercise of authority during his year in Dakar.

Joost Van Vollenhoven was born July 21, 1877, to Dutch parents living in Algeria. He became a naturalized French citizen upon entering the Ecole Coloniale in 1899. He graduated first in his class four years later and received his doctorate in law at the same time. His thesis on the *fellah algérien* was later published. He was fluent in Dutch, English, French, German, and Arabic. His outstanding qualifications were immediately recognized when he joined the colonial service in 1904. After a brief internship in Dakar, he was promoted directly to the rank of secretary general (second class); he thus skipped the rank of administrator, at which most new recruits from the Ecole started. In 1908, he was posted to Equatorial Africa, to serve as secretary general in Brazzaville under Governor General

Merlin. Three years later, at the age of thirty-four, he was promoted to governor and posted back to Paris. There, the minister of colonies appointed him head of his cabinet. In 1914, after having spent a year as a finance director in Paris, Van Vollenhoven was appointed secretary general of Indochina, under Albert Sarraut. When Sarraut left during the first months of the war, Van Vollenhoven served as interim governor general of Indochina. He nevertheless requested that he be relieved of these administrative duties, in order to enlist in the army. In 1915, his request was granted; he received his commission as sergeant and returned to France in early 1916. He was wounded twice that year, and had just recovered from his injuries and requested a return to the front, when he was appointed governor general of French West Africa by Messimy.[11]

As this brief biographical sketch suggests, Van Vollenhoven's rise in the ranks of the colonial administration had been phenomenal. Indeed, as a seasoned office administrator who had already served in West Africa under Roume, Equatorial Africa under Merlin, and Indochina under Sarraut, he represented the best of a new generation of colonial civil servants trained at the Ecole Coloniale and fully committed to the rational *mise en valeur* of the empire. He was also the first career colonial administrator since Ernest Roume to arrive in Dakar without any field experience in ruling Africans. Despite his impressive credentials, Van Vollenhoven had never served as a circle *commandant*. The new governor general would compensate for this lack of experience by bringing in lieutenant governors he trusted, and by retaining Maurice Delafosse as his political advisor. Van Vollenhoven's appointment to Dakar coincided with a policy shift in Paris, where the new colonial minister had decided that West Africa could serve the metropole by supplying it with raw materials and foodstuffs as well as men. The governor general thus arrived overseas determined to rationalize the bureaucracy in the interest of both immediate *ravitaillement* and long-term economic development. To achieve this goal, he issued an impressive number of circulars reorganizing the federation's finances and central bureaus, and specified "conditions of action" for efficient administration at the circle level.[12]

Van Vollenhoven's most important contribution as governor general, however, was not bureaucratic reform, but his decision to issue new instructions for governing West Africa. These instructions, though not nearly so imbued with a respect for and an interest in the

African past as were Clozel's, reiterated his predecessor's conclusion that it was necessary to appoint traditional chiefs as French auxiliaries wherever possible. At the same time, he displayed special concern for the *évolués*. In addition to these circulars, Van Vollenhoven left behind a detailed statement explaining why such policy and attitude changes were required. All these documents reflected the influence of Delafosse, who provided the governor general with a coherent historical explanation for the recent revolts in the federation. These directives would serve as guidelines for future governors general throughout the interwar period. Following upon Clozel's circulars, they provide further proof that Dakar was moving away from the radical measures of the past, and that a new consensus was emerging on how best to govern and develop the federation.

One of Van Vollenhoven's first actions as governor general was, like Clozel, to issue a circular instructing his subordinates to reappoint traditional chiefs to office under the French. This was necessary, he went on to explain, because "a society can only progress when it is solidly policed." Earlier administrations had ignored this fundamental reality. They had often presumed to rule Africans directly through their own agents—the interpreters, guards, and secretaries who staffed the local *commandant*'s bureaus—because they thought the traditional chiefs were exploitative and despised. This policy, the governor general maintained, while justifiable perhaps in the abstract, was fatally flawed in practice. On the one hand, French administrators were too few to supervise adequately the agents who carried out their demands. On the other, the agents chosen had all too frequently no legitimacy in the eyes of their African subjects. Viewed as interlopers who abused the powers granted them by the colonial administration, these agents had weakened both the authority of Africa's indigenous ruling class and the prestige of the French in whose name they operated. In the process, they had contributed to the crisis of the war years. To reverse this tendency, local administrators were now to discover who the traditional lineage heads were, grant them sufficient funds to maintain their customary retinue, and avoid using the *indigénat* against them. Where no chiefs existed, the French were to choose the candidate most acceptable to the local population. New consideration for chiefs did not signify, however, that the precolonial elite was to continue ruling in its own right. On this point, Van Vollenhoven was inflexible: "There are not two authorities in the circle, French authority and native authority; there is only one. Only the *commandant* of the circle commands; he alone is responsible. . . . The native chief is only an instrument, an auxiliary . . . the native chief never speaks in his own name, but always in the name of the *commandant* of the circle and by formal or tacit delegation from the latter."[13]

In subsequent directives Van Vollenhoven also recognized that a new elite, irrevocably detached from traditional society, had come into being under French rule. To ensure their loyalty, he recommended raises in the salaries of African administrative personnel and a less condescending attitude toward the *évolués*. Both recommendations hinted that a reassessment of educated Africans as well as the old elite was taking shape in Dakar under Van Vollenhoven's administration. Van Vollenhoven's personal perspective on how best to reorient native policy was perhaps most evident in a final memorandum the governor general sent to the minister on December 20, 1917. Written by Delafosse, in his capacity as advisor for native affairs, but revised by Van Vollenhoven, this remarkable document explained in greater detail why Van Vollenhoven was adopting new measures. It also left little doubt that, in the wake of various challenges to its authority, Dakar was consciously repudiating an earlier way of thinking about ruling Africans. Finally, this document made clear that in rejecting certain policies, Van Vollenhoven was not abandoning France's mission in West Africa.[14]

In the initial draft, Delafosse accused Van Vollenhoven's predecessors of creating anarchy in West Africa. The situation in the federation, he wrote, was not good. French security was an illusion; the French themselves were hated. The Government General alone was to blame for this. It had failed in its responsibility of exercising control from above, particularly with regard to native affairs. It had not defined any clear-cut principles. Instead, a combination of incompatible terms had been invoked—assimilation, association, *apprivoisement*—without producing the desired effects:

> The first step for those advocating assimilation should have been the creation of schools. Yet there exists a ridiculously small number of them. . . .
> What can we offer those who attend? A few jobs as interpreters barely remunerated, without future, in which the unfortunate employees drag out a disappointing existence, rejected by both black and European society. . . .
> Association? . . . Before we came there existed political institutions perfectly adapted to the country and to the level of civilization of its inhabitants . . . all that we have ignored. . . . It would, however, have been easy and logical to associate these institutions in our undertakings. On the

contrary we have held them at arm's length. The chiefs we have chosen have been treated like servants. . . . *Apprivoisement?* . . . The objective was to draw the hesitant toward us, to end the privations, to penetrate the population with the idea that our intervention was synonymous with progress, moral and material improvement, justice, security. . . .

I have seen lots of reports referring to slaughtered tyrants, the French peace, economic development . . . but I have also seen circles where the *commandant* has substituted himself for the former tyrant, without any benefit to the local populations.[15]

More often than not, Delafosse continued, Dakar had destroyed existing institutions without putting anything better in their place. The situation was worse than in the first years of French occupation. "Our native policy has regressed, not progressed." He attributed this situation to a lack of interest in, and respect for, the cultures France had undertaken to change. Ponty, he pointed out, had held in contempt all scientific inquiry. The African people had a history of their own, which, he concluded, "we do not have the right to ignore nor disdain, on the grounds that it is not written and does not appear on university curricula. It is the history of a human race and, for this reason alone, cannot remain unknown to men, whomever they might be, and particularly not to men who have received the mission to continue [this history]."[16] Delafosse's criticisms of past administrations were not, however, entirely fair. Dakar had not suffered so much from inconsistency in its vision as from too much emphasis on one principle: the eradication of "feudal" vestiges. Numerous exceptions had been made in the application of this policy, which may have caused Dakar's apparent indecisiveness; but there was nothing chaotic about the decision to make exceptions. And although no scholar, Ponty was certainly aware of the prestige attached to scientific knowledge, as his directives on public health and hygiene indicate. Toward the end of his administration, as Christopher Harrison has shown, Ponty also began to rely on "expert" advice, at least in the realm of Muslim policy.[17] In the final version of the memoradum, Van Vollenhoven did not substantially alter Delafosse's conclusions. His tone was nevertheless milder; and the accent, not surprisingly, was less on criticizing his predecessors and dwelling upon the need to respect African institutions, and more on assessing the unanticipated consequences of earlier policies for French rule and the implications of such consequences for the future. Indeed, as far as Van Vollenhoven was concerned, the most salient fact to emerge from the situation he had inherited was not

that Dakar had ignored a civilization that deserved to be preserved—
although he did not rule out this notion; rather, it was that French
"civilizing" actions had caused a breakdown of social relations in
West Africa, which now threatened French hegemony and had to be
reversed.

There had been, Van Vollenhoven began, a deplorable absence of
unified doctrine in West Africa over the past thirty years. On account of lack of documentation and the problems posed by organizing these vast territories, actions had been undertaken piecemeal,
often with the best of intentions. This approach had, through no one
individual's fault, "necessarily and fatally" disrupted African society. The first elements contributing to this disorganization had been
the establishment of French peace and the introduction of the railroad; they had broken down the isolation in which Africans had
lived for centuries. Such isolation, Van Vollenhoven intimated, deserved to be ended. It was, in and of itself, the "fruit of barbarism."
This isolation nevertheless had had certain advantages: "Traditions
remained alive, custom was rigorously observed, social and family
discipline was everywhere respected, and everywhere punishment
for deviation was ruthlessly applied."[18]

Having broken down the isolation of African society, France then
applied its laws and suppressed the great commands. The principle
that custom should be respected only insofar as it did not conflict
with civilization was not understood by those it was designed to
benefit; imprisonment did not appear, either to the victim or the
criminal, to be a sufficient penalty for their crimes, and only served
to undermine further traditional authority:

> We created civil justice, but native society was scared by the rights we
> granted to individuals, particularly to women and to young people, [who
> began] challenging with impunity conjugal and paternal authority, age-
> less foundations of the African family. We suppressed the great com-
> mands, feared and respected, but we also deprived the collectivity of the
> tyranny that constituted a solid framework. . . . I do not criticize these
> measures . . . only assert that these reforms have profoundly troubled the
> natives who . . . observe that the rigorous hierarchy of yesterday has been
> replaced [today] by a well-intentioned but emasculated one.

In addition to the disarray created in rural West Africa, which was
evidenced by, among other things, Islam's tremendous inroads, there
was "profound discontent and growing disillusion among the minority who rallied to our cause out of either affinity or self-interest,

and who have not found in the new West Africa advantageous employment." He wrote, "We must distinguish between the masses, who must pursue their evolution in their own milieu, and the elite, who must evolve more and more in our milieu." The latter, he insisted, were no longer "natives" and should not be treated as such. "They have raised themselves. . . . It is to them that we have the greatest responsibilities. They are the young, the avant-garde, the example." They have heard the speeches, Van Vollenhoven pointed out, but do not see the civilization promised them: no schools, no hospitals, no modern technology, no prosperity. Thus, he concluded, alongside the unhappy rural masses, an elite ready to follow "the wrong shepherds" has now sprung up.[19]

The breakdown of traditional authority structures, the emergence of urban *évolués* bitterly resenting the lack of opportunity open to them: this, Van Vollenhoven summed up, was already the situation on the eve of World War I. "Imagine, then, the anguish of a population that, for three centuries now, has served as a 'reservoir'! That has never seen its children again, shipped off first to the Americas, then for the conquest of Equatorial Africa, of Madagascar, of Morocco, and finally to Europe." Colonial recruitment had thus pushed African forbearance to the breaking point; the subsequent revolts made glaringly obvious the fragility of French rule after thirty years of "liberation." These people, Van Vollenhoven reminded the minister, once were welcoming; now they neither "like us or trust us." The situation was not yet desperate. But immediate action was necessary to redress the balance in France's favor.[20]

This letter, coupled with Van Vollenhoven's actions, confirms that the events of the war years had shaken Dakar from its ideological moorings. Yet, if a new concern for French interests, along with repudiation of past methods for uplifting Africans, permeate this text as well as the other circulars cited above, another concern also emerges: that of a civilizing mission still unfulfilled, and a continuing commitment to somehow completing France's original goals. Despite Van Vollenhoven's insistence that France had acted precipitously in disrupting the old order, his words did not imply that the republican fight against this African ancien régime should be abandoned. Similarly, although Van Vollenhoven lamented "the disintegration [*désorganisation*] caused by the implantation of those essentially moral principles that had led to colonization in the first place," he also maintained that the Government General had not acted vigorously enough in providing schools, hospitals, and prosperity—in a word, the "civilization"—promised during the conquest. These references to civilizing Africans presaged an important transformation in the content of the *mission civilisatrice*. In many ways this transformation had already begun under Clozel and Van Vollenhoven, but it would be most evident under their successors, Martial Merlin and Jules Carde.

The Advent of Association, 1919–1930

In 1919, the Government General of French West Africa would, for the first time since the beginning of the war, be ruled by one man for longer than two years. That year Martial Merlin was appointed to Dakar, where he would remain until 1923. Martial Merlin was no newcomer to the federation. He arrived in Dakar with a record of long and distinguished service in France's different African territories, including a recent posting as governor general of the French Equatorial African federation.[21] At the age of fifty-eight, he belonged to the the first generation of civilian administrators serving in West Africa, a group that also included Roume, Ponty, and Clozel.[22] Merlin had almost succeeded Roume at the head of the federation in 1908.[23] His own experience in West Africa dated to the early 1890's in the colony of Senegal, where he had promoted a policy of collaboration with aristocratic chiefs in the interests of both cheap and efficient indirect administration. This experiment anticipated on a local level the policies that Dakar began to adopt for the entire federation and that Merlin would now continue. At the same time, it provided the basis for the revised approach to uplifting Africans that Merlin formulated in the 1920's. Both initiatives would be designated by the term "association."

Association was not, of course, an original concept in 1919. As Raymond Betts has shown, Parisian theorists since the expansion of the empire under the Third Republic had advocated some form of government by association for their overseas territories, predicated upon respect for indigenous cultures, and administration through preexisting native political structures. If the first tenet of association had influenced the Government General before the war, the notion that precolonial institutions in West Africa should be preserved had seemed inappropriate under Roume and Ponty. In the 1920's, however, this French version of indirect rule also began to appear relevant in Dakar. In addition, the Government General now faced far greater pressure from the metropolitan government to implement a policy by that name. The most powerful colonial minister of the interwar years, Albert Sarraut (1921–1925), proclaimed that a new era of "association" was about to begin throughout the empire, one in which old and new elites would everywhere be granted representative assemblies of some kind.[24] Sarraut justified this largesse as part of France's reward to its subjects for contributing to the war effort. This directive from Paris, reiterated throughout the interwar years, dovetailed with Dakar's own thinking and made compliance easy. After the war, the Government General increasingly spoke of its obligation to extend gradually democratic rights to selected Africans—in order to associate them in their own administration.

What exactly did Dakar mean by these terms? Its doctrine of association rested on two premises. The first was that some form of sharing power with the old and new elite in West Africa was necessary to preserve French authority. The second was that this power sharing, in the proper doses and surrounded by the proper safeguards, was also in the best interests of its subjects and thus consistent with France's civilizing mission in West Africa. The idea that association was integral to French survival made its formal appearance in Dakar shortly after Merlin's arrival. An administrative report from 1920 hinted at Dakar's change of heart, when it noted that the "fierce struggle against chiefs" had been a misguided crusade, inspired by the republican ideology of France's newly triumphant bourgeoisie. Such a crusade was out of touch with African realities and had to be abandoned:

> The prewar years had been a time when the administrative cadres were filled with young people just out of school, sons of bourgeois living off annuities or children of the lower classes educated with the help of scholarships. . . . Both groups left France, not because they had to, but out of love for the free life. Because of a lack of more experienced personnel, they were given extensive circles; and since the command sent down from the upper echelons of the administration was to liberate the slaves, to ruin the great commands, to eradicate feudal vestiges, they put all their youthful energy and secret instincts at the service of the oppressed against the slave holding oligarchy of the chiefs. . . . It was a splendid massacre, in which the ones followed in their predecessors' footsteps. . . .
>
> This was the easy part. The difficulty began when it became necessary to rebuild the destroyed edifice. At first the difficulties were not appar-

ent . . . impressive groupings were formed which inspired their architects with great optimism. . . . Unfortunately, it quickly became evident that the new groupings were artificial and that their administration was impossible. . . . Their improvised chiefs completely lacked authority.[25]

Merlin developed these ideas more fully in a letter to the minister of colonies, Albert Sarraut, in 1921. The situation in West Africa had never been "more favorable. Peace reigns everywhere. But of what does [this peace] consist? Is it the atavistic and resigned submission of a 'cursed race,' as one of my predecessors put it, after the repression of the peoples of the West Volta in 1917? Is it, on the contrary, the loyal patriotism of our subjects, as another of my predecessors stated, after the recruitment of 1916? I think the truth is much more nuanced, much more complex." Merlin continued,

We came as conquerors . . . we appeared as liberators. . . . We released them from the tyrannical domination of a bloody oligarchy. . . . In exchange for a light head tax, each person was guaranteed complete liberty for himself and his family to live, to own, even to enrich himself, and in all circumstances to have justice done. . . . But the deepest source of their loyalty lies in the tranquillity that we assured them. It is this [tranquillity] that makes the French peace not simply a façade, or a figure of speech, but an objective, substantial and durable reality, capable of resisting the most violent attacks.[26]

This tranquillity, however, had a price, and France quickly earned the hatred of those who lost when peace was achieved: dispossessed sovereigns, warrior chiefs, *marabouts*, witches, fetishists. For a long time, these elements "managed to lure us into a false sense of security by their cleverness." They were nevertheless waiting for the right moment to reassert their preeminence—they were at the root of the revolts of 1916 and 1917. The problem now was to determine what attitude to adopt toward them and, more specifically, what portion of French sovereignty to accord or refuse them. "Let there be no mistake," Merlin warned, "regarding this issue: it is the most important one facing our colonial policy." He then continued:

What have the English done? They have allowed to persist, under the semblances of a doctrinaire liberalism, all that is oppressive in the feudal regime that was in place when they arrived. This fundamentally aristocratic regime, which did not allow them to recruit even a twentieth of the men we were able to during the war, is now condemned by all important colonial figures [because it risks alienating the mass of African subjects].

Less liberal in its proclamations, but more democratic in terms of its effects, our policy consisted, in contrast, in preserving for ourselves alone all sovereignty. In conciliating the masses, however, we alienated the sympathy of the dispossessed chiefs, who were reduced to simple intermediaries. Is there not room for a mixed policy that simultaneously respects the *amour propre* of the ruling classes and the essential rights of the masses?[27]

Merlin's comparison with Britain here suggests how self-conscious the French still were about their own republican mission to free Africans from aristocratic oppression. However, Merlin's conviction that France now had to consider a "mixed policy" was a departure from the very ideals the governor general celebrated as the essence of French "democratic" actions in West Africa: the preservation of all sovereignty in the hands of the administration. Before the war the question of power sharing had not arisen in Dakar for the simple reason that the African "ruling classes" were considered too barbaric to rule through. Now Dakar was suggesting that it should "respect" them in order to prevent future rebellions. As Merlin made clear elsewhere, this policy would also help the French against the second threat that Dakar was facing: new demands by the *évolués*.

The uprooted [*déracinés*] . . . have not found everywhere an organization strong enough to contain [*encadrer*] them. . . . Already before the war the *paix française* encouraged little by little the dispersion of the natives and diminished the solid cohesion of the villages where the authority of the elders used to hold sway uncontested. A growing individualism slowly but surely began to destroy the powerful African collectivity. . . . It is now necessary for us to reconstitute this cohesion . . . and to restore to village chiefs their authority.[28]

In other circulars, Merlin's fears with respect to the *évolués* were more evident:

The ideas of emancipation, which the backers of the anti-European movement are attempting to spread in Africa, are obviously destined to create illusions among the young educated blacks, agents of the administration or of commerce, desiring to equal the white man, and to incite them to dream of aspiring for themselves, to the exclusion of any foreign element, the role of educators and leaders of the indigenous societies. On the other hand, the masses have up until now stayed attached to the land and faithful to their ancient customs. The stories of the liberated soldiers, returning home from the metropole or the coastal cities, have perhaps awakened in them new feelings. There is no one who does not understand the profound importance, vital even, for our work of colonization, which this possible, probable even, evolution presents, this "disenchantment" of a half-asleep society discovering all at once new horizons, a more active and more individualistic conception of life, the possibility for a man to exist with well-defined personal rights outside of his family, clan and tribe.

But this new disposition, in favoring the intellectual development and the material progress of the natives, also renders them more vulnerable to the self-interested calls and fallacious promises of professional agitators. It thus behooves us to confront these unhealthy stimuli with the notions of order and social discipline, which should direct the evolution of the black races and preserve Africa from upheavals, whose certain effect would be to annihilate the work of civilization that has begun and return the continent to its ancient barbarism.[29]

In lamenting past policies and assumptions and thinking up ways to prevent future attacks on French authority, Merlin was not suggesting, however, that the aspirations of this new elite be ignored altogether. To the contrary, just as he was envisaging some form of power sharing with chiefs, the governor general also recommended that the *évolués* be given their own say in decision making. In a confidential letter to the minister, written while Diagne was mounting his campaign for political equality for Africans, Merlin insisted that he certainly "did not oppose" the goals the *évolués* and Diagne stood for. "I told [M. Diagne]," Merlin continued, "that we had the same ultimate objective, that of encouraging the progress of the indigenous populations along the path of civilization." Rather, Merlin explained, he opposed Diagne's means: "What separates us is the question of extent . . . he wants to go too fast, while I intend to show consideration for the transitions." And Merlin concluded, "In point of fact, I am firmly convinced that reasonable and carefully considered democratic measures are likely to engender, to the benefit of civilization, more solid and lasting habits [*acquisitions*], than measures inspired by a demagoguery that is as imprudent as it is utopian."[30]

Such measures did not remain entirely hypothetical. During his tenure in office, Merlin made several policy changes that were consistent with his rhetoric. The first of Merlin's measures was promulgated on May 5, 1919, and provided for the creation of *conseils de notables* (councils of notables). A series of additional decrees appeared on December 4, 1920. These various measures, taken together, can be divided into two categories: those designed to increase the representation of African notables on the governor general's and the lieutenant governors' administrative councils, and those that created new councils at the village and circle levels, composed solely of Africans. The measures in the first category provided for the appointment of two African *évolué* subjects to the administrative councils of the member colonies, and nine African chiefs, one from each colony, to the Council of the Government General in Dakar.[31] The measures in the second category constituted the main thrust of the Government General's attempt to associate Africans in their own administration in the rural areas, and resulted in a number of explanatory circulars.[32] They provided for the creation of a local council of notables in every circle, composed of eight to sixteen village and canton chiefs or other notables chosen by the governor. According to the 1919 decree, these notables would be consulted by the local administrator on such matters as tax rates, the allocation of *prestations*, the furnishing of census statistics, and the selection of market days.[33] Such councils, over which the *commandant* would preside, were to have no powers of their own. The administrator would explain what had to be done in the circle and why these measures were in the best interest of the Africans. He would also listen to the chiefs' grievances or opinions on predetermined subjects. In the process, the notables would get to know the colonizing power better, understand its motives for being in West Africa, and learn to appreciate French administrative methods.[34]

Along with new councils of notables, the second category of decrees provided for the transformation of all African communities into *communes* with municipal responsibilities. Three degrees of *communes* were envisaged: native *communes*, mixed *communes*, and *communes de plein exercise* with the full range of privileges allowed municipalities in France.[35] African *communes*, which were what villages could expect to become, were to be run by an administrator-mayor with the help of a commission of elders appointed by the governor and presided over by one of its members, presumably the village chief. They could consider matters of local interest—taxes, *prestations*, census rolls, maintaining public order, public hygiene—but their opinions were nonbinding. In addition to providing a forum for the expression of grievances, *communes* were to help educate the village elders in modern administrative techniques: "Only assemblies at the circle (council of notables) and communal level, where the questions discussed are of immediate practical interest . . . permit [Africans] to collaborate effectively with the local administration and prepare their education in public affairs." Such collaboration would represent an important improvement over past practices, when "the social function of a village was reduced to the execution, pure and simple, through the chief as intermediary, of administrative orders."[36] Cities alone qualified for mixed-*commune* status, and in 1921, Porto Novo, Abidjan, Conakry, Kayes, and Bamako were all granted that rank. Mixed *communes*, run by a joint commission of Europeans and educated Africans who met certain requirements and were headed by an administrator-mayor, had more autonomy than native *communes*; they still had no electoral privileges.[37] No city was considered evolved enough to be promoted to the status of the Four Communes of Senegal in the interwar period.

These various reforms, although similar to Dakar's earlier decisions to return chiefs to office, went beyond them in two respects. They introduced the principle of consultation, and they acknowledged for the first time the aspirations of the *évolués*. Merlin apparently believed that future misunderstandings could be avoided if the administration had a means of keeping up with the sentiments and aspirations of those among their subjects who had appeared most unhappy with French rule: traditional notables and the younger generation. Rural *communes* and councils of notables also appeared designed to help the administration in a more subtle way. As Merlin's emphasis upon public education suggests, he saw in these institutions a chance to make the rural elite more modern leaders in their own right. Implicit in this argument was the assumption that only by becoming more forward-looking could chiefs hope to retain their prestige before the impatient and uprooted *évolués*, and thus prevent the latter from challenging the French.

Merlin's reforms to associate Africans in policy making thus marked another phase in native policy during the postwar decade. The new governor general, however, also began to embrace a rhetoric of civilization different from that of his predecessors. In the 1920's, Dakar did not discreetly initiate certain political changes while maintaining intact its former doctrine that all chiefs were bloody tyrants and that Africans had to evolve gradually in their own cultures. It simultaneously revised its official definition of how best to uplift Africans. The two phenomena were not unrelated. As an analysis of the statements by Merlin that accompanied his reforms will show, Dakar's postwar ideology changed in exactly the same direction as its native policy. During the interwar period, the policy of association was seen not only as politically expedient but also as essential to the civilizing of Africans.

Merlin's postwar reinterpretation of France's civilizing mission in West Africa included a number of new elements, each of which coincided with a certain aspect of the policy of association. In his 1921 letter to the minister discussing Diagne, which was quoted above, Merlin had maintained that "carefully considered democratic measures" would further the "cause of civilization" better than hasty ones. The juxtaposition of "democratic measures" and "civilization" suggests that in the postwar period, power sharing had suddenly become a theme of France's mission in West Africa. In the presentation of his decree creating councils of notables and *communes* in West Africa, Merlin made even clearer that he considered his actions to be democratic in nature, and therefore consistent with the republican concerns that had always informed French actions in West Africa:

> [These measures] achieve for the first time . . . the principle of participation of all the political, economic and social interests present [in the colony] in our attributions of sovereignty. In all the parts of the both massive and complex organism that constitutes the French West African Federation, from the Council of the Government General, which is in one sense the brain, to the native *commune*, which is like the cell, we are everywhere associating in our administration those affected by it. And we are doing this not in a fragmentary manner, under the pressure of circumstances, but thanks to a complete and well-thought-out program . . . flexible enough to be adapted to all milieux according to their degree of evolution, liberal enough to satisfy all legitimate aspirations.[38]

Another new theme was a revised assessment of Africa's traditional ruling class. In the postwar era a cardinal principle of French ideology was that the precolonial African chieftaincy was less exploitative and more representative than had earlier been believed. Merlin revealed this belief when he created councils of notables and *communes* and in reference to the policy of appointing traditional chiefs to office. "The institution [of councils and communes]," he wrote, "represents one phase in the reconstitution of the cadres of native society that we inconsiderately destroyed. It aims at restoring to life those councils of notables that existed in fact in the majority of communities and that constituted the representative body of common interests before the French conquest." He later observed:

> We condemned too quickly the use of the *commandement indigène* . . . a premature generalization hid from us the advantages we could derive

from an undoubtedly imperfect social organization, but one which was nevertheless long adapted to local mores and satisfactory generally since it was in sum the spontaneous reflection of natural needs and aspirations of our subjects. . . . Through lack of careful scrutiny, we did not see the patriarchal and familial side of this organization that we destroyed, instead of ameliorating or adapting it to the new function that we wished it to play. Our error was to believe that in acting this way we were fulfilling the deepest wishes of our natives. . . . But deprived of their traditional guides they did not understand the excellence of our intentions, and it was a great surprise for us to discover in the course of rebellion the permanence of an entire hierarchy of occult chiefs, whom we believed to have long ago died out. We thus began to realize the dangers of our policy of liberation.[39]

This more benign image of the precolonial West African elite in general, and chiefs in particular, would be reiterated throughout the 1920's and 1930's. It undoubtedly reflected Merlin's own understanding of West African political organization acquired through his years in Senegal; yet other factors also help account for Dakar's change of heart. Certainly, the more conservative climate in France made respect for the African aristocracy more thinkable than in the prewar era. Closer to home, the recent research of Maurice Delafosse on West Africa confirmed the governor general's reinterpretation of the *commandement indigène*. Merlin's words echoed arguments Delafosse first made in *Haut-Sénégal-Niger* (1912), regarding political organization in the Western Sudan. Delafosse argued that only after the French defeated the recently formed empires of Samori and Umar had "the traditionally constituted native states" of West Africa been able to reemerge and live in peace with one another. These political units were surprisingly diverse—the household; the *quartier*, made up of the extended family; the village; the canton; the kingdom (or confederation if it was ruled not by a king but a council of chiefs); and the empire:

These different stages of native political association can coexist in a single state and merely form the administrative divisions of this state. Thus an empire can include several kingdoms, each divided into cantons which encompass in turn several villages composed of several *quartiers*. But political development can be arrested at any one of these stages, which then itself becomes a state in its own right: we have native political units that are only cantons—indeed they are the most numerous today; we have states that consist of a single village, which can be found among a few peoples in the [Western] Sudan and especially among peoples living in the forest.[40]

Each of these political units, empires excepted, traditionally had its own, for the most part popularly accepted, chief responsible for administering the "affairs of state." At the level of the village and the canton, these chiefs were usually descendants of the family responsible for founding the political unit. At the level of a kingdom, in contrast, power was genuinely feudal: a seignorial class of aristocratic chiefs—often canton chiefs themselves—limited the authority a hereditary king could accumulate. Only at the level of the empire, Delafosse concluded, was authority noncustomary, that is to say, acquired by force.[41] Delafosse thus supported Merlin's argument that the authority of most African chiefs was "patriarchal" and "familial" in nature, and not necessarily resented by their subjects. He completed this picture by emphasizing that councils in West Africa had traditionally counterbalanced the authority of chiefs:

> We should recall that the village chief, or the one so-called, is generally nobody and the village council is everything. We will remember that the canton chief is but little if he does not have the support of his private council and the confidence of his cantonal assembly. We should try not to forget that a chief cannot truly exercise power if he has not received the investiture of the competent assembly and that the word of a chief even legally exercising his functions has no value unless it expresses the opinion of the people represented by their traditional spokesmen.[42]

Beyond Delafosse's contribution, a more professional and scientific interest in traditional African society was emerging among members of colonial and academic circles in Paris in the 1920's. An important sign of this change was the Colonial Ministry's decision in 1925 to help fund a new Institut d'Ethnologie at the University of Paris, jointly founded by Delafosse, the Durkheimians Marcel Mauss and Lucien Lévy-Bruhl, and the liberal anthropologist Paul Rivet.[43] For the first time in France, the discipline of ethnology was associated with a university. Within a year of the Institut's founding, the Ecole Coloniale was offering several new courses of its own in West African history, customary law, and languages, and sending its students to the Institut for additional training. There they learned how to conduct ethnographic fieldwork and were encouraged to take a scholarly interest in the people of the circles that they would be administering.[44] These initiatives confirm that the new valorization of African institutions taking place in Dakar was also occurring at the highest level of the colonial administration, not to mention the university milieu itself. These metropolitan developments encouraged the Government General's emphasis upon preserving precolonial cultures.

Yet, although this discovery of "authentic" African civilizations by the minister of colonies and the Ecole Coloniale was promising, too much should not be made of it. Like the colonial administration's sudden postwar realization that France should allow Africans to participate in their own government, its favorable reassessment of traditional African political institutions occurred only after Dakar and Paris had determined that returning the chiefs to relative authority was in France's best interest. The war had exposed the need for chiefly collaboration and better contact with the majority of their subjects. By now maintaining that chiefs were both more representative and less exploitative than had earlier been believed, the administration could appoint the same African aristocrats to office that it had earlier condemned, and still claim to be respecting its traditional commitment to the African masses. The timing of France's change of heart on this point suggests the need for maintaining French hegemony, not a genuine interest in the precolonial institutions of West Africa.

Indeed, whether even the metropolitan scholars, responsible with Delafosse for the creation of the Institut d'Ethnologie, had such an interest is open to question. The ethnologists teaching there insisted that their mandate was simultaneously scientific and utilitarian— that is, they were to study colonial peoples, but always in order better to control them. As Lévy-Bruhl explained it, the principal reason for founding the Institut was the "urgent" need in the colonies for practical ethnological information gathered by professionals. "When a colony contains peoples of inferior civilization, or very different [civilizations] from our own, good ethnologists are as necessary as good engineers . . . and good doctors." Successful *mise en valeur* required an "exact and profound knowledge of [local] languages, religions and social cadres, which must not be tampered with lightly," to avoid insurrections.[45] As these quotations suggest, the research agenda of the "scientific" Institut members had, on paper at least, the same political and economic objectives as the colonial administrators they were now training.[46]

Merlin articulated one last civilizing theme, which also contrasted with the emancipationist doctrine of the prewar years. This was the idea that, as Africa's traditional and popularly accepted rulers, chiefs and ruling notables offered the best vehicle for introducing change into the countryside, and should and would now be used as such by the administration. Association of chiefs and councils would not mean that rural African society would simply be restored to the precolonial status quo. Instead, civilization would continue, but this time would be truly adapted to the African environment. Rather than destroying African institutions and attempting to rebuild, association would allow France to reform African society from within. This idea was best expressed in an internal memorandum in 1921, which claimed that by respecting traditional forms of political authority in West Africa and simultaneously encouraging the public education of chiefs, association would allow "all classes of African society to evolve within an organization that is familiar to them and that, far from being incompatible with a superior civilization, will render such civilization more accessible to the mass of our subjects."[47]

Like his other arguments, this belief overlapped with the needs of the colonial state in a specific way. We have seen how Merlin created councils to ensure the public education of chiefs in the rural areas, in order to enhance their prestige in the eyes of the masses and prevent further dissolution of social bonds. Now Dakar was arguing that this education would also promote civilization. According to Merlin's revised rhetoric, the interests of the colonial state and its subjects could be met by means of one and the same policy: that of a close association between old and new elites in the running of the federation. This same view, and the policies to which it gave rise, would continue under his successor, Jules Carde. This continuity was all the more noteworthy, given that Merlin and Carde could not have differed more in background and experience.

Jules Carde (1923–1930) was born on June 3, 1874. Like Van Vollenhoven, he grew up in the French colony of Algeria. Carde was the only governor general of West Africa of his generation not to attend the Ecole Coloniale; rather, he began his career in the prefecture of Alger and then entered the colonial service. His first posting was to Madagascar in 1898. The fact that Carde did not have an Ecole Coloniale or a law degree did not count against him in his bid for high office. Instead, it may have made him more ambitious, for Carde rose quickly through the ranks of the colonial hierarchy. In 1909, he served as an administrator in Ivory Coast, and then as the cabinet chief to the governor general of Equatorial Africa, Gabriel Angoulvant. Carde was made a governor in 1916, and in 1917 he was handpicked by Van Vollenhoven to serve as secretary general of the West African federation. Van Vollenhoven thought highly of Carde, writing, upon his own resignation, that he could not say enough about the man and calling him a true *chef*, ultimate praise from someone who had made a cult of leadership abilities.[48] After the war, Carde was posted to Cameroon as *commissaire de la République* to organize France's League of Nations mandate and preside over the transition from military to civilian rule. He arrived in Dakar from Cameroon, where he had received high marks for inaugurating the colony's *mise en valeur*.

If Carde's predecessor, Martial Merlin, was a typical old-school administrator formed in the field, Carde was more in the mold of Van Vollenhoven, whose energy and pragmatism if not charisma Carde often recalled. With Carde, we pass fully into the new generation of leadership in French West Africa whose rise to power Van Vollenhoven had inaugurated in 1917–1918, but which Merlin's subsequent appointment had interrupted. This generation included Governors General Carde, Van Vollenhoven, Angoulvant (interim governor general, 1917–1918), and Carde's successor, Jules Brévié (1930–1936), all of whom were born between 1860 and 1870. Typical of this new leadership was support for the policy and ideals of association, and a renewed commitment to *mise en valeur*. Carde's ties to this new generation were particularly strong, since he had served under Governors General Angoulvant and Van Vollenhoven before being appointed governor general himself.

Carde's acceptance of the premises of association became clear shortly after he arrived in Dakar in 1923. He immediately endorsed Merlin's policy of devolving a portion of French authority upon West Africa's old elite and educating them in public affairs. "Local administrations," Carde reported to Paris in 1925, "are pursuing tirelessly the education and strengthening of *le commandement indigène*. . . . Everywhere a serious effort is being made to develop, reinforce or create an armature whose need is made every moment more pressing." He concluded by reiterating that "regenerating *le commandement indigène* by infusing it with an unwavering loyalty, this is the primordial task of our policy of sovereignty in West Africa." Carde was not content, however, to rely on consultation to achieve this regeneration. Thinking ahead, he made school attendance and the learning of French obligatory for all sons of chiefs, notables, and the rich generally: "The prestige that is conferred upon

birth must be strengthened by the respect that knowledge confers."
Forced by budgetary restrictions to make a choice about whom to
instruct, administrators should begin with the aristocracy; even if
the latter were not later employed by the French, they rarely became
déclassés. And for the majority who did become chiefs, their time
in French schools would make them better collaborators and exem-
plars.[49] In this context, Carde showed the same conviction as Merlin
that the interests of the masses and those of Dakar could be reconciled when educated chiefs participated in policy making. Chiefs,
strengthened and trained, would become the intermediaries through
which new ideas penetrated the countryside. "It is through the inti-
mate association of all the different elements of authority in this
country," Carde insisted in 1923, "that we will most securely guide
the higher destinies of [our subjects]":

> [But] chiefs must be the most solid pressure point of the lever with which
> we propose to elevate the masses. Their training must be furthered, but
> without the impatience of before . . . our action must necessarily adapt
> itself to the particular circumstances it encounters. And since there can
> be no question of democracy everywhere . . . it should first be given to the
> ruling class. Our efforts must be directed toward consolidating the tradi-
> tional social armature, toward creating it wherever it does not exist, it is
> toward constituting an intelligent aristocracy that we must first apply our
> efforts.[50]

Finally, for Carde as well as Merlin, another purpose of strengthening and educating chiefs was to offset the new elite's growing insubordination. "It is not possible," he wrote in 1928, "to arrest the
evolution of the latter"; one must "direct it and control it by maintaining intact this traditional armature." Carde regretted the unanticipated consequences that prewar educational policies had had for
this group:

> To our worries, which the last resistances of barbarism have created,
> must be added the worries of watching the deviations of those at the
> avant-garde of evolution, those who are exercised by vain ambitions. At
> the head of this avant-garde, we find those who have been educated in our
> schools, whom we have employed in our administration. Abruptly torn
> from their milieu, without yet possessing sufficient aptitudes to adapt to
> their new milieu, these uprooted Africans suffer from their isolation,
> chafe against their lack of power, and, ceding to the perfidious suggestions
> that aggravate racial hatreds, soon become rebels. Such is the inevitable
> price paid for too rapid evolutions.[51]

However, Carde was willing throughout his tenure to take additional "democratic measures" to placate this rebellious avant-garde and to justify these measures as part of a continuing march toward civilization. In 1924, he exempted the *évolués* from the *indigénat*, as Van Vollenhoven had exempted the chiefs in 1917.[52] The following year he wrote to the minister that Merlin's decrees of 1919–1920 instituting association "no longer harmonize with the new conditions of Africa's social development," and suggested that the time had come to create a limited electoral college for chiefs and *évolués*. All those who could legitimately claim to speak in the name of the collectivity were to be admitted. This college would elect to the councils of the individual colonies and the council of the Government General those members of the African community previously designated by the administration.[53] In 1928, Carde expanded upon this measure by allowing African subjects to qualify for certain administrative positions formerly reserved to citizens.[54]

In initiating these measures, Carde emphasized their liberal and uplifting nature and insisted that they were having the desired effect. Each new initiative acknowledged the progress the *évolués* had made, and prepared the way for future progress. The electoral college was appropriate because, thanks to the benefits of French education and moral instruction, an elite was slowly being created. It was not enough, he continued, to congratulate themselves on having created this new elite. Since they had shown African leaders a new form of existence, which this elite desired to make its own, chiefs and *évolués* must be more closely involved in the undertakings of the administration. By 1930, Carde would look back upon his years in office convinced that he had contributed decisively to the moral progress of the African elite and, by extension, that of the African masses, which had begun the day the French first set foot in West Africa:

> Thanks to the security, thanks to the amelioration in the economic conditions of existence, the ancient families of native chiefs naturally began to base their superiority upon new "values," which the sheer strength of force no longer sufficed to uphold. Even though they have jealously preserved the advantages of certain local traditions, they have evolved under French authority, of which it was only in their best interest to become the auxiliaries. The development of education and the special access that their sons have been given to this institution, have allowed them to assimilate certain modes of thinking and action to which their contact with

material progress made them initially receptive, but whose moral aspect is now developing in an ever more marked fashion.[55]

Independent of these chiefs, Carde added, certain particularly talented individuals had increasingly taken advantage of these educational and administrative opportunities. They, together with the rural notables, formed a "true elite" who occupied a preeminent position in the social organism and whose aspirations were respected by the local administration.

It is interesting to note in conclusion how fully Carde's outlook here anticipated certain ideas that officials in Paris, on their own, put forward in the late 1920's. We have already seen that between 1925 and 1927 the Conseil Supérieur des Colonies and the colonial minister began to have doubts about the worthiness of any African for French citizenship. In debating this issue, however, the Conseil also recognized that it would not do to ignore completely the aspirations of "deserving subjects." To keep them "in the humiliating and materially disadvantageous conditions" of serfs was only to invite further revolt.[56] The ideal solution was to create a new legal category between subject and citizen for the majority of "evolved" Africans— that of *indigènes d'élite*.[57] This native elite would enjoy special prerogatives, including the right to vote in local elections and exemption from the *indigénat*. The colonial minister was sufficiently impressed with the idea to prepare a *projet de décret* on the subject and submit it to the various governors general for comment.[58]

In the end, the new status never became law, in part because Carde refused to approve the project. Carde's point was a simple one; West Africa did not need an official status for "deserving Africans," because such a status already existed de facto, if not de jure, thanks to the initiatives he had already taken and would continue to take regarding the *évolués*. As Carde explained it to the minister, he did not want to be hampered by the creation of a new legal category to which specific rights were automatically attached. In addition, in the most politically advanced parts of the federation, the subjects would see this category as a new means of avoiding the extension of citizenship, and it would generate more discontent than it alleviated.[59] Although Dakar and Paris diverged slightly on the method, both revealed their commitment to creating—alongside a renewed aristocracy—a new elite who would remain more African than French.

Association Assessed

The doctrine of civilization through association, developed closely with the new policy of chiefs and *évolués* collaborating, was deemed essential to preserving French hegemony in West Africa. To what extent, we may now ask, did policy and ideology serve the Government General and promote progress as claimed? With respect to the *évolués*, this question was partially answered in the preceding chapter. Throughout the 1920's, a portion of the new elite continued to pressure the Government General for greater concessions than those contained in the doctrine of association. Far from being content with Dakar's policy of gradual democratic measures, this group aspired to equality with the colonizer in policy making. In this sense, Dakar's doctrine of limited power-sharing was a failure for the long-term interests of the Government General. Within thirty years—rather than the centuries Dakar had originally imagined—the federal authorities would have to accept *évolués* as equals and turn power over to them altogether. In the short term, however, association helped preserve French rule, by offering a counterdoctrine to the *évolué* ideology of assimilation. This justified giving but a small part of French sovereignty to the new elite, instead of the full equality they demanded. Colonial officials were thus able to preserve, for the entire interwar period, the very authority that was being contested, without appearing as die-hard racists before world or metropolitan opinion.

The policy of association with regard to the *évolués* did not serve the cause of civilization as defined by the French in the 1920's. Association was supposed to allow educated Africans a portion of France's sovereignty and prepare for the public education of others. The first objective was achieved only marginally by Dakar's policies; the second, not at all. Dakar's various measures to allow *évolués'* participation in the administration—their appointment to administrative councils, the creation of mixed *communes*, the institution of an electoral college, and the opening (after qualifying) of administrative positions formerly reserved to citizens—were concessions of the most minimal kind. At best, the *évolués* were now to be consulted in matters concerning them.

Just how minimal Dakar's interwar concessions were can be seen in the administration's subsequent treatment of Africans who applied for jobs formerly open exclusively to the French. According to the new legislation, in order to gain admission to the *cadre supérieur*, Africans had to pass the same exams as Europeans. In 1929, Carde sent a circular saying that none of that year's African candidates had passed the requisite exams, and complaining that their preparation had been deplorable. The Africans had had the arrogance to assume that, Carde continued, authorization to apply meant automatic admittance. He pointed out that the new measure was only for those who were truly worthy, by virtue of their education and their morality.[60] Admission to the *cadre supérieur* would remain, in other words, as selective as admission to citizenship. Such limited participation in this and other realms hardly qualified as power sharing, much less an education in public administration. Dakar as much as acknowledged both failures after World War II, when it abandoned the policy of *évolué* association for the doctrine of political assimilation for all educated Africans.

Dakar's postwar policy and ideology of association with respect to chiefs did help consolidate French authority in the countryside, although not as completely as Dakar had intended. As the continued protests of the new elite attest, association of chiefs did not reestablish the older generation's control over a new generation born under colonial rule. However, after 1918, chiefs in West Africa did not revolt again; instead, they loyally served the colonial administration, for a variety of reasons. First, their defeat during the war convinced them that rebellion would be fruitless. Second, the kind of association that chiefs were being offered differed substantially from that of the *évolués*. For the chiefs, association meant, not so much the empty "privilege" of sitting on councils in urban areas, or the right to take exams only to be rejected, but the opportunity to accrue real power and wealth as French intermediaries in the countryside. While ostensibly supervised by French administrators, these chiefs would have considerable freedom to act as they chose, as long as they collected the taxes and labor the local *commandant* demanded. French personnel was too scarce, after the war as before, to exercise any real control over the chiefs. In the interwar years, the French did not hesitate to give chiefs privileged access to new agricultural technology, capital resources, and land in an effort to use them, in keeping with their ideology, to introduce new farming methods in the countryside. Astute chiefs in the service of the French could amass personal fortunes. A final reason for collaborating was that, as Dakar had accurately realized, customary chiefs and other notables had suffered a real loss of authority because of social changes introduced by the French. Much like the colonial administration, they deeply resented the claims of a new younger generation to speak for the majority of Africans; these demands for assimilation threatened to detach the masses further from their traditional deference. For the old elite, therefore, association appeared to offer a way to stem the decline in their personal prestige.

These motives did not bode well for advancing the cause of civilization as defined by the French. Once entrenched in office, the old elite often took advantage of the very peoples whom they were supposed to be guiding, and enriched themselves at their expense. This flagrant abuse of power was particularly true under Carde. During his administration, the 2,200 canton chiefs employed in West Africa became notorious for their corruption and excessive labor demands.[61] Meanwhile, the councils and *communes*, deemed essential for educating these chiefs and for staying in touch with popular sentiment, had either never been organized or had served only to communicate the *commandant*'s wishes to the assembled notables. Indeed, as early as 1921, Merlin had admitted that the creation of *communes* was premature, and no effort was made to establish them in the 1920's.[62]

The councils of notables fared only slightly better. Also in 1921, the lieutenant governor of Guinea reported that none had been established in his colony because of the "insufficient evolution" of the chiefs in question. In 1924, the lieutenant governor of Dahomey insisted that councils of notables existed in every circle in his colony and that they were convened twice a year. But a mission of inspection criticized the governor for apparently resenting the chiefs' opinions when they disagreed with his own. Ten years later, in 1931, the colonies of Ivory Coast and Guinea had not created councils of notables, although every other colony had them. In a letter to the minister a year later, Dakar gave a positive assessment of the councils and their progress.[63] Nevertheless, Dakar's circulars belied this verdict: the governor general admitted that the efforts to allow Africans' participation in administering the country had not always been successful. At no point were the councils of notables permitted to become what Raymond Buell had predicted in 1926 on his visit to West Africa: "When each of the one hundred and fourteen circles of West Africa establishes such a council, the mechanism of criticism may become formidable."[64] As a result, the old elite, far from "assimilating certain modes of French thinking" and helping to uplift the rest of the population, continued to lose legitimacy in the eyes of their subjects. In this case, as with the *évolués*, Dakar's new ideology of promoting progress through association was patently at odds with the social and political realities of the 1920's.

Causing this egregious gap between what French ideology promised and the results obtained were certain contradictions in the way the association of the old elite was conceptualized in the first place. The measures taken by Merlin to respect the representative functions of the chieftaincy, including the creation of *communes* and assemblies of notables, could not possibly encourage the public education of chiefs. Despite Merlin's claims to the contrary, the December 4 decrees failed to endow the various assemblies with the powers to function as anything but mouthpieces for the administration. A circular drawn up by the lieutenant governor of the Sudan in 1921, regarding the new rural assemblies, and which Dakar subsequently distributed to all the governors as a model for their colonies, confirms that the Government General saw association as little more than an obligation to inform notables of their duties as determined by the colonial government.

> The Sudan is not a settler colony and the collaboration of the natives is indispensable to us. Up until now this collaboration has been obtained without difficulty by authoritarian means. But it would reveal a strange blindness to imagine that our native subjects will tolerate indefinitely such methods. The events of exceptional gravity that have occurred in various foreign colonies since the war demonstrate that upon attaining a certain degree of evolution, subjected races no longer accept being kept out of their government. This movement will occur in our colony and if we refuse to envisage it, if we do not prepare for it through a methodical and progressive participation of the most enlightened and influential elements in the administration of the territory, we will dredge between ourselves and the natives a chasm, which nothing will be able to overcome.[65]

Having made his plea for association on pragmatic grounds, the author then explained what he meant by "methodical and progressive participation." It amounted to "explaining" French policy to the most influential members of the community, who, having heard why the French were implementing certain measures, would presumably acquiesce more readily: "Our objectives are sufficiently elevated to be explained publicly without danger. All our efforts aim at improving the lives of our subjects and it is not apparent what interest we could have in hiding [this goal]. You know anyway that most of the ordinary difficulties of our administration derive from the ignorance of the natives and that it is enough to enlighten them to obtain their submission."[66]

Other inconsistencies were pointed out as early as 1921 by Lieutenant Governor Antonetti of Ivory Coast, when Merlin submitted the decrees of 1920 for comments to all his subordinates. Antonetti argued that the institution of councils as designed by Merlin could actually backfire. "Just as our authority would stand to gain from decisions based upon reasonable opinions [expressed by the chiefs]," he wrote Merlin, "it would stand to lose from requesting consultation and then ignoring the advice proffered." And, inevitably, Antonetti continued, chiefs would make complaints that the French would not be able to redress. Transforming chiefs and their councils into formal administrative bodies would cause them to lose immediately their legitimacy in the eyes of the population. Chiefs, he argued, were being consulted more by the administration anyway, as they evolved; to grant such consultations a legal existence would constitute a mere *trompe l'oeil*. He concluded by adding that chiefs were often the oldest and most conservative members of the community and therefore least apt to be the instruments of the progress that France aspired to achieve in West Africa. If anyone, the young *évolués* were best prepared to understand "the realism of our native policy." Until the administration could balance these two different groups, Antonetti warned, it would be impossible to form genuine assemblies.[67]

This critique had no impact on Dakar's thinking. Merlin went ahead and passed his reforms, and Carde continued to maintain that the French were forming an "intelligent aristocracy" and introducing "democratic measures" that were restoring "the social cohesion" of the community. Ironically enough, even as the French sought to strengthen chiefs through association, they continued to erode their authority in other ways. For example, a logical measure to have taken, as part of the new policy of power sharing and reconstitution of the traditional social armature, would have been to restore to chiefs at least some of their powers to punish criminal actions. Instead, a new revision of the 1912 decree on native justice, issued by Carde in 1924, removed such prerogatives where they still existed.[68] Although visibly at odds with the new more positive view of chiefs, this 1924 revision was in every other sense a continuation of earlier trends in judicial organization. It reaffirmed the necessity to uphold customary civil law.[69] And it completed the transfer, under way since 1903, of legal jurisdiction for criminal offenses from the chiefs to the French administration.[70] These reforms directly conflicted with the expressed postwar ideal of strengthening the traditional authority of Africa's indigenous elite.

The French were not entirely unaware of the gap between their promises and actual events. Although Merlin and Carde either were genuinely oblivious to, or else chose to ignore, the abuses by chiefs and their declining status and popularity, Carde's successor, Jules Brévié, understood the situation all too well. Upon taking office, he immediately declared that a "crisis" of the chiefs' authority existed in the countryside. This crisis was particularly upsetting not only to Brévié but also to Paris, because it forced them to confront the fact that chiefs, far from regaining their former ascendency over the population and helping civilization penetrate the masses, had become weaker under ten years of association. Such weakness meant that the new generation was no more "in hand" than it had been in the early 1920's.[71] Brévié, however, did not then question the fundamental assumptions or structure of association as defined by Merlin; nor did he advocate a new flexibility toward the *évolués*. He simply reiterated these assumptions and, in a new set of circulars, expanded the existing structure of association.[72] In the 1930's, Brévié decided that Merlin's legislation regarding *communes* had been too ambitious; he instituted new consultative councils at the village and canton level, in yet another attempt to ensure that chiefs stayed in touch with local sentiment. He also recommended that more attention be paid to selecting and educating chiefs. Such measures would, Brévié explained, restore the chieftaincy to its original representative function and would prevent abuses.[73]

This concept remained as flawed in the 1930's as it had been in the 1920's. Contrary to what Brévié maintained, chiefs, even with their restored councils, could not be "both the representatives of the ethnic collectivities and the agents of the administration whom they were required to obey." And even as the federal authority noted the problem of "an aristocracy that was not evolving quickly enough to retain control of the milieux which these chiefs were supposed to be guiding," the Government General continued to maintain that traditional notables remained the best instruments of the progress France wished to effect.[74] Respected but also taught by the French, these chiefs, Brévié insisted, could still become "animated by our thought, infused with our desire to assure a better future to the native."[75] To this end, administrators were to make sure that chiefs "had access to the new conditions of existence" that were developing around them. "Without this effort," Brévié warned his subordinates, "the evolution of the masses will precede that of their natural chiefs, and the chasm that already exists in some places between the new and the old generation will grow deeper. . . . Chiefs must be convinced . . . to precede the young along the path to progress, in order to maintain intact their prestige and their moral ascendency."[76] Such an outlook, for all its apparent emphasis upon progress, essentially sought to contain the consequences of the *mission civilisatrice* rather than recognize the social, cultural, and economic changes that colonial rule had engendered. Despite Brévié's insistence that chiefs could become ideal enlightened collaborators, accepted by their peoples as their "natural" leaders, no such evolution took place in the 1930's. Their authority continued to decline, and their abuses remained unchecked. French ideology and policy, however, refused to confront this reality.

This refusal is easily explained. In West Africa, association still offered sufficient advantages to the Government General for Dakar to turn a blind eye to the gap between its stated objectives and what was actually taking place. These advantages included the loyal allegiance of chiefs who had earlier revolted, and the containment of *évolué* demands. To have admitted that the chiefs were unable to represent both the French and the masses would have meant finding new intermediaries for administering the federation. The Government General understood that the only possible alternative intermediaries to these chiefs were paid French administrators or members of the new elite. The first option was unacceptable, for reasons of cost; the second was eliminated because, as Dakar realized, the new elite would have demanded a greater say in policy making than the chiefs they replaced. The only safe choice, when it came to preserving Dakar's authority intact, was to retain the old regime in office.

There was, however, another reason favoring the persistence of the doctrine of association, which will be examined in more depth in the next chapter. In the interwar years, Paris began to pressure Dakar to embark upon a more vigorous and more successful policy of *mise en valeur*. The federal authorities thus had a greater need to secure the loyalty of rural elites and shore up their prestige, for the implementation of *mise en valeur* would inevitably require an increase in taxes and labor requisitions from the local populations. As in the past, the French were in no position to extract these resources "directly"; they required African intermediaries. Precolonial chiefs appeared to be the obvious candidates in the 1920's, since they required minimal pay and were known to their subjects. Ironically, the very *mise en valeur* that these chiefs facilitated would only widen the chasm between the masses and chiefs that Brévié feared, and which the policy of association had originally been conceived to prevent.

Ever since the publication of Raymond Betts's *Assimilation and Association in French Colonial Theory, 1890–1914*, historians have been familiar with the theoretical content of the doctrine of association, as elaborated in France at the end of the nineteenth century. Recently, Gwendolyn Wright has shown how associationist ideas influenced colonial architecture and urban design in French Morocco, Indochina, and Madagascar between 1900 and 1940. Neither account, however, explored the relationship between the idea of association and the ideology of the *mission civilisatrice*. The example of French West Africa in the 1920's suggests that the rhetoric and policy of association had an important civilizing dimension from the outset.

Yet if association was always embedded in a larger civilizing discourse, the republican idea of the *mission civilisatrice* had not always invoked the concept of association—at least not in French West Africa. The development of this concept constituted an important shift in French ideology in the 1920's, compared to the prewar years, when no mention of the term occurred in Dakar. The changes signaled by the term "association," it is true, appear subtle enough. The new themes in Dakar's civilizing rhetoric—extending "democratic" privileges and "representative government"—remained as republican as the abolition of "feudalism" and emancipation from slavery that they replaced. Nevertheless, the face of tyranny and the means to combat it had changed. In the 1920's, "premature" demands for freedom had become civilization's greatest impediment; its newest obligation, gradual initiation into the modern democratic process through traditional structures and limited concessions to the *évolués*.

Such caution in approaching the civilizing process was not unprecedented in French West Africa. Education and the administration of justice had already been "adapted" to the African environment in the name of respect for existing institutions, and the French had always been wary of extending citizenship too rapidly. But there remains something significant about the shift in the realm of native policy which civilization through association represented. What disappeared was a certain commitment to the idea of universal man, everywhere equal in potential and deserving of emancipation. Within the various impulses of the *mission civilisatrice* between 1895 and 1914, racism and pragmatism had, of course, also been amply represented. Yet, compared to the interwar years, there had also been a current of egalitarian sentiment. Although French was still to be taught, barbaric custom to be banished, and medicine distributed, the era of large gestures was receding. Henceforth an important part of French civilizing efforts would be preoccupied with wooing the elite, traditional and modern. In West Africa as in France, an intensifying respect for hierarchy in all its forms—social, sexual, and racial—represented the Third Republic's true face in the 1920's.

CHAPTER 7

Civilization Through Coercion

HUMAN 'MISE EN VALEUR' IN THE 1920'S

If our subjects have shown a sincere willingness to break out of their atavistic laziness and misery, they are still far from attaining a modern rhythm of activity. There are even some who persist in the belief that they have earned the right to sloth, the moment they have put aside the minimal reserves for maintaining a vegetative life. We will make them understand that nobody has the power to escape from the law of work, and that any claim to personal freedom loses a great deal of its psychological value once the human collectivity, in the name of irresistible progress, whose elements or merits are not open to discussion, imperiously demands the integral development of all the resources that nature puts at its disposal.

— Governor General Jules Carde[1]

In 1905, the Government General of French West Africa had abolished the legal existence of slavery throughout its territories. In advocating the abolition of slavery, Dakar nevertheless failed to make clear what form of labor should replace it. Implicit in the 1905 decree was a belief in the superiority of free labor and the law of the marketplace; both beliefs were unquestioned tenets of liberal republicanism. Yet a pervasive feature of the French colonial system in West Africa was administrative recourse to forced labor, which the Government General made no effort to conceal. To the contrary, it insisted that use of force was required to help Africans progress; this justification was particularly evident in the 1920's, when a new demand in Paris for the *mise en valeur* of the federation encouraged Dakar to develop a coherent labor doctrine and regulate its labor practices. It is this theme of "civilization through coercion," especially as it emerged between 1918 and 1930, that this chapter explores.

Dakar's willingness to regulate the use of forced labor in the 1920's should have conflicted with the free-labor ideology that had led to the nonrecognition of slavery in 1905. Two racist beliefs helped mitigate this contradiction for the French. The first was the conviction that Africans, once they had filled their grain reserves for the coming year, refused to take on any further labor. The second was a belief that the French knew what was in the best interests of the colonized and could thus force Africans to cooperate in their plans, if the latter did not spontaneously offer their labor. Armed with these convictions, many French argued that coercion, though unpalatable, was often temporarily necessary to inculcate in the African an absent work ethic, without which the free-labor principle could not operate. In the face of an African labor shortage, Dakar also maintained that coercion alone would ensure sufficient manpower for essential civilizing projects, such as the construction of infrastructure and cash-crop cultivation. Since the development of railroads and production for export would benefit West Africa as much as France, the Government General reasoned, it had the right forcibly to mobilize Africans to work on both projects—as long as the worker was adequately protected.

The belief that France knew what was in the best interests of Africans was a by-product of industrialization in Europe. The overwhelming superiority of French technology to any in Africa convinced the French that they held a monopoly on civilization. The belief in African laziness also derived from the absence of industrial achievements in Africa comparable to those in the West. Confronted with their subjects' "failure" to exploit the economic potential of the federation, French officials attributed this situation to moral depravity. Both the apparent failure of freed slaves in the West Indies to prosper after emancipation, in the 1830's, and the "scientific" findings of French physical anthropology after 1850, encouraged the image of the lazy African; the wartime use of colonial labor combined with the growth of eugenic thinking and the flood of new immigrants in the metropole gave racist stereotypes another lease on life in the 1920's.[2]

Crucial as racist stereotypes were to French claims for the civilizing potential of forced labor, the concomitant insistence that such coercion was legitimate only if it did not harm the interests of the worker also needs explaining. This proviso was one important way in which republicans explained away the larger incongruity of democratic France resorting to forced labor. The timing of Dakar's decision to regulate forced labor, however, also reflected postwar France's intensifying interest in racial regeneration. The French sought to improve their own racial stock, and the same concern affected the policy of overseas administrators, especially as they became aware of just how scarce their African human resources were in the federation. The burgeoning pro-natalist and eugenics movements in France cut two ways for Africans. Both doctrines encouraged the idea that these workers were inferior to white workers, and therefore it was France's duty and right to coerce them into productivity. But these same doctrines also insisted, in theory at least, that France's African workers now had to be more adequately fed, paid, and vaccinated, so they would grow more numerous and more robust.

The French administration in West Africa was hardly the first "post-emancipation" state to suppress slavery only to justify and regulate other forms of compulsory labor.[3] Such behavior was typical of nineteenth-century industrializing societies, seeking both at home and in their colonies to transform existing modes of labor organization through law and state authority, and to adapt them to the new demands of a capitalist economy. These economies could not condone the personal tyranny and violence associated with slavery and the slave trade. They required, instead, a system of "free" labor enforced by an objective authority, in which workers internalized such supposedly absent values as self-discipline and temperance. The challenge in this context was to make workers do independently what the new capitalist economy necessitated. Faced with this challenge, European states, committed in theory to free labor, did not hesitate to resort to various coercive forms of social control to achieve the desired objective.[4] The same process can be seen in French West Africa between 1895 and 1930 in general, and in the 1920's in particular. Determined to integrate African producers into the cash economy, the Government General first refused to recognize slavery, then rationalized a system of forced labor designed to tie the African peasant to the world market.

'Mise en Valeur' in the 1920's

Most forms of forced labor in West Africa first came to be debated and regulated in the 1920's. Before then, it was taken for granted that using coercion fell within the purview of France's *mission civilisatrice*. Individual governors were left to take the initiative as they saw fit, and they were only occasionally reminded by Dakar that part of their duties was "to bring the population to increase production" and to "know how to force their subjects to get back to their agricultural tasks."[5] Local administrators regularly forced Africans to work as porters and to help build the railroads and roads in their circles.[6] This said, there were two exceptions to the prewar disinterest in labor regulation. The first were *prestations*, legalized in 1912 under Ponty, which were annual labor requisitions every African over the age of fifteen owed the administration; they were not to exceed twelve days per year. French citizens, the *évolués*, and Europeans in general were automatically exempt. The labor made available was to be used exclusively in the circle and devoted to small-scale public works of immediate interest to the community—roads, bridges, and the upkeep of local buildings. The administration was to make sure that fulfillment of an African's *prestations* never interfered with planting and harvesting. Those who could afford it could buy out of their *prestations*, thus furnishing the administration with a supplementary source of income. The French justified this particular alienation of liberty on the grounds that it served the community's immediate interests. In addition, *prestations* still existed in France and did not constitute an exorbitant infringement of the individual's rights.[7] The legalization of *prestations* formed a clear precedent for regulating federation-wide recruitment of Africans for infrastructure construction and private concessions in the 1920's.[8]

The second precedent occurred not in Dakar, but in Ivory Coast under the governorship of Angoulvant. Interim governor general for both AEF and AOF from 1918 to 1919, he had made a name for himself between 1908 and 1916 as "pacifier" and "developer" of Ivory Coast. At that time, Angoulvant had successfully defeated the local Baule population, who resisted French rule. He also became infamous in colonial circles for his outspoken belief that the French had to force Africans to grow certain cash crops, in order to help the local populations progress. To implement such a policy, he said:

> We must completely modify the black mentality in order to be understood. . . . Let us be honest: at present, the native is still detached from our institutions. . . . For a long time yet, it will thus be necessary for our subjects to be brought to progress against their will. . . . The role of the administration is a particular one. . . . It will involve the special intervention of our authority: we shall exercise this authority in essence to make Africans work, a notion they do not [yet] have.[9]

Along with the earlier regulation of *prestations*, Angoulvant's theories regarding labor anticipated many of the ideas that Dakar began to espouse more systematically in the 1920's. This time, however, the justification would occur at a federal rather than a local level and would emphasize the need to treat the forced laborer fairly. Several factors account for the Government General's specifying conditions under which coercion was legitimate. The state had experimented successfully during the war with mobilizing and allocating French and immigrant labor in France; this precedent paved the way for greater government intervention in metropolitan and colonial labor markets in the 1920's. The market for foreign labor, in particular, became increasingly "unfree" in France in this period.[10] A genuine desire to offer their subjects a better deal after their war contribution also counted for something. But underlying these factors was a more basic reason still: the emergence of a renewed emphasis upon *mise en valeur* in Paris and Dakar, as well as a changing concept of how to tap the federation's economic potential.

Before World War I, the Government General had been content to limit its development strategy to the construction of infrastructure and *assainissement*. The result had been, Roume's efforts notwithstanding, little real *mise en valeur*. Dakar's earlier attempts at development had not been a complete failure. Between 1902 and 1914, Senegalese peanut production expanded steadily as the railroad reached from its base in Dakar toward the Niger River. Palm oil and palm kernel production, which had long existed in Dahomey, continued to rise, although less dramatically than peanut exports during the same period.[11] Rubber exports buoyed the local budgets of Guinea and Ivory Coast until 1913, when world rubber prices collapsed and led to a decline in local production.[12] Outside these areas of commercial growth, however, there existed little new trade of which Dakar could boast in 1914. Contrary to early optimistic predictions, the railroad had not automatically created islands of civilization and prosperity wherever it penetrated.[13] Only in colonies that had ready access to ports and where a strong export-oriented marketing network was already in place did Roume's railroads generate the commodity production anticipated by the French. Most of the railroad system initially planned by Dakar, including the Senegal-Niger link, had not been built. On the eve of World War I, what the French still believed to be the Western Sudan's vast potential had not even begun to be developed.

Both Dakar's approach to and complacency regarding *mise en valeur* would change during the war. When hostilities broke out, members of the colonial lobby and the Colonial Ministry began to believe that the empire could provide France with the raw materials required by the war effort. This idea had led to the immediate enactment of *ravitaillement* in West Africa, under Van Vollenhoven's supervision. From this policy, it was a small step toward envisioning a whole new role for West Africa in the postwar metropolitan economy. A colonial conference organized by Colonial Minister André Maginot in 1917, to which administrators, businessmen with colonial interests, and politicians were invited, determined that West Africa should remain a producer of raw materials; it also insisted on increasing production of fatty oils and of cotton, cocoa, and timber. In this context, the need for rational development was emphasized even more than before the war. The conference recommended an expansion of public works, more scientific research into crop yields, modernization of African farming techniques, and greater investment in the social welfare of their subjects. Maginot's successor at the Ministry of Colonies, Henri Simon, created the department's first Direction of Economic Affairs, to plan postwar colonial development. Simon's successor, Albert Sarraut, further developed the principles of the Maginot Conference before the Chamber of Deputies in 1921, when he outlined his famous investment program for the rational development of France's overseas territories. Sarraut suggested that more than one billion francs be earmarked for investment in railways, ports, and irrigation in West Africa, as well as schools, health care, and research facilities; he failed, however, to offer a realistic plan for financing this program.[14]

Nothing came of Sarraut's investment plans; in the postwar depression, France turned to its colonies for funds, rather than the other way around. But the idea that West Africa could and should produce more did not disappear. From World War I to the Great Depression, the Colonial Ministry and the Direction of Economic Affairs reiterated this idea. Individual industries that would benefit from an increase in colonial commodities, and several new scientific organizations with an interest in agricultural research overseas, also lobbied the government for intensified *mise en valeur*.[15] Thanks to these pressures, colonial administrations everywhere in the 1920's adopted Sarraut's commitment to increase colonial productivity. In the process, they came to reconsider many of their earlier assumptions about expanding commercial exchanges. Nowhere was this more true than in West Africa. In addition to expanding infrastructure, the Government General now created specialized agricultural services in each colony.[16] More important, it determined that special attention would have to be paid to the individual producer. In practice, this would mean spending more on educating him, improving his health, and motivating and mobilizing him to grow the desired commodities.

Beyond a renewed interest in rational *mise en valeur*, a second factor helps explain the development of a labor policy in Dakar in the interwar years. This was the discovery that West Africa lacked not only the basic infrastructure for transporting its presumed potential wealth to sea but also the basic manpower to generate this wealth in the first place. Recruitment between 1914 and 1917 had exposed the extent to which the peoples of West Africa were impoverished and unevenly distributed among the member colonies. The presence of a sufficient number of healthy African workers to carry out a policy of colonial development in a given part of the federation could not be taken for granted. West Africa, in short, suffered from an even greater demographic crisis than France. For this reason, too, more intervention in every aspect of labor—productivity, availability and reproduction—was clearly required. The governor general most responsible for inaugurating Dakar's postwar labor policies was Jules Carde (1923–1930).

Carde arrived in Dakar with no illusions about state funding for *mise en valeur*. The challenge he faced was how to make the federation more productive by relying solely on its own resources. This challenge encouraged him to confront squarely the issue of African labor. Carde's background also predisposed him to take an interest in mobilizing African workers. Carde had served as Angoulvant's head of economic affairs in 1909–1910 in Ivory Coast, at the very moment Angoulvant was pioneering the forced cultivation of cocoa. Seven years later, he had been chosen by Van Vollenhoven as his secretary general. He had thus been intimately involved in the *ravitaillement* effort, which had also relied upon coercion to intensify African production of raw materials and foodstuffs. Carde's intense commitment to *mise en valeur* was evident in the public works program he supervised while in office. One priority was to continue the infrastructure projects envisioned by Roume and endorsed by Sarraut. He made remarkable progress on this commitment, despite the depleted finances of the Government General. In a period when personnel expenses continued to rise, Carde determined that public borrowing to help finance his objectives was impossible. Instead, he urged each member colony to restrict its administrative costs and to raise taxes, and thus use local funds for infrastructure projects that had been financed out of the general budget. These included, principally, shorter railways, wells, schools, and health care facilities. The general budget would be reserved for major public works essential to the federation's prosperity: the completion of intracolony railroads, especially the Thiès-Kayes line linking the port of Dakar to the Niger River; the dredging of ports; the improvement of the navigability of the Senegal and Niger Rivers; and work on the Niger River dams. These latter projects were designed to bring the hinterlands of the different coastal colonies, and the landlocked territories of Sudan and Niger, into the orbit of *mise en valeur*, primarily through cotton production.

Along with renewed emphasis upon public works, however, Carde stressed the need to consider the health, education, and working habits of the African producer—what Carde called the *mise en valeur* of West Africa's human resources:

> In all likelihood, the greatest portion of our future exports will come from the native producer, living less and less off of uncultivated produce and more and more off the product of his own labor. . . . Indeed the true interest of developing a permanent communications network, in fact that which in the last analysis justifies and guarantees the financial sacrifices required by such public works, is neither the relative natural richness of a particular area, nor the greater or lesser worth of its harvest, but the intensity and the quality of the labor that we can tap, not of course from an ignorant and denuded native, but from the same individual, once properly equipped and instructed.[17]

Carde developed these ideas in more detail in December 1925, before the members of the Council of the Government General. At that time, he voiced frustration at the assumption prevalent in the metropole that all that was needed to "amplify and activate the organization of the colonies, and thus to procure France the necessary raw materials to free it from foreign dependency" was billions of francs for infrastructure. Even if money were available, he explained, the lack of able-bodied men would prevent its being put to use:

> Possessing an area of 4.8 million km and a population of 13 million, that is to say 2.6 inhabitants per square km, it is impossible for West Africa to increase its production in raw materials and at the same time to constitute a physical plant in the short time spans often envisaged. . . . If one

considers that the population, whose native hardiness has been ruined by interminable wars, centuries of slave trade and periodic famine and epidemics, is further reduced on the one hand by the *tirailleurs* recruited by conscription—a small enough number granted, but that immobilizes a physical elite—and on the other by the farmers engaged in agriculture for export, and that it is obliged to feed itself as well, one is forced to admit that the number of workers available for public works projects is fairly limited.

And he continued, somewhat ominously:

The *mise en valeur* of a new country like West Africa must, in effect, take place according to a geometric progression. Local conditions subject this progression to an unvarying law, which must be discovered, then integrally applied without overstepping it. Those who are too impatient will not, as they think, restore the economic and financial health of our country. They will be cruelly deceived at the expense of criminal waste.

Carde added as one solution a repopulating of the country, "by giving to its starving inhabitants health and strength through a policy of 'full-stomachs.'"[18] "You know," he repeated in 1927, "that *faire du noir* is one of the principal goals that I have assigned myself in French West Africa."[19]

True to his words, Carde would spend much of his time in office trying to ensure that the production of cash-crop exports and the "production of men" would progress simultaneously. One result was that African health care and nutrition now figured more prominently on the Government General's agenda. Dakar had always attached special importance to the civilizing impact of public hygiene. But where the emphasis had once been on urban *assainissement*, it now shifted to preventing disease and lowering mortality rates among the African populations throughout the federation. This shift certainly echoed metropolitan trends; as we have seen, postwar anxiety about increasing and ameliorating the French race led Parliament to pass social hygiene measures that it had resisted before the war. A major circular from Colonial Minister Daladier to all governors general in 1924 illustrated the government's intention to take this tack overseas. Daladier stressed "the absolute necessity to extend as fully as possible to our colonies the services of preventive medicine, hygiene and assistance, whose principal goal is to assure the sanitary protection of the collectivities and to protect them from the causes of mortality or decay [*dépérissement*] which prevent the development of the native races."[20] In addition to combating such devastating diseases as syphilis, tuberculosis, leprosy, sleeping sickness, and malaria among the colonized, Paris innovated in another way. It demanded a shift from individualized curative medical care, based in hospitals, dispensaries, and maternities, to mobile medical units staffed by indigenous auxiliaries—doctors, midwives, nurses, vaccinators, and sanitary guards—supervised by Europeans. They would go directly to the masses and map the incidence of disease, innoculate and distribute serums, and demonstrate modern prophylactic methods and puericulture. Demographic statistics were also to be kept. Surveillance, and education and hygiene at home, held the key to the "sanitary control" and "physical regeneration of the races."[21]

Dakar, however, had not needed Paris to point the way. The reorganization of the AMI in 1912 had recommended that medical personnel tour their districts regularly for the same reasons. During the war, the demands for African manpower made prevention of the endemic and epidemic diseases and the fight against infant mortality among Africans a new priority of the Government General. At the same time, a drastic drop in the number of doctors in the federation—from around 100 in 1912 to 67 in 1921—also put health care back on the agenda.[22] Several new initiatives testified to this concern. One of the recruitment bonuses of 1918 was a new medical school for training African doctors and midwives. An African maternity was created in Dakar in 1919, and an Office of Social Hygiene in Dakar started in 1921.[23] Most revealing were two circulars by Merlin which anticipated every point Daladier raised. The ideal originally formulated by Roume of combining "hygiene and medical assistance" for Africans, Merlin noted, was impossible at the moment; the "least urgent" therefore had to be sacrificed to strategies for "conserving the race." Administrators were now to take seriously the *assainissement* of villages; there was to be only one hospital and maternity per colony; simple dispensaries and mobile medical consultations were to be the rule; doctors were to have cars at their disposal. Detailed instructions followed on prophylaxis against malaria (only in areas where Africans and whites cohabited), yellow fever, smallpox, typhus, leprosy, tuberculosis, dysenteries, sleeping sickness, and trachoma.[24]

Carde could not but approve these measures; indeed, he developed them in considerably more detail, and then was relentless in demanding that his subordinates act upon them.[25] He stressed improv-

ing African birthing methods and child care. French-trained midwives were to work with their traditional counterparts, not supplant
them; recognizing the need to educate mothers in their homes,
Carde instituted the same system of visiting nurses just started in
France.[26] Because of him, and with help from Paris, the number of
European doctors had risen to 188 by 1930. Credits for health care
rose from 10,310,930 francs in 1924 to 46,922,180 francs in 1930.[27]
Carde's overall approach to medical assistance nevertheless mirrored
his approach to public works: that is to say, more had to be done
with less. "Preventive and social medicine" could not occur at the
expense of "economic development." Thus colonies were to increase
health care expenditures, but to no more than 12 percent of their
budgets.[28] Expensive European doctors, while indispensable as su-
pervisors, were only a small part of the solution. Carde was suspicious of doctors; he accused them of refusing the social and mobile
role that Dakar was assigning them, preferring to stay in their dispensaries. Existing French and African personnel—teachers, administrators and their wives, engineers, *tirailleurs* and their wives, even
missionaries—could demonstrate modern prophylaxis as or more effectively. What were needed were more African auxiliaries trained
within each colony, who could take the message of preventive hygiene directly to villagers of similar ethnicity. It was up to the governors and local administrators, Carde repeated, to coordinate and
direct this essential effort.[29]

Improved health care for Africans had always been part of the
Third Republic's civilizing agenda in West Africa. While laudable in
principle, the Government General's sanitary policy had been self-
serving and little had genuinely benefited its subjects. Dakar's postwar attitude toward health care was, if anything, less disinterested—
although for that very reason there also now existed greater potential
that something concrete would actually be done for Africans. In the
end, however, Carde's greater emphasis upon improving the "quality
and quantity" of the African races imposed one more responsibility
on French administrators while giving them little incentive and inadequate means to comply. The 1920's saw a major change in the
orientation of African medical assistance, but with few immediate
results for those Dakar most wished to reach: Africans living far
from a dispensary.[30]

Meanwhile, the same search for expanded manpower that informed its hygiene and medical care directives also led the Govern-

ment General to formulate guidelines on African labor. These were
not intended to render existing forms of forced labor obsolete. In the
interwar period, as before the war, no one in the colonial administration questioned France's right to mobilize African labor forcibly—
it was still assumed that Africans were lazy and incapable of understanding where their own interests lay. Rather, the purpose of such
guidelines was twofold. They were to compel Africans who had remained outside the export economy to contribute to the *mise en valeur* of their territories. Only then would additional funds be available for social investment. And they were to make more efficient
the forms of forced labor practiced before and during the war, to ensure that Africa's most precious resource was not wasted. The only
innovation was that the need to inculcate in Africans "the universal law of labor" now became an articulated tenet of French civilization ideology in West Africa.

In addition to further regulation of both *prestations* and the
forcible recruitment of African workers for public works, this rationalization and regulation took two forms, which will be examined
below: compulsory cash-crop cultivation, and forced labor for private enterprises. Both were the object of governmental directives in
1924–1925; at this same time, but independent of Dakar, inspectors
in the federation also began to debate labor conditions in West Africa. A dialogue developed between the inspectors and the Government General on the proper way to administer labor in West Africa.
As the first comprehensive statements of the colonial administration's position on coercion, Dakar's regulations and the reports of
the missions of inspection provide a valuable look at French attitudes on force as part of the civilizing mission in the 1920's.

Compulsory Cash-Crop Cultivation: The Case of Cotton Production

Although the actual incidence of coercion by the French in West
Africa is impossible to quantify in the 1920's, the persistence of
prestations indicates that forced labor continued everywhere in the
upkeep of local roads and administration buildings. The promulgation of directives encouraging cotton cultivation and legitimating
the use of force suggests, moreover, an upsurge in coercion wherever
this crop was tried out in the 1920's. Finally, forced labor for infrastructure and on European-owned concessions in this period seems

to have most affected colonies with either labor shortages or labor excesses. Areas with low population density would almost certainly encourage coercion; areas where a surplus of manpower was believed to exist would serve as a recruiting ground for those same labor-poor colonies. Three colonies in particular fit one or more of these descriptions, and they appear to have been the ones where coercion was most prevalent: Ivory Coast, the Western Sudan, and the recently created colony of Upper Volta.[31] The administration resorted to force in Ivory Coast because of a chronic labor shortage, a perceived enormous cash-crop potential, and rich forest reserves. The Western Sudan and Upper Volta were susceptible to heavy coercion because of their suitability for cotton production and supposed manpower excess, respectively. The following overview of statements on cotton production reveals how the Government General justified compulsory cash-crop cultivation in the 1920's.

Cotton was one of the cash crops most in demand by the metropole after the war, and expectations for its successful introduction in West Africa were greatest. Indeed, the idea of expanding cotton cultivation in the African interior had already led, between 1918 and 1923, to grandiose plans for irrigating the Niger Valley under Carde's predecessor in office, Martial Merlin.[32] During that period, a private consortium of cotton interests put forth a concept of building dams and a system of irrigation canals along the Niger. This consortium was convinced that, once the river was regulated, the Western Sudan could become a vast cotton plantation capable of making France self-sufficient in what had become an increasingly expensive imported commodity. Merlin had supported this *politique de l'eau* in 1920, as a way of developing an untapped West African resource and the logical complement to the federation's railroad network. Funds for the project had been included in Colonial Minister Albert Sarraut's plan for *mise en valeur* of the empire.[33]

As the above description suggests, the Niger Valley project was in the Roume tradition of *mise en valeur* through large-scale infrastructure. Carde, though committed to public works, was initially hostile to the project. The whole point of the irrigation scheme, Carde argued, was to make the African more productive. If this was the case, it made more sense to raise the peasant's standard of living than to "offer ourselves the luxury of useless and expensive programs, and then have to eat our words."[34] Considerable pressure must have been brought to bear on the governor general to change his mind, because within a year he had agreed to go forward with the proposed construction. Over the next six years he would allocate fifty-two million francs from the federal reserves to its completion.[35] Carde nevertheless insisted on experiments in rice farming, too. He also declared that if no cotton were ever harvested in the Niger Valley, he would still complete the works in question in an effort to free the peoples of the interior once and for all from the misery of famine. He optimistically envisioned the day that rice cultivation in the valley would eradicate starvation, help repopulate the hinterland, provide additional manpower to develop the coastal colonies, and facilitate increased production of oleaginous crops in the Sudanese zones by eliminating the need to grow any foodstuffs there.[36]

Carde's initial rejection of the Niger project offers not so much a lesson in altruism as a concrete example of his approach to making the federation more profitable. In labeling the Niger project wasteful, the governor general was not contesting the validity of its purpose—cotton cultivation. Indeed, Carde issued his own circular stressing the need for increased cotton production. Rather, Carde was simply contesting Merlin's means to that end. Limited financial and human resources, and unrelenting pressure from Paris to transform Africa into the supplier of raw materials, were facts of life in Dakar in the 1920's.[37] Carde thus determined early on that the best way to increase production, in the short term, was to work within the existing framework of African peasant agriculture.

Within a year of taking office, Carde sent out a major circular "organizing the production of textiles in French West Africa." He began by noting that Sarraut had given priority to cotton production, and so Dakar had formulated guidelines for French administrators in the West African savanna, where production would naturally be concentrated. The completion of the Thiès-Kayes-Niger railroad the year before, linking the Niger River to the Atlantic Ocean at Dakar, had finally created, Carde noted, the means for bringing the interior into international commerce. However, the railroad alone would not "provoke the continuous production of cotton in this country." Coordinated measures were necessary if the local peasant, who for centuries had grown cotton to satisfy his own needs, was to produce the quality and the quantity of cotton sufficient for French industry. Motorized transportation to the railroad and a proliferation of accessible marketing centers, where cotton could be sorted and sold at "fair" prices, were prerequisites that local administrators should do their utmost to encourage. Once these conditions were met, Carde noted optimistically, not only would cotton tonnage for export increase; a parallel rise in Africans' buying European cotton cloths could be expected, as local producers sold more and more of their own cotton in exchange for manufactured goods. Local governments should research seed selection, to determine which strains were best suited to their circles.[38]

These prescriptions all involved ways the administration could encourage production by easing access to markets. Noticeably absent were scientifically based recommendations for improving yields, or alterations in primitive farming methods.[39] This was because Carde's primary assumption was that it was possible to "draw from native cultivation," without modifying traditional farming methods, a much greater yield of cotton than the few hundred tons produced:

> It is incontestable that the areas devoted to this industrial plant can be largely extended without any great changes by the farmer. I am certainly not suggesting that these extensions occur at the expense of foodstuff production. Indeed, as it is, the native usually alternates cotton plants with his food plantings. It will suffice to increase both if these two cultivations are associated in a greater proportion than is currently the practice.

A crucial factor in the increased production Carde had in mind, in other words, was greater effort by the Africans themselves. This immediately raised the question of whether such an effort could be taken for granted, even if all the proper incentives were adopted to secure it in the first place. Carde tended to doubt it:

> The present organization [of native societies], which generally rests upon patriarchy, is particularly resistant to modern concepts of intensive production. The Sudanese farmer is not, in the true sense of the word, a producer. If the export of agricultural products has increased since the reign of *la paix française*, it is because the need to pay his taxes, on the one hand, and the attraction of European merchandise that has been offered to him in most places, on the other, have induced the black man to sell an ever increasing portion of his harvest to the merchant, but without modifying his habits or his way of life. His capacity for work, which is mediocre, has not appreciably increased.[40]

His conclusion posed a dilemma: how to break down this resistance, which meant certain failure. In a section entitled "Action upon the native in view of the development of production," Carde rejected coercion, only to revalidate it later. His words deserve to be quoted at length, because they illustrate not the crudeness of French justifications of forced labor—indeed, if anything, Carde's analysis reveals a sophisticated understanding of the limited ends that coercion could usefully serve—but the good-faith belief that certain conditions legitimated coercion.

> To increase [the native's capacity for labor] it has often been suggested that administrative regulations be instituted to force the native to produce. The least that can be said about this legislated coercion is that it is ineffectual. First, because it conflicts headlong with our own ideas of what constitutes personal liberty and second, for reasons that too often are neglected and that are of a geographical nature. The Sudan is not an island! It is a relatively populous hinterland, bordered by foreign colonies some of which have significant labor needs. And just because the reasons that used to cause the peoples of the Niger and the Volta frequently to migrate have since disappeared, there is no reason to believe that their current tendency to settle down would persist in the face of administrative measures that directly challenged their own customs. There is every reason to believe that, instead of the abundant labor that we had hoped to acquire in this manner, a vast migratory movement toward Gold Coast and Nigeria would quickly manifest itself. Thus regulated coercion cannot be the instrument by which the African native is brought to respect, better than he does today, the universal law of labor.[41]

Carde's reasons for rejecting a regulated use of coercion to help Africans "better respect the law of labor" are revealing. Although he mentions that coercion would be an affront to "our ideas of personal liberty," his main objection was that force would be counterproductive. His words suggest that excessive reliance on coercion was characteristic of the past, and that one of his principal aims was to discourage such practices in the future. However, if systematic violence were to be avoided, there were times when coercion was both legitimate and recommended:

> Sometimes the native, victim of his own carelessness, restricts his plantings to the point where they no longer suffice to feed him. . . . It is therefore necessary to try and improve his food intake, and if, in so doing, we run up against his indolence, it behooves us to force him to create food reserves. . . . Motivated by the strictly humanitarian goal of protecting the native against his own nature, such intervention is justified every time the African in question is capable of furnishing the additional effort necessary to procure the supplementary income to improve his present condition, and as long as this intervention is sufficiently explained, and does not exceed his capacity for understanding.[42]

The 1924 circular confirms the combination of racist and liberal assumptions in French thinking at the time. Although Carde accepted the stereotype of the lazy African, this did not prevent him from applying the principles of economic liberalism to African labor, once it had been forcibly mobilized. One classic tenet of free-labor ideology was a belief that the free market would ensure equitable remuneration and decent working conditions. These fair prices, and the material rewards to which they gave access, provided the incentive to work harder and better. Carde's insistence that forced labor in West Africa prove remunerative to the farmer subjected to its provisions reflected this ideology. His very emphasis upon the notion that fair prices be paid for crops grown under compulsion suggests that the Government General's long-term objective remained a free-labor economy in which the self-directed laborer worked to satisfy ever-expanding wants.

Carde aired his views on coercion more frankly in his reply to an inspector on mission in 1926. This answer further illustrates that Carde condoned selective coercion not only for cash-crop cultivation but also for several measures necessary for *mise en valeur*, in good faith that it would help the African progress. Carde began by asserting that it had become a commonplace to say that the African did not like to work. What, then, should the administration do when such laziness threatened to jeopardize works of public interest? In this situation, the answer had already been given, not by France, but by the League of Nations. Carde pointed out that this august body, which expressed "the will of all civilized nations in pursuit of a more generous humanity," had stipulated in 1926 that "the colonial power undertakes to prohibit forced or obligatory labor, except for public works and essential services and in return for an equitable remuneration." This statement was the international recognition of the law of labor, which no country concerned with the future of the "retarded" peoples under its tutelage could ignore without danger. This law should, if necessary, be the point of departure for a salutary obligation to work; such an obligation, he added, was no different from all the other obligations that an educator must impose, or else fail at his mission. Moreover, conceived in the best interest of the African, this coercion could only enhance his life by making possible the completion of public projects from which he would be the first to benefit. To speak of compulsory labor or forced labor in this context was an exaggeration: "Too often it is forgotten that, in our civilized countries, the harsh necessities of life impose different constraints from those that a generally mild and generous nature imposes upon the native. In organized societies, man must work to survive, and this obligation, even though it is written in no law, weighs as heavily upon us as if it were."[43]

Carde then argued that "this same coercion is no less justified when it is a question of reacting against the native's lack of foresight, in order to induce him to cultivate crops" from which he could benefit. There had already been numerous examples of "the beneficial effect of our intervention in this direction among peoples" whose inertia "was condemning them to the most precarious existence." Ivory Coast was a case in point, "where the native today is accumulating considerable profits from cocoa cultivation, to which he has enthusiastically given himself over, but which had to be imposed by force at the outset." Compelling Africans to work for private companies was similarly justified. There could not be, of course, any question of "forced labor," with all the excesses and brutal obligations that this term conjured up. Rather, "it was simply a matter of ascertaining whether the administration did not have the duty to interest itself in that important part of the *mise en valeur* of new countries, which the efforts of settlers and merchants constituted, the duty to interest itself in an active way, by actually intervening if necessary, to help the latter procure the element necessary to help them succeed."[44] Indifference by the administration, in such a situation, could condemn several praiseworthy efforts to failure. Here, too, the administration would be wrong not to interfere, so long as the labor thus procured was guaranteed proper treatment. There is a certain irony in Carde's justification, for the League of Nations certainly never intended to sanction the use of force to provide labor for private enterprises or for cash-crop cultivation. As we shall see, both forms of obligation would be condemned in 1930 by the very body of opinion in whose name Carde was authorizing them.

Such an open discussion of forced labor was new in the 1920's. It was undoubtedly the result of Dakar's attempt to satisfy the metropole's sudden demand for raw materials, without ruining the labor resources necessary for subsequent *mise en valeur*. As Carde put it at the beginning of the 1924 circular, "it is necessary to foresee and organize future [production], while extracting the utmost possible from the present." Others, however, also addressed the issue of forced crop production after the war; one of the most important of these, as the above exchange of views suggests, was the colonial Inspectorate. Between 1918 and 1932, many more colonial inspectors were sent on mission to West Africa than before the war. Their reports provide invaluable information on how local governments implemented Dakar's circulars exhorting them to increase production; for, if Paris was pressuring Dakar, the Government General was unquestionably pressuring its subordinates for quick results. For example, the 1924 cotton circular was followed by another two years later that recalled its basic points; a further directive went out in 1930.[45] More generally, all circulars from the minister relating to *mise en valeur* were passed on to the individual lieutenant governors, with comments by the governor general. The results of this pressure were not what Dakar had ostensibly requested. Cotton production went up only marginally; meanwhile, force was used indiscriminately, with disastrous consequences for the local populations. The peoples of two colonies in particular suffered the most in the interwar period: Upper Volta and Ivory Coast.[46]

Upper Volta not only belonged to the Sudanese savanna earmarked by Carde as suitable for cotton. It also had a reputation as a densely populated colony whose "surplus" labor could be exported to neighboring labor-poor colonies with no ill effect. Two missions of inspection visited the colony between 1925 and 1932.[47] The second, led by Inspector Sol, discovered that none of the abuses identified by his predecessor had been corrected. For nine years, Inspector Sol wrote sarcastically in his final summation, the colony of Upper Volta had had the privilege of being governed by a man of action, Lieutenant Governor Hesling. He was driven by a single idea: to make the empire supply the metropole with certain raw materials, particularly cotton, that France was currently buying on foreign markets.[48] This ambition in itself was not, the inspector argued, to be condemned. What was unacceptable was the way Hesling and his successor had tried to achieve this objective. The governor had sanctioned full-scale use of force to make the Africans under his control grow not only cotton but also peanuts, sisal, and kapok, all at the expense of their own foodstuffs. Such crops were being grown not on private plots, but in collective fields known by the Africans, tellingly, as *champs du commandant*. Finally, the administration also required that farmers take the harvests to specific trading posts, to be sold at a fixed price, usually arbitrarily low.[49] If anyone refused, he was punished by the *indigénat*. A scandalized Sol wrote:

The high administration decides to intensify the cultivation of cotton and to hand the crop over to the representatives of European merchants; [it then] holds a palaver in which good advice alternates with threats; cotton must "yield." If these suggestions are not followed, the cultivation of the crop is then declared either a *prestation* or a public service—the illegality of such obligations does not, incidentally, seem to bother anyone. If the cotton is not forthcoming, the result is the same everywhere: punishment. It doesn't matter what the natives think . . . that they regard this as a new tax. It does not matter that to furnish this quota they neglect their own millet. . . . He "yielded" what he was supposed to. . . . It is a regime of tyrants and all tyrants are far from being good ones.[50]

Meanwhile, he concluded, there existed an almost infallible legal way of obtaining what was desired: to offer to pay for the service solicited.[51]

This conclusion suggests that Sol was moving away from the notion that forced labor in any form was acceptable. Subsequent statements belie this impression and provide further insight into the racism that permeated official thinking. If adequate remuneration did not induce Africans to work, then outright requisition was legitimate on one condition—that it be surrounded by greater guarantees:

The moral right to use coercion [is] the automatic corollary to the idea of colonization. . . . Colonial rule rests upon an act of violence. Its only justification lies in the intention to substitute a more enlightened authority for the one in place, one capable of conducting the conquered peoples to a better existence. . . . We have committed ourselves to this task. . . . However, reliance upon the African's self-interest alone does not suffice [to achieve the stated objective]. New needs have not appeared, because the values of our two civilizations are not the same and we wish to substitute our own for theirs. This result can only be achieved by exerting pressure upon individual actions. Such pressure is legitimate, on the sole condition that it is in the best general interest as well as that of the natives.

Sol ended his report to the minister with a plea for a return to legality, to avoid a repeat of Hesling's regime: "It is better, from every point of view, even from that of world opinion, to exercise loyally and with caution a coercion recognized as necessary and rigidly regulated, than to display a façade of liberalism, behind which an infinitely heavier and more odious arbitrariness can run rampant."[52]

Ivory Coast was also repeatedly criticized for the brutality of its compulsory cotton production in the 1920's. In 1918, the first of many inspections exposed a system of administrative intervention that compromised rather than furthered, as the lieutenant governor himself claimed, the "generous goals of France's civilizing mission"; this situation would not change during the next fifteen years, despite repeated calls to order.[53] Inspector Kair discovered that Lieutenant Governor Antonetti was forcing the producers in the north to grow cotton in collective fields, instead of their own food crops, and to sell it at artificially low prices fixed by the administration, in collusion with a representative of one of the trading firms. Such procedures, Kair concluded, were nothing less than a kind of state management that recalled the arbitrary methods of the concessionary companies; these methods, he added, had long since been condemned. Far from making the well-being of the African its central preoccupation, the administration seemed primarily interested in ensuring that taxes were paid. The questions of porterage, and of whether the price the producer received for the crop he had been forced to grow was sufficient, were secondary. The lamentable consequences of such an outlook included the fact that the African worker had nothing to eat when he returned home; that he did not have enough money to buy anything from the trading post where he went to trade in the first place; and that the producer who really planted and harvested his crop ended up working exclusively for the collectivity, which went against the individualistic traditions of the peoples in question. The crowning irony was that the administration's goals for industrial production were not even being met. Such policies, Kair pointed out, were sacrificing the long-term development possibilities of the colony for marginal short-term gains.[54] Was it not sad, he queried, to realize that the victim of such policies had begun to consider himself "less our associate than our slave"?[55]

Kair went on to express his outrage that such a regime had been allowed to come into existence. Its every facet confounded traditional French economic ideas, as well as those regarding native policy. Did the administration think that it could oblige the native to undertake other tasks than those the African himself had chosen, once he paid his head tax and fulfilled the *prestations*? Did it believe that Africans had to sell their products at an arbitrarily low price that had nothing to do with supply and demand?[56] If so, the lieutenant governor was wrong. There was ample legislation on when force was permissible in the public interest and the interest of civilization. Antonetti's coercive policies had not, however, been included. Nor was it likely that they ever would be. Although nothing was easier for the administration than to legalize measures it deemed appropriate for the interests involved, the practices in question here would be impossible to reconcile "with the conception that French public opinion, the Parliament and the government all have of the policy we should follow with regard to the native populations."[57] According to this conception, and here Kair did not go so far as Carde, the administration could only encourage the African to produce indirectly, through the payment of taxes and the creation of new needs and wants. This latter goal would be achieved when the local merchants decided, as happened everywhere else, to go to the producer himself, rather than remain in the *chef-lieu* and rely upon the administration to force the African to come to them.[58]

Like Sol's reports, Kair's attest to the existence of widespread abuse in the cultivation of cotton in West Africa. Confronted with the same evidence, however, both Inspectors displayed more or less the same attitude as Carde toward forced labor: that coercion was legitimate as long as it benefited the colonized. Indeed, the substance of the inspectors' critique was not that compulsory cash-crop cultivation was in and of itself immoral—not even Kair drew that lesson—but, rather, that the ends to which coercion was being put in these instances did not justify the means. Although this emphasis reflected a genuine concern for the well-being of their subjects, it also conveniently coincided with France's own long-term economic interests in West Africa. It was more desirable and efficient to have Africans producing cotton on their own, and at prices high enough to allow them to consume imported French goods, than to have to continue forcing them to grow cash crops. This market integration would never take place if the French continued to mistreat their labor as the inspectors had documented, or if the Africans were diverted from food production to the point that their health suffered.

Yet what made good sense to the inspectors on mission made less to the governors in the field, for one reason in particular: in colonies like Upper Volta and Ivory Coast, there was no market into which Africans could be "benignly" coerced. This absence helps explain why so many abuses were occurring there. With no indigenous trading network to tap into, the lieutenant governors of those colonies had two choices when it came to *mise en valeur* in the interwar years. They could either have waited, as Kair recommended, for merchants to come to the producer; such a development was dependent upon the construction of roads and the arrival of the automobile. Or they could force Africans to produce the desired commodity and

themselves organize its sale and distribution; this use of coercion, if
it went beyond the spirit of Carde's circular, did not go against its
letter, since the governor general had not explained how local administrators should behave without a viable marketing system.[59]
Given the pervasive belief that Africans did not wish to work, the
lieutenant governors predictably took the second option. The obligation to grow cash crops for the administration also often appeared
as the only guarantee that "lazy" Africans would be able to pay their
taxes. Antonetti argued that an "abusive" use of compulsion was the
only policy worthy of France for this very reason—despite the fact
that it lacked, and probably would continue to lack, a legal basis.[60] In
reply to Kair's criticisms, he said:

> May I continue to use temporarily and until the necessary evolution has
> taken place, the methods that have worked to date to ensure that the na-
> tives have sufficient funds to pay their taxes and increase their produc-
> tion and commercial activity, or must I abandon them immediately at the
> risk of seeing a drop in local tax receipts—a decline that would obviously
> in turn slow down or bring to a halt altogether certain public works,
> roads, etc., as well as the continuing expansion of such social assistance
> programs as health care and education—and resign myself to reducing my
> budget? Needless to say the punishments that I would then be meting out
> under the *indigénat*, for all those who defaulted on their taxes, would
> hardly take the place of the receipts lost because of the lack of foresight
> by a population incapable of procuring on its own enough money to cover
> its obligations.[61]

Antonetti's attitude indicates that the questions that the high administration was beginning to ask regarding compulsory cash-crop
cultivation had little relevance for those administrators in colonies
that lacked a tradition of export agriculture. Under these circumstances, the inspectors' conviction that regulation would prevent the
excesses uncovered in Ivory Coast and Upper Volta was illusory. In
1930, these officials nevertheless saw their wish for greater regulation of coercion finally realized. A ministerial decree regulating
"obligatory public labor" listed for the first time the kinds of forced
labor that the government considered legal, including compulsory
cash-crop cultivation for two purposes, education and experimenta-
tion. Both forms required prior approval from the governor general
before they could be instituted.[62] This decree was the French government's definitive judgment on legitimate force in cash cropping
until 1946, when, in conformity with the recommendations of the

Brazzaville Conference, another decree formally abolished all forms of coercion in West Africa.

Given the timing of its passage, one is tempted to argue that the 1930 law was Paris's response to the Colonial Inspectorate's reports being filed throughout the 1920's. More likely, however, pressure from the International Labor Office (ILO) induced the government to act.[63] In 1926, that bureau had decided to investigate the extent to which slavery was still practiced throughout the world. This investigation was later broadened to include research into forms of forced labor, particularly in the European colonies. After four years and several conferences, the ILO drew up an international treaty condemning certain forms of forced labor—including compulsory cultivation programs—and encouraging its signatories to abolish all coercion within five years. The French along with the Portuguese refused to sign the treaty. Represented by the now more cooperative Blaise Diagne, France claimed that the treaty favored Great Britain, whose territories in West Africa were more advanced economically and much more populous than its own. In order, however, not to appear too illiberal compared to London, Paris promptly issued its own decree regulating forced labor in general, and compulsory cash-crop cultivation in particular, in its colonies.[64]

Forced Labor and Private Enterprise: The Example of Ivory Coast

A second form of coercion, which also underwent legitimation and regulation in West Africa in the 1920's, was used to recruit African workers onto European-owned concessions; this practice, like compulsory crop cultivation, had long existed in certain parts of West Africa without any legal foundation. It was particularly prevalent in the Sudan and Ivory Coast, two notoriously underpopulated regions toward which French capital began to gravitate in the postwar years; and in Upper Volta, which administrators counted on to provide migrant labor to the cocoa farms and timber companies of Ivory Coast.[65] The most important indication that Dakar's attitudes toward this form of coercion were also changing was the adoption of the first labor code in 1925, instituting a uniform system of individual wage contracts whose provisions the administration was to oversee and enforce.[66] The official aim of this code was to regulate conditions for Africans working on European farms or concessions.

It established for the first time a standard type of individual written contract, which spelled out the respective legal rights and obligations of each party.

Like Carde's circular on cotton cultivation, the labor code of 1925 represented a new, but incomplete, clarification of the Government General's position on the use of forced labor in West Africa. The code appeared to be an attempt to move toward a free-labor market, since it explicitly stipulated that the contracts were to be voluntary. But the code did not actually deny administrators the right to recruit wage laborers by force in the face of labor shortages, and many clauses in Carde's decree seemed designed with forced labor in mind. This ambiguity suggested that the new legislation's primary purpose was not to end compulsory wage labor but to rationalize labor recruiting for private employers and to improve working conditions for Africans on European farms and concessions. Once again, the Government General made clear that it considered such coercion compatible with France's civilizing mission, as long as the workers were fairly paid and well treated.

The decision to create a work code in West Africa in 1925 was a specific response to heightened demands for wage labor by Europeans in the colony. With the adoption of the Niger irrigation project and a new awareness of the economic potential of Ivory Coast, French entrepreneurs began to consider investing in West Africa on a greater scale than ever before.[67] As early as 1920, however, they expressed concern over the availability of African workers, without whom their enterprises—which were to consist largely of cotton, cocoa, and forest plantations—were doomed to failure. These concerns were not unfounded, since the areas in which they proposed to settle were underpopulated. The Niger Valley, which was expected to produce record tonnages of cotton, had an estimated population of only 310,000 farmers.[68] The forest zone of Ivory Coast suitable for cocoa production and timber harvesting was also labor-poor. Moreover, cutting and transporting timber was backbreaking work and unlikely to attract volunteers. Exacerbating this situation were the meager wages the European companies offered. Meanwhile, the one area with manpower, the Mossi *réservoir d'hommes*, was already freely directing its "surplus" labor to work on African-owned cocoa farms in Gold Coast. Wages were considerably higher in that colony compared to Ivory Coast, and the workers were not subject to *prestations* and other forms of corvée labor.[69] Finally, in the same areas where European settlers hoped to invest, they would directly compete with the administration for labor, as the Government General pursued its expansion of public works.

Confronted with these impediments to labor recruitment, private enterprises did not hesitate to demand official intervention to secure them the workers they needed to guarantee a return on their investment. It was the administration's responsibility, they insisted, to reroute the migrant labor away from the British and into the French territories, and to mobilize the underutilized labor of the local inhabitants for their benefit.[70] The local government should also provide redress for desertion by employees, which they claimed was a chronic problem among naturally "lazy" African workers. As one sympathetic colonial official put it:

> It is desertions that at this time make native labor so unreliable. The true cause of such desertions is not to be found either in the at times excessive demands of the employers, or the supposed inadequacy of the salaries, which today are fair. They seem to derive almost solely from the native indolence of the blacks, which encourages them to break their contracts signed under moral pressure, whose benefits they don't understand.[71]

Despite the potential conflict of interest between its own labor needs and those of European settlers, Dakar proved sympathetic to the labor concerns expressed by private French businessmen. The latter could play an important role in making the federation more productive, particularly in the absence of any government funds. "The indigenous populations," a report drawn up in Dakar in the early 1920's maintained, "are incapable of developing their country alone . . . their negligence too often leads them to cultivate land insufficient for obtaining the produce necessary for satisfying their yearly needs. Certain tribes suffer famines every year as a result. To obtain the desirable results, a close collaboration between European (capital and brains) and native (labor) will thus be required for several years to come." This collaboration would eventually give way to *mise en valeur* by the African himself. But the African would first have to be "brought [in his own interest] to our side, abandoning the miserable existence he leads to learn the necessity of work that will procure him a better life." Dakar also agreed that the African worker was unreliable and needed to be taught greater discipline. All these factors encouraged the Government General to begin drafting a labor code in 1923 (finished in 1925), one of whose principal functions was to "grant employers a certain security against the employee who did not feel like staying on the job."[72]

In keeping with the administration's self-perceived role as tutor to the "childlike" races of West Africa, however, the new code had another function: to ensure that "the legitimate rights, well-being and security of the laborers," as well as those of the employers, were protected. As Carde explained to the Council of the Government General in 1924, he had been surprised when he arrived in Dakar to find that, despite the large concessionary companies in the Western Sudan and Ivory Coast in need of abundant wage labor, no regulation existed regarding working conditions. This sudden interest in workers' rights can, like the new instructions regarding cash-crop production, be attributed to Dakar's heightened awareness that it could not afford to waste its precious human resources through ill-treatment. An analysis of the new code's provisions nevertheless reveals the administration's definition of those rights. Freedom not to work was certainly not one of them. "The goal of this *projet de réglementation de travail*," a member of the governor general's council indicated, "was to bring certain particularly backward populations of West Africa to civilization through work, and especially to make them understand that the law of labor is the basis of all progress."[73]

The provisions of the code fell into two groups: those that satisfied the settlers' primary demands, and those that protected the workers. Among those in the first group, legally regulating private requests for labor posed considerably more difficulties than did discouraging desertion once a contract had been signed. To solve the latter tendency, Dakar instituted the system known as the *pécule*, which sanctioned withholding a portion of salaries owed until the contract in question had expired.[74] The *pécule* system was designed to keep Africans working. It also created a fund from which the employer could automatically collect fines. Lastly, it was to be remitted to the chief in the circle from which the worker had been recruited, and the chief would make it over to its rightful owner when he returned. In this way, the French hoped to secure a steady and disciplined work force, prevent vagrancy, and ensure that taxes were paid. The French legitimated holding a portion of Africans' salary on the grounds that the African often spent his money on useless goods while on the job, thus winding up with nothing to show for his labor. The *pécule*, it was argued, would teach him the virtue of saving and indoctrinate him with the proper work ethic. The new code also set up arbitration councils, in which labor disputes were to be settled fairly.[75]

Along with regulating the *pécule*, the new code imposed various obligations upon employers. These constituted the second group of provisions in 1925. The employer was responsible for transportation to and from the place of work. In order to guarantee all workers adequate remuneration, the decree allowed the administration to determine a minimum wage. A whole section of Carde's 1926 arrêté on the code's local application was devoted to work hygiene, prophylaxis, and medical care: "humanitarian reasons," but also "the future of colonization" required such measures, "in order to prevent the abusive use of unfortunately limited [human] resources." To protect the health of African workers, maximum work hours, one day of rest, free medical attention, housing and minimum food rations were regulated in considerable detail; each worker was to pass a preliminary health examination at hiring, a second one once he arrived at his worksite, several during his contract, and a final one at the end of his contract; no contract was to exceed two years, or be shorter than fifteen days; compensation for job-related accidents was also required, although no minimum amount was determined by decree.[76] In 1930, Carde issued guidelines specifying further the hygiene and health measures that employers had to implement.[77]

Exceptionally precise when it came to workers' physical needs, the code remained ambiguously silent on whether the administration could recruit African labor, if it were not volunteered. The notion of individual wage contracts suggested that the theory behind the new decree was to develop and regulate a free-labor market. This impression was reinforced by article 10 of the code, which required that administrators verify the free consent of each contracting worker before officially stamping a contract under which the above provisions were enforceable. Yet article 1 of Carde's 1926 arrêté, on local enforcement, provided for the creation of *offices de travail*. Staffed preponderantly by employer representatives and administrative personnel, they resembled in their purpose the immigrant labor placement offices in France: they were to coordinate "rationally" the supply of and demand for labor.[78] Such an institution almost automatically implied continued administrative intervention in labor recruitment. Indeed, statements by both Carde and the Ministry of Colonies appeared to take for granted that the ideal of two freely consenting parties would remain just that—an ideal—and that com-

pulsory recruitment for private enterprises would continue as long
as necessary. A 1925 Paris memorandum maintained that the text
of the new code "will certainly ameliorate employer-employee relations and will determine the responsibilities of each. It will not completely resolve the question of recruitment. Administrative intervention will still be necessary, but should conserve its character:
that is to say be paternal, and not cover up a more or less disguised
form of obligatory labor, by requiring the native to undertake ardu-
ous and sometimes insufficiently remunerated tasks."[79] This description of administrative intervention recalls that of Carde in his
1924 circular on cotton production. Carde echoed the Ministry's
words, in his own description of the code, shortly after it had been
approved by the council:

> The labor code proposes to grant the legal basis to contracts that they
> have lacked to date. When it has entered native mores, it will make it
> more difficult to commit the abuses that have been discovered recently
> on the part of employers and employees, and will guarantee the native ac-
> ceptable moral and material means of existence. It will nevertheless not
> alone solve the question of labor recruitment, which conditions the econ-
> omy of all of West Africa and particularly that of Ivory Coast.[80]

The colonial service thus had no illusions about the degree of coercion that would be necessary to secure adequate numbers of workers for European enterprises, and it was prepared to cooperate in
their recruitment regardless of whether such practices were legally
acknowledged in the code. In this context, there is perhaps no more
revealing statement than that made by Carde in private to his former secretary general in 1930, shortly after the governor general left
AOF. Reflecting upon a recent report by Inspector Kair in Ivory
Coast accusing the local administration of repeatedly breaking the
law by pressuring Africans to work for Europeans, Carde noted:

> Everyone knew, and the missions of inspection that came to AOF also
> knew, about the actual help the authorities gave to private individuals,
> not only in Ivory Coast but in other colonies of the group (Sudan, Upper
> Volta, Guinea, Dahomey) for recruiting labor. Illegal, perhaps, this aid was
> nevertheless justified for reasons that no one, among people of good faith,
> questions. This aid [to private enterprises] could only be defended if it
> granted the workers the full guarantees provided by the decree and re-
> spected the multiple instructions that I sent out. How valid were these
> legal provisions? In practice, as you pointed out, their validity depended
> on the manner in which they were applied. In theory, I believe that they
> were, and remain, entirely adequate.[81]

Adequate was not, however, the Colonial Inspectorate's impression of Dakar's labor guidelines. Throughout the 1920's the same Inspector Kair who had complained about forced cotton cultivation in Ivory Coast warned the administration about abusive forcible recruitment for European cocoa planters and forestry concessions there. Indeed, after revisiting the colony in 1930, Kair claimed that local government's continued "excesses" had precipitated the ILO's movement to organize an international treaty condemning forced labor generally.[82] Kair's reports attributed such abuses in part to an exceptional number of Europeans in the colony, and in part to the ambiguities of Carde's new labor legislation.[83]

Since the war, Kair complained, Europeans in ever greater numbers had arrived in the colony to farm cocoa and tap its forest reserves, both of which required extensive African labor. But these new *colons* had proceeded in a manner that defied the laws of economics, "not to mention those of simple humanity." Spectacular profits had been made, but purely because wages were withheld from a labor force coerced into working for Europeans.[84] Particularly grievous was the fact that none of the guarantees in the 1925 decree had been respected. Kair discovered that at no point was the worker informed of his rights; his legal work hours were ignored; the minimum wage, established by the Government General to protect the worker, had become the maximum wage protecting the employer's interests; minimum food rations were the maximum allotment; no effort was made to recognize workers' differing dietary traditions; sickness often ensued, with only one-fourth of wages paid out over eight days as compensation; a contract nevertheless could not be invalidated on the basis of poor health.[85] Kair concluded that it would have been simpler for the administration to have subsidized the forest and cocoa concessions outright, through an additional tax upon the African. This tactic would have had the merit of allowing the latter to opt for the labor of his choice, and thus have helped form a labor force better equipped to help the French in the future. Instead, the African's natural repugnance for work had only been heightened by the oppressive regime in Ivory Coast.[86]

How had this come about, after the labor code that ostensibly condemned these practices? The answer, Kair soon discovered, lay within the code itself, which he now began to scrutinize. Entering a contract under the provisions of the 1925 decree was supposed to be voluntary. But the obligations imposed were so draconian, it was impossible to imagine anyone choosing to accept them. Why, for example, would an African agree to having his wages withheld? The only possible conclusion was that the decree's primary purpose was to establish the conditions for administrative cooperation in labor recruitment. This conclusion was borne out by the situation in Ivory Coast, where the new legislation applied only to workers recruited by force. Indeed, the inspector added, no African worker would ever voluntarily consider opting for such a contract, for fear of being confused with a *recruté* and being subject to the same onerous work constraints. Kair concluded this section of his report by asking whether the French had seen the African entrepreneur and other readers of the text as "idiots," when they had proposed to regulate the "free" labor market in West Africa. If so, they were mistaken.[87]

Kair's criticisms did not, however, lead him to the conclusion one might have expected: that the use of administrative pressure for recruiting workers in the private sphere was immoral and wasteful. Rather, while arguing that the administration should not continue "directly" to recruit workers for private individuals, he accepted that "administrative intervention" could be tolerated, provided its incidence was better controlled than in the past. Administrators in Ivory Coast were certainly guilty of having pursued a policy that flouted every principle of France's civilizing mission. Nevertheless, it was not the recourse to coercion that was at fault; it was that insufficient discretion was exercised—itself a reflection of a code that did not say what it meant. If the administration felt it necessary to aid these planters, if the only way to get Africans to work was through administrative pressure, there was, Kair insisted, nothing shameful about admitting it. At least it could be checked. He ended by suggesting that in the future "administrative pressure" should only be allowed if it conformed to a plan approved ahead of time by the local administration, which would determine how many workers could be recruited in a specific area, how long they would work, and what kind of job they would be doing. This plan would, in turn, take into account the labor needs and resources of each region, the aptitude of each ethnic group for a certain kind of work, and its physical capacity for and resistance to work generally.[88]

This plea did not go entirely unheeded. On the one hand, the metropolitan government, in its 1930 decree regulating obligatory public labor, officially forbade the administration's direct engagement in recruiting labor for private gain.[89] On the other, the local administration admitted that the ideal remained free labor, but that "pressure" would still be necessary for a period of five years.[90] It then created a system of mobile inspections, whose responsibility would be to ensure better respect for the provisions of the 1925 decree. At the same time, the Government General accepted Kair's recommendations for programs to distribute labor in given areas. The need for such programs had been anticipated by Carde on the eve of his retirement from office, when the first effects of the depression were being felt in West Africa. The governor general had pointed out that the time had come to plan production on a yearly basis, in order to put an end to capricious and abusive administrative interventionism, in cash-crop production and in labor recruitment. Such programs, annually approved in council, would provide, Carde declared, the legal basis that intervention lacked, and guarantee that its use would be commensurate with the African's own aptitude and best interest. Carde wrote in 1929:

> Here is a native who has paid his taxes, carried out his *prestations*, completed his military requirement and all other legal obligations. We impose upon him an additional obligation, which will undoubtedly procure him appreciable advantages, but whose utility he does not recognize immediately. If morally the right to act this way can be extracted from the definition of colonialism, the text that would render it legal does not exist. This text must be instituted, and in the present state of the political evolution of West Africa, its most rational materialization consists of an annual program of agricultural production to be approved in this Council.[91]

Such measures did not resolve altogether the ambiguity about coercion in recruiting African wage laborers, particularly in Ivory Coast. This ambiguity was deliberate; while most members of the colonial establishment agreed in theory that free labor was superior to forced labor, they also remained convinced that without "pressure" Africans would not work for Europeans. Deprived of a labor force, the Europeans would then be obliged to leave the colony. Yet without them, the administration believed, no progress of any kind would take place in West Africa. The most enlightened course of action, in this context, was to end the abuses associated with forced labor, without actually abolishing forced labor itself. Official policy in the 1920's reflected this conviction. As Carde reaffirmed in 1928:

> A nation that uses the law of labor, which is imposed upon humanity, in such a way that its subjects find, there where they go to work for the future of their country, material conditions superior to the ones in their vil-

lages; that they acquire a taste for hygiene, cleanliness, the notion of remunerated labor, and return to their homes better armed against life than
when they left; such a nation . . . is completely and nobly fulfilling the
civilizing mission that it inherited.[92]

While working conditions were increasingly regulated, the question
of how Africans were to be recruited was not directly addressed in
any labor legislation.

"All administrative measures tending to modify the organization
of native society can, by the disruption they cause to time-honored
habits, have negative repercussions upon the resistance of the
race."[93] For this reason, Carde cautioned his subordinates in 1926
against interfering in marriage customs, family arrangements, or trying to move from collective forms of labor to individual ones. As
this quotation suggests, the French by the 1920's had found another
argument—besides the fact that the African chieftaincy was more
"familial" and "representative" than first thought—for now "respecting" African institutions previously condemned through a policy of association: the medical/biological one. This emphasis upon
race regeneration—which previous historians of the doctrine of association have (like its civilizing content) failed to note—was entirely in keeping with the intensifying interest in *mise en valeur* in
the interwar years, and the larger eugenicist and pro-natalist trends
emerging in the metropole at this time. These developments help
make clear why it was only in the 1920's that Dakar began to explore and articulate its own attitudes toward labor.

Most striking about Carde's words is that, for all the ostensible
concern with preserving the African race through a policy of respecting custom, no one in Paris or Dakar questioned the appropri-
ateness of inculcating in Africans the disruptive "law of labor." At
best, the new interest in improving Africans physically led to the
regulation of forced labor. It did not cause the French ever to question the policy of forced labor. In the grand scheme of things, "learning to work" was considered too universal a perquisite of civilization to be withheld from Africans, while the racist belief that Africans were inherently lazy and unable to think for themselves was
too ingrained to ever make free labor the only option.

The different African peoples of Ivory Coast or the Sudan worked
on their own as hard as any producers throughout the world. When
the French argued that the inhabitants of these colonies were indo-

lent, they meant that the Africans did not work as the administration wished they would. That is to say, they did not grow the crops that the Government General desired, or did not choose to work for Europeans rather than on their own plots of land, or failed to volunteer to build railroads and roads planned by the local administration. The decision by individual Africans not to undertake any of these tasks was determined by rational economic calculations. It made no sense to grow crops for which there was no demand, or from which the African farmer could not profit. Wages on European concessions and for public works projects were usually too low to make the displacement worthwhile. French ideology effectively obscured these explanations for African behavior, by focusing upon the African's supposed psychological barrier to labor. Although there was some attempt to improve Africans' health care and diet, older stereotypes refused to die. Indeed, they gained new potency in the particularly race-conscious and commodity-hungry 1920's.

The peoples of West Africa did not passively submit to their own exploitation. Resistance took a variety of forms: flight, noncooperation, and strikes. In some cases, the presence of coercion achieved the desired results, but not in the manner anticipated by the French. Flight from forced-labor demands in their own circles was a powerful motivation for inhabitants in the interior to engage "voluntarily" in migrant wage labor in Senegal and Gold Coast, then eventually in Ivory Coast. From migrant laborers these workers often went on to become independent cash-crop farmers. In neither case, however, did they learn the "law of labor" from the French. Indeed, if anything, administrative recourse to forced labor delayed the integration of West Africa into the world market—a fact Inspector Kair underscored. Rather, these individuals were responding to opportunities that Dakar had helped create, but never fully understood or controlled. For this situation, the ideology of the *mission civilisatrice* was partially responsible, both before and after World War I.

Conclusion

It is June 1995, and I have just returned from a conference in Dakar, commemorating the centenary of the founding of French West Africa.[1] The conference was organized in large part by the National Archives of Senegal, but much of the funding for the conference came—not surprisingly—from France. Although the French press paid little attention to the event, Chirac's new Ministre de la Coopération, Jacques Godfrain, participated in the opening ceremonies. He spoke warmly of France's continuing relationship with its former West African colonies, and of the permanence of the bonds that existed between them—bonds whose nature, of course, had changed since decolonization. He also listed the principal achievements of the federation during its existence. The high points that Godfrain identified for the period 1895 to 1930 are worth repeating. The years 1895 and 1902 marked key moments in the bureaucratic organization of the Government General. In 1912 the Ecole William Ponty for training African teachers was created, and education for the masses was inaugurated. In 1914, Blaise Diagne was elected to the French Parliament, which represented a major step forward for African democracy. In 1918 the Ecole de Médecine was founded, followed in 1924 by the Institut Pasteur of Dakar. And in 1923 the Senegal-Niger railroad was finally completed. The next milestone Godfrain mentioned was the creation of a girls' lycée in 1938.

This list contains few surprises, but in light of the arguments put forward in this book, it invites several comments. On the most elementary level, what is striking is how little official French discourse has changed, despite the disappearance of the empire. The benefits it brought to West Africa, France still maintains, were education, health care, railroads, and democracy. The only discordant note sounded here by the minister relative to the governors general of the first part of the century is the praise accorded Diagne's successful election to the Chamber of Deputies. At the time, French administrators were sure that this was not how to go about democratizing African societies. More subtle, but equally revealing in the minister's review of French colonization, is the long gap in his narrative between the founding of Institut Pasteur in 1924 and the next *date-clé*—1938, when Dakar innovated in the realm of female education. From 1924 to 1938 there was, apparently, nothing to commemorate. We now know why: association and human *mise en valeur* left few legacies of which the French could conceivably be proud, and the interwar years were among the most coercive of the colonial period.

[margin handwritten note: colonial dark age]

Another keynote speaker at the conference was the eminent Guinean historian and critic of colonialism, Boubacar Barry. Barry did not dwell on past iniquities: he was not there to accuse the French, at least not directly. Rather, he began his remarks by considering what remained of the old French West African federation. And he identified three legacies: the actual archives of French West Africa, located in Dakar; the franc CFA, which until recently was pegged to the French franc, and is used throughout France's former sub-Saharan colonies; and the French language, which remains the official language of the independent West African nations that once made up the federation. Barry did not comment extensively on the first two, but he did have something to say about the continued use of French. Did it not, he suggested, limit the options of Africans in the modern world? Was it not perhaps time to choose another language, the language of many of their neighbors—English?

Barry's comments, too, provide a telling coda to the story of France's colonization of West Africa. In contrast to French officials, he intimated that the *mission civilisatrice* was largely a lie. French West Africa was itself an imaginary political construct; all that remains of the colonial administration are the reams of paper that any bureaucracy generates, and the official memory that the conservation of archives represents. Economically, France linked West Africa to the world market on unequal terms. This linkage and subordination continue, as witness France's 1995 decision to devalue the franc CFA by half. Last but not least, Francophone West Africans remain imprisoned within a language not of their choosing, nor that of an increasing number of the world's inhabitants. Far from graciously accepting the proffered French hand of continuing "friendship," Barry made clear that West Africans should begin to look for new "friends" elsewhere.

Two starkly different views, in short, of France's past (and future) in West Africa. Which view better approximates what "really" happened? This book has argued that the answer is not so obvious or straightforward as it might at first seem. Certainly, official French colonial ideology in West Africa narrated a sequence of events that differed dramatically from how many Africans lived them. Rather than assume that French perceptions were deliberately duplicitous, I have sought to account for the persistent French misunderstanding of Africans and their civilizations. Colonialism was as much a state of mind as it was a set of coercive practices and system of resource extraction. Those responsible for determining French policy in West Africa behaved according to a certain "civilizing" logic—a twisted logic, perhaps, but one that was internally coherent and made perfect sense to contemporaries. If one does not know the content of France's civilizing mission or the ways it served to justify French actions, the acquisition, evolution, and endurance of the empire in Africa cannot be fully explained.

The preceding chapters have examined this sense of mission in detail. What larger conclusions can now be drawn about the *mission civilisatrice* in West Africa, the nature of modern French republicanism, and the relationship between colony and metropole? The study of the *mission civilisatrice* in Dakar reveals, first, that there was a continuous republican idea of empire in French West Africa between 1895 and 1930. This idea can be attributed to the continuity of the democratic tradition in France under the Third Republic. As heirs to the universalizing impulses of 1789, French republican policy-makers never questioned that Africans had to learn to feel French, though they insisted that their subjects evolve within their own cultures. The conviction that democratic France had a special obligation to improve the lives of all Africans, and not just those of an indigenous elite, was also widely held. Moral improvement would occur through a selective extension of the rights of man to Africans: the abolition of slavery, "feudal" tyranny, and barbaric custom first, and then the gradual initiation into representative government. Modern science and technology would develop Africa's human and natural resources and raise the standard of living. And in exchange for their largesse, French administrators had no qualms imposing on their *sujets* many of the obligations of *citoyens*: taxes of course, but also conscription, so that Africans, too, might defend the motherland.

Although continuously "republican," the French idea of empire contained more universalizing and egalitarian tenets before World War I than after. Between 1895 and 1914, a powerful rhetoric of emancipation and social and cultural transformation emerged among policy makers in Dakar. French administrators called for the eradication of slavery and the aristocracy, in the name of the individual's right to freedom; they proclaimed the need for mass education and the spread of the French language, and they built railways and improved public health in the name of France's republican traditions. This liberalism had its well-defined limits. Only a few Africans were ever expected to become French citizens, and Africans were to love France and Africa simultaneously. Nevertheless, Dakar's particular reading of local conditions and how they could be bettered remained deeply informed by the language of the rights of man all the way up until World War I.

The upheaval of World War I altered this progressive interpretation of the *mission civilisatrice*. In the course of recruiting soldiers and intensifying production for the war effort, Dakar began to reassess what it meant to civilize Africans. The wartime and postwar generation of governors general felt their predecessors had made mistakes. African chiefs were not tyrants, but genuine representatives of democratically organized collectivities. The new educated elite was not turning out as Dakar had expected. The policy of *mise en valeur*, predicated upon the construction of railroads, had neglected the most important factor in West Africa's agricultural productivity: the human element. A more conservative vision of the *mission civilisatrice* thus emerged, in which the prewar preoccupation with transforming African society yielded to a greater respect for the precolonial aristocracy—who were now to become associated in the civilizing process—and an emphasis upon power sharing generally. And a greater concern for inculcating in Africans "the law of labor" and new strategies of race preservation—what the French referred to as *faire du noir*—replaced the tenet of civilizing through railroads and modern sanitation.

The gradual attenuation of progressive values in French civilizing discourse suggests a second conclusion—one that takes us back to France and, more particularly, to the history of French republicanism in the modern era. French historians are currently debating just how "republican" the Third Republic was at the turn of the century. Some historians have called the period between 1871 and 1914 one of "internal colonization" in the metropole, during which the young Third Republic built schools, roads, and railroads and introduced modern hygiene and uniform standards of justice and conscription in order to transform "peasants into Frenchmen."[2] These historians have argued for the distinctiveness of the first half of the Third Republic, specifically the Belle Epoque, seeing it as an era of ascendant republican values "speaking in the accents of citizenship and patriotism."[3] According to this view, liberal values were more resilient in fin-de-siècle France than elsewhere on the Continent.[4] Other scholars, however, are not so sure; they have maintained that any reform passed in the pre–World War I era had more to do with stemming social unrest and the nation's biological decline than a genuine desire to emancipate the masses. France, the argument implicitly runs, was more conservative and modern than liberal in this era.[5]

There is evidence to back both perspectives, but the history of the civilizing mission in West Africa suggests that the first view is closer to the truth. One of my central discoveries has been that republican sentiment was stronger in Dakar before the Great War. A more modern understanding that the health of all depended upon regulating that of the individual may well have spurred public health initiatives overseas. But Dakar's native, educational, and judicial policies and discourse confirm that being a liberating force *outre-mer* constituted an integral part of what it meant to be civilized, French, and republican in the prewar period.

The evolution of French civilization ideology in Dakar after the war also reveals the fate of the Third Republic. Recent research on subjects as different as attitudes toward women, the growth of corporatism, and social insurance has repeatedly reached the same conclusion: that by the mid-1920's, the Third Republic had acquired a decidedly illiberal orientation, which only became more pronounced in the 1930's. During and after the war, new technocratic and corporatist ways of organizing society, the economy, and the state, which were still contested and resisted at the end of the nineteenth and the beginning of the twentieth century, triumphed over those political forces that gave priority to the rights of citizens. In Parliament, there was a gradual shift as conservative forces rode the wave of anxiety and disillusionment that four years of total war, fought mostly on French soil and at the cost of 1.4 million lives, had created. Movements that placed the national interest above that of the individual—such as pro-natalism, eugenics, and social hygiene—now received greater support from the government and the public at large, which were openly more xenophobic and race conscious than in the past. Republican liberties and universal values were on the defensive, while nostalgia for time-honored traditions helped to mask and negotiate the many transformations that were taking place.[6]

Changes in Dakar's outlook in the 1920's only further substantiate these findings. The Government General backed away from its earlier language of the *droits de l'homme*, and began emphasizing the need to ameliorate the African races and to preserve chiefs whose power was "familial." Whatever local developments encouraged this shift in policy and rhetoric, it was also evidence of comparable trends in France. Through the lens of the civilizing mission, the more pronounced liberalism and heightened conservatism of the pre- and postwar Third Republic stand out.

Does the light shed on the fate of the Third Republic by French actions overseas mean, then—as Gwendolyn Wright has persuasively argued—that "the colonies provided more than the ideal laboratory so often evoked, and more than the mirror we might refer to today. They functioned like a magnifying glass, revealing with startling clarity the ambitions and fears, the techniques and policies that pertained at home, here carried out almost without restraints."[7] This statement raises yet another issue regarding modern imperialism that I have sought to address: the nature of the relationship between metropole and colony. A third finding here is that this relationship is not straightforward. The metaphor of the magnifying glass certainly captures one essential facet of the bond between center and periphery: the decisive influence of the metropole upon colonial ideas and actions. Between 1895 and 1930, a number of French tenets in West Africa clearly reflected and distorted impulses at work in France, whether anti-"feudal" or antidemocratic, social hygienicist or racist.

Yet overseas policy was not just the product of metropolitan trends. For all their freedom, colonial administrators—at least at the

level of the Government General—operated within a complex web
of constraints. Foremost among these were the local African conditions and institutions that the French sometimes ignored, sometimes destroyed, and sometimes remolded, but never escaped. The
history of the civilizing mission in Dakar is replete with examples of
African influences upon French actions. In the prewar era, the threat
posed by such formidable African adversaries as Samori, Amadu, and
Umar also helped determine the Government General's anti-"feudal" rhetoric. By the same token, the shift in French rhetoric that
occurred in the 1920's cannot be adequately understood until factors
particular to West Africa as well as to the metropole are taken into
consideration. The stirrings of nationalist protest threatened equally
the interests of the French and Africa's old elite. The two now appeared natural allies while concessions to—but also containment
of—the *évolués* became imperative. Recruitment had revealed that
the indigenous population was so malnourished that a matter of
practical necessity was the development of Africa's human resources. Along with the intensifying racism and paternalism in
France, these local factors were responsible for Dakar's postwar discourse of association and race regeneration. In the end, official
French cultural assumptions in West Africa in the twentieth century
are best understood as the combined product of colonial and metropolitan influences.

And there is another way that the image of the colonies as a magnifying glass fails to capture the full complexity of the metropoli-
tan-colonial relationship, as the evidence garnered here implicitly
suggests. A volume edited more than ten years ago, entitled *Double
Impact*, was devoted to the proposition that in the age of the "new
imperialism," ideas not only radiated outward from France to colonial Africa; developments in the African colonies also had a decisive
impact on ideas in the metropole. We have, in fact, caught tantaliz-
ing glimpses of West Africa's influence upon the culture of metropolitan France—in realms that the contributors to this volume did
not apparently contemplate.[8] Take, for example, the more racialized
turn of the *mission civilisatrice* in the 1920's. As Africans within
the federation asked for rights that the republican civilizing mission
had promised, a new sexual and cultural distancing from all people
of color occurred in Paris as well as Dakar. Given the simultaneity
of these events, there is every reason to assume that the revolts of
the colonized contributed as much as developments in Europe itself

to the increasingly conservative politics and culture of metropolitan France. Indeed, if "inferior" people of color had not challenged French authority in the colonies, the interwar emphasis upon regenerating the white French race at home might not have been so great.

The new respect for the precolonial aristocracy that emerged in Dakar in the 1920's can also deepen our understanding of postwar developments in France. In addition to local unrest in the federation, metropolitan insecurities regarding France's place in the world clearly contributed to a more benign French view of "traditional" chiefs. But it is also likely that the need for and acceptance of chiefs' collaboration throughout the empire reinforced the Third Republic's rightward drift at home. In this context, the timing of the founding of the new Institut d'Ethnologie at the University of Paris appears particularly relevant. Republican policy makers and academics discovered in "traditional" African institutions, which they were now officially studying, a bulwark against the assimilationist demands of the new colonial elite. But might they not have also discovered in "primitive" Africa an idealized premodern and patriarchal world reminiscent of the one they had ostensibly lost at Verdun, and now wished unconsciously to resurrect? Could not disillusionment with republicanization overseas have helped to create suspicion of democratic values in the metropole? There is surely much more to the history of association in Dakar and Paris than the nervous reactions of an insecure colonial state.

What was true of the empire's impact on the culture of the metropole in the 1920's must be true in other decades as well. Republican France has had a long history of partially and sometimes fully excluding certain groups from the larger democratic polity in the twentieth century—immigrants, Jews, and women, as well as colonial subjects, come to mind. The fact that until 1962 France had an empire in which such exclusion was the norm suggests that the practice of colonialism may well have reinforced and enabled these other forms of discrimination in the metropole in ways that have not yet been recognized. Another major conclusion of my study is that this cross-fertilization of ideas, habits, and trends between the Republic and the empire existed, and that it deserves more serious attention than it has received. With a few important exceptions, political and cultural historians of modern France are still not placing France and its colonies in the same historical frame.[9] In this, they constrast sharply with the historians of French science (cited in the Introduction and Chapter 2), whose investigations into the complex interplay between "core" and "periphery" in the development and dissemination of modern scientific knowledge are now well under way. These historians do not agree on the relationship between Western science and imperialism. But they do agree on the centrality of the relationship itself and on the need to examine it.[10] The rewards of such an approach for modern French historians promise to be equally rich. In this book, using the colonies as a window on the metropole has highlighted several important trends in the history of the Third Republic. Examining the empire's impact on all facets of life in the metropole will explain even more of France's evolution in the twentieth century.

Finally, it seems appropriate to ask at the end of this study what the subsequent history of the *mission civilisatrice* in France and West Africa will be. I have argued that by the war years, the more universalistic elements of France's early overseas mission had mostly exhausted themselves, leaving a heightened sense of difference and a conservative rhetoric of civilization. Would the republican idea of empire in France and West Africa subsequently recover any of its earlier egalitarianism? Here, the intertwined histories of republicanism in France and the growth of nationalist protest in Africa remain instructive. When the Popular Front came to power, there was a brief shift in Paris's and Dakar's rhetoric and policies regarding forced labor. Marius Moutet, Léon Blum's new Socialist minister of colonies, hoped to remedy the notorious abuses attached to forced labor in Ivory Coast and to authorize substantial new social investments in the federation. And Governor General de Coppet did succeed in making the application of the *prestations* more equitable throughout the West African colonies.[11] Meanwhile, the comprehensive investigation of conditions throughout the French Empire undertaken by the Popular Front's Commission Guernut paved the way for wider scrutiny of the colonies after World War II.

The advent of the Vichy regime marked a brief return to the most abusive and authoritarian tendencies of the 1920's in Dakar and Paris. The reformist agenda of de Coppet and Moutet was nevertheless taken up by the new Fourth Republic, anxious to reward African loyalty and forge a more constructive relationship with the empire. At the same time, World War II further radicalized urban and educated Africans and made imperative real concessions to the educated elite overseas. In 1946, forced labor was abolished in the empire, and the language of assimilation returned with the creation of the French Union and the decision to make all colonial subjects French citizens. Without abandoning the canton chiefs, the French authorized political parties and assiduously wooed the *évolués*. The French government also came to accept the principle that they would have to invest public funds in the empire if it were ever to prosper. Such funds were finally forthcoming in the 1950's.[12]

These shifts did not resolve the ambiguities that had always marked France's republican empire. Despite the reforms of the Popular Front and the early Fourth Republic, French governments continued to deny the colonized the full rights of metropolitan citizens. Although forced labor was abolished in 1946, the latter-day investment in the empire did not challenge the premises of *mise en valeur* articulated in the 1920's. African economic well-being was still conceived exclusively in terms of integrating the federation into the world economy through the export of cash crops. Indeed, that tenet has survived in the form of development economics.[13] The main difference between now and then is that whereas the colonial powers assumed that African poverty was primarily the result of the African producer's moral deficiencies, modern economics attributes this poverty to social factors. Last, the current discrimination against children born on French soil of foreign parents suggests that republican France has not yet divested itself of the racist thought that peoples of nonwhite ethnicity cannot become truly French. As the interwar years showed, the combination of increased immigration, social dislocation, and rising nationalism can easily turn liberals into neo-traditionalists, xenophobes, and racists—who maintain an official rhetoric of republican fraternity and progress.

France since the Enlightenment and the Revolution has succeeded in spreading its egalitarian credo and civilization across the globe. Ironically enough, it was least successful in this enterprise during the modern colonial period, when its claims to a civilizing mission in the name of the rights of man were greatest. The parts of the world where French culture is most welcome today are not necessarily those where the *tricouleur* once waved—as Boubacar Barry's rejection of the French language indicates. Intellectuals in Francophone Asia and Africa in particular have an ambivalent relationship to France, because their countries were colonies; among the South American intelligentsia, in contrast,—and in academic circles in North America, for that matter—French ideas are eagerly embraced as an alternative to the cultural hegemony of a capitalist and neo-imperialist United States.

The moral of this story is obvious but worth repeating: France's culture and democratic ideals have taken root most firmly overseas when not accompanied by a "mission" to civilize predicated upon first becoming rulers in another people's land. The question is why it took a country with as strong a republican tradition as France so long to see the discrepancy between ideal and reality, between ends and means. Racist assumptions about Africans, the spoils the empire yielded, and the prestige it bestowed upon *la grande nation* are only half the answer. Equally to blame was a civilizing ideology that was never *only* racist in content. While racism was always present between 1895 and 1930, it came shrouded first in emancipationist rhetoric and subsequently in scientific "respect" for traditional cultures. Both claims made it difficult for many liberals to see how inconsistent the very notion of a civilizing mission was with the Republic's universalist commitments. If the empire endured as long as it did, it was in part because French racism often worked hand-in-glove with more progressive values. As the French today struggle to build a genuinely pluralistic society, there are still lessons to be learned from the civilizing delusions of their recent past.

Reference Matter

Notes

PREFACE

1. On July 22, 1993, the newly elected conservative government amended the French naturalization laws (Code de la Nationalité) to make the acquisition of French citizenship more difficult for children of foreigners born in France.

INTRODUCTION

1. Throughout this book, "primitive," "savage," "civilization," and "barbarism" and all forms thereof generally refer to contemporaneous perceptions and should be read as if in quotation marks.

2. In studying the official secular discourse of civilization under the Third Republic, I am not suggesting that this was the only version of the *mission civilisatrice* that obtained in France in this period. Catholics also embraced the idea of a special French mission to civilize and invested it with their own set of meanings. This said, there were some civilizing premises articulated by the republican elite—for example, the need to eradicate poverty and slavery in Africa—that all French endorsed (although not necessarily for the same reasons). How Catholics approached French colonization, and how republicans viewed the civilizing efforts of missionaries, remains a rich topic for historical investigation.

3. A recent exception to this trend is Miller's excellent essay "Unfinished Business," which touches upon some of the same themes I am exploring. Through an analysis of literary sources, Miller, too, seeks to understand a "certain pattern of forced and dubious reconciliation between the ideals of the French Revolution and France's nationalistic and imperialistic tendencies" (p. 107).

4. Kanya-Forstner has made the case for military imperialism in *Con-*

quest of the Western Sudan. The classic study of imperialism first and foremost as a patriotic venture is Brunschwig, *Mythes et réalités.* Brunschwig's views are amplified in Andrew and Kanya-Forstner, "French Colonial Party" and "French Business and the French Colonialists." For a rebuttal, see Abrams and Miller, "Who Were the French Colonialists?" Persell, *French Colonial Lobby,* suggests that nationalism, coupled with the commercialism of France's bourgeoisie, best accounts for the dynamics of French colonialism at the turn of the century; Lagana, *Le parti colonial français,* argues that economic motivations were preeminent. Laffey, "Roots of French Imperialism," has also demonstrated the role commercial interests played in French imperialism. The most comprehensive economic history of the French empire is Marseille, *Empire colonial et capitalisme français.*

5. Cooper and Stoler have reached a similar conclusion in their introduction to a new collection of essays, *Tensions of Empire.* I thank Fred Cooper for sharing this introduction with me.

6. See, in particular, Betts, *Assimilation and Association;* Murphy, *Ideology of French Imperialism;* Lewis, "One Hundred Million Frenchmen"; Girardet, *L'idée coloniale en France;* Cohen, *French Encounter with Africans;* Adas, *Machines.* S. Roberts, *History of French Colonial Policy,* and Buell, *Native Problem,* also discuss administrative doctrines as part of their overall studies of French colonialism.

7. For example, Schneider, *Empire for the Masses;* Campion-Vincent, "L'image du Dahomey"; Pruneddu, "La propagande coloniale"; Lejeune, *Les sociétés de géographie;* August, *Selling of the Empire;* Ageron, "L'exposition coloniale de 1931"; Lebovics, *True France;* Blanchard et al., *L'Autre et Nous;* Bancel, Blanchard, and Gervereau, eds., *Images et colonies;* Marseille, *L'âge d'or.*

8. The pioneering works in postcolonial studies are all by literary specialists: Said, *Orientalism;* Bhabha, "The Other Question"; Spivak, *In Other Worlds.* Two recent volumes in the field edited by historians, and which include essays on French colonialism, are Dirks, *Colonialism and Culture;* and Prakash, *After Colonialism.* Said's most recent work, *Culture and Imperialism,* also includes a discussion of French-language texts.

9. The only area of French West Africa in which French attitudes have been examined closely is the Four Communes of Senegal. See Crowder, *Senegal;* Idowu, "Assimilation in 19th Century Senegal"; Cruise O'Brien, *White Society.* Two studies that have begun to explore how the experience of colonization affected French ideas about Africans are M'Bokolo's short article, "Du 'commerce licite'"; and the essays contained in Johnson, ed., *Double Impact.* Lebovics has decisively shown how important the empire was to the construction of French national identity in the interwar years; but in his chapters on the Colonial Exposition of 1931 and the growing nationalist movement in French Indochina, he has juxtaposed, rather than fully articulated the connection between, events overseas and trends within the metropole. See Lebovics, *True France,* chaps. 2–3.

10. Headrick, *Tools of Empire* and *Tentacles of Progress*; Petitjean, Jami, and Moulin, eds., *Science and Empires*; McClellan, *Colonialism and Science*; Pyenson, *Civilizing Mission*; Adas, *Machines*; Osborne, *Nature, the Exotic, and the Science of French Colonialism*; Bonneuil, *Des savants pour l'empire*; P. H. Martin, *Leisure and Society in Colonial Brazzaville*; Wright, *Politics of Design*; Rabinow, *French Modern*.

11. Pyenson has rightly been criticized not only for failing to explicate the term "civilizing mission," but for putting forward an excessively uncritical and Eurocentric view of the complex relationship between science and empire. Worboys and Palladino, "Science and Imperialism." For Pyenson's defense of his position, see Pyenson, "Cultural Imperialism" and *Civilizing Mission*, pp. xi–xv.

12. Current research on the gendered nature of French colonialism also promises to shed new light on such civilizing efforts, but this literature is still in its infancy—particularly regarding the Third Republic. See Stoler, "Rethinking Colonial Categories" and "Making Empire Respectable"; Clancy-Smith and Gouda, eds., *Domesticating the Empire*.

13. Several studies of French administrators exist, but they are not specifically concerned with the ideas of the governors general of French West Africa: Deschamps, *Méthodes et doctrines*; Delavignette, *Les vrais chefs de l'empire*; Cohen, *Rulers of Empire*; Brunschwig, *Noirs et blancs*. One important exception is Johnson, "William Ponty." In the case of French West Africa, there are now studies on individual aspects of the French administration, such as its educational and Islamic policies. Most of these studies have not gone beyond 1920; they will be cited when appropriate. No comprehensive overview of the policies of the Government General exists for the period before World War II.

14. Long neglected, the history of republican ideology is coming back in fashion. Indispensable are Nicolet, *L'idée républicaine*, first published in 1982 and just reprinted; Agulhon, *La République, Histoire vagabonde, La République au village, 1848*, and *Le Cercle dans la France bourgeoise*; Furet, *La Gauche et la révolution*, and Furet and Ozouf, eds., *Le siècle de l'avènement républicain*; Nord, *The Republican Moment*; and Stone, *Sons of the Revolution*.

15. Rabinow, *French Modern*, p. 196.

16. On French ideologies of racism, past and present, see Guillaumin, *L'idéologie raciste*; Taguieff, *La force du préjugé*.

CHAPTER I

1. Quoted in Godechot, *La grande nation*, 1: 71; Laurens, *L'Expédition d'Egypte*, p. 34; Lochore, *History of the Idea of Civilization*, p. 54.

2. Lejeune, *Les sociétés de géographie*, chap. 3.

3. Quoted in Murphy, *Ideology of French Imperialism*, pp. 15, 23.

4. Leroy-Beaulieu, *De la colonisation* (1874), p. vii. References to France's work of civilization are found throughout the book.

5. Quoted in Ageron, *France coloniale*, p. 65.

6. Gambetta was the earliest colonial enthusiast of the three, endorsing future expansion already in 1870. Cohen, "Gambettists and Colonial Expansion."

7. Quoted in Ageron, *France coloniale*, pp. 65–66; Robiquet, ed., *Jules Ferry*, 5: 210–211; Thobie, in Meyer et al., *Histoire de la France coloniale*, vol. 1, *Des origines à 1914*, 618–619.

8. See Girardet, *L'idée coloniale*; Schneider, *Empire for the Masses*.

9. Quoted in *Le livre des expositions universelles*, pp. 90–91; Lyautey, "Le sens d'un grand effort."

10. Febvre, "Civilisation"; Beneton, *Histoire de mots*, pp. 29–38; Stocking, *Victorian Anthropology*, pp. 11–12. Febvre, "Civilisation," makes it clear that before the French coined the term "civilization," they had used the term "police" (*un peuple policé*) to describe the contrast between European societies and barbaric ones. But by the 1770's this word no longer adequately expressed the image the French had of themselves, for "police" failed to reflect French achievements in the moral and scientific realms. For a more detailed account of the history of the idea of the civilizing mission in France, see Conklin, "Of Titians and Camels."

11. Febvre, "Civilisation," pp. 14–23. See also Duchet, *Anthropologie et histoire*; Chaunu, *L'Amérique et les Amériques*; Williams and Williams, *Great Map of Mankind*; Pagden, *European Encounters*.

12. This becomes clear from a close reading of the colonial officials' reports cited in Duchet, *Anthropologie et histoire*. It should be noted, however, that the philosophes—famous for their denunciation of the brutality of the Spanish conquest of America—did approve of the "civilizing" work certain missionaries were carrying out in the New World. Although not enthusiastic about the religious content of missionary activity, Abbé Raynal in his *Histoire philosophique*, Voltaire in the *Essai sur les moeurs*, and Buffon in the *Histoire naturelle* all noted the success with which the Jesuits in Paraguay and the Quakers in North America had overcome the "ferocity" of the local inhabitants and remade them in their own image. This approval suggests that the Enlightenment figures, too, were close to conflating colonization with civilization. See, in addition to Duchet, *Anthropologie et histoire*, pp. 210–211, Benot, *Révolution française* and *Diderot*.

13. Duchet explores these connections between philosophes and colonial bureaucrats in some detail. See Duchet, *Anthropologie et histoire*, pp. 125–136; and also Cohen, *French Encounter with Africans*, pp. 136–137; Lokke, *France and the Colonial Question*, pp. 35–60. For metropolitan attitudes toward slavery generally in the second half of the eighteenth century, see Pluchon, *Nègres et Juifs*; Blackburn, *Overthrow of Colonial Slavery*; Boulle, "In Defense of Slavery"; Seeber, *Anti-Slavery Opinion in France*; Popkin, "The Philosophical Basis of Eighteenth-Century Racism"; Debbasch, *Couleur et liberté*; Drescher, "The Ending of the Slave Trade"; Geggus, "Racial Equality, Slavery, and Colonial Secession"; Peabody, *There Are No Slaves in France*.

14. Cohen, *French Encounter with Africans*, p. 136; Duchet, *Anthropologie et histoire*, pp. 145–151.

15. This sentiment led some to recommend a reform of the Code Noir that regulated the conditions of slavery. Others thought slavery should be abolished altogether, as long as this abolition was gradual and guaranteed compensation to slave owners. Lokke, *France and the Colonial Question*, pp. 67–68; Adas, *Machines*, p. 108; Sala-Molins, *Le Code Noir*.

16. For contemporary attitudes toward intermarriage and the civilizing potential of commerce, see Duchet, *Anthropologie et histoire*, pp. 219–220; Cohen, *French Encounter with Africans*, p. 178; Pagden, *European Encounters*, p. 169.

17. For a recent summary of Enlightenment views on despotism in China, see Spence, *Search for Modern China*, pp. 132–136; French attitudes toward Islam in North Africa are discussed in Thomson, *Barbary and Enlightenment*; and Laurens, *Les origines intellectuelles*. Both of these show more effectively than Said's *Orientalism* how Islam by the end of the eighteenth century was no longer considered a culture that could be known sympathetically and then used to show the inadequacies of European civilization.

18. On the barbarism of Egyptians and the civilizing impact of rational government and commerce, see, for example, Volney, *Voyage en Egypte*, p. 111; Abbé Raynal actually called for the French conquest of the Barbary Coast in the name of civilization. Raynal, *Philosophical History*, 4: bk. 11, pp. 38–41.

19. Godechot, *La grande nation*, 1: 71.

20. For an interpretation along these lines, see, for example, Blanning, *Origins of the French Revolutionary Wars*, pp. 179–184.

21. This is the viewpoint adopted by Godechot, *La grande nation*.

22. The colonial nature of the Egyptian expedition has been recognized by an older generation of historians, including Lokke, *France and the Colonial Question*; Charles-Roux, *France, Egypte et la Mer Rouge* and *Bonaparte, gouverneur d'Egypte*. Their work, however, suffers from a particular bias; writing when the French Empire was reaching its apogee, they tended to see in Napoleon's actions the origins of later colonial policies adopted by the Third Republic. The most recent analysis of the expedition also recognizes the colonial nature of the invasion: Laurens, *L'Expédition d'Egypte*.

23. Quoted in Laurens, *L'Expédition d'Egypte*, p. 39.

24. For an assessment of the scientific achievement of the Institut, see Gillispie, "Aspects scientifiques de l'Expédition d'Egypte." Lorcin discusses the Institut in the context of the French conquest of Algeria, but we differ slightly about its role in the emergence of the *mission civilisatrice*. For her, the civilizing mission is still only a suggestion in Egypt; I see the Institut as its first formal expression. Lorcin, *Imperial Identities*, pp. 103–104.

25. Godechot, *La grande nation*, 1: 111–121, 163–168, 280; Laurens, *L'Expédition d'Egypte*, pp. 128–130, 168, 280–284, 288–297; Moiret, *Mémoires*, pp. 77–78.

26. Pinkney adopted this perspective in *Decisive Years*, pp. 142–146.

27. For evidence of this civilizing rhetoric, see Lochore, *History of the Idea of Civilization;* Ageron, *France coloniale;* Julien, *Histoire de l'Algérie,* vol. 1, *La Conquête.*

28. Julien, *Histoire de l'Algérie,* 1: 162–163; Turin, *Affrontements culturels;* Marcovich, "French Colonial Medicine."

29. Lorcin, *Imperial Identities,* pp. 41–49 104–107; Julien, *Histoire de l'Algérie,* 1: 162–163; Pyenson, *Civilizing Mission,* pp. 87–93; Taylor, "French Scientific Expeditions," p. 244. Lorcin argues that there were more similarities than differences between the Egyptian Institut and the Algerian Commission. Until a more systematic comparison of the Egyptian and Algerian expeditions is made, any conclusion about the differences between the two groups remains tentative. On the role science played in French colonization of Algeria between 1830 and 1870, see Lorcin, *Imperial Identities,* pt. 2; Osborne, *Nature, the Exotic, and the Science of French Colonialism,* chap. 6; for the period 1870–1940, Pyenson, *Civilizing Mission,* pp. 93–127.

30. Osborne, "The Medicine of the Hot Countries" and *Nature, the Exotic, and the Science of French Colonialism,* pp. 87–97.

31. Leroy-Beaulieu, *De la colonisation* (1874), pp. 326–338. For an assessment of Leroy-Beaulieu's colonial views, see Warshaw, *Paul Leroy-Beaulieu,* chap. 6.

32. Ageron in particular has noted the predisposition of French explorers, officers, and early colonial settlers in North Africa and sub-Saharan Africa to view indigenous African societies as "feudal" and, like Leroy-Beaulieu, to attack them on those grounds. Ageron, *France coloniale,* p. 69.

33. The question of assimilation and French attitudes toward it under the Third Republic will be discussed in more detail in Chap. 3.

34. Turin, *Affrontements culturels,* pp. 33–73, 115; Frémeaux, *Les bureaux arabes,* pp. 191–227.

35. I am necessarily telescoping here a shift in French rhetoric that took place gradually between 1830 and 1870. For additional information about French attitudes during this period, see Frémeaux, *Les bureaux arabes;* Perkins, *Qaids, Captains, and Colons;* Christelow, *Muslim Law Courts;* Lorcin, *Imperial Identities;* Clancy-Smith, *Rebel and Saint;* Rey-Goldzeiguer, *Le royaume arabe;* Schnapper, *La politique et le commerce français;* Emerit, *Les Saint-Simoniens;* Richter, "Tocqueville on Algeria"; Masson, "L'opinion française."

36. Klein, "Slavery and Emancipation," pp. 171–172.

37. For a discussion of African slavery in the eighteenth century in Lower Senegal, see Searing, *West African Slavery;* for the Senegambia generally, Barry, *La Sénégambie du XVe au XIXe siècle;* for the Western Sudan before the French conquest, Meillassoux, ed., *L'esclavage en Afrique précoloniale.*

38. Hopkins, *Economic History of West Africa,* chaps. 2–3.

39. Ibid., chap. 4. Peanut production will be examined more closely in the next chapter.

40. My account is drawn from Crowder, *West Africa Under Colonial*

Rule; Ajayi and Crowder, eds., *History of West Africa*, vol. 2; Kanya-Forstner, *Conquest of the Western Sudan*; Hargreaves, *West Africa Partitioned*, 2 vols.

41. Similar concerns led to the creation of Government Generals elsewhere in the empire: in Algeria (1896) and Madagascar (1897). The Government General of Indochina, created on paper in 1887 but still barely functional, was also reorganized in 1897.

42. The Colonial Ministry was created in 1894. Before then, responsibility for the colonies had been divided between an undersecretary, who had no power in his own right, and the minister of the marine, who was in charge of the colonial army. The creation of a Colonial Ministry under civilian rather than military control, like the creation of the Government General, signaled a growing sensitivity in Paris to the importance of colonial consolidation and commercial development in place of further expansion. For the first twenty years of its existence, however, the new ministry lacked the prestige of other more established cabinet posts. During those years, the Colonial Ministry proved unable to assert any real control over colonial affairs because of the rapid turnover in its personnel and a lack of clear-cut organization. The officers of the colonial army in West Africa had powerful supporters of their own in Paris at least until the outbreak of the Dreyfus affair. Kanya-Forstner, *Conquest of the Western Sudan*, pp. 202–262; Berge, *Le sous-secrétariat*; Leitch, "Colonial Ministry."

43. The need for resolving the conflicts between the different governors and the military was the primary reason put forth to justify the creation of the federation in the report to the minister on the question. Décret, June 16, 1895, *JORF, Lois et Décrets*, June 17, 1895, p. 3385.

44. For the history of the Government General, see Newbury, "Formation of the Government General" and "Government General and Political Change"; Vodouhe, "La création de l'Afrique occidentale française"; de Benoist, "La balkanisation de l'Afrique occidentale française"; Leitch, "Colonial Ministry."

45. Décret, June 16, 1895, *JORF*, p. 3385.

46. Newbury, "Formation of the Government General," pp. 120–121. Another reason why the Sudan was dismembered at this time was that earlier that year the army had finally captured Samori and completed the occupation of Lake Chad. Both feats rendered the presence of the colonial army somewhat superfluous, since it could now be argued that the Western Sudan was effectively "pacified."

CHAPTER 2

1. Quoted in François, *L'Afrique occidentale française*, pp. 315–316.

2. ANSOM, EE 3766 (3), personnel file. Roume is the only governor general in this study to have attended Polytechnique.

3. Maclane, "Railways and 'Development Imperialism,'" p. 508.

4. Charges of conflict of interest would be levied in the popular press

against Roume in 1909, when he was accused of retiring only to become a banker to the colony he had formerly headed. See for example the article in *Gil Blas*, "Coulisses de la Finance," Oct. 23, 1909, in Fonds Auguste Terrier 5925, Institut de France.

5. The Union was organized in 1893, as "an association of principal French firms with interests in the colonies," to give impetus to a more commercially oriented French colonial policy. Its emphasis on *mise en valeur*, rather than continued expansion, distinguished it from its rival organization, the Comité de l'Afrique Française, founded three years earlier. Although members of the Comité almost always offered an economic rationale for their traditional imperialist designs, their preeminent argument for promoting colonization was political. In contrast, the Union, under the direction of Marseille businessman Jules Charles-Roux and the liberal economist and politician J. Chailley-Bert, dedicated itself exclusively to making overseas possessions more productive. Both organizations remained powerful until the eve of World War I, but after 1900 the Union wielded the most influence in government circles and won the most support for its programs. Persell, *French Colonial Lobby*, pp. 17, 20–22, 27; Andrew, *Théophile Delcassé*, p. 32; Chailley-Bert, *Dix années de politique coloniale*, pp. 37–54.

6. Persell, *French Colonial Lobby*, chap. 6; Bonneuil, *Des savants pour l'empire*. Although his study of *mise en valeur* is devoted to the interwar years, Bonneuil points out some of the policy's prewar antecedents.

7. As early as 1892, it had become commonplace to assert in colonial circles that, especially in West Africa, an "era of exploitation" should now replace the "era of conquest." Quoted in Andrew, *Théophile Delcassé*, p. 31. The term *exploitation* here is used in the French sense, which does not carry the pejorative connotations it does in English. In French, *exploitation* can best be translated as "development." Also see Guy, *Les colonies françaises*.

8. Osborne, *Nature, the Exotic, and the Science of French Colonialism*, p. 190 n. 80.

9. Persell, *French Colonial Lobby*, p. 100; Laffey, "Roots of French Imperialism."

10. The literature on these developments is growing rapidly; I have found the following particularly useful: Rabinbach, *Human Motor*; Rabinow, *French Modern*; Ewald, *L'état providence*; Donzelot, *Policing of Families*.

11. De Benoist, "La balkanisation de l'Afrique occidentale française," p. 35.

12. Decree of Oct. 15, 1902, *Annuaire du gouvernement général de l'AOF*, 1912, pp. 24–26.

13. ANS, 18 G 3, Roume, "Instructions aux Lieutenants Gouverneurs," Nov. 11, 1902.

14. Two of the earliest railroads to be planned in West Africa were a line to connect the ports of Dakar and Saint-Louis and a Senegal-Niger link de-

signed to connect the Senegal and Niger Rivers. Conceived together in the early 1880's, the two projects soon became separate. Government funds for the Dakar–Saint-Louis line were voted by Parliament in 1882 and the line itself completed in 1889. It extended 265 km and cost a total of 22,244,000 fr. Between 1881 and 1904, 555 km of the Senegal-Niger link had been completed at a cost of 54,626,000 fr. The only other pre-1900 railroad begun in West Africa was undertaken by the colony of Guinea out of its own funds. It advanced even more slowly: between 1891 and 1900, only 153 km had been built. Pheffer, "Railroads and Aspects of Social Change," pp. 226–227; "Les grands travaux," p. 378. For additional details, see Maclane, "Railways and 'Development Imperialism,'" pp. 506–507.

15. ANS, 5 E 1, Conseil de Gouvernement, 1902. The port of Dakar was constructed as a naval base and a commercial harbor between 1898 and 1908, at a cost of 21 million fr. Headrick, *Tentacles of Progress*, pp. 160–161.

16. This loan was to be allocated as follows: sanitation (*travaux d'assainissement*): 5,450,000 fr.; Dakar port construction: 12,600,000 fr.; railroads: Kayes-Dakar–Saint-Louis line, 5,500,000 fr.; Guinea line, 17,000,-000 fr.; Ivory Coast line and port, 10,000,000 fr.; debt interest: 11,648,055 fr. (Guinea) and 2,654,662 fr. (Senegal). François, *L'Afrique occidentale française*, p. 136.

17. For a contemporary account of Roume's program of public works and the 1903 loan, see François, *L'Afrique occidentale française*, pp. 135–139.

18. Newbury, "Formation of the Government General," p. 125.

19. ANS, 18 G 4, Circulaire, Gouverneur général to lieutenants gouverneurs, Jan. 24, 1905.

20. Under *assainissement*, Roume included both medical care and public hygiene. I therefore discuss them together here.

21. The 1906 loan was to be allocated as follows: railroads: Guinea line, 30,000,000 fr.; Ivory Coast line, 22,000,000 fr.; Dahomey line, 13,000,000 fr.; Thiès-Kayes-Ambidedi line (part of the link between Senegal and the Sudan), 13,500,000 fr.; port construction and river dredging: Dakar, 4,750,000 fr.; Senegal and Niger Rivers, 2,000,000 fr.; Ivory Coast ports, 3,000,000 fr.; medical assistance: 3,000,000 fr.; military housing: 5,000,-000 fr.; telegraph lines: 2,500,000 fr. François, *L'Afrique occidentale française*, pp. 142–143.

22. Roume put the botanist Auguste Chevalier in charge of a permanent scientific mission in West Africa from 1905 to 1913. Chevalier inventoried the federation's flora, especially in the rain forest. No agricultural services, however, were established in the individual colonies until after the war. Bonneuil, *Des savants pour l'empire*, pp. 27–31.

23. ANS, H 18, Roume, Discours, Comité Supérieur d'Hygiène et de Salubrité Publiques de l'AOF [a consultative committee made up largely of federal agents, medical personnel, and French representatives from Senegal], Dec. 12, 1904; Roume, Discours, Comité Supérieur d'Hygiène et de Salubrité Publiques de l'AOF, June 20, 1905, *JOAOF*, pp. 322–324. Numer-

ous medical reports from his own bureaus help account for Roume's interest in prophylaxis against disease-bearing mosquitoes. See ANS, H 12, "Rapport sur les transformations à apporter dans la police sanitaire en AOF et la réorganisation du service sanitaire destinée à en assurer le bon fonctionnement," Dr. Rangé to gouverneur général, no. 34, Jan. 29, 1904; ANS, 5 E 7, "Rapport du Dr. Le Moal de sa mission d'étudier d'après les nouvelles données les causes d'insalubrité des agglomérations et les moyen d'y remédier," Dec. 12, 1904, Conseil du Gouvernement Général, Documents, 1904; ANS, H 18, "Etude sur la moustique en AOF. Leur rôle pathogénique. Prophylaxie," n.d., also by Le Moal. Roume clearly preferred mosquito eradication to the prophylactic use of quinine for the control of malaria. This confirms William Cohen's findings that the French did not use prophylactic quinine much in this period, although it challenges his claim "that the French means of combating malaria had not changed dramatically since the beginning of the nineteenth century" (Cohen, "Malaria and French Imperialism," p. 29). Mosquito eradication was a new policy, which all colonial powers were adopting at this time. Curtin, *Death by Migration*, pp. 131–140. Nevertheless, I concur with Cohen's larger point, that colonialism helped to reduce malaria in French West Africa, rather than the reduction of malarial incidence leading to the French conquest of the region.

24. Décret, Apr. 14, 1904, *JORF, Lois et Décrets*, Apr. 17, 1904, p. 2398, art. 1, and p. 2399, art. 16; ANS, H 19, extrait du décret "relatif à la protection de la santé publique en AOF," Apr. 14, 1904.

25. Décret, Apr. 14, 1904, *JORF*, p. 2398, art. 1.

26. See for the Four Communes of Senegal, arrêté no. 6, Jan. 5, 1905, *JOAOF*, pp. 11–12; for Conakry (Guinea), arrêté no. 58, Jan. 16, 1905, *JOAOF*, pp. 30–31; for Kayes and Bamako (Upper Senegal-Niger), arrêté no. 468, May 25, 1905, *JOAOF*, pp. 289-290; for Dahomey, arrêté no. 123, Feb. 4, 1905, *JOAOF*, pp. 81–82; and for Ivory Coast, arrêté no. 124, Feb. 4, 1905, *JOAOF*, pp. 83–84. For discussions of how the April 14, 1904, decree was adapted to Senegal, see the minutes of the Comité Supérieur d'Hygiène et de Salubrité Publiques de l'AOF, April and June 1905 sessions, *JOAOF*, pp. 201–202, 217–221, 227–235, 322–330.

27. A circular in April requesting the lieutenant governors to report on the major causes of depopulation in their colonies further confirmed Roume's interest in fighting the high mortality and morbidity rates in Africa. ANS, 5 E 8, Inspecteur des Services Sanitaires Civiles, "Résumé du rapport général sur la dépopulation et sur les moyens d'y remédier," Conseil de Gouvernement, Documents, 1905. Roume never followed up on this original investigation.

28. ANSOM, AP 3236, Roume, Discours, Comité Supérieur d'Hygiène et de Salubrité Publiques de l'AOF, June 17, 1904; Roume's interim replacement also developed these ideas in a letter to the minister announcing his intention of recruiting civilian doctors for the federation. Until then, all medical personnel were attached to the colonial troops. ANSOM, AP 3240,

Gouverneur général par intérim [hereafter p.i.] to ministre des Colonies, no. 1285, Sept. 9, 1904.

29. Arrêté no. 131, Dec. 10, 1904, *JOAOF*, pp. 84–86, later modified by arrêté no. 24, Jan. 7, 1907, *JOAOF*, pp. 11–15.

30. This figure was given in Roume's speech to the extraordinary session of the Council of the Government General, convened in May 1906 to ratify the decision to raise a second loan for the federation. Roume explained that three million francs of this new loan would be used to build twenty new medical stations—one per doctor. ANS, 5 E 10, Conseil extraordinaire, May 1906.

31. ANS, 5 E 8, "Résumé du rapport général sur la dépopulation," 1905. The ordinance creating the group of medical assistants was arrêté no. 28, Jan. 7, 1906, *JOAOF*, pp. 28–30. Also see provisions for their training in arrêté no. 24, Jan. 7, 1907, *JOAOF*, p. 14. Roume rejected the possibility of creating a medical school in Dakar, such as existed in Madagascar and Indochina, because of the insufficient "development of our African populations." Instead, *aides-médecins* were to be trained in each circle by European doctors. Roume, Discours, Conseil de Gouvernement, Dec. 4, 1905, *JOAOF*, p. 587. The annual meeting of the Council of the Government General provided a forum for major policy statements by the head of the federation. His opening speeches were reprinted in France and commented upon in the metropolitan press. Despite their propagandistic overtones, these speeches usually reflected the personal views of the governor general and indicated the orientation of colonial policy for the coming year.

32. Arrêté no. 29, Jan. 7, 1906, *JOAOF*, pp. 30–31.

33. ANS, 5 E 8, "Résumé du rapport général sur la dépopulation," 1905; ANSOM, AP 3240, Gouverneur général p.i. to ministre des Colonies, no. 1285, Sept. 30, 1904.

34. Roume, Discours, Conseil de Gouvernement, Dec. 15, 1904, *JOSD*, p. 682; ANS, 5 E 8, Conseil de Gouvernement, Documents, 1905.

35. Hargreaves, *West Africa*, p. 112.

36. Roume, Discours, Conseil de Gouvernement, Dec. 15, 1904, *JOSD*, p. 682.

37. ANS, 5 E 1, "Projet d'emprunt des 65 millions: exposé des motifs du projet de loi," Conseil de Gouvernement, Documents, 1902.

38. ANSOM, AP 3236, Roume, Discours, Comité Supérieur d'Hygiène et de Salubrité Publiques de l'AOF, June 17, 1904; see also ANSOM, AP 3240, Gouverneur général p.i. to ministre des Colonies, no. 1285, Sept. 9, 1904; Roume, Discours, Conseil de Gouvernement, Dec. 15, 1904, *JOSD*, p. 684.

39. Quoted in François, *L'Afrique occidentale française*, pp. 314, 141. François is an indispensable source for the early history of the Government General because of the numerous original documents he reprinted in his volume, many of which I have not found in the archives. Unfortunately, he did not always cite the exact dates or sources of the documents he was reprinting.

40. Leroy-Beaulieu, *De la colonisation* (1886), p. 314.

41. Persell, *French Colonial Lobby*, p. 40; also see Chailley-Bert, *Dix années de politique coloniale*. Deherme, *L'Afrique occidentale française*, p. 14. The same ideas were endorsed by another publicist and future governor of Senegal, Camille Guy. Guy, *Les colonies françaises*.

42. M. Delafosse, *Broussard*, pp. 46–47. This book appeared first as a series of articles in the *Bulletin du Comité de l'Afrique Française* in 1909.

43. Régismanset, *Questions coloniales*, p. 95. The most virulent critic of the *mission civilisatrice* in this period, however, was the Socialist Paul Vigné d'Octon, author of *Les crimes coloniaux de la Troisième République*. Suret-Canale has briefly discussed d'Octon's polemic in "A propos de Vigné d'Octon."

44. Maclane, "Railways and 'Development Imperialism,'" pp. 507, 511.

45. For a discussion of the American railway and its cultural impact, see Schivelbusch, *Railway Journey*, chap. 6. Like the French in West Africa, the Americans had linked transportation and civilization in the mid-nineteenth century. This celebration of the creative impact of the railroad was, according to Schivelbusch, fundamentally different from the European reaction to the steam engine. In Europe, the mechanization of transportation had been associated—at least initially—with the destruction of a traditional artisan culture. But in both Africa and the United States, the perception was that steam power "gained a new civilization from hitherto worthless wilderness" (p. 91).

46. The colonial lobby was responsible for promoting the notion that the West African colonies were an imperial treasure-house, waiting to yield its bounty in direct proportion to the kilometers of railway laid across the great African expanses. This propaganda created unrealistic expectations from the outset about the ease with which the African interior could be rationally exploited. On the myth of the wealth of the Sudanese interior, see Cohen, "Imperial Mirage."

47. Quoted in Elwitt, *Making of the Third Republic*, p. 161.

48. See also Brunschwig, "Note sur les technocrates"; Pheffer, "Railroads and Aspects of Social Change," pp. 16–21.

49. On the education provided at Polytechnique and the attitudes it fostered, see Shinn, *L'Ecole Polytechnique*. Richard F. Kuisel notes the neo-Saint-Simonianism of late-nineteenth-century *polytechniciens* in *Ernest Mercier*, p. 46. Elwitt has called attention to the close association between *polytechniciens* and railroad interests in the early Third Republic in *Making of the Third Republic*, pp. 115, 131, 152, 154.

50. Silverman, *Art Nouveau in Fin-de-Siècle France*, pp. 1–5.

51. Silverman argues that fears of socialism, and industrial stagnation relative to Germany and the United States in the 1890's, led the republican elite "from technological monumentality to artisanal work of high quality as the source of French modernity." Instead of massively industrializing, "France would compensate for industrial deceleration with civilizing graces"—that is to say, by now promoting high-quality goods made by tra-

ditional French artisans (Silverman, *Art Nouveau in Fin-de-Siècle France*, pp. 52–53).

52. Mandell, *Paris 1900*, p. 67. Mandell concludes that the 1900 exposition, unlike earlier ones, was essentially a failure: "It put on full view a glut of facts and of material goods, exposing to all the selfish pursuit of wealth and power that motivated society at large. . . . The widespread, optimistic Saint-Simonian faith was dispelled in the fin-de-siècle spirit of lassitude, scepticism, introspection and irony" (pp. 120–121). Rosalind Williams also argues that the attitude toward technology at the 1900 exposition was confused, and that the entire enterprise was much criticized for its promotion of consumerism (*Dream Worlds*, chap. 3). For a contrasting view, see Weber, *France: Fin de Siècle*, p. 81.

53. As part of its commitment to promoting science and technology, the Third Republic expanded and overhauled the university system, founded the Ecole Pratique des Hautes Etudes and, in conjunction with private interests, established new commercial and industrial schools in major cities. Day, "Education for the Industrial World"; Lundgreen, "Organization of Science and Technology in France"; Paul, *From Knowledge to Power*, pp. 5–14, 35–59, 143–163.

54. Elwitt, *Making of the Third Republic*, p. 146.

55. Weber, *Peasants into Frenchmen*, chaps. 12, 28–29; also see Price, *Modernization of Rural France*; Annie Moulin, *Peasantry and Society in France*, chap. 3.

56. McKay, *Tramways and Trolleys*, pp. 149–150.

57. Kern, *Culture of Time and Space*, p. 213.

58. Pheffer, "Railroads and Aspects of Social Change," p. 165. This is the best available study of the Dakar–Saint-Louis railroad. According to Pheffer, the original reason for building the line in Senegal was to conquer the independent and hostile province of Cayor which lay between the ports of Saint-Louis and Dakar. The governor was nevertheless delighted when it boosted the colony's trade as well.

59. Nord, "Welfare State in France," p. 833.

60. Headrick, *Tools of Empire*, chap. 3; Curtin, *Death by Migration*, pp. 62–67 and chap. 5.

61. For a fuller discussion of these developments, see Salomon-Bayet et al., *Pasteur et la révolution pasteurienne*; Latour, *Pasteurization of France*; Léonard, *Les médecins de l'ouest*, vol. 3; A. M. Moulin, "Bacteriological Research."

62. On the growing concern over cholera and typhoid, see Hildreth, *Doctors, Bureaucrats, and Public Health*, pp. 123–129. The high valuation of medicine and visibility of doctors under the Third Republic and the medical model of national decline are analyzed in Nye, *Crime, Madness and Politics in Modern France*, chap. 2; Ellis, *Physician-Legislators*.

63. Latour, *Pasteurization of France*; A. M. Moulin, "Bacteriological Research."

64. Curtin, *Death by Migration*, pp. 132, 136; Dozon, "Quand les pastoriens traquaient la maladie du sommeil," p. 31.

65. Tropical medicine was an international movement. Worboys dates its birth in England around 1910 ("Emergence of Tropical Medicine," pp. 85–87). For Latour, tropical medicine in France was born with the spread of Pasteur Institutes to the colonies at the end of the nineteenth and beginning of the twentieth century (*Pasteurization of France*, pp. 143–144).

66. Bonneuil, *Des savants de l'empire*, p. 105.

67. A. M. Moulin, "Bacteriological Research," pp. 338–343; idem, "Patriarchal Science," pp. 311–314. According to Moulin, French society at large was much more easily "pasteurized"—that is to say, accepting of the existence of dangerous microbes that had to be combated—than the medical community itself, which had to confront in Pasteur's doctrines a revision of its theories as well as its practices. This view is an important corrective to the more sweeping claims made by Latour, Léonard, and Salomon-Bayet et al. about the "Pasteurization of France" in this period. Moulin's findings nevertheless confirm that the germ theory of disease entered popular culture and political discourse quite rapidly in late-nineteenth-century France.

68. Bruno, *Le tour de la France par deux enfants*, p. 305; Dozon, "Quand les pastoriens traquaient la maladie du sommeil."

69. For the early history of the hygiene movement, see Coleman, *Death Is a Social Disease*, and La Berge, *Mission and Method*; on the political activities of the hygienists under the Third Republic, see Ellis, *Physician-Legislators*, chap. 6; their relations with the state bureaucracy are examined in Hildreth, *Doctors, Bureaucrats, and Public Health*, chaps. 2–3; the ideology of *l'hygiéniste* is explored in Murard and Zylberman, "De l'hygiène comme introduction à la politique expérimentale" and "La raison de l'expert"; Mitchell, *Divided Path*, is also useful. For an excellent overview of the developments in public health in this period, see Nord, "Welfare State in France," pp. 833–836.

70. This desire to "civilize" the masses through improved hygiene was shared by France's rural practitioners, although they disagreed profoundly with the hygienists on how to realize this goal (as discussed below). See Léonard, *Les médecins de l'ouest*, 3: 1193–1194.

71. Shapiro, *Housing the Poor of Paris*, p. 135; Hildreth, *Doctors, Bureaucrats, and Public Health*, pp. 118, 133–137.

72. Ellis, *Physician-Legislators*, pp. 172–182.

73. As Hildreth and Mitchell have shown, this group was also affected by the bacteriological revolution—but in a very different way from their hygienist brethren. These small-town practitioners cared little about Pasteur's findings. However, they did see in the new prestige now attached to public health an opportunity to drive out unlicensed traditional practitioners who were competing with them and extending their own private practices. Hildreth, *Doctors, Bureaucrats, and Public Health*, p. 224; Mitchell, *Divided Path*, pp. 139–140.

74. The hygienists preferred a state-managed system of public hospitals and dispensaries for all of France; the practitioners advocated a system of privatized home care in which the government reimbursed doctors for each visit. Hildreth, *Doctors, Bureaucrats, and Public Health*, pp. 237–238, 252–254.

75. The principal provisions of the 1902 public health bill included setting uniform standards of salubrity for all of France, stiffening penalties for infractions, and codifying and updating regulations for the control and reporting of all contagious diseases. Shapiro, *Housing the Poor of Paris*, pp. 147–153; Ellis, *Physician-Legislators*, pp. 187–190; Hildreth, *Doctors, Bureaucrats, and Public Health*, pp. 137–139.

76. Hildreth, *Doctors, Bureaucrats, and Public Health*, p. 328.

77. This laboratory was moved from Saint-Louis to Dakar in 1913. Calmette, "Les missions scientifiques de l'Institut Pasteur"; Marcovich, "French Colonial Medicine," p. 104.

78. Roume, Discours, Comité Supérieur d'Hygiène et de Salubrité Publiques de l'AOF, June 20, 1905, *JOAOF*, p. 323; in this same speech, he cited the example of the recent successful *assainissement* of Ismailia (Egypt), where malaria had been wiped out thanks to mosquito eradication. Roume, Discours, Conseil de Gouvernement, Dec. 9, 1905, *JOAOF*, p. 589.

79. Circulaire no. 101c "a. s. de la lutte entreprise contre les maladies endémiques et epidémiques," Gouverneur général to lieutenants gouverneurs, Apr. 4, 1909, *JOAOF*, p. 211; circulaire no. 50c "a. s. de la lutte entreprise contre les maladies endémiques et epidémiques," Gouverneur général to lieutenants gouverneurs, May 26, 1910, *JOAOF*, p. 349; circulaire "relative à l'application des réglements de l'hygiène pendant l'hivernage," Gouverneur général to lieutenants gouverneurs, May 22, 1911, *JOAOF*, p. 315; circulaire no. 109c "a. s. de la prophylaxie de la fièvre jaune," Gouverneur général to lieutenants gouverneurs, Nov. 30, 1911, *JOAOF*, pp. 791–792; circulaire no. 60c "relative à l'application stricte des réglements sanitaires pendant l'hivernage," Gouverneur général to lieutenants gouverneurs, May 14, 1913, *JOAOF*, pp. 537–538; arrêté "promulguant en AOF le décret du 2 septembre 1914, étendant dans les colonies les dispositions de décret du 14 août 1914, édictant des mesures exceptionnelles en vue de prévenir et de combattre les maladies infectieuses," Oct. 20, 1914, *JOAOF*, pp. 924–925. None of these circulars mention the use of quinine, although a circular from 1923 indicated that quinine and mosquito netting were the two forms of prophylaxis in use. Circulaire no. 28 bis, "a. s. de la prophylaxie des affections endémo-épidémiques," Gouverneur général to lieutenants gouverneurs, Feb. 15, 1923, pp. *JOAOF*, pp. 165–166.

80. Circulaire no. 50c, May 26, 1910, *JOAOF*, p. 349.

81. A. M. Moulin has also recognized the greater ability of public authorities and medical hygienists in the colonies to work together. She attributes such cooperation to "more stressing considerations" there than the

metropole ("Bacteriological Research," p. 342). I think the explanation is more complex; metropolitan developments were as critical as local factors in shaping Roume's public health policies.

82. Medical assistance in West Africa is more difficult to compare to metropolitan initiatives than public health legislation. Unlike the 1904 decree on public health, the AMI was not an adaptation of preexisting legislation in France. Certainly, in West Africa (as was not true in France), the delivery of medical care was entirely by the state. This arguably could not have been otherwise; but it is interesting to note how similar the federal authorities' approach was to the hygienists' thwarted ideal in France. The emphasis on building hospitals and dispensaries, for example, was the same system Parliament rejected when it passed the Medical Assistance Law of 1893.

83. See, in particular, arts. 1 and 15, décret, Apr. 14, 1904, *JORF, Lois et Décrets*, Apr. 17, 1904, p. 2398; and arts. 1 and 19, loi, Feb. 15, 1902, *JORF, Lois et Décrets*, Feb. 19, 1902, pp. 1173–1174.

84. Calmette, "Les missions scientifiques de l'Institut Pasteur," p. 132; Nattan-Larrier quoted in Latour, *Pasteurization of France*, p. 144.

85. Roume, Discours, Conseil de Gouvernement, Dec. 4, 1905, *JOAOF*, p. 587.

86. ANS, 5 E 8, "Résumé du rapport général sur la dépopulation," 1905.

87. Although no study of the finances of the Government General exists, individual monographs confirm this tendency to increase tariffs, particularly during the 1920's and the Great Depression. For example, Péhaut, *Les oléagineux*, p. 608; Searing, "Accommodation and Resistance," chap. 4; Hopkins, *Economic History of West Africa*, p. 260. It should also be recalled that Dakar's monopoly on customs tariffs encouraged local administrations to increase indirect taxes to increase their budgets, which resulted in higher costs to the African consumer of imported goods. On this point, see Weiskel, *French Colonial Rule*, pp. 172–174.

88. Ponty first discussed the loan in his 1911 speech to the Council of the Government General (Discours, Conseil de Gouvernement, June 20, 1911, *JOAOF*, pp. 261–371). The governor general had just completed a three-and-a-half-month tour of the federation, which convinced him that a new loan was necessary.

89. The relevant figures are cited below. This assessment is also based on a comparison of the economic performance of the federation before and after World War I. After the war, exports from West Africa increased substantially; although several factors account for this improvement, one important reason appears to have been the administration's new emphasis on forcing Africans to grow the desired crops. This improvement in the postwar economy will be discussed in Chap. 7.

90. See Pelissier, *Les paysans du Sénégal*; Brooks, "Peanuts and Colonialism"; Swindell, "SeraWoolies, Tillibunkas and Strange Farmers."

91. The colony of Senegal had the most skilled workers of any territory in the federation. A decree of June 6, 1905, regulated their emigration from

the colony. In essence, no one had the right to recruit Senegalese workers without the authorization of the administration. ANS, K 32, "Renseignements sur la main d'oeuvre indigène," n.d. (ca. 1912–1913). What interest there was in labor legislation before the war came from Paris. The Colonial Ministry twice asked the Government General for information regarding the applicability of metropolitan labor legislation to the federation and encouraged local initiatives in this domain. See, in particular, circulaire ministérielle no. 1726, May 26, 1909, attached to circulaire no. 159c "a. s. de la législation ouvrière," Aug. 8, 1909, *JOAOF*, pp. 378–379, and circulaire ministérielle "questionnaires sur les accidents du travail . . . ," June 10, 1912, *JOAOF*, pp. 455–458.

92. Despite the creation of an Inspectorate of Agriculture headed by Chevalier, no local agricultural services were created until after the war. The most important initiative for increasing African production was the creation of peasant *sociétés de prévoyance* in 1910. Conceived originally as voluntary cooperatives for seed distribution and local credit, the few that existed were taken over by the administration in 1915. Arrêté no. 802, July 21, 1910, *JOAOF*, pp. 483–485; ANS, 5 E 21, "Rapport sur les sociétés indigènes de prévoyance," Conseil de Gouvernement, Documents, 1909; ANS, 5 E 38, "Avant-projet de la réorganisation des sociétés indigènes de prévoyance," Conseil de Gouvernement, Documents, 1913; ANS, circulaire no. 39 "a. s. des sociétés indigènes de prévoyance, de secours et de prêts mutuels," Gouverneur général to lieutenants gouverneurs, Apr. 15, 1916; Boyer, *Les sociétés indigènes de prévoyance*. Although in 1904 and again in 1909 the Colonial Ministry requested that it be provided with an annual head count of the federation's subjects, establishing such a census was next to impossible before World War I. Field administrators gathered such statistics haphazardly, when they complied at all. Gervais, "Contribution à l'étude de l'évolution de la population de l'AOF," pp. 6–21.

93. Circulaire no. 20c "a. s. de la réglementation de la main d'oeuvre indigène et du régime du travail," Gouverneur général p.i. to lieutenants gouverneurs, June 3, 1912, *JOAOF*, pp. 180–181. Clozel was lieutenant governor of Upper Senegal-Niger at the time. The possibility of introducing individual labor contracts to West Africa had been raised earlier by the minister of colonies, in 1908. A decree of May 28, 1907, had created such contracts for the French Congo, and the minister felt that they would logically complement France's policy of slave liberation. ANS, K 26, Ministre des Colonies to gouverneur général, no. 107, Feb. 27, 1908. The governor general solicited advice from his subordinates in a circular dated April 24, 1908. At that time, Clozel had argued that such contracts were unnecessary, given the absence of concessionary companies in the colony. Lieutenant Governor Angoulvant of Ivory Coast thought they were a good idea as long as they did not make labor recruitment more difficult. The lieutenant governor of Guinea insisted that the administration was making sure that former slaves were now freely working for other people. These letters

are also contained in ANS, K 26. The issue was not raised again until Clozel's 1912 circular.

94. ANS, K 32, "Renseignements sur la main d'oeuvre indigène" (ca. 1912–1913).

95. ANS, 2 G 13–30, "Rapport d'ensemble-situation économique," Gouverneur général to ministre des Colonies, 1913.

96. According to statistics provided by Guiraud, *L'arachide sénégalaise* (p. 37), peanut exports increased from 148,843 metric tons (34,575,000 fr.) in 1903 to 242,084 metric tons (59,229,000 fr.) in 1913. This was in direct proportion to the increase in total federal revenues, suggesting the extent to which the federation's prosperity was pegged to the trade in Senegalese groundnuts. Figures from 1917 confirm the extent to which Senegal led the federation in wealth. While its foreign trade amounted to 275,997,615 fr., the respective figures for the next two richest colonies, Guinea and Ivory Coast, were 36,650,245 fr. and 25,839,820 fr. Searing, "Accommodation and Resistance," 1: 276.

97. Bado, "La maladie du sommeil."

98. I realize that even this point is debatable; policies of eradicating single pathogens may well save fewer lives than funds directed toward lowering infant mortality.

99. Circulaire no. 840 bis, Gouverneur général to lieutenants gouverneurs, June 1, 1912, *JOAOF*, pp. 386–392; see, in particular, art. 2. Two additional circulars focused on fighting sleeping sickness among Africans. But in both cases, these were initiated by the Ministry of Colonies, which was subsidizing the research into the disease. Dakar on its own showed little interest in the question. Circulaire ministérielle "a. s. des moyens propres à combattre et à rayer la trypanosomiase en AOF," Jan. 27, 1908; *JOAOF*, pp. 177–180; arrêté no. 769, July 15, 1911, and circulaire no. 69c "a. s. des mesures de prophylaxie à prendre contre la trypanosomiase," Gouverneur général to lieutenants gouverneurs, Aug. 29, 1911, *JOAOF*, pp. 451–452, 642–644; and Dozon, "Quand les pastoriens traquaient la maladie du sommeil," pp. 33–34.

100. Circulaire 840 bis, June 1, 1912, *JOAOF*, pp. 386–392, art. 33; ANS, 5 E 26, Inspecteur des services sanitaires, "Rapport," Conseil de Gouvernement, Documents, June 1911.

101. ANS, H 13, Circulaire confidentiel, "a. s. de l'application des règles sanitaires," Gouverneur général to lieutenants gouverneurs, May 14, 1913. In 1911, compliance with the April 14, 1904, sanitary regulations regarding standing water was so poor that Dakar raised the penalties; arrêté no. 1271, Nov. 10, 1911, *JOAOF*, pp. 753–754.

102. ANS, Commission Permanente, Dec. 21, 1914; see also ANS, H 20, arrêté "sur les mesures d'hygiène extraordinaires nécessaires à l'assainissement de la ville de Dakar," July 24, 1914. This measure was inspired in part by the realization that many Africans carried the parasite but showed no clinical symptoms of malaria. All Africans thus posed a danger to Europeans.

103. ANS, H 22, Rapport "sur le service d'hygiène de la ville [de Dakar]: historique, mesures à prendre," n.a., 1921.

104. On the history of the plague in Dakar, see Bruno Salleras, "La peste à Dakar en 1914"; Seck, *Dakar*, pp. 134–139; M'Bokolo, "Peste et société urbaine à Dakar"; Headrick, *Tentacles of Progress*, pp. 165–167.

105. ANS, 5 E 40, Inspecteur Général des Services Sanitaires, "Note," Conseil de Gouvernement, Documents, 1920–1921; Cohen, "Health and Colonialism in French West Africa"; Domergue-Cloarec, "Politique coloniale française."

106. ANS, H 12, "Rapport du chef du Service de Santé au Sénégal sur le cours des aides-médecins stagiaires et résultats obtenus," May 5, 1911. According to Bouche, there were only 42 Africans trained, or being trained, as *aides-médecins* in 1909 (*L'enseignement*, 2: 851 n. 182).

107. ANS, H 12, "Rapport du Comité des Travaux Publics des Colonies, a. s. du projet type pour la construction de groupe d'assistance indigène," Oct. 14, 1907. The number of *groupes*—which were to consist of a dispensary, a house for the doctor, and a pavillion for the sick—was later reduced to twelve. For an account of their progress between 1908, when the credits for their construction actually became available, and 1913, see ANS, 5 E 24, 25, 26, and 38, Conseil de Gouvernement, Documents, sessions of 1910, 1911, 1912, and 1913. In the meantime, the colonies had built their own makeshift dispensaries, which numbered 113 in 1912. ANS, 5 E 30 and 31, Conseil de Gouvernement, Documents, 1912, and ANS, 5 E 44, Conseil de Gouvernement, Documents, 1913.

108. Ministre des Colonies, "Instructions relatives au développement des services de médecine préventive, hygiène et assistance dans les colonies," Dec. 30, 1924, *JOAOF*, p. 109.

CHAPTER 3

1. Roume, Discours, Conseil de Gouvernement, Dec. 4, 1905, *JOAOF*, p. 592.

2. Bouche, *L'enseignement*, 1: 2. Ageron makes a similar point about the importance of education in France's interpretation of its *mission civilisatrice*, but he does not assume that that was its only theme (*France coloniale*, p. 67).

3. Weber, *Peasants into Frenchmen*, chap. 18.

4. The classic study of association remains Betts, *Assimilation and Association*. Contemporaries agreed that the new doctrine would work best where the local population was homogeneous and relatively "civilized." In the prewar era it was accepted that Indochina and Madagascar fulfilled those conditions, but Africa did not. Betts himself noted that a strong moral sentiment informed the theory of association in France before 1914, despite this theory's claim to be based on scientific principles. It is this moral dimension of prewar French colonial doctrine in West Africa that I wish to explore, and that I prefer to designate as "republican." The doctrine of associ-

ation was eventually applied in West Africa in the 1920's, and this change will be explored in detail in Chap. 6.

5. The standard work on education in French West Africa is that by Bouche, *L'enseignement*. Yet it does not explicitly explore the ideological outlook of those making educational policy in West Africa; moreover, although Bouche suggests in her introduction that there was no conflict between the dictates of France's civilizing mission and the need to educate Africans to serve in the administration, she fails to follow up on the point. In fact, her title suggests the opposite. It is the ideological content of French schooling in West Africa that I will explore.

6. On republican schools generally, see Prost, *Histoire de l'enseignement en France*, chaps. 9, 12, 14, 16; Zeldin, *France 1848–1945*, chap. 4; Chanet, *L'école républicaine*. On republican education as a preparation for citizenship, see Rosanvallon, *Le sacre du citoyen*, pp. 362–390; Nord, "Republican Politics and the Bourgeois Interior," pp. 201–205; Auspitz, *Radical Bourgeoisie*.

7. Weber, *Peasants into Frenchmen*, p. 309.

8. Garcia, "L'organisation de l'instruction publique"; Harding, "Les écoles des Pères Blancs." These articles, like Bouche's work, provide an indepth analysis of the school system created by the French without specifically examining the assumptions upon which the system rested.

9. François, *L'Afrique occidentale française*, p. 167.

10. A policy of both cultural and political assimilation was applied to a select group of French colonies after 1789: the islands of Guadeloupe, Martinique, and Réunion, French Guyana, and the French cities of India and of coastal Senegal. They all had two points in common, which explain why France was willing to assimilate their populations. Each was fairly small, and each had been founded under the ancien régime, which meant that by the nineteenth century there had been at least a hundred years of contact and intermarriage between the French and other local inhabitants. In contrast, none of the new colonies in the nineteenth century offered comparable conditions for acculturation—a reality the French were already beginning to come to terms with in Algeria. Bouche, *Histoire de la colonisation*, vol. 2, *Flux et reflux*, pp. 100–108.

11. In 1857, Senegalese Muslims were granted their own courts for all noncriminal matters. A new decree in 1905 confirmed the right of Muslims in the Four Communes to preserve these courts, and officially organized their composition; see Saar and Roberts, "Jurisdiction of Muslim Tribunals"; Schnapper, "Les Tribunaux musulmans." For the history of the Four Communes, see Johnson, *Emergence of Black Politics*; Crowder, *Senegal*; Idowu, "Assimilation in 19th Century Senegal."

12. The best account of education in the Four Communes before the creation of the Government General is provided by Bouche, *L'enseignement*, 1: 119–214. My description of their schools is based on her findings.

13. The *assimilés* as a group were not necessarily converts to Christianity; some remained practicing Muslims. There was no legal definition of the

term *assimilé* until 1912, although an attempt was made in 1903 to determine who exactly belonged in this category and what rights the term conferred. For a good discussion of the different groups in the Four Communes, see Idowu, "Assimilation in 19th Century Senegal," pp. 202–207.

14. ANS, 5 E 4, Camille Guy, "Rapport sur l'enseignement," Conseil de Gouvernement, Documents, 1903.

15. The history of the late-nineteenth-century colonial doctrine that subject peoples had to evolve in their own cultures, and its links to the new social sciences in France, has yet to be written. In his all-too-brief chapter "The Scientific Attitude," Betts suggests how the work of Durkheim, Fouillée, and Gustave Le Bon encouraged a new emphasis on preserving indigenous institutions (*Assimilation and Association*, chap. 4). Another helpful introduction is Wooten, "Colonial Administration." For the emergence of the social sciences and their general relationship to the study of Africa, see E. Williams, "Anthropological Institutions"; Cohen, *French Encounter with Africans*, chap. 8; T. N. Clark, *Prophets and Patrons*, chap. 6; Dias, *Musée ethnographique*, pp. 30, 53–59, 182–183, 247–251.

16. Bouche, *L'enseignement*, 2: 477.

17. ANS, 5 E 4, Camille Guy, "Rapport sur l'enseignement," Conseil de Gouvernement, Documents, 1903.

18. Arrêté "organisant le service de l'enseignement dans les Colonies et Territoires de l'AOF," Nov. 24, 1903; reprinted in *L'enseignement aux indigènes*, 1: 501–519.

19. Arrêté, Nov. 24, 1903, Titre I.

20. Kelly, "Presentation of Indigenous Society," p. 524.

21. ANS, 2 G 8–7, "Rapport sur l'enseignement," Gouverneur général to ministre des Colonies, 1908.

22. An entire section of the arrêté of November 24, 1903, was devoted to the organization of a program of postprimary professional training. See Titre II, arts. 16–24.

23. For the organization of a normal school for the federation, see also arrêté, Nov. 24, 1903, Titre IV. For a complete history of this school and its later influence, see Sabatier, "Educating a Colonial Elite."

24. ANS, "Rapport annuel sur le fonctionnement de l'école, 1911–1912 (L'école normale de Saint-Louis)." This report is attached to ANS, Circulaire no. 111c "a. s. du recrutement des élèves de l'Ecole Normale," Oct. 28, 1910.

25. E. Williams, "Anthropological Institutions," pp. 343–346; Cohen, *Rulers of Empire*, pp. 48–49.

26. Roume, Discours, Conseil de Gouvernement, Dec. 4, 1905, *JOAOF*, p. 590; circulaire no. 45c "a. s. du développement des écoles de village," Gouverneur général p.i. to lieutenants gouverneurs, Feb. 27, 1908, *JOAOF*, p. 116.

27. Lapie quoted in Prost, *Histoire de l'enseignement en France*, p. 278; Roume, Discours, Conseil de Gouvernement, Dec. 15, 1904, *JOSD*, p. 685.

28. On the importance of the _leçon de choses_ in France, see Prost, _Histoire de l'enseignement en France_, pp. 278–279, and the school regulations of Jan. 18, 1887, and June 20, 1923, reprinted in Gay and Mortreux, eds., _French Elementary Schools_, p. 52.

29. Circulaire no. 45c "a. s. du développement des écoles de village," Gouverneur général p.i. to lieutenants gouverneurs, Feb. 27, 1908, _JOAOF_, p. 116.

30. Not everyone agrees on the "progressive" nature of the republican school system. For a more critical view, see Elwitt, _Making of the Third Republic_, chap. 5; L. Clark, _Schooling the Daughters of Marianne_, chap. 2; Gildea, _Education in Provincial France_, chaps. 7–8. Although the metropolitan schools were also instruments of social control, their commitment to molding responsible and freethinking citizens deserves equal emphasis.

31. Froidevaux, "L'enseignement indigène dans les colonies françaises"; Hardy, _Une conquête morale_, p. 187.

32. Guy quoted in Bouche, _L'enseignement_, 2: 568.

33. Circulaire no. 44c "relative aux programmes scolaires," Gouverneur général to lieutenants gouverneurs, May 1, 1914, _JOAOF_, p. 462.

34. Ford, "Which Nation?," p. 37. For the republican emphasis upon French linguistic unity in the nineteenth century, also see Dias, "Langues inférieures"; Chanet, _L'école républicaine_, chap. 6.

35. This policy was typical of Archinard, who had during the conquest era organized a special school for the sons of chiefs. This school was first reorganized by the 1903 decree, then eliminated altogether in 1909 as an anachronism. Arrêté no. 630, June 9, 1909, _JOAOF_, p. 273.

36. Guy, "Compte-rendu de la Distribution des Prix de l'Ecole Normale de Saint-Louis," July 15, 1905, _JOAOF_, pp. 432–434.

37. ANS, 2 G 9–2, "Rapport d'ensemble de la Guinée," Lieutenant gouverneur de la Guinée to gouverneur général, 1909.

38. After signing the 1903 arrêté, Roume issued no subsequent federation-wide circulars on the subject.

39. "Native" policy (_politique indigène_) was the term the French used to designate policy toward Africans; more specifically, it tended to refer to the political, as opposed to the social or economic, aspects of French decision making. Many of these political policies in turn reflected France's moral commitment to uplift Africans. The problems of both slavery and relations with existing African rulers, for example, were considered by Dakar to belong to the realm of "native" policy. I have decided to retain the term because, despite its racist overtones, it accurately reflects a way of thinking about Africans typical of the colonial era which cannot be translated any other way. Hereafter, native policy will appear without quotation marks.

40. In committing themselves to respecting "customary law," the French did not explain exactly what they meant. On the one hand, the administration believed that the precolonial legal form was comparable in function to European law, although obviously inferior to it. On the other hand, the

French did not assume that this custom was in any way static, and constantly stressed that any attempt at codification would interfere with the custom's natural evolution under French rule. The nature of precolonial indigenous law, and its transformation during the colonial period, has come in for some debate. The classic statement on the fundamental historical continuity of "customary law" is Elias, *Nature of African Customary Law*. Recently, scholars have begun to examine how precolonial legal forms were decisively shaped by new social forces introduced during the colonial period in different parts of Africa. More often than not, these scholars have argued, the "customary law" the Europeans applied was invented and tells us little about precolonial traditions of law. See Chanock, *Law, Custom and Social Order*; Snyder, "Colonialism and Legal Form" and *Capitalism and Legal Change*; Mann and Roberts, eds., *Law in Colonial Africa*, pp. 21–23. This same invented "custom" can, however, tell us a great deal about the European colonizer. In my discussion the French terms "customary law" and "custom" appear without quotation marks, because they accurately capture the way the French thought about the legal systems of the peoples they were ruling.

41. My remarks about native policy are relevant for the term "native" courts. Because this was what the French called their special African courts, and the term helps to convey the ideology of the period, it has been retained. The phrase native courts will appear hereafter without quotation marks.

42. Arrêté no. 12 "promulguant dans les Colonies et les Territoires du Gouvernement Général de l'AOF le décret du 12 décembre 1905, relatif à la répression de la traite en AOF et au Congo français," Jan. 4, 1906, *JOAOF*, p. 17.

43. French refusal to intervene in civil customs affecting women generally seems to have persisted throughout the colonial period. It is presumably linked to a similar refusal in the metropole to grant women the same rights as men under the Third Republic. Although there was some interest in emancipating women from oppressive marriage customs and paternal authority—and this interest would increase in the 1920's and 1930's—the administration's official attitude was that such social change should proceed at its own pace. This attitude eventually brought French administrators into conflict with French missionaries, particularly in the Western Sudan, who sought to free their own female converts from their subordination within the African household and have them marry according to the precepts of the Catholic Church. But there appears to have been nothing comparable in West Africa, for example, to the "female circumcision" debates which convulsed colonial Kenya in the 1920's. For further (limited) information on French attitudes toward family and marriage customs, see Robert, *L'évolution des coutumes*; de Benoist, *Eglise et pouvoir colonial*.

44. On the administration of justice before 1903 and Roume's view of it, see ANSOM, APC 54/7, Léonce Jore, "Les institutions judiciaires indigènes de l'AOF," n.d. [ca. 1924], chap. 1; AP 1645/3, Roume, "Note pour le min-

istre," July 15, 1903, which discusses the inadequacies of previous attempts to organize a system of native justice in the different colonies and provides an overview of the earlier legislation; Meunier, *Organisation et fonctionnement de la justice indigène*, pp. 42–44.

45. On the history of the *indigénat*, see Asiwaju, "Control through Coercion."

46. For a discussion of this law and how it was applied, see Meunier, *Organisation et fonctionnement de la justice indigène*, pp. 20–32. Besides reprinting the relevant decrees regarding the judicial system in West Africa before 1914, Meunier provides a contemporary, and largely sympathetic, analysis of the entire system.

47. On Muslim courts, see note 11, above.

48. ANSOM, AP 1645/3, "Procès-verbal de la Commission chargée de la réorganisation de la justice dans les territoires du Gouvernement Général de l'AOF," first session, May 18, 1903.

49. Ibid., session of May 20, 1903.

50. Ibid.; ANSOM, AOF VIII, Justice, Lieutenant gouverneur de la Côte d'Ivoire to ministre des Colonies, no. 28, Feb. 2, 1901.

51. Roume summarized the lieutenant governors' criticisms of the professional magistrature in his "Note pour le ministre," July 15, 1903.

52. Gouvernement Général de l'AOF, *Justice indigène*. The 1903 decree also reorganized the administration of French justice in the federation. The provisions for native justice are listed under Titre VI of this decree and are reprinted in Meunier, *Organisation et fonctionnement de la justice indigène*.

53. All Africans who were not considered *assimilés* qualified as subjects of the French Empire. From a legal point of view, an *assimilé* was treated like a European and came under the jurisdiction of the French courts. The commission had recommended that the status of *assimilé* be defined and had suggested its own interpretation. Individuals who should be able to claim *assimilé* status, according to their report, included (1) any individual registered to vote; (2) employees of the administration; (3) any individual registered in the *état-civil*; (4) any individual who within a specified period obtained a notarized act certifying that he was born or has resided for more than five years within a district under the jurisdiction of French law; (5) any foreigner. ANSOM, AP 1645/3, session of May 22, 1903. Meunier argues that this definition was left out of the final decree because it would unintentionally place several categories of individuals under the jurisdiction of French laws against their wishes. The issue would be taken up again in 1912. Meunier, *Organisation et fonctionnement de la justice indigène*, p. 87.

54. ANSOM, AP 1645/3, Roume, "Note pour le ministre," July 15, 1903.

55. Gouvernement Général, *Justice indigène*, pp. 30, 29.

56. Ibid., p. 31.

57. ANS, 2 G 3–3, "Rapport politique," Gouverneur général to ministre des Colonies, second semester, 1903.

58. The most famous examples of administrators known for compiling

sensitive accounts of customary law before World War I are Governor Clozel of Upper Senegal-Niger and Maurice Delafosse. In 1909 it was Clozel, not Governor General Ponty, who ordered the administrators of his colony to complete the classification of customary law requested by Dakar in 1905. Robinson, "Ethnography and Customary Law in Senegal," pp. 232–233; Wooten, "Colonial Administration." Determining how interested French administrators were generally in the peoples they were ruling is no easy task. Sibeud has shown that many French administrators in sub-Saharan Africa were motivated to study local peoples under their authority for practical reasons as well as a desire to establish themselves professionally by publishing their research in France in the most prestigious social science journals of their day ("La naissance de l'ethnographie africaniste," pp. 639–644, 651–657). Unfortunately, no overall study of the content of this colonial ethnography exists; it was clearly of uneven quality, although the best-known authors, such as Maurice Delafosse, Charles Monteil, and François Clozel, paved the way for the creation of the Institut d'Ethnologie at the University of Paris in the 1920's (as will be discussed in Chap. 6).

59. It is worth noting that the number of administrators with legal training increased steadily: 23 percent (1900–1906), 29 percent (1906–1914). Nevertheless, their training was exclusively in Roman law. Cohen, *Rulers of Empire*, p. 35.

60. For the antislavery movement in France before and during the Second Republic, see Jennings, *French Reaction*; Martin, *L'abolition de l'esclavage*; Daget, "Les mots." The best existing account of French attitudes toward slavery in West Africa before 1905 is Renault, "L'abolition de l'esclavage"; also of interest is Boutillier, "Les captifs en A.O.F." For the administration's own view of the history of French anti-slavery in West Africa since 1848 see ANS, K 24, "Historique de la question de l'esclavage depuis 1848." This memorandum was written by administrator Poulet and dated March 18, 1905. French views are also discussed in Roberts and Klein, "Banamba Slave Exodus," pp. 382–383; R. Roberts, "End of Slavery"; Klein, "Slavery and Emancipation"; Mbodj, "Abolition of Slavery in Senegal." Klein's forthcoming comprehensive study of slavery and emancipation in French West Africa should be especially illuminating on the question of French views of slavery and African responses for the entire period under discussion here.

61. Renault, "L'abolition de l'esclavage," p. 6.

62. This flagrant disregard for the provisions of the 1848 law was justified on political grounds. The French did not want to antagonize unnecessarily the slave owners, most of whom were chiefs in the protectorate zones, with whom the maintenance of good relations was perceived as paramount to French survival.

63. Schoelcher, "Abolition définitive de l'esclavage au Sénégal," *Le Rappel*, Feb. 15, 1881, quoted in Schoelcher, *Polémique coloniale*, 1: 260–263. Unfortunately, it was not long before the administration lapsed into its old

ways. Schoelcher, "Toujours l'esclavage au Sénégal, *Le Rappel*, Dec. 19, 1882, quoted in Schoelcher, *Polémique coloniale*, 2: 191–192.

64. For additional details on the French conquest, see Kanya-Forstner, *Conquest of the Western Sudan*, chap. 1. An excellent account of the colonial army's treatment of slavery in the Western Sudan is R. Roberts, *Warriors, Merchants, and Slaves*. Bouche, *Les villages de liberté*, discusses the army's attempts in the Sudan to liberate slaves and regroup them into *villages de liberté*; these villages are also mentioned briefly in R. Roberts, *Warriors, Merchants, and Slaves*, p. 144. The role of *villages de liberté* in the pacification of Ivory Coast is touched upon in Weiskel, *French Colonial Rule*, pp. 104, 109. For a discussion of slave recruitment, see Echenberg, "Slaves into Soldiers."

65. Deherme, *L'Afrique occidentale française*, p. 475.

66. For contemporary accounts of this decision, see André, *De l'esclavage à Madagascar*; Lebon, *La politique de la France*, pp. 159–173.

67. Quoted in Deherme, *L'Afrique occidentale française*, p. 482. Georges Deherme was the author of the Government General's report on slavery; he later published his findings in his book *L'Afrique occidentale française*, but his original manuscript can also be consulted in ANS, K 25.

68. Circulaire, Délégué du gouverneur général to commandants de cercle, Haut-Sénégal et Niger, Feb. 1, 1901, quoted in Deherme, *L'Afrique occidentale française*, p. 484.

69. Renault, "L'abolition de l'esclavage," pp. 54–56.

70. ANS, K 15, Letter regarding the Brussels General Act (1890), signed by Roume, n.d.; ANS, K 16, Note regarding slavery, signed by Roume, n.d.; ANS, K 15, Letter regarding the Brussels General Act (1890).

71. Arrêté no. 12 "promulguant dans les Colonies et les Territoires du Gouvernement Général de l'AOF le décret du 12 décembre 1905," Jan. 4, 1906, *JOAOF*, pp. 17–19.

72. Deherme, *L'Afrique occidentale française*, pp. 493–494, 496.

73. Roume, Discours, Conseil de Gouvernement, Dec. 4, 1905, *JOAOF*, p. 592.

74. This is the viewpoint of Roberts and Klein, "Banamba Slave Exodus"; and Searing, "Accommodation and Resistance."

75. In the section of his book entitled "Action sociale," Deherme gives an idea of the prevailing French view of African attitudes toward work and of slavery's supposedly pernicious influence on Africans' ability to labor without the threat of force. See, in particular, Deherme, *L'Afrique occidentale française*, pp. 499–517.

76. ANS, K 15, Letter regarding the Brussels General Act (1890).

77. These instructions are quoted in Deherme, *L'Afrique occidentale française*, p. 490.

78. ANS, K 24, Gouverneur général to administrateurs et officiers commandants de cercle en territoire civile de la Mauritanie, Mar. 22, 1906; Roberts and Klein, "Banamba Slave Exodus," pp. 386–387; ANS, 2 G 8–1,

Lieutenant gouverneur du Haut-Sénégal et Niger to gouverneur général, no. 91, Feb. 5, 1909.

79. The effects of abolition in the Middle Niger Valley are discussed in R. Roberts, *Warriors, Merchants, and Slaves*, pp. 175–213, who emphasizes the extent to which slaves freed themselves once the French had created the conditions for emancipation. The full impact of slave emancipation upon the populations in French West Africa has not yet been documented. In addition to Klein's and Searing's work on Senegal, see Moitt, "Slavery and Emancipation in Senegal's Peanut Basin"; for the Western Sudan, see Klein's summary of the literature in "Slavery and Emancipation," pp. 182–190; R. Roberts, "End of Slavery"; the decline of slavery in Dahomey is discussed by Manning, *Slavery, Colonialism, and Economic Growth*, pp. 188–193, and among the Baule in Ivory Coast, by Weiskel, *French Colonial Rule*; for the Guinea coast, see Klein, "Slave Resistance." For a French administrator's assessment of the decline of slavery by the 1920's in the Western Sudan, see de Kersaint-Gilly, "Essai sur l'évolution de l'esclavage."

80. Renault, "L'abolition de l'esclavage," pp. 57–58. On this point, I disagree with Fall, who sees Renault as concluding that French attitudes toward slavery in Senegal were entirely hypocritical (Fall, *Le travail forcé*, p. 34). I think Renault presents a much more nuanced picture of the French, and that he argues for a real change in France's commitment to combat slavery with the advent of the Government General in West Africa.

81. Débats, Chambre des Députés, Mar. 19, 1896, *JORF*, pp. 1001–1008; André, *De l'esclavage à Madagascar*, pp. 165–169; Lebon, *La politique de la France*, pp. 160–167.

82. Débats, Chambre des Députés, March 19, 1896, *JORF*, pp. 1007, 1009.

83. Décret, Feb. 7, 1897, *JORF, Lois et Décrets*, Feb. 10, 1897, pp. 895–897.

84. The new law in no way altered the privileged status of the *assimilés* of the Four Communes of Senegal, who considered themselves citizens—even though they had not been individually naturalized. Idowu, "Assimilation in 19th Century Senegal," pp. 196–197.

85. ANSOM, AP 2759/2, Politique indigène: naturalisation des indigènes, législation et projets. Gouverneur général to ministre des Colonies, no. 1015, May 30, 1907. Roume's proposed decree, entitled "Projet de décret," is attached to this letter.

86. ANSOM, AP 2759/2, "Note pour le Ministre au sujet du projet de décret de Roume," Aug. 5, 1907. The author of this note, Albert Duchêne, raised these questions. He wanted to know whether Roume would require each Senegalese born in the Four Communes to apply for naturalization individually in order to continue to exercise his electoral rights. If this were the governor general's intention, a clause would be needed to make the objective of the decree clear. Roume replied that the decree in no way affected the current status of the Senegalese in question. AP 2759/2, Gouverneur général to ministre des Colonies, Nov. 23, 1907. Although this position sug-

gests that Roume was not hostile to the privileges of the *assimilés,* it is difficult to know his attitude for sure. In my analysis, I have emphasized the liberal nature of Roume's proposal as it affected subjects outside the Four Communes. Other historians, however, have seen in the attempts to introduce a naturalization law to West Africa a ploy by the French administration to challenge the exceptional political privileges of the *originaires.* Once a naturalization law existed, the argument goes, most *originaires* would not have been able to satisfy the conditions for naturalization. This is Idowu's perspective in "Assimilation in 19th Century Senegal," pp. 214–215. French attitudes toward the *originaires* will be discussed in more detail in Chap. 5.

87. On the question of who qualified to exercise rights in French republican doctrine, see Rosanvallon, *Le sacre du citoyen,* pp. 393–441.

88. On bourgeois domesticity and "republican motherhood," see Smith, *Ladies of the Leisure Class;* Landes, *Women in the Public Sphere;* Fraisse, *Reason's Muse;* McMillan, *Housewife or Harlot;* L. Clark, *Schooling the Daughters of Marianne;* Hause, *Women's Suffrage;* Moses, *French Feminism.*

CHAPTER 4

1. Quoted by Ponty, *Justice indigène,* p. 33.

2. Sonolet, *Moussa et Gi-gla,* p. 114.

3. ANSOM, EE II, 1137 (6), personnel file; *Annuaire du Ministère des Colonies,* 1912, p. 883; Johnson, "William Ponty," pp. 129–136. Johnson provides an excellent introduction to Ponty's republicanism. We differ, however, in our approaches. Unlike Johnson, I am more interested in the larger republican culture that Roume and Ponty shared in West Africa before World War I than in Ponty's individual achievements. For a fictionalized account of Ponty's years in office, see the novel by the colonial administrator Robert Arnaud (who wrote under the pseudonym Robert Randau), *Le chef des porte-plume.*

4. This difference in interests was obvious even to contemporaries. Consider, for example, the following statement, which appeared in the journal of the colonial interest group, the Comité de l'Afrique Française: "If M. Ponty has not altered the [economic] program established by M. Roume, if instead he has made every effort to bring about its execution, he has nevertheless been able to infuse his administration with a new element which . . . will give his government a very personal stamp. To put it succinctly, M. Roume created a financial and administrative organization and inaugurated a native policy, M. Ponty is completing and perfecting the former and giving full scope to the latter" ("La pénétration de la Côte d'Ivoire," p. 193). A similar assessment was made by Humbert, "L'AOF sous l'administration de M. W. Ponty."

5. ANS, 4 G 6, Mission Guyho, 1907, "Rapport sur les rouages centraux du Gouvernement Général," Dec. 5, 1907.

6. Colonial inspectors constituted an elite corps in the French colonial service. Their members were sent throughout the empire to verify accounts

and policy decisions of the local administrations. They then filed lengthy reports with the colonial minister summarizing their findings, and they could recommend measures of redress against incompetent officials at all levels of the overseas bureaucracy. Missions to West Africa were rare before World War I, when metropolitan interest in the federation was intermittent at best. After the war, they became more numerous. Colonial inspectors' ability to check abuses was always limited, but their reports are an invaluable "outside" source of information on administrative practices in the colonies. See Garner, "Watchdogs of Empire."

7. ANSOM, AP 3065, "Dépêche relatif aux critiques formulées par les Missions d'Inspection qui ont opérées en 1908 dans plusieurs colonies de l'AOF," Ministre des Colonies to gouverneur général, Apr. 19, 1909.

8. ANS, 4 G 6, Gouverneur général to ministre des Colonies, no. 1701, Aug. 13, 1909.

9. William Ponty, Discours, Conseil de Gouvernement, June 21, 1909, *JOAOF*, p. 289. While the word *apprivoisé* literally translates as "tamed," Johnson has argued that the best equivalent to Ponty's usage in English is "acclimated to French authority" ("William Ponty," p. 142). I agree with this translation, although I would add that to *apprivoiser*, for Ponty, was also to civilize. Ponty was the only governor general to use the term regularly.

10. For individual case studies of military policy see, for Senegal, Diouf, *Le Kajoor au XIXe siècle*; Searing, "Accommodation and Resistance," 1: 56–81; Barry, *La Sénégambie du XVe au XIXe siècle*, pp. 281–395; Klein, *Islam and Imperialism in Senegal*; Robinson, *Chiefs and Clerics*, pp. 28–69, 104–138; for Dahomey, Lombard, *Structures de type 'féodal'* and *Autorités traditionnelles*, pp. 146–147; for Guinea, Suret-Canale, "La fin de la chefferie en Guinée"; Derman, *Serfs, Peasants and Socialists*, pp. 43–48; for Upper Volta, Skinner, *The Mossi of the Upper Volta*, pp. 139–160; Madiéga, "Esquisse de la conquête."

11. For the ways in which French policy exacerbated social disintegration, see Diouf's superb analysis of Faidherbe's policy in Cayor in the 1860's. Diouf, *Le Kajoor au XIXe siècle*, chaps. 11–16 and conclusion.

12. This has been the traditional view of French administration in the Western Sudan, although recent research suggests that it needs to be qualified. R. Roberts has shown that in parts of the Middle Niger, the army attempted to resurrect certain pre-Umarian states and to identify legitimate heirs who would be loyal to the French (*Warriors, Merchants, and Slaves*, pp. 154–161). For the literature on French direct administration, see, for example, Lombard, *Autorités traditionnelles*, pp. 106–108; and the following exchange: Deschamps, "Et maintenant, Lord Lugard?"; Crowder, "Indirect Rule: French and British Style."

13. Searing has shown the extent to which the old policy of protectorates was preserved in Cayor, Walo, and Jolof in the 1890's by the administration of Martial Merlin ("Accommodation and Resistance," 1: 86–171). Among the Baule peoples in Ivory Coast, whom the French only began to conquer

after 1898, the first civilian administrators also preferred a protectorate system based on respecting traditional institutions. See Weiskel, *French Colonial Rule*, pp. 142–154. In Upper Volta, the French chose to maintain rather than suppress the various kingdoms of the Mossi. The Mossi Nabas, or kings, were, however, quickly reduced to ceremonial figureheads within the colonial hierarchy. Recent research on the military territory of Niger has revealed a combination of approaches until 1908. In the north a system of uniform canton chiefs emerged; in parts of western Niger, on the other hand, a protectorate solution was sometimes adopted to cement certain earlier alliances with local leaders. Fuglestad, *History of Niger*, pp. 66–70.

14. For example, in a letter from Lieutenant Governor Clozel to Roume in 1907, Clozel wrote that he would attempt to take into account as much as possible "the principles repeatedly posed by the Governor General, that is to say, the disappearance of the great native commands." ANS, 5 E 15, Lieutenant gouverneur de la Côte d'Ivoire to gouverneur général, no. 30, May 20, 1907. In 1917, the lieutenant governor of Guinea also makes a reference to the "instructions of 1907 aimed at destroying the great native commands." ANS, 5 E 40, Conseil de Gouvernement, Documents, 1917. These instructions were not, of course, always followed, for individual governors realized that dismantling the commands in question could have disastrous implications for maintaining French rule, since they presupposed sufficient European personnel or African collaborators to take the place of the displaced sovereigns.

15. Roume, Discours, Conseil de Gouvernement, Dec. 4, 1905, *JOAOF*, p. 586.

16. ANS, 2 G 3–3, "Rapport politique," second semester, Gouverneur général to ministre des Colonies, 1903.

17. Searing, "Accommodation and Resistance," 1: 236–237.

18. Ponty was influenced by the ideas of Gallieni as much as those of his direct superior, Archinard. Gallieni had preceded Archinard as commander of the French forces on the Upper Niger River. He, too, was a firm believer in France's *mission civilisatrice* and architect of a *politique des races*. For Gallieni's native policy, see Michel, *Gallieni*, pp. 147–234; Rabinow, *French Modern*, pp. 146–162.

19. ANS, 17 G 38, Circulaire, Gouverneur général to lieutenants gouverneurs, Sept. 22, 1909. Ponty's policy toward chiefs has often been discussed in the context of French native policy generally, but its ideological character has not always been recognized. Johnson, for example, overlooks the antichief sentiment in the *politique des races* ("William Ponty," pp. 141–151). Cohen, Harrison, Searing, and Amselle, on the other hand, argue that Ponty was particularly sensitive to African forms of "feudalism," and my findings confirm their insights (Cohen, *Rulers of Empire*, pp. 75–76; Harrison, *France and Islam*, pp. 73–89; Searing, "Accommodation and Resistance," chap. 3; Amselle, *Logiques métisses*, pp. 182, 239). There is also an older literature that has long acknowledged French hostility in general to

chiefs in West Africa. But these studies fail to distinguish between the different attitudes within the French administrative hierarchy, and imply that antichief sentiment persisted from the advent of civilian rule until independence. This is the impression conveyed by Crowder, "West African Chiefs"; Villandre, "Les chefferies traditionnelles"; Cornevin, "Evolution des chefferies traditionnelles" (2 parts). In fact, the official attitude toward chiefs changed not only with personnel, but in the wake of such watersheds as World War I. The change in attitudes toward chiefs in the 1920's is the theme of Chap. 6.

20. ANS, 17 G 38, Circulaire, Sept. 22, 1909. As this quotation indicates, there was an equally strong anticlerical dimension to the *politique des races*, which further demonstrates the hold of republican values on Ponty. Ponty was convinced that Africans were doubly oppressed by an alliance of feudal chiefs and Muslim elites, and this belief led to ideologically inspired campaigns against the religious aristocracy in this period as well, at least until 1912. Harrison has thoroughly analyzed this dimension of French thinking (*France and Islam*, chaps. 3–5).

21. Marty, "La politique indigène," p. 7. Paul Marty worked in Ponty's Arab bureau and upon Ponty's death published a eulogy of the governor general that summarized his major initiatives while in office.

22. ANS, 17 G 38, Circulaire, Sept. 22, 1909.

23. These instructions are quoted in Marty, "La politique indigène," p. 7.

24. Circulaire "a. s. de l'impôt de capitation en AOF," Gouverneur général to lieutenants gouverneurs, Jan. 30, 1914, *JOAOF*, p. 152; circulaire no. 75c "a. s. des tournées devant être effectuées par les Administrateurs," Gouverneur général to lieutenants gouverneurs, Sept. 6, 1911, *JOAOF*, p. 623.

25. ANS, Circulaire no. 57c "a. s. de la politique indigène et du fonctionnement de l'Inspection des Affaires Administratives," Gouverneur général to lieutenants gouverneurs, Aug. 12, 1911; ANS, 2 G 9–5, "Rapport d'ensemble, situation politique et administrative," Gouverneur général to ministre des Colonies, 1909.

26. ANS, 2 G 3–3, "Rapport politique," Gouverneur général to ministre des Colonies, 1903. This report contained a section on each colony, including Upper Senegal-Niger, from which this passage is taken.

27. Circulaire, Jan. 30, 1914, *JOAOF*, p. 152.

28. These assessments of the effect of the *politique des races* upon policy making throughout the federation are contained in ANS, 17 G 39, Affaires Politiques, Gouverneur général to ministre des Colonies, "a. s. des chefs indigènes," Aug. 1917; Chef des affaires civiles to directeur des Finances, "a. s. des remises d'impôt aux indigènes," Apr. 23, 1917.

29. ANS, 17 G 39, Chef des affaires civiles to directeur des Finances, Apr. 23, 1917. Despite his arcane language, Delafosse was one of the first and best ethnographers of his time. Delafosse's ideas and role in advising the Government General will be discussed more fully in Chap. 6.

30. In the case of Dakar's Islamic policy, the appropriate dates here are 1902 to 1912. In 1912, an ideologically inspired campaign against *marabouts* in the Futa Jallon led to open revolt, and Dakar's official attitude toward Islam began to change. A Service des Affaires Musulmanes was founded in 1913 to promote the scientific study of Islam, on the grounds that without knowledge of its "sociological laws" one would be unable to guide "native society." The arrival of Paul Marty, an Islamic expert sent by the Colonial Ministry in 1912 to advise the governor general on Muslim affairs, also explains this "scientific turn." Under Marty's direction, a more pragmatic and benign view of African Islam emerged, which emphasized preserving its institutions rather than eradicating them. This development presaged a comparable reassessment of chiefs that would occur, as we shall see, during World War I. Harrison, *France and Islam*, pp. 105–117.

31. Circulaire no. 29c "a. s. de l'unité de fonctionnement de la justice indigène en AOF," Gouverneur général to lieutenants gouverneurs, Mar. 6, 1910, *JOAOF*, pp. 161–162.

32. Ponty, *Justice indigène*, p. 31.

33. ANS, 5 E 24, "Note sur la situation politique," June 10, 1910, by the Chef du service des Affaires administratives et indigènes. This note discusses Ponty's circular of March 6, 1910.

34. Since Roume's first attempt to have a naturalization law passed in 1907, a Cour de Cassation ruling of July 24, 1907, had established that the Senegalese of the Four Communes could be considered citizens only if they were individually naturalized (which meant, for Muslims, giving up what the French called "leur statut personnel" and accepting the provisions of the Civil Code). It was thus now possible to go ahead and establish the legal criteria for acquiring citizenship. ANSOM, AP 2759/4, "Note sur l'opportunité d'un décret permettant aux indigènes de l'AOF d'accéder à la qualité de citoyen français," Mar. 15, 1911.

35. In addition to the criteria suggested by Roume in 1907, two were suggested by Ponty in his note of March 15, 1911: a certificate of primary studies and verification of tax compliance by property owners. The administration was concerned that it protect itself against "overly hasty or excessive numbers of naturalizations inspired by motives of immediate personal gain rather than by a natural evolution toward the ideas of civilization and of progress." ANSOM, AP 2759/4, "Note." Article 6 stipulated that citizenship was personal, but could be extended to a wife married under French law and any children from that union that had been registered on the *état-civil*. Arrêté no. 907 "promulguant en AOF le décret du 25 mai 1912 fixant les conditions d'accession des indigènes de l'AOF à la qualité de citoyen français," June 12, 1925, *JOAOF*, pp. 395–396.

36. Ponty, *Justice indigène*, p. 32.

37. Ibid., p. 42.

38. Ibid., pp. 21–22.

39. Ibid., p. 78.

40. Ibid., p. 79. Article 48 had figured in the 1903 decree and was apparently retained in the 1912 reform as continuing proof of French liberalism. For a further discussion of when Africans could use French courts, see Opoku, "Traditional Law under French Colonial Rule."

41. Ponty's emphasis on respecting local customs as part of France's civilizing mission could, in light of his admission that maintaining such custom was crucial to the preservation of public order, be interpreted as a convenient pretext for not extending the full guarantees of French law to Africans in order to better subjugate them. Aissi, in his study of the legal system in French Equatorial Africa, where the administration of justice was very similar to that introduced in West Africa, has adopted this perspective ("La justice indigène"). Although there is no question that in practice native justice was discriminatory and preserved full powers of repression to colonial authorities, the legal system elaborated by Ponty cannot be said to have been devised with only this end in mind. French actions in West Africa were far too complex to allow the attribution of all policy decisions to economic or political motivations.

42. ANSOM, APC 54/7, Léonce Jore, "Les institutions judiciaires indigènes." In the first draft of the 1912 reform, the village chiefs retained their powers to punish. According to the author of this draft, although abuses by these chiefs had been noted, preserving their right to punish petty offenses would "fortify their authority and . . . enhance their prestige, in keeping with our native policy." ANS, M 81, Lieutenant Gouverneur Guyon, "Avant-projet de la réorganisation de la justice. Titre VI—justice indigène," 1910. Most lieutenant governors, however, recommended that village chiefs be stripped of the right to punish even the most minor infractions. The only exception was the lieutenant governor of Dahomey, who argued that village chiefs should retain responsibility for maintaining order. He pointed out that the French had no choice but to rule through a form of "attenuated protectorate" (*protectorat atténué*) and thus had to leave some powers to local chiefs. ANS, M 83, Lieutenant gouverneur du Dahomey to gouverneur général, no. 137, Apr. 29, 1911. This point of view conflicted with Ponty's commitment to encourage direct contact through curtailing the chiefs' powers, even at the village level, and was not incorporated into the final draft of the decree. See later drafts, also by Guyon, of the proposed decree in ANS, M 83, Lieutenant Gouverneur Guyon, "Avant-projet de la réorganisation de la justice indigène," Jan. 25, 1911.

43. This issue had been raised as early as 1905, when administrators discovered that they technically could not appeal province chiefs' judgments they considered unfair. The prosecutor general, who was responsible for interpreting the decree, was opposed to extending such an appeal, on the grounds that the administrator himself would then be less than impartial and that the objectivity of the lower courts would be affected. ANS, M 80, "Extrait de la lettre du Procureur général chef du service judiciaire de l'AOF à gouverneur général," no. 962, Nov. 11, 1905. Roume, however, felt that

the administrator did constitute an impartial and independent third party who should be allowed to intervene in "cases where the solution was not immediately evident to those members of the native courts as of yet imperfectly prepared for their new and important mission as judges. It is necessary indeed, that in the accomplishment of their delicate task, the latter be guided and educated, in a manner of speaking, by us." Roume then issued instructions to the lieutenant governor of Dahomey granting administrators the right to appeal judgments from the lower courts. ANS, M 94, Gouverneur général to procureur général, no. 816, Mar. 21, 1906, and Gouverneur général to lieutenant gouverneur du Dahomey, Dec. 12, 1906. Ponty subsequently confirmed these instructions in 1910 and 1911; the 1912 reform formalized this interpretation and extended it to the entire federation. ANS, M 94, Lieutenant gouverneur du Dahomey to gouverneur général, no. 391, Nov. 5, 1911, and Gouverneur général to lieutenant gouverneur du Dahomey, no. 438, Dec. 14, 1911.

44. Here again, it is interesting to note the contradictions in the Government General's outlook. Considerations of public order had, in the case of civil law, dictated little interference in African custom; now the same considerations were being evoked to justify intervention.

45. ANS, M 95, "Note sur le droit d'appel," Service d'Administration Générale et des Affaires Politiques, Mar. 8, 1908. The vagueness of the 1903 decree on this point led Guyon, the head of this service, to recommend that all administrators prosecute crimes allowed by custom when they felt such action was warranted. In 1910, this same question was taken up again by the Service d'Administration Générale et des Affaires Politiques (now renamed the Service des Affaires Politiques, Administratives et Economiques). In a note prepared by the head of this service, it was pointed out that the "felonies" reserved to the circle courts for sentencing were inadequately defined and left too much responsibility in the hands of the province courts. At the same time, however, precedent had actually extended the competence of the circle courts beyond that of the lower courts. This situation, the author argued, should be formalized by a new decree specifically listing the felonies reserved to the circle courts for prosecution. The 1912 reform incorporated just such a list. ANS, M 15, "Note sur la compétence quant aux faits des tribunaux de cercle du Chef des Affaires Politiques, Administratives et Economiques," no. 1497, 1910.

46. Ponty, *Justice indigène*, p. 82.

47. These provisions were contained in article 36 of the 1912 decree. Ibid., p. 84.

48. Because of the seriousness of these crimes, they came under the jurisdiction of the circle courts, presided over by a French administrator. Ibid., art. 19, pp. 11–12.

49. Circulaire "a. s. des pouvoirs disciplinaires," Gouverneur général to lieutenants gouverneurs, Sept. 28, 1913, *JOAOF*, pp. 909–910.

50. Ponty, *Justice indigène*, pp. 85, 86.

51. Ibid., art. 37, pp. 19–20.

52. Maurice Delafosse described African custom on this point: "In general the natives of West Africa do not distinguish between criminal and civil offenses: in principle, any judicial affair amongst them is a civil matter between two parties, one of whom claims to have been injured by the other. It follows that the role of the court consists principally in determining whether there really is a wronged party, by whom he was injured and what reparation should be accorded to him: it is thus the principle of compensation . . . that supersedes that of punishment, and the latter may not even figure in the sentencing, even if according to Western jurisprudence, a crime has been committed." Delafosse, *Haut-Sénégal-Niger*, 3: 153.

53. This point was made by an administrator in a response to an early draft of the new decree drawn up by the attorney general. He objected that it was wrong to make French, rather than customary, law the basis for determining crimes, and argued that if anything, the *commandants'* judicial responsibilities should be curbed, not expanded. ANS, M 80, J. N. Valzi, "Note au sujet des projets de modification au décret du 10 novembre 1903," Oct. 5, 1907. On the other hand, a sampling of the sentencing by the lower courts in the colony of Senegal in cases of matrimonial disputes, reveals that the administration did not hesitate to set aside traditional punishments for adultery, such as mutilation or confiscation of property, as too "barbaric" to respect, and substituted short prison sentences. See Saar, "Jurisprudence des tribunaux indigènes," pp. 151-152.

54. Professional judges predominated in the composition of the Chambre d'homologation. This court was presided over by a judge from the French Appeals Court in Dakar; other members of the court included two French counselors, two functionaries from the Government General, and two African assessors. The last had only a consultative voice.

55. Ponty, *Justice indigène*, arts. 22–28, pp. 13–16.

56. Chambre d'homologation, arrêt Sept. 14, 1909, affaire Ango, Kalley et Taddo, du cercle de Niamey, in Joucla and Gilbert-Desvallons, eds., *Jurisprudence*, p. 33.

57. Chambre d'homologation, arrêt Nov. 26, 1907, affaire Toïné et deux autres, and arrêt June 8, 1908, affaire Déridié Bamba et un autre, both in Joucla and Gilbert-Desvallons, *Jurisprudence*, pp. 35, 27.

58. Chambre d'homologation, arrêt June 11, 1907, affaire Mama Couloubaly, and arrêt Feb. 22, 1910, affaire Seyni Saloum, both in Joucla and Gilbert-Desvallons, *Jurisprudence*, pp. 20–21, 69.

59. ANS, M 80, J. N. Valzi, "Note au sujet des projets de modification au décret du 10 novembre 1903," Oct. 10, 1907.

60. ANS, M 83, Lieutenant gouverneur du Haut-Sénégal et Niger to Lieutenant Gouverneur Guyon, Apr. 29, 1911, and Lieutenant gouverneur p.i. du Dahomey to gouverneur général, no. 137, Apr. 29, 1911.

61. ANS, M 161, Lieutenant gouverneur du Haut-Sénégal et Niger to gouverneur général, no. 127, Aug. 25, 1912.

62. On this point, also see Saar, "La Chambre Spéciale d'Homologation," p. 104.

63. The result of this single-mindedness, according to Saar, was that "the introduction of principles contained in the French penal code occurred in West Africa, and on numerous points, well before the official decree of April 30, 1946, attributed exclusive powers of criminal jurisdiction to French courts" (ibid., p. 115). The opposite point of view has also been put forth by the author of a history of the administration of justice in West Africa published in 1955: André Robert maintains that the attempt to introduce French criminal principles from above had no impact upon African society before 1946 (Robert, *L'évolution des coutumes*, pp. 57, 86, 147, 191, 202–216). The numerous quotations I cite suggest that Saar's assessment is the correct one, although it must be assumed that the degree to which French principles infiltrated custom varied tremendously throughout the federation.

64. Ponty, *Justice indigène*, p. 31; ANS, M 85, "Note au sujet du décret du 16 août 1912," n.d. [ca. 1912–1913]. This note was prepared by Ponty's staff to reply to a letter from a notorious "pro-native" deputy, Maurice Viollette, criticizing the new decree as reactionary.

65. ANS, M 97, Gouverneur général to ministre des Colonies, no. 711, Apr. 10, 1919.

66. Groff, "The Dynamics of Collaboration," has recently shown how a traditional officeholder, working as a linguist for the French in Ivory Coast, successfully used the courts to contest an illegal expropriation of his wealth by the local administration; R. Roberts, "The Case of Faama Mademba Sy," has examined how the French used the courts to diminish the powers of Mademba, king of Sansini. These studies, along with those by Saar, suggest that the courts were used by both the French and Africans, although to what extent awaits further research.

67. ANSOM, APC 54/7, Léonce Jore, "Les institutions judiciaires indigènes de l'AOF."

68. ANS, 2 G 8–7, "Rapport sur l'enseignement," Gouverneur général to ministre des Colonies, 1908; circulaire no. 82c "relative à l'enseignement dans les colonies de l'AOF," Gouverneur général to lieutenants gouverneurs, Aug. 30, 1910, *JOAOF*, p. 565; William Ponty, Discours, Conseil de Gouvernement, June 20, 1911, *JOAOF*, p. 370; see also circulaire no. 42c. "a. s. de l'augmentation de la population scolaire en AOF," Gouverneur général to lieutenants gouverneurs, Apr. 19, 1913, *JOAOF*, pp. 493–494.

69. Circulaire no. 16c, Feb. 2, 1910, *JOAOF*, p. 84.

70. ANS, 2 G 8–7, "Rapport sur l'enseignement," 1908, Gouverneur général to ministre des Colonies, first version; circulaire no. 16c, Feb. 2, 1910, *JOAOF*, p. 84.

71. Circulaire no. 44c "relative aux programmes scolaires," Gouverneur général to lieutenants gouverneurs, May 1, 1914, *JOAOF*, pp. 461–462; Ponty, Discours, Conseil de Gouvernement, Dec. 18, 1908, *JOAOF*, p. 586.

72. Ponty, Discours, Conseil de Gouvernement, June 20, 1910, Sept. 12, 1912, *JOAOF*, pp. 405, 732.

73. Circulaire no. 29c "a. s. de l'emploi de la langue française," Gouverneur général to lieutenants gouverneurs, May 8, 1911, *JOAOF*, p. 286; circulaire no. 82c, Aug. 30, 1910, *JOAOF*, p. 565.

74. This is Bouche's point of view. For a full discussion of Hardy's reforms, see Bouche, *L'enseignement*, 2: 778–865.

75. Circulaire "a. s. de l'application des arrêtés du 6 juin 1908, concernant le personnel de l'Enseignement en AOF," and arrêté no. 632 "organisant le cadre des Inspecteurs de l'Enseignement," Gouverneur général to lieutenants gouverneurs, June 6, 1908, *JOAOF*, pp. 326–327; circulaire no. 52c "relative au cours d'adultes," Gouverneur général to lieutenants gouverneurs, Feb. 21, 1909, *JOAOF*, p. 114.

76. Circulaire no. 82c, Aug. 30, 1910, *JOAOF*, p. 566; circulaire no. 29c, May 8, 1911, *JOAOF*, pp. 286–287.

77. See esp. circulaire no. 62c "a. s. de la refonte des textes de l'enseignement en AOF," Gouverneur général to lieutenants gouverneurs, Aug. 24, 1911, *JOAOF*, pp. 575–576; and circulaire no. 16c, Feb. 2, 1910, *JOAOF*, p. 84, which argued that although compulsion was not possible, all African employees of the French should be "the first to provide this elementary example of devotion to our institutions and comprehension of our ideas which consists of sending their children to school."

78. Circulaire no. 44c, May 1, 1914, *JOAOF*, pp. 463–482.

79. Hardy, *Une conquête morale*; Sonolet and Pérès, *Le livre du maître africain*.

80. Circulaire no. 44c, May 1, 1914, *JOAOF*, pp. 463, 464; Hardy, *Une conquête morale*, pp. 183–196, 267–274.

81. Circulaire no. 44c, May 1, 1914, *JOAOF*, pp. 471, 473–474.

82. Sonolet et Pérès, *Le livre du maître africain*, p. 119; Gay and Mortreux, eds., *French Elementary Schools*, pp. 34, 99–102.

83. Sonolet, *Moussa et Gi-gla*. Sonolet, a former *chargé de mission* in West Africa, abridged the same textbook under a different title in 1924 for use in France—so that young French children could become acquainted with West Africa, its inhabitants, its riches and the "admirable progress France is bringing about there." Sonolet, *Les aventures de deux négrillons*.

84. Sonolet, *Moussa et Gi-gla*, p. 74.

85. Ibid., chaps. 27 and 49.

86. Ibid., pp. 123–125, 110. Also see p. 89.

87. Ibid., pp. 80, 52–53, 82, 138.

88. Ibid., pp. 39, 50, 83, 248; this point was stated again in the conclusion. In Bruno's 1922 edition of *Le tour de la France par deux enfants* (used in metropolitan schools) the term does not come up in the same way. There are many references to what an *homme* does and does not do; but the emphasis is on becoming an *honnête homme* and a good *Français* (pp. 17, 20, 23, 95, 100, 102, 144, 180, 212, 234, 243, 289).

89. Hardy, *Une conquête morale*, p. 341; ANS, 5 E 40, "Rapport sur l'enseignement," Conseil de Gouvernement, Documents, 1917. Georges Hardy had been inspector of education in West Africa since 1912 and would be appointed director of the Ecole Coloniale in 1926. He thus had the opportunity to shape policy not only in the colonies but in Paris as well.

90. Deherme, *L'Afrique occidentale française*, p. 498.

91. In 1912, Dakar concluded that the results from the first few years of the normal school's existence were "satisfactory but not brilliant" and requested that the governors take more interest in preparing candidates from their colonies for admission. Circulaire no. 111c, "Inspection des écoles et rapports mensuels d'inspection," Gouverneur général to lieutenants gouverneurs, Oct. 28, 1912, *JOAOF*, p. 688. A circular from the previous year had made the same complaint. ANS, Circulaire no. 103, Gouverneur général to lieutenants gouverneurs, Nov. 11, 1911.

92. ANS, 2 G 14–56, "Situation de l'enseignement, 1913–1914," Gouverneur général to ministre des Colonies. According to this report, Senegal (pop. 1,250,000) led the federation in education: 4,500 students in 48 schools, 40 French teachers and 60 African ones. The Sudan, in contrast, with a total population four times that of Senegal (pop. 5,000,000), had an enrollment of 3,000 students and a teaching staff of 30 French and 28 African instructors. This great discrepancy is partially explained by the fact that more than half of the schools in Senegal were located within the Four Communes. Bouche, *L'enseignement*, 2: 614, 637. All these statistics were provided by the colonial administration and are undoubtedly inflated, since they did not correspond to any objective standard regarding what constituted a school or provide any information on how long a student attended classes. Population estimates are no more accurate. The governmental circulars' descriptions of how little progress had been made furnish a more reliable indication of the lamentable state of education in West Africa in 1913.

93. ANSOM, AP 3052, Mission Kair, Côte d'Ivoire, 1920–1921, "Rapport no. 16," Apr. 9, 1921.

94. Only in the 1930's would Dakar contemplate, for the first time, some instruction in African languages. See, for example, ANS, Circulaire no. 107, Gouverneur général to lieutenants gouverneurs, Apr. 8, 1933, which discussed "enseignement populaire." Even then, however, the emphasis remained upon teaching Africans "spoken French."

95. Débats, Chambre des Députés, Dec. 19, 1912, *JORF*, p. 3306.

96. ANS, H 13, Circulaire confidentiel, "a. s. de l'application des règles sanitaires," Gouverneur général to lieutenants gouverneurs, May 14, 1913. An edited version of this circular appeared in the *JOAOF*, which avoided any mention of segregation.

CHAPTER 5

1. ANS, 2 G 27–21, "Rapport politique," Gouverneur général to ministre des Colonies, 1927.

2. For the decree and accompanying instructions, see arrêté "promulguant en AOF le décret du 7 février 1912 sur la réorganisation du recrutement des troupes indigènes," Mar. 16, 1912, *JOAOF*, pp. 196–197; "Instructions sur le recrutement des troupes noires," Aug. 22, 1912, *JOAOF*, pp. 550–552.

3. Michel, *L'appel à l'Afrique*, p. 407. See also Lunn, "Memoirs of the Maelstrom"; Davis, *Reservoirs of Men*; Summer and Johnson, "World War I Conscription"; Echenberg, "Paying the Blood Tax."

4. ANS, 5 E 26, Conseil de Gouvernement, Procès-verbal, 1911; ANSOM, Téls., Arrivées, Gouverneur général to ministre des Colonies, Aug. 27, 1914.

5. Michel, *L'appel à l'Afrique*, p. 11; Lunn, "Memoirs of the Maelstrom," pp. 92–99.

6. Débats, Chambre des Députés, Dec. 13, 1912, *JORF*, p. 3166.

7. Débats, Chambre des Députés, Dec. 19, 1912, *JORF*, pp. 3285, 3286.

8. Michel, *L'appel à l'Afrique*, pp. 42–44, 64–66.

9. Lunn, "Memoirs of the Maelstrom," pp. 111–127.

10. These reports can be found in ANSOM, AP 3034/1, 2, and 5.

11. ANSOM, Téls., Arrivées, Gouverneur général to ministre des Colonies, Oct. 30, 1915.

12. The description of the Bambara revolt is based on Michel, *L'appel à l'Afrique*, pp. 54–56.

13. Quoted in ibid., p. 56.

14. Ibid., pp. 100–116; ANSOM, AP 3038, Mission Demaret, Haut-Sénégal et Niger, 1919; Capron, *Communautés villageoises bwa*.

15. In Dahomey, Africans resisted recruitment even before open revolt broke out in 1916. D'Almeida-Topor, "Les populations dahoméenes"; Garcia, "Les mouvements de résistance au Dahomey."

16. Fuglestad, "Les révoltes du Touareg du Niger."

17. ANSOM, AP 3049, Mission Demaret, Haut-Sénégal et Niger, 1919, Dossier P, Extrait de la correspondance officielle, no. 123, Sept. 14, 1917.

18. ANS, 4 D 72, "Rapport sur le recrutement," Gouverneur général to ministre des Colonies, Sept. 25, 1917. Van Vollenhoven hoped to supply the metropole with both cereals and oleaginous products. Before arriving in Dakar, he reached an agreement with the major trading firms in West Africa granting them the exclusive right to purchase these products at fixed prices. Dakar then instructed administrators to encourage Africans to intensify cultivation of both foodstuffs and cash crops, instructions which led to widespread coercion. Although production went up, a shortage of available shipping meant that the merchandise stockpiled on the coast never reached France; instead, the bulk of it rotted in coastal ports. The only exception was the Senegalese peanut crop; exports in peanuts increased 40 percent between 1916 and 1917. Michel, *L'appel à l'Afrique*, pp. 200–221, 265–282; for

a case study of the *ravitaillement* effort in one colony, see Picciola, "Quelques aspects de la Côte d'Ivoire."

19. Arrêté "promulguant en AOF les décrets du 14 janvier, 1918," Feb. 2, 1918, *JOAOF*, pp. 51–52.

20. Michel, *L'appel à l'Afrique*, p. 243; Lunn, "Memoirs of the Maelstrom," p. 193.

21. ANSOM, AP 145/6, "Etude sur l'état juridique des indigènes du Sénégal" and "Projets de décrets relatifs à leur statut personnel," n.d. [ca. 1912]. These various documents drawn up by the federal authorities summarized Dakar's position on Senegalese citizenship under Ponty. Ponty sent all these position papers to Paris in 1913 with a cover letter, in which he explained his own desire to see the mulattoes granted immediate naturalization. Gouverneur général to ministre des Colonies, no. 1661, Aug. 6, 1913. No action was taken before World War I, during which a new law resolved the *originaires'* legal status.

22. Muslim *originaires* had no interest in using French courts for civil disputes, naturally preferring their own Muslim courts for these matters. ANS, M 87, Gouverneur général to ministre des Colonies, no. 2470, Dec. 23, 1913.

23. Ponty, *Justice indigène*, p. 3.

24. ANS, M 83, Conseil de Gouvernement, Documents, 1911.

25. Ponty, *Justice indigène*, p. 36. This passage is in boldface type.

26. ANS, M 87, Lieutenant gouverneur du Sénégal to gouverneur général, no. 963, Dec. 13, 1913. As this remark suggests, the lieutenant governors were strongly opposed to the *évolués'* privileges—such as the right to elect their own deputy and to control their own budget. They saw in the 1912 reform an ideal opportunity for undoing, or at least containing, the damage done by an earlier generation's premature and arbitrary introduction of assimilative legislation. For these men, it was a cardinal principle that French institutions should be kept out of the countryside, because such institutions were invariably unadapted to the African mentality. The lieutenant governors also argued that French courts, with their drawn-out procedures and high expenses, placed the African at a decided disadvantage (the native courts were free). If non-naturalized *originaires* were placed under the jurisdiction of French law, they pointed out, Africans involved in cases with them would inevitably be dragged before an incomprehensible and unfamiliar jurisdiction. Underlying these arguments was the assumption that the only proper goal for the French in West Africa was to lead their African subjects gradually from an "inferior" state to a more advanced one. For these views, see ANS, M 83, Lieutenant gouverneur de la Côte d'Ivoire to gouverneur général, no. 447, Apr. 26, 1911, and Lieutenant gouverneur du Sénégal to gouverneur général, no. b 726, June 6, 1911.

27. ANS, M 87, Gouverneur général to lieutenant gouverneur du Sénégal, no. 1282, Dec. 29, 1913, and Gouverneur général to ministre des Colonies, no. 2470, Dec. 23, 1913. These arguments fell upon sympathetic

ears in Paris. Early in 1914, the minister of colonies cabled Ponty to return to the status quo of 1903 as regarded all the *originaires*. Paris, not fully aware of the distinctions that the local administration made between Muslim and Catholic, *assimilé* and *évolué* inhabitants of the Four Communes, determined that "the loyalty of the Senegalese" and the services that they had rendered merited exceptional measures in their favor, and that they should continue to be under the jurisdiction of French courts in urban areas throughout West Africa. This represented a compromise. It signified that, in the rural areas outside Senegal, the *évolués* would, like all other Africans, come under the jurisdiction of the native courts. ANS, M 87, Ministre des Colonies to gouverneur général, no. 230, Feb. 27, 1914.

28. Buell, *Native Problem*, 1: 950. These measures are also discussed by Lamine Gueye, a French-educated lawyer and *originaire* activist during the interwar years, in his work on the rights of Senegalese born in the Four Communes; see *De la situation politique des Sénégalais*, pp. 29–31. For the educational reform of 1914, see circulaire 44c "relative aux programmes scolaires," May 1, 1914, *JOAOF*, pp. 461–482.

29. Johnson's *Emergence of Black Politics* is the standard account of Diagne's career and Senegalese politics in general in this period. For the war's impact on Diagne's political career, see Searing "Accommodation and Resistance," 2: 364–416.

30. For the debates surrounding the 1915 law, see Débats, Chambre des Députés, July 1, 8, 1915, *JORF*, pp. 1032–1034, 1072–1076. The two laws in question can be found in *Bulletin des Lois*, 1915, 3: 1932, and 1916, 8: 1650.

31. ANS, M 87, Gouverneur général to ministre des Colonies, no. 142, Feb. 2, 1916. Reply to dépêche, Dec. 12, 1915, "relative à la délivrance de jugements supplétifs d'actes de naissance et au statut des indigènes du Sénégal." See also M 87, Gouverneur général to ministre des Colonies, no. 491, Apr. 12, 1916.

32. ANSOM, AP 170/5, Rapport Angoulvant "a. s. de la proposition de loi tendant à accorder la qualité de citoyen français aux natifs des communes de plein exercise du Sénégal," Gouverneur général p.i. to ministre des Colonies, Sept. 3, 1916.

33. Searing, "Accommodation and Resistance," 2: 462–476. The colonial service was divided into three levels, or *cadres*: the lower level *cadre commun*, in which Africans served; the *cadre secondaire*, to which a few Africans were admitted but where most low-level personnel were Europeans; and the *cadre supérieur* or *métropolitain*, reserved, as of 1914, to French citizens holding degrees available only in the metropole. Diagne stressed equal pay for equal work for African and French employees and the opening of the *cadre supérieur* to Africans.

34. ANSOM, AP 145/9, Blaise Diagne, "Projet de décret modifiant le décret du 7 décembre, 1917," n.d. [ca. 1919]; Blaise Diagne to ministre des Colonies, June 5, 1919.

35. For a more detailed discussion of Diagne's political activity and the

Government General's response, see Searing, "Accommodation and Resistance," chap. 6.

36. ANS, 17 G 233 FM, "Note," 1921.

37. ANSOM, AP 145/9, Blaise Diagne to ministre des Colonies, June 5, 1919. On Diagne's "Frenchness," see Langley, *Pan-Africanism*, p. 289; Lambert, "From Citizenship to *Négritude*," p. 240; Johnson, *Emergence of Black Politics*, pp. 150–155; July, *Origins of Modern African Thought*, pp. 393–411.

38. ANS, 17 G 233 FM, "Note," 1921.

39. Buell, *Native Problem*, 1: 967–980.

40. On Senegalese nationalism in this period, see Johnson, "Impact of the Senegalese Elite"; Gueye, *Itinéraire Africain*; Lambert, "From Citizenship to *Négritude*," pp. 244–249.

41. ANS, M 106, "Rapport de M. Henri Labouret, Chef de Cercle, Lobi, Haute Volta," Dec. 20, 1919.

42. Although some research has been done on West African protest movements in the 1920's, it remains fragmentary, one reason being that these movements were much less extensive than in the 1930's. The activities of West Africans in Paris are discussed in Spiegler, "Aspects of Nationalist Thought"; Dewitte, *Les mouvements nègres en France*; Langley, *Pan-Africanism*, chap. 7. For the growth of West African cultural nationalism, see Manchuelle, "Assimilés ou patriotes français?" and "Le rôle des Antillais."

43. The Government General was particularly distressed by the tactics used—the workers had issued an ultimatum to the Compagnie Dakar-Saint-Louis that if their demands were not met by a certain date a work stoppage would ensue. Because that threatened shipment of the valuable peanut crop just being harvested, Dakar, under pressure from the local Chamber of Commerce, urged a settlement. ANS, K 35, "Note au sujet de l'ultimatum adressé par les cheminots du DSL," Ingénieur en chef Mouneyres, Apr. 12, 1919; Chambre de Commerce, Rufisque, to gouverneur général, no. 754, Apr. 26, 1919; telegram, President du Conseil Général to ministre des Colonies and to Blaise Diagne, député, Apr. 14, 1919.

44. ANS, 17 G 296 FM, Correspondance, Gouverneur général p.i. to gouverneur général, Apr. 17, 1923. As the interim governor general said in this letter: "I have just dispersed across West Africa the Committee. . . . These messieurs, emboldened by the exaggerated expectations which people had and by the impunity with which certain of their demonstrations were allowed [to take place], dared to make a totally misplaced and improper request concerning Hassell. I am packing them off to the four corners of the federation. This should have the most salutary effect." There is an Achille Hassell, listed as *administrateur des colonies*, in the 1922–1923 *Annuaire du Ministère des Colonies*, pp. 491–492. Although no colony is mentioned, his earlier postings had all been in Africa. One must presume that this is the Hassell to whom the interim governor general is referring.

45. Buell, *Native Problem*, 2: 34; ANS, 2 G 25–8, "Rapport politique," Gouverneur général to ministre des Colonies, 1925.

46. For nationalist protest in Dahomey during the interwar period, see Manning, *Slavery, Colonialism, and Economic Growth*, pp. 261–280; Moseley, "Indigenous and External Factors"; Anignikin, "Les origines du mouvement national."

47. According to Manchuelle, "Le rôle des Antillais," the Ligue des Droits de l'Homme had extensive contacts with the Senegalese and Dahomeyan elite in this period.

48. Hunkanrin graduated from the normal school in Gorée in 1906 and taught for three years; then he accepted a more lucrative job in a commercial trading house. Accused of stealing merchandise, he was sentenced to a year's imprisonment in Dakar. Shortly thereafter, he fled to Nigeria, apparently afraid of being arrested, under the provisions of the *indigénat*, for subversive activities. Diagne secured for Hunkanrin a position in France in 1919 on the military staff in charge of colonial troops. Their friendship, however, cooled when Hunkanrin began to attend anarchist meetings in Paris and to further his contacts with the Ligue. His subsequent movements are obscure, but in 1920 he was returned to Porto Novo for civil prosecution and imprisoned in the neighboring coastal port of Cotonou. Ballard, "The Porto-Novo Incidents of 1923," pp. 61–68.

49. Spiegler, "Aspects of Nationalist Thought," pp. 39–48; Dewitte, *Les mouvements nègres en France*, pp. 66–68; Harrison, *France and Islam*, pp. 154–155. According to Ballard, "The Porto-Novo Incidents of 1923," Hunkanrin spent as much time protesting native policy in Dahomey as he did seeking an extension of citizenship. This preoccupation with local grievances can be attributed to the complicated kingship politics in Porto Novo. The French had established a protectorate over the Kingdom of Porto Novo in 1882, but then systematically reduced the king's powers, in keeping with their anti-aristocratic ideology. This prompted traditional claimants to the throne to agitate for a return of the kingship to its original role; Hunkanrin and his associates embraced this platform as a vehicle for criticizing the administration.

50. Ballard, "The Porto-Novo Incidents of 1923"; Harrison, *France and Islam*, pp. 150–155.

51. ANSOM, AP 3056, Mission Cazaux, Dahomey, 1923–1924, "Rapport no. 71."

52. From the Second Congress of the Third International in 1920 until the advent of the Popular Front, the PCF maintained that the fight for colonial emancipation was one of the party's revolutionary goals. True to its ideals, the PCF waged bitter battles in its press in support of the two most important colonial uprisings in the French Empire during the interwar period, the Rif War in Morocco, led by Abd El-Krim, in 1925, and the Vietnamese uprising at Yen Bay in 1930. Monéta, *La politique du parti communiste français*; Liauzu, *Aux origines des tiers-mondismes*.

53. ANS, 2 G 23–9, "Rapport politique," Gouverneur général to ministre des Colonies, 1923.

54. The best-known nationalists included the Dahomeyan Tovalou Houénou, who founded the Ligue Universelle pour la Défense de la Race Noire; the Senegalese Lamine Senghor, who led the Comité de la Défense de la Race Nègre; and two Sudanese, Tiemoho Garan-Kouyaté and Abdou Koité, who led the Comité's successor, the Ligue de la Défense de la Race Nègre, from 1925 to 1936. Langley, *Pan-Africanism*, chap. 7; Dewitte, *Les mouvements nègres en France*, pp. 74–89, 125–216.

55. ANS, K 35, telegram, Gouverneur général to ministre des Colonies, Apr. 15, 1919; 6 E 48, Conseil de Gouvernement, Documents, 1924; 2 G 23–9, "Rapport politique," Gouverneur général to ministre des Colonies, 1923.

56. ANS, 2 G 26–8, "Rapport politique," Gouverneur général to ministre des Colonies, 1926.

57. ANS, 17 G 296 FM, Correspondance, Gouverneur général to gouverneur général p.i., May 9, 1923.

58. ANS, circulaire no. 13, Gouverneur général to lieutenants gouverneurs, Jan. 13, 1932. The Government General also issued periodic circulars urging the formation of secret services in each colony to facilitate the compilation of the desired data. Governors were to submit detailed monthly reports on the *état d'esprit* prevalent in their colonies. ANS, circulaire no. 64, Gouverneur général to lieutenants gouverneurs, Sept. 17, 1921; circulaire no. 25, Gouverneur général to lieutenants gouverneurs, Feb. 2, 1923; circulaire no. 164, Gouverneur général to lieutenants gouverneurs, Sept. 11, 1925. These disparate instructions culminated in 1931 in a decision to institute a central service of public safety and general information in Dakar, "rendered necessary by the disturbing development of extremist propaganda in all milieux." ANS, circulaire no. 76, Gouverneur général to lieutenants gouverneurs, Feb. 2, 1931.

59. ANS, circulaire no. 146, Gouverneur général to lieutenants gouverneurs, May 8, 1928. For the history of the press in Senegal and Dahomey, see Boulègue, "La presse au Sénégal avant 1939"; Pasquier, "Les débuts de la presse au Sénégal"; Codo, "La presse dahoméenne."

60. Schneider, *Quality and Quantity*, chaps. 3–5; Stovall, "Color-blind France?"; Schor, *L'opinion française et les étrangers*, pts. 1–2; Cross, *Immigrant Workers*, chaps. 6–8; M. L. Roberts, *Civilization without Sexes*. Cross points out that after experimenting with colonial labor in France during World War I, both government and employers rejected it in the 1920's as unproductive and too expensive. Nevertheless, 471,330 Algerians entered France in this period; they faced greater discrimination than any other group (*Immigrant Workers*, pp. 42–44, 123–126).

61. For the history of these movements, see Schneider, *Quality and Quantity*, pp. 124–128; Murard and Zylberman, "De l'hygiène comme introduction à la politique expérimentale"; Pedersen, *Family, Dependence and the Origins of the Welfare State*, chaps. 2, 5; Talmy, *Histoire du mouvement familiale*, vol. 1; Knibiehler, *Cornettes et blouses blanches*.

62. Schneider, *Quality and Quantity*, pp. 141–142.

63. Schor, *L'opinion française et les étrangers*, pp. 529–542; Cross, *Immigrant Workers*, pp. 177–178; Brubaker, *Citizenship and Nationhood*, pp. 111, 215.

64. ANS, 17 G 40 FM, Direction des Affaires Politiques et Administratives, "Note au sujet de l'exécution des instructions contenues dans la note du 17 octobre, réglementation intéressant la politique indigène et la police générale de l'AOF," Nov. 1921; ANSOM, AP 3045, Mission Kair, Soudan, 1922–1923, Gouverneur général p.i. to lieutenant gouverneur du Dahomey, Apr. 11, 1923, contained in "Rapport," May 16, 1923.

65. Buell, *Native Problem*, 1: 947; see also ANSOM, AP 1525, Naturalisations, AOF. These records, which are incomplete, show eighteen naturalizations in 1920, then only four in 1923, and six in 1924. They do not indicate how many applied.

66. French reassessment of the policy of granting "worthy" Africans citizenship began in 1924 and lasted until 1933. In 1924, Colonial Minister Daladier drew up a *projet de loi* designed to transform citizenship from a favor granted to individual subjects at the discretion of the colonial administration into an automatic right if certain criteria were met. Such a law, if passed, would have represented a significant liberalization of citizenship. It appears to have been motivated in part by a desire to unify the existing legislation throughout the empire (each colony had its own set of criteria for extending citizenship); in part by agitation by the Ligue Française pour la Défense des Droits de l'Homme et du Citoyen, which was in favor of the project (ANSOM, AP 2759–3, Ligue to Président de la République, Dec. 20, 1920); and in part by the residual debt that France felt it owed its subjects for their contribution to the war effort. It is unclear whether this law ever came before Parliament, and those who drafted the law seem to have been ignorant of the stakes involved. The proposed legislation did, however, give rise to a prolonged investigation by the legal branch of the Conseil Supérieur des Colonies into the conditions regulating naturalization in the empire. ANSOM, AP 1638, "Projet de loi; accession des indigènes à la naturalisation," 1924; ANSOM, AP 145–6, "Proposition de loi par M. Valude," 1922. For the law's provisions, see Roustans, "L'accession à la qualité de citoyen français."

67. ANS, 17 G 59 FM, "Rapport sur la condition légale des sujets dans les colonies françaises et sur les prérogatives qui en résultent," M. Tesseron, Directeur Honoraire au Ministère des Colonies, 1925; and Conseil Supérieur des Colonies, sessions of March 30 and June 15, 1927, "Rapport de M. Bernard Lavergne, Professeur à la Faculté de Droit à Lille."

68. Another innovation was that the age for applying for naturalization was dropped from 21 to 18 (as was the case in France after 1927). Nevertheless, any African under the age of 21 had to have the consent of his father and family council; such paternal consent was not required for foreigners in France and was an additional hurdle for the first generation of educated Af-

ricans. Arrêté no. 117 a.p. "promulguant en AOF le décret du 21 août 1932, relatif aux conditions d'accession des indigènes de l'AOF à la qualité de citoyens français," Jan. 19, 1933, *JOAOF*, pp. 155–157; for the local application of the decree, see arrêté no. 118 a.p., Jan. 19, 1933, *JOAOF*, pp. 157–160. The 1918 decree on naturalization for *ancien combattants* was also revised by a decree of April 19, 1933, which unified conditions for veterans throughout the empire; see arrêtés no. 1410, 1411 a.p., June 17, 1933, *JOAOF*, pp. 605–607, 611–612.

69. ANS, circulaire no. 11 "a. s. de l'accession des indigènes à la qualité de citoyen français," Gouverneur général to lieutenants gouverneurs, Jan. 19, 1933.

70. At the turn of the century, the assumption was that women and children were too weak to survive in West Africa. "We do not believe it will be possible for a long time yet for white children to be born and brought up in the equatorial or tropical climates of Africa" (Barot, *Guide pratique*, p. 329). That opinion had changed by the 1920's, as is evident in such books as Chivas-Baron, *La femme française aux colonies;* Faure, ed., *La vie aux colonies.*

71. Barot, *Guide pratique*, p. 331. The director of African affairs at the Colonial Ministry, Gustave Binger, wrote the preface to this book. On French attitudes toward concubinage in West Africa before World War I, also see Bathily, "Aux origines de l'Africanisme," pp. 94–97; Cohen, *Rulers of Empire*, p. 122.

72. M. Delafosse, *Broussard*, p. 79. Although he eventually married in France, Delafosse began his career by taking a Baule wife, with whom he had two children. He recognized both of them legally, before he returned to France.

73. Hardy, *Ergaste*, pp. 31–32, 78.

74. Maunier, *Sociologie coloniale*, vol. 1, *L'introduction*, pp. 112–113, 117, 171.

75. Faure, *La vie aux colonies*, pp. 68, 101.

76. Hardy, *Ergaste*, pp. 30, 121.

77. Chivas-Baron, *La femme française aux colonies*, p. 187; Faure, *La vie aux colonies*, p. 56.

78. Faure, *La vie aux colonies*, p. 11.

79. Chivas-Baron, *La femme française aux colonies*, pp. 146, 186–187.

80. Dakar had exhibited an interest in *métissage* in 1910, when it circulated a questionnaire on the subject to all lieutenant governors. But the initiative for this measure came from the Paris-based Société d'Anthropologie, which contacted Governor General Ponty and asked him to distribute the questionnaire among the colony's administrators. There is little sense in the original questionnaire or the answers to it that the federal administration felt threatened by the offspring of mixed marriages in this period. See "Enquête sur les croisements ethniques."

81. See, in particular, Mazet, *La condition juridique des métis*. A whole

series of novels from the interwar years also explored the plight of the *métis*. For example, Chivas-Baron, *Confidences de métisse*; Cendrieux, *François Phuoc, métis*; Wild, *L'autre race*; Favre, *L'orientale* 1930. These novels stressed such themes as the *métis'* hatred for their French fathers, the inability of the *métis* to fit into French society, and the incompatibility of the two races.

82. Maunier, *Sociologie coloniale*, vol. 1, *L'introduction*, p. 114. Another clear example of eugenicist thinking penetrating colonial circles is provided by two articles that appeared in *La Revue Indigène*—a colonial journal devoted to "native affairs"—on the eve of World War I. The first article reported on the latest findings of the Eugenics Society: that "children of mixed parentage resemble most the parent in whose original habitat they are born and raised." This meant that French-Indochinese children were "destined to return rapidly to the Indochinese type." And the article concluded, "Is it because they have known this law for a long time that the English have avoided in general *métissage* in the colonies?" ("La science et les métis"). Another article by French colonial employees argued that no Indochinese could acquire the requisite degree of civilization to be admitted to the colonial service at the same pay as Europeans. As proof, the signatories cited "the regression which takes place when descendants of *métis* intermarry"; they "return slowly but surely to the inferior origin" ("Lettre des Amicales").

83. According to this decree, if a *métis* could provide proof of his or her French culture, this along with his or her white features was sufficient for citizenship. See arrêté no. 2568 a.p. "promulguant en AOF le décret du 5 septembre 1930, fixant la condition juridique des *métis* nés de parents inconnus en AOF," Nov. 14, 1930, *JOAOF*, pp. 944–946.

CHAPTER 6

1. ANS, 17 G 40 FM, Direction des Affaires Politiques et Administratives, "Note a. s. de l'exécution des instructions contenues dans la note du 17 octobre, réglementant intéressant la politique indigène et la police générale de l'AOF," Nov. 1921.

2. Whether France was assimilationist or associationist has been a recurrent debate in French colonial historiography. The debate is to some extent a useless one, since most students of the subject agree that from the end of the nineteenth century on, France was both. The more interesting questions are, in what context and for what reasons was one of these tendencies dominant? And, when one tendency did dominate, what did the term mean to those policy makers wielding it, and how did the doctrine affect their actions? These are the questions I propose to explore in this chapter. Betts did not broach these more specific issues in his *Assimilation and Association*, although this work remains an indispensable starting point for any scholar of association. For an approach similar to mine, see Wright's *Politics of Design*, a fine account of the influence of associationist ideas on colonial architecture from 1900 to 1940.

3. Between the tenures of Van Vollenhoven and Merlin, the Governments General of both Equatorial and West Africa were temporarily headed by Gabriel Angoulvant. This appointment was always considered an interim one; I will therefore not discuss him directly, although his name will come up in this chapter and in Chap. 7.

4. See, in particular, Hobsbawm, "Introduction: Inventing Traditions."

5. The details of Clozel's career are contained in his personnel dossier, ANSOM, EE II 845 (I). For an analysis of Clozel's policies as governor of Ivory Coast, see Weiskel, *French Colonial Rule*, chaps. 4–5; for more personalized accounts of the man, see M. Delafosse, "Clozel, un grand africain disparu"; and L. Delafosse, *Maurice Delafosse*.

6. Clozel and Villamur, eds., *Les coutumes indigènes*; Clozel, *Dix ans à la Côte d'Ivoire*.

7. These include M. Delafosse, *Haut-Sénégal-Niger*, *Les noirs de l'Afrique*, *L'âme nègre*, *Les civilisations nègro-africaines*, *Les nègres*. For additional biographical details, see L. Delafosse, *Maurice Delafosse*. No major study of Delafosse's contribution to ethnography exists, despite his pioneering fieldwork in West Africa. Nor has his influence on native policy received adequate attention. This neglect is beginning to change. In addition to Wooten, "Colonial Administration," see Grosz-Ngaté, "Power and Knowledge"; Van Hoven, "Representing Social Hierarchy"; Harrison, *France and Islam*, pp. 102–105, 144–149, 155–156; Bazin, "A chacun son bambara." For a contemporary view of his work, see "Mémorial Maurice Delafosse."

8. ANS, 17 G 39, Chef du Service des Affaires Civiles to directeur des Finances, Apr. 23, 1917. This letter refers to Clozel's initiatives while governor general.

9. This letter was actually drafted by Maurice Delafosse in his capacity as Clozel's chief of political affairs. For the draft, see ANS 17 G 60, Gouverneur général to ministre des Colonies, Feb. 20, 1917. For the final version, see Fonds Auguste Terrier 5925, "Rapport sur la réorganisation de l'AOF après la cessation des hostilités," Gouverneur général to ministre des Colonies, no. N339, Mar. 15, 1917.

10. Clozel would die suddenly a year later while traveling in Morocco, on May 10, 1918.

11. The details of Van Vollenhoven's life are available in a variety of sources: *Une âme de chef*; Général Mangeot, *La vie ardente de Van Vollenhoven*; Prévaudeau, *Joost Van Vollenhoven*. He continues to fascinate, as two recent articles attest: DeGroot, "Joost Van Vollenhoven"; Cornevin, "Joost Van Vollenhoven."

12. ANS, circulaire no. 37, Gouverneur général to lieutenants gouverneurs, Apr. 12, 1917, and circulaire no. 64 "a. s. du ravitaillement de la métropole," Gouverneur général to lieutenants gouverneurs, June 7, 1917; circulaire no. 82 "fixant les rapports du Gouvernement Général avec les Administrations locales," Gouverneur général to lieutenants gouverneurs, July 28, 1917; circulaire no. 118 "a. s. de l'administration des cercles," Gou-

verneur général to lieutenants gouverneurs, Nov. 1, 1917; circulaire no. 132, "a. s. du contrôle financier," Gouverneur général to lieutenants gouverneurs, Dec. 31, 1917.

13. Circulaire no. 88 "a. s. des chefs indigènes," Gouverneur général to lieutenants gouverneurs, Aug. 15, 1917, *JOAOF*, pp. 467, 468–471, 472.

14. ANS, 17 G 61, Gouverneur général to ministre des Colonies, Dec. 20, 1917.

15. ANS, 2 G 17–4, draft dated Sept. 22, 1917 in Maurice Delafosse's handwriting. In mentioning association here, Delafosse is probably referring to the native policy being advocated in Paris since 1900. To reiterate, I have found no use of the term "association" by the Government General before 1918.

16. Ibid.

17. Harrison, *France and Islam*, pp. 106–107. And Ponty participated in the Société d'Anthropologie's scientific survey on *métissage* between 1910 and 1912 (see Chap. 5, n. 80). Delafosse's criticisms of Ponty can be explained in two ways. First, neither Ponty's creation of a Muslim affairs department in 1913, nor his association with the Société d'Anthropologie, would have impressed Delafosse. It was late to embark in 1913 upon the study of Muslim society—the damage from Ponty's earlier anti-aristocratic crusade had been done. And Delafosse's pioneering ethnography was incompatible with the racist physical anthropology for which the Société d'Anthropologie, under the leadership of Paul Broca, was best known. Second, Delafosse was fighting for his career in West Africa when he drafted this memorandum. He was hoping finally to become governor of a colony but, because of political differences with Angoulvant, would be transferred back to Paris after the war. His disappointment is palpable in these pages. For the details regarding the end of Delafosse's career in West Africa, see L. Delafosse, *Maurice Delafosse*, pp. 309–360.

18. ANS, 17 G 61, memorandum, Dec. 20, 1917.

19. Ibid.

20. Ibid.

21. ANSOM, EE II 1726 (I) and (II); EE II 1629, personnel file. Merlin served as the governor general in Afrique équatoriale française (AEF) from 1908 to 1917, when he was transferred to Madagascar. In 1923 he would be appointed governor general of Indochina. Merlin often cited Roume as an inspiration for his own policies in Dakar, which included relaunching the program of public works originally conceived by Roume and interrupted by the war. It has often been assumed that Merlin's appointment was a deliberate counter to Diagne's influence, although there is no direct evidence to support this conclusion.

22. See Delafosse's own account of these early years in the field, *Broussard*.

23. ANSOM, EE II 1726 (I), Ministre des Colonies to gouverneur général p.i., no. 113, Feb. 18, 1909. At the time of Ponty's appointment the minister explained to Merlin that this decision was not to be interpreted as a mark of

disfavor. That appointment, the minister continued, resulted from circumstances that Merlin "would understand later." The implication is that Merlin was the logical choice to replace Roume when the latter retired.

24. Sarraut, *La mise en valeur*, p. 105. Sarraut first presented his ideas on colonial development to Parliament in 1921, then published them two years later in the work just cited.

25. ANS, 17 G 293 FM, "Note a. s. du rôle des chefs," n.d. [ca. 1920].

26. ANS, 17 G 293 FM, Gouverneur général to ministre des Colonies, Mar. 26, 1921.

27. Ibid.

28. ANS, 5 E 44, "Note sur la situation politique de l'AOF en 1920," Conseil de Gouvernement, Documents, 1920.

29. ANS, circulaire confidentielle a. s. du Congrès panafricain de Bruxelles et de Paris, Gouverneur général to lieutenants gouverneurs, Sept. 17, 1921.

30. ANS, 17 G 233 FM, Gouverneur général to ministre des Colonies, confidentielle et personnelle, Aug. 14, 1921.

31. Arrêté "promulguant en AOF le décret du 4 décembre, 1920 portant réorganisation des communes mixtes et des communes indigènes en AOF"; arrêté "promulguant en AOF le décret du 4 décembre, 1920 réorganisant le Conseil de Gouvernement, la Commission permanente de ce conseil et le Conseil du Contentieux administratif de l'AOF," Jan. 16, 1921, *JOAOF*, pp. 90, 95.

32. Merlin admitted that the appointment of Africans to the administrative councils was not the most important part of his plan to associate Africans. As he put it, "The introduction of natives to our councils is a delicate process. In the higher administrative assemblies, their effective collaboration implies an administrative and judicial culture that they rarely possess. In the elected assemblies [such as the General Council of Senegal] they allow themselves to be caught up in the political and personal aspects of the discussions, forgetting that their role is purely administrative and economic." ANSOM, AP 3052, Mission Kair, Guinée, 1921, "Rapport no. 77," Mar. 12, 1921.

33. *Prestations* were the free-labor obligations each adult African owed the administration; this labor was for local projects such as roads or bridges that would theoretically benefit the community as a whole.

34. Arrêté "promulguant en AOF le décret du 21 mai, 1919 portant création de conseils de notables indigènes en AOF," June 6, 1919, *JOAOF*, p. 405; circulaire no. 74 "relative à la création de Conseils de notables," Gouverneur général to lieutenants gouverneurs, June 6, 1919, *JOAOF*, p. 410.

35. Arrêté, Jan. 16, 1921, *JOAOF*, p. 90; circulaire no. 3 "relative à l'organisation du régime municipal en AOF," Gouverneur général to lieutenants gouverneurs, Feb. 12, 1921, *JOAOF*, p. 175. The decree regarding the three degrees of *communes* was actually a reform of existing legislation regarding municipal government. The first decree in this area dated back to

April 5, 1884. This decree had been amended on December 19, 1891, and then again under Ponty by the decree of May 15, 1912.

36. ANSOM, AP 3052, Mission Kair, Guinée, 1921, "Rapport no. 77," Mar. 12, 1921, réponse du gouverneur général; circulaire no. 3, Feb. 12, 1921, *JOAOF*, p. 177.

37. African members had to be over twenty-five, fluent in French, and one of the following: a retired agent of the administration, a member of the Legion of Honor or recipient of a medal of valor, a recipient of a military pension, a merchant paying the *patente* (license for the exercise of a trade), an owner of registered property, or a notable with property noted as such by the local administrator. The commission deliberated upon the same matters as *communes de plein exercise*. Merlin discussed his ideas for reorganizing the mixed *communes* in ANSOM, AP 170/6, Gouverneur général to ministre des Colonies, no. 371, Feb. 2, 1919.

38. ANS, 17 G 293 FM, Gouverneur général to ministre des Colonies, Mar. 26, 1921.

39. Circulaire no. 3, Feb. 12, 1921, *JOAOF*, p. 175; and 17 G 40 FM, Direction des Affaires Politiques et Administratives, "Note," Nov. 1921.

40. Delafosse, *Haut-Sénégal-Niger*, 3: 143, 124–125.

41. Ibid., pp. 125–143.

42. Delafosse, "Participation des indigènes de l'AOF à l'administration locale," Apr. 16, 1918, *Dépêche Coloniale*, in ANSOM, AP 170/3. Although after Van Vollenhoven's departure Delafosse retired early from the colonial administration, he remained a tireless defender of the ideas and policies he had attempted to implement during the war. His articles continued to appear in the colonial press until his premature death in 1926. This particular article came from a series published in the *Dépêche Coloniale* during the last year of the war, and devoted to the question of how to improve native policy. See also Delafosse, "Sur l'orientation nouvelle" and "Les points sombres."

43. No comprehensive study of the founding of the Institut d'Ethnologie exists. Pieces of the story can be gleaned from Bender, "Development of French Anthropology," pp. 145–148; T. N. Clark, *Prophets and Patrons*, p. 214; Lebovics, *True France*, pp. 32–36; Clifford, *Predicament of Culture*, pp. 61, 123–124; Dias, *Musée ethnographique*, pp. 247–255. For antecedents to the Institut, see Sibeud, "La naissance de l'ethnographie africaniste."

44. Cohen, *Rulers of Empire*, p. 93 and chap. 6; Clifford, *Predicament of Culture*, p. 61. Another example of the administration's "ethnographic" turn is provided by the French approach to education in West Africa in this period. In 1912, Georges Hardy had founded a pedagogical journal for teachers within the federation, the *Bulletin de l'Enseignement de l'AOF*; in the interwar years, this journal instructed French and African teachers to collect local ethnographic information, and published much of it. Drawing heavily upon Lévy-Bruhl's categories, such studies were to provide the materials for teaching different Africans about their own past, thus preventing the formation of more *déclassés*. These efforts also reflected and contributed

to the rehabilitation of traditional African institutions then occurring. Kelly, "Interwar Schools," pp. 172–175; Manchuelle, "Assimilés ou patriotes français?," pp. 348–354.

45. Lévy-Bruhl, "L'Institut d'Ethnologie," p. 234.

46. The issue of how involved professional French anthropologists (as opposed to colonial administrators with some Institut training) were in French imperialism in the 1920's is, of course, a vexed one. Jean Copans has argued that, despite the practical orientation Lévy-Bruhl wished to give the new Institut d'Ethnologie, the fieldwork produced by the professionals there was less closely allied to the interests of the colonial state than that of Britain's International African Institute (also founded in 1926). Whereas the latter consciously dedicated itself to producing concrete information about African institutions—past and present—essential to indirect rule, the Durkheimian orientation of French interwar ethnology led to a more philosophical exploration of African cosmogony and total social facts. A positive aspect of this approach was that the different races of the world were seen as fundamentally equal. Copans, *Critiques et politiques,* pp. 90–97. Yet Institut ethnographers have also been criticized for reifying the "traditional" aspects of African cultures at the expense of their modern features, and assimilating all African societies into a larger *civilisation noire* whose underlying structures were everywhere the same. In these ways, their work may have inadvertently contributed to the growing sense among administrators and the public of how different Africans were from whites, thus the intensifying racism of the interwar years. On these points, see Clifford, *Predicament of Culture,* pp. 61, 88–89; Grosz-Ngaté, "Power and Knowledge," pp. 501–507. Considerably more research is needed, however, on the work of the Institut faculty and the ethnography their students produced before any definitive conclusions can be reached on the Institut's relationship to colonialism in the interwar years.

47. ANS, 17 G 40 FM, Direction des Affaires Politiques et Administratives, "Note," Nov. 1921.

48. ANSOM, EE II 814 (I), personnel file.

49. ANS, 2 G 25–8, "Rapport politique," Gouverneur général to ministre des Colonies, 1925; circulaire "sur la réorganisation de l'Enseignement," Gouverneur général to lieutenants gouverneurs, May 1, 1924, *JOAOF,* pp. 311, 326–327.

50. ANS, 2 G 23–9, "Rapport d'ensemble," Gouverneur général to ministre des Colonies, 1923.

51. ANSOM, CG 60/B 36, "Rapport politique," Gouverneur général to ministre des Colonies, 1928.

52. A decree of December 7, 1917, had exempted certain agents of the colonial administration, including chiefs. In 1918, all those who had served in the African troops were also exempted. In 1924, the Government General again reformed the *indigénat,* this time exempting all Africans serving in the administration, a group defined as subjects who were members of any

official councils or committees, recipients of any French medal, holders of the *brevet* or higher degree, licensed traders and certain property owners, and women and children. Arrêté "promulguant en AOF le décret du 15 novembre, 1924 portant réglementation des sanctions de police administrative en AOF," June 20, 1925, *JOAOF*, p. 575.

53. The African subjects who would qualify for admission were functionaries who had served five years (except members of the police and those whose jobs required no special qualifications); canton and province chiefs; merchants who paid the *patente* and who met the qualifications required for election in the Chambers of Commerce; urban property owners whose property was valued at 5,000 fr.; rural property owners who cultivated their land year round (the amount of land required was to be determined by the lieutenant governors); recipients of the Legion of Honor; and Africans who had rendered exceptional service to France. Eligible voters also had to be over the age of twenty-five, reside within the federation, and have no criminal record. ANS, 18 G 128 FM, Gouverneur général to ministre des Colonies, no. 58, Mar. 6, 1925; arrêté "promulguant en AOF les décrets du 30 mars, 1925," Apr. 18, 1925, *JOAOF*, pp. 340–341.

54. Arrêté "promulguant en AOF le décret du 23 février, 1928 déterminant l'accession des indigènes non-citoyens originaires des colonies du groupe de l'AOF à certains emplois publics," May 22, 1928, *JOAOF*, pp. 366–367. This decree opened up the elite *cadre supérieur* to noncitizens who passed the qualifying exam.

55. ANS, 18 G 128 FM, circulaire "relative à l'application des décrets du 30 mars, 1925," Gouverneur général to lieutenants gouverneurs, Apr. 18, 1925; ANSOM, AP 1638/3, Gouverneur général to ministre des Colonies, no. 1072, Oct. 8, 1930.

56. ANS, 17 G 59 FM, Conseil Supérieur des Colonies, sessions of March 30 and June 15, 1927, "Rapport de M. Bernard Lavergne, Professeur à la Faculté de Droit à Lille."

57. ANS, 17 G 59 FM, Conseil Supérieur des Colonies, Procès-verbaux for March 30 and June 15, 1927. The idea of an intermediary status between citizen and subject was first debated in these meetings. Discussion continued the following year; ANSOM, AP 1638, Conseil Supérieur des Colonies, Procès-verbaux for June 13, 1928.

58. ANSOM, AP 1638, Ministre des Colonies to vice président du Conseil d'Etat, "a. s. de l'institution dans certaines de nos possessions d'une catégorie de sujets ou protégés dites indigènes d'élite." His report and *projet de loi* are attached to this correspondence. The governors general of Madagascar, Equatorial Africa, and French Somaliland favored the proposal to create the new category.

59. ANSOM, AP 1638, Gouverneur général to ministre des Colonies, no. 1072, Oct. 8, 1930.

60. ANS, circulaire no. 084, Gouverneur général to lieutenants gouverneurs, Mar. 18, 1929. Sabatier confirms that few Africans were able to

enter the higher cadre before World War II ("'Elite' Education in French West Africa," pp. 263–264).

61. The Government General implicitly admitted this problem in 1932, when an important circular on local assemblies argued that while canton chiefs would remain the principal agents of the French in the countryside, they would no longer collect taxes. This task would be left to the village chiefs. See circulaire no. 421 a.p., Gouverneur général to lieutenants gouverneurs, Sept. 28, 1932, *JOAOF*, p. 941.

62. See ANSOM, AP 3052, Mission Kair, Guinée, 1921, "Rapport no. 78," Mar. 19, 1921, Observations du gouverneur général.

63. ANSOM, AP 3052, Mission Kair, Guinée, 1921, "Rapport no. 67," Apr. 30, 1921; and AP 3056, Mission Cazaux, Dahomey, 1923–1924, "Rapport no. 62," Apr. 30, 1924; ANS 18 G 54 FM, Gouverneur général to ministre des Colonies, no. 28, Jan. 28, 1932.

64. See circulaire no. 421 a.p., Sept. 28, 1932, *JOAOF*, p. 938; Buell, *Native Problem*, 2: 1000–1001.

65. ANS, 18 G 54 FM, circulaire no. A 27, Lieutenant gouverneur p.i. du Soudan to administrateurs de la colonie, Apr. 15, 1921.

66. Ibid.

67. ANS, 18 G 54 FM, Lieutenant gouverneur de la Côte d'Ivoire to gouverneur général, no. 791 g.p., Apr. 12, 1921.

68. Arrêté "promulguant en AOF le décret du 22 mars, 1924 réorganisant la justice indigène," May 22, 1924, *JOAOF*, p. 398; circulaire "sur la réorganisation de la justice indigène," Gouverneur général to lieutenants gouverneurs, May 22, 1924, *JOAOF*, p. 395. Revision of the 1912 decree had been under consideration since Van Vollenhoven's tenure; Merlin drew up the first project of reform in 1921 and circulated it for comments both among his administrators and the staff in Paris. When Governor General Carde took over from Merlin in 1923, he modified Merlin's proposals, which were then accepted and passed into law.

69. This time, however, Dakar found it necessary to interfere with this custom when it sanctioned marriage practices the French deemed uncivilized. See ANS, circulaire no. 91, Gouverneur général p.i. to lieutenants gouverneurs, Oct. 5, 1920, regarding the case of the "morality and legality of the marriage of a native minor contracted without the consent of the interested party."

70. In this context, the most important innovation of 1924 was to appoint European administrators to the presidency of subdivision courts in the place of African notables. The 1924 decree also tried to decentralize the hierarchy of courts by creating in each colony a Chambre coloniale, to which appeals of lower-court rulings could be made. Extensive documentation of the debates that the reform of the 1912 decree engendered and of the various drafts of the decree can be found in the ANS, M 119 FM, files on justice; and in ANSOM, AP 1645. A comparative discussion of all three decrees on justice is contained in Léonce Jore's unpublished and unfinished manuscript, "Les institutions judiciaires indigènes de l'AOF," in ANSOM, APC 54/7. A

published summary of the 1924 provisions is available in Moreau, *Les indigènes de l'Afrique occidentale française.*

71. It is interesting to note that at the same time that Brévié arrived in Dakar, the minister of colonies, concerned by growing unrest in Indochina, suddenly began to take an interest in the problem of rural chiefs' authority throughout Africa. A directive sent to the African governors general by the minister explained that "certain African *chefferies* have disappeared or constitute a mere façade. The traditional command structures of the native collectivities have proven too weak to resist the new aspirations of a generation whose tendencies disconcert and surprise the old notables. The old social armature is coming apart." This circular went on to recommend that new measures be taken to consolidate chiefs' authority. ANS, 18 G 66 FM, circulaire no. 10, Ministre des Colonies to gouverneurs généraux, Oct. 9, 1929; see also circulaire no. 1 c.s., Ministre des Colonies to gouverneurs généraux, June 10, 1930. When Governor General Brévié received the minister's circulars, he requested that his governors submit reports on the extent to which Van Vollenhoven's directives of 1917 and the decrees of 1919 and 1920 had been implemented. ANS, 18 G 66 FM, circulaire no. 342, Gouverneur général to lieutenants gouverneurs, Sept. 17, 1930. These reports revealed how little had been accomplished in the way of genuine association. They are contained in ANS, 18 G 54 FM, and are summarized in Gouverneur général to ministre des Colonies, no. 28, Jan. 28, 1932. ANS, 18 G 66 FM, Gouverneur général to ministre des Colonies, no. 1060, Oct. 1, 1930, also discusses the current state of native policy in West Africa.

72. Jules Brévié was governor general from 1930 to 1936. His commitment to the same policy is all the more telling because he fit the profile of the "ethnographer-administrator" much more than either of his fellow Ecole Coloniale graduates, Carde and Van Vollenhoven. Brévié had had considerable field experience in the Western Sudan and showed an all-consuming interest in native policy while in office. He was enormously well read, and in 1923 published *Islamisme contre "naturisme" au Soudan français: Essai de psychologie politique coloniale.* This book, to which Maurice Delafosse wrote the introduction, compared animism to Islam in West Africa. Brévié also knew Lévy-Bruhl, and their correspondence can be consulted in ANS, 17 G 327 FM, Correspondance Brévié. One of his final gestures before leaving Dakar was to found the Institut Français sur l'Afrique Noire, devoted to the study of African civilization.

73. As in the past, however, no deliberative powers were to be granted any African assembly. The right to the final say in policy making had to be reserved to the colonizer, "in order to apply it in the direction of the moral and material improvement of the African populations." ANS, 18 G 54 FM, "Rapport au sujet des assemblées indigènes," May 10, 1932. A description and the attributes of the new assemblies were provided by Brévié in his circulaire no. 421 a.p., Sept. 28, 1932, *JOAOF*, pp. 938–942, and "arrêté type," ANS, 18 G 66 FM.

74. Circulaire no. 415, a.p., "Les Chefs," Gouverneur général to lieutenants gouverneurs, Sept. 27, 1932, *JOAOF*, pp. 903, 904.

75. Circulaire no. 421 a.p., Sept. 28, 1932, *JOAOF*, p. 939.

76. Circulaire no. 415 a.p., Sept. 27, 1932, *JOAOF*, p. 904.

CHAPTER 7

1. Carde, Discours, Conseil de Gouvernement, Nov. 22, 1928, *JOAOF*, p. 845.

2. For French reactions to the emancipation of slaves in Haiti, see Geggus, "Haiti and the Abolitionists."

3. For a survey of forced labor practices in countries that had abolished slavery, see Kloosterboer, *Involuntary Labor*. Kloosterboer discusses forced labor in Madagascar but not in other French territories in Africa. A comparative study of several post-emancipation societies can also be found in Foner, *Nothing but Freedom*.

4. For an excellent discussion of this Europe-wide trend, see Cooper, *From Slaves to Squatters*, pp. 24–34.

5. ANS, Q 55, Gouverneur général to lieutenant gouverneur de la Guinée, Aug. 29, 1913.

6. Fall has extensively documented both of these forms of forced labor before World War I (*Le travail forcé*, chaps. 2–3).

7. *Prestations* were regulated by the arrêtés of Nov. 11, 1912, Dec. 31, 1917, Sep. 23, 1918, and Feb. 2, 1933, which allowed each lieutenant governor to establish the details of enforcement in his colony. *Prestations* had been introduced in France in 1836 for the upkeep of local roads. They were not to exceed three days a year and could be commuted to a cash payment if desired. On the use of *prestations* in France in the second half of the nineteenth century and the controversies this institution generated, see Price, *Modernization of Rural France*, pp. 264–266. For their impact in French West Africa, see Fall, *Le travail forcé*, chap. 6.

8. Much of the infrastructure construction in the interwar period used labor forcibly recruited by the administration. In 1926, this form of labor was partially regulated through the creation of the S.M.O.T.I.G. (Service de la main d'oeuvre pour les travaux d'intérêt général). Regulations stipulated that the reserve or "deuxième" portion of Africans drafted for military service could be used for public works projects. The idea for such recruitment can be traced to World War I, when Africans were sent from one part of the federation to another as a solution to the local labor shortages. The decision to force Africans to work on construction sites as part of their military service was justified on the grounds that they would acquire valuable skills and that public works were necessary to raise the standard of living. For case studies of the use of military labor, see Echenberg and Filipovich, "African Military Labour"; Fall, *Le travail forcé*, chap. 5.

9. Quoted in Weiskel, *French Colonial Rule*, p. 243.

10. On immigrant labor in France in the interwar years, see Cross, *Immigrant Workers*.

11. Between 1895 and 1920, total peanut production in French West Africa rose from 51,600 tons to 291,732 tons. Péhaut, *Les oléagineux*, p. 459. During the same period, palm oil production in Dahomey fluctuated between a low of 4,077 tons in 1897 and a high of 22,514 tons in 1919. Palm kernel production was also inconsistent, increasing slightly from an average of 21,177 tons in 1895 to 29,342 tons in 1920. Péhaut, *Les oléagineux*, pp. 575–576; Manning, *Slavery, Colonialism, and Economic Growth*, pp. 217–223.

12. The rubber trade was more important in Guinea than in Ivory Coast. In Ivory Coast, rubber production expanded from approximately 125 tons in 1896 valued at 440,000 fr., to a high in 1906 of 1,519 tons valued at 6,400,000 fr. After 1907, production declined because supplies dwindled and the administration decided to "pacify" the colony; Weiskel, *French Colonial Rule*, pp. 174–176. In Guinea, rubber exports increased from an 1893–1895 average of 1,000 tons valued at 3,500,000 fr., to a 1909–1912 high of 1,808–2,040 tons valued at 15,000,000 fr. Goerg, *Commerce et colonisation*, p. 338.

13. In Guinea, for example, the Government General had assumed that the local populations would simply move their villages alongside the railroad. Instead, they sometimes fled villages that happened to be located in the railway's path. Mangolte, "Le chemin de fer de Konakry au Niger," pp. 94–95. In the Middle Niger Valley, in contrast, the railroad between Kayes and Bamako did increase commercial activity, but not in the manner the administration had hoped. Thanks to the railroad, the regional grain and cloth market expanded as local inhabitants increased production of both commodities for local consumption. Cultivation of export commodities, including cotton for which the administration and French textile manufacturers had high hopes, failed to develop. Prohibitive transportation costs kept Sudanese cotton from being competitive on the world market. R. Roberts, *Warriors, Merchants, and Slaves*, chap. 4.

14. *Conférence Coloniale instituée par M. A. Maginot*; Heisser, "Impact of the Great War"; Sarraut, *La mise en valeur*. The same emphasis upon rational development is evident in Sarraut, "La mission civilisatrice de la France." Two other important publicists for the postwar *mise en valeur* of West Africa were Cosnier, *L'Ouest africain français*; Pelleray, *L'Afrique occidentale française*. For a critical assessment of the new orientation toward *mise en valeur* in Paris in the 1920's and 1930's, see Coquery-Vidrovitch, "Colonialisme ou impérialisme."

15. Dramatic postwar increases in U.S. and Indian cotton prices encouraged a new interest in the empire by French textile manufactures, while the war had convinced the soap and oil industries that West Africa could and should become France's exclusive supplier of peanuts. Heisser, "Impact of the Great War," pp. 126–127; Marseille includes an excellent discussion of both industries in the interwar years in *Empire colonial et capitalisme français*, pp. 159–234. Numerous new organizations promoting a more scientific approach to colonial agriculture also appeared after the war. The

most important in the 1920's were the Comité d'Action Agricole et Colonisatrice, the Académie des Sciences Coloniales, and the Association Colonies-Sciences. These groups believed that modern applied science and agricultural experts held the key to successful overseas development. Thanks to their efforts, greater resources were devoted to research on colonial agriculture in Paris and Dakar during the interwar years. Bonneuil, *Des savants pour l'empire*, pp. 1–65 and conclusion.

16. For additional details, see Bonneuil, *Des savants pour l'empire*, pp. 42–52. Merlin in particular was enthusiastic about the aid scientific research could bring to the colonies; see his remarks on the general budget in ANS, 6 E 46, Conseil de Gouvernment, Procès-verbal, 1922.

17. "Circulaire relative à l'intensification de la production agricole et pastorale en Afrique occidentale française," Feb. 25, 1930, p. 6.

18. Carde, Discours, Conseil de Gouvernement, Dec. 2, 1925, *JOAOF*, pp. 1036–1037.

19. Carde, Discours, Conseil de Gouvernement, Dec. 5, 1927, *JOAOF*, p. 837.

20. "Instructions relatives au développement des services de médecine préventive, hygiène et assistance dans les Colonies," Ministre des Colonies, Dec. 30, 1924, *JOAOF*, p. 106.

21. Ibid., pp. 106–112.

22. ANS, 5 E 44, Inspecteur Général des Services Sanitaires, "Renseignements sur le service," Conseil de Gouvernement, Documents, 1921.

23. ANS, H 14, Dr. Adam and Dr. Nogue, "Rapport sur la mortinatalité et mortalité infantile en AOF," Aug. 1922.

24. ANS, circulaire no. 19, "a. s. de l'assistance médicale indigène," Gouverneur général to lieutenants gouverneurs, Apr. 12, 1921; instructions no. 28 bis, "a. s. des affections endémo-épidémiques de l'AOF," Gouverneur général to lieutenants gouverneurs, Feb. 15, 1923, *JOAOF*, pp. 165–166. This circular embodied instructions the Inspecteur Général des Services Sanitaires had recommended in 1922. ANS, 6 E 46, Conseil de Gouvernement, Procès-verbal, 1922.

25. Circulaire "sur le fonctionnement des services d'Assistance médicale," Gouverneur général to lieutenants gouverneurs, Mar. 12, 1924, *JOAOF*, pp. 179–180; ANS, circulaire no. 23, Gouverneur général to lieutenants gouverneurs, Feb. 9, 1925; instruction "relative à l'orientation et au développement des services d'Assistance médicale indigène," Gouverneur général to lieutenants gouverneurs, Feb. 15, 1926, *JOAOF*, pp. 193–200; instructions "relatives au fonctionnement des services de Santé et d'Assistance," Gouverneur général to lieutenants gouverneurs, Mar. 5, 1927, *JOAOF*, pp. 258–261; instruction "sur le fonctionnement administratif de l'Assistance médicale indigène en AOF," Gouverneur général to lieutenants gouverneurs, May 1, 1927, *JOAOF*, pp. 393–396; circulaire no. 279 bis s.s.m., "Instructions relatives: a) à l'orientation et au développement des services d'Assistance médicale indigène en AOF; b) à l'hygiène et à la protection san-

itaire des travailleurs recrutés par les particuliers," Gouverneur général to lieutenants gouverneurs, Aug. 1, 1930, *JOAOF*, pp. 697–706.

26. Instruction, Feb. 15, 1926, *JOAOF*, pp. 193–200; ANS, 2 G 26–2, "Rapport Annuel," Santé, 1926; circulaire no. 279 bis, Aug. 1, 1930, *JOAOF*, pp. 697–706. On visiting nurses in France, see Knibiehler, *Cornettes et blouses blanches*, p. 147.

27. ANS, 2 G 24–35, "Rapport Annuel," Santé, 1924; ANS, 2 G 30–49, "Rapport Annuel," Santé, 1930. The Colonial Ministry actively recruited doctors for service overseas after issuing its 1924 directive.

28. Instruction, Feb. 15, 1926, *JOAOF*, pp. 193–200; ANS, circulaire "annexe à la circulaire du 10 mars, 1924 sur la préparation des budgets de l'exercise 1927," Gouverneur général to lieutenants gouverneurs, Mar. 10, 1926.

29. All these ideas were spelled out in circulaire no. 279 bis, Aug. 1, 1930, *JOAOF*, pp. 697–706.

30. This is the drift of circulaire no. 279 bis. The number of people hospitalized yearly actually decreased between 1927 (26,867) and 1931 (24,700); ANSOM, AP 3240, Dr. Blanchard, "L'oeuvre sanitaire en AOF (secret)," Dec. 31, 1940. The 1929 annual report showed that no colony was close to spending 12 percent on health care (Guinea was highest with 8.4 percent, Ivory Coast was lowest with 4.7 percent); ANS, 2 G 29–8, "Rapport Annuel," Santé, 1929. A mission of inspection suggested, however, that greater percentages were in fact budgeted but not spent—the reason, "lack of personnel." ANSOM, AP 3064, Mission Kair, Niger, 1929, "Rapport no. 6," July 7, 1929. After 1931 a new loan led to greater investment in African health care programs, but the orientation toward preventive medicine stayed the same. Until more local studies on the interwar years are undertaken, any conclusion about the impact of Carde's directives must remain tentative.

31. In 1919, the boundary of Haut-Sénégal et Niger was redrawn to create two separate colonies, Western Sudan and Upper Volta, and the military territory of Niger. In 1922, Niger was made a colony. The primary reason for carving out the new colony of Upper Volta was the realization that its principal ethnic group, the Mossi, was sufficiently numerous to offer an ideal labor source for public work projects in the rest of the federation, and for the labor-poor colony to its south, Ivory Coast. Upper Volta contained an estimated population of three million—one fourth the total population of French West Africa—of whom more than a million were Mossi. Exact population figures for this period are unknown. Dakar believed that creating a separate administration for this labor source would facilitate its reallocation, by force if necessary, throughout West Africa. A secondary reason for creating Upper Volta was political. The widespread revolts during the war in western Volta suggested the need for closer supervision by the French administration.

32. The belief that the Western Sudan was suited to cotton cultivation for export was as old as the federation itself, and proved to be a dream that would not die. In 1903, the local administration in the Sudan and a manu-

facturers' association, the Association Cotonnière Coloniale, had experimented with new seeds and encouraged local producers to increase their crops. They had, however, stopped short of coercing Africans to grow the desired commodity, either because they believed in free labor or feared revolt. When Africans failed to respond, the Association Cotonnière lost interest. Henry, *Le coton dans l'Afrique occidentale*; R. Roberts, *Warriors, Merchants, and Slaves*, pp. 169–173; Schreyger, *L'Office du Niger au Mali*, pp. 7–13.

33. For a history of the early irrigation schemes for the Niger, see Schreyger, *L'Office du Niger au Mali*, chaps. 1–3.

34. Quoted in Schreyger, *L'Office du Niger au Mali*, p. 42.

35. Ibid., p. 47.

36. These ideas were developed in his 1924 and 1929 speeches to the Council of the Government General. Carde, Discours, Conseil de Gouvernement, Nov. 12, 1924, *JOAOF*, pp. 659–671, and Nov. 25, 1929, *JOAOF*, pp. 1018–1036. The Office du Niger never did produce much cotton, but small amounts of rice were eventually grown there. For an excellent analysis of French efforts to coerce Africans to settle in the Niger Valley and become "model farmers," see Van Beusekom, "Colonial Rural Development."

37. Several circulars, in addition to the one discussed later, revealed the pressure on Dakar from Paris for cotton in particular and raw materials in general. For example, the Ministry demanded in 1924 that a yearly map be drawn and sent indicating cotton production per circle. ANS, circulaire ministérielle no. 7132, Ministre des Colonies to gouverneur général, Dec. 19, 1924. In 1926, Carde wrote to his subordinates that, although the minister was pleased with their efforts to develop the federation's agricultural potential "in order to procure for the metropole the raw materials it needed," he wanted more specific annual agricultural reports. ANS, circulaires no. 40, Gouverneur général to lieutenants gouverneurs, Mar. 15, 1926, and no. 063, Gouverneur général to lieutenants gouverneurs, Apr. 5, 1926. In October of that year, the minister again made it clear that he wanted more results in every domain; the words "concrete results" were even underlined. Dépêche ministérielle, no. 4833, Oct. 23, 1926, reprinted in ANS, circulaire no. 239, Gouverneur général to lieutenants gouverneurs, Nov. 30, 1926. In December, the Ministry recommended that a policy of "agricultural specialization by region" be introduced in West Africa as part of the ongoing effort to supply the metropole with raw materials and provisions. ANS, Dépêche ministérielle, no. 5758, Ministre des Colonies to gouverneur général, Dec. 21, 1926.

38. "Circulaire relative à l'application de l'arrêté du 6 mars, 1924," Mar. 15, 1924, pp. 1, 2–28.

39. Although scientific research into colonial agriculture grew dramatically in France in the 1920's, Carde would have little to do with it. He was no less suspicious of agronomists sent by the Ministry of Colonies than he was of doctors sitting in their dispensaries. He appeared to see them as met-

ropolitan "experts" who sought to apply their particular "expertise" to the colony without learning about its peoples or the administration's political and economic priorities. Dakar was still enamored of science and technology, but it wished to control their application in an era of growing technocracy. On Carde's hostility to agronomists, see Bonneuil, *Des savants pour l'empire*, pp. 67–68, 97.

40. "Circulaire relative à l'application de l'arrêté du 6 mars, 1924," Mar. 15, 1924, pp. 25, 11.

41. Ibid., p. 12.

42. Ibid., pp. 12–13.

43. ANSOM, AP 3059, Mission Merly, Dakar, 1925–1926, "Rapport no. 63," Feb. 2, 1926.

44. Ibid.

45. ANS, circulaire no. 087, Gouverneur général to lieutenants gouverneurs, Apr. 20, 1926; "Circulaire relative à l'intensification de la production agricole et pastorale en Afrique occidentale française," Feb. 25, 1930.

46. The peoples of the Middle Niger Valley, where the French began constructing dams in the 1920's, were also forced to grow cotton. The worst abuses were in the 1930's, when progress on the dams and irrigation canals was slow. These abuses are discussed in Van Beusekom, "Colonial Rural Development," chap. 4; Magasa, *Papa-commandant a jeté un grand filet devant nous*; Herbart, *Le chancre du Niger*.

47. The first mission took place in 1925 and was led by Inspector Picanon. He discovered guards in the fields, whose job was to force Africans to grow cotton. One can measure "the weight of this coercion by the number of guards deployed." Concluding that the colony lacked a viable marketing network, he recommended that more specific regulations on the use of force be issued. ANSOM, AP 3057, Mission Picanon, Haute Volta, 1925, "Rapport no. 119," Feb. 23, 1925.

48. ANSOM, AE 105, Mission Sol, Haute Volta, 1932–1933, "Rapport no. 35," Nov. 1932.

49. The low prices paid to the African producer can be explained by the lack of competition which existed in West Africa among the import-export houses who bought the African peasant's crops. The export duties which these firms had to pay, which helped to finance the budget of the Government General, also encouraged merchants to pay artificially low prices to the African producer.

50. ANSOM, AE 105, Mission Sol, "Rapport no. 35," Nov. 1932.

51. Recent research on the subject of forced labor in Koudougou, one of the ten circles in Upper Volta, confirms the inspectors' findings of compulsory cash-crop cultivation in that colony after 1925. Koudougou was the most densely populated circle of the colony, with an estimated 350,000 people. Between 1925 and 1928, cotton production increased from 214 tons to 710 tons. According to official reports, this increase resulted from administrative pressure. During the same period, millet harvest decreased from

112,000 to 105,000 tons. In 1929 and 1930, however, production fell dramatically to 44,250 tons and 40,000 tons. Cordell and Gregory, "Labour Reservoirs and Population," pp. 207-212. The same trends are evident in the circle reports of Ouahigouya; Marchal, ed., *Chronique d'un cercle de l'AOF*, pp. 93–155. The impact of Hesling's cotton policy upon the local population in the four southern circles of Upper Volta has also been examined by Gervais, "Creating Hunger," pp. 114–117.

52. ANSOM, AE 105, Mission Sol, "Rapport no. 35," Nov. 1932.

53. The inspections in question took place in 1918–1919, 1924–1925, and 1930–31. These reports are available in ANSOM, AP 3047, AP 2760, AE 101, and AP 3066. Kair supervised all three of these missions, so he knew the colony and its problems well. For an in-depth analysis of the earliest use of force in the colony for cash-crop cultivation, see Weiskel, *French Colonial Rule*, chap. 6. The administration intensified the use of coercion during World War I in response to the Government General's request for foodstuffs and commodities for the metropole.

54. ANSOM, AP 3047 bis, Mission Kair, Côte d'Ivoire, 1918–1919, "Rapport no. 44," Aug. 22, 1919.

55. ANSOM, AP 3047, Mission Kair, Côte d'Ivoire, 1918–1919, "Rapport no. 45," Mar. 26, 1919.

56. ANSOM, AP 3047, Mission Kair, Côte d'Ivoire, 1918–1919, "Rapport no. 61," Feb. 21, 1919.

57. ANSOM, AP 3047, Mission Kair, Côte d'Ivoire, 1918–1919, "Rapport no. 60," Kair to ministre des Colonies, Sept. 8, 1919.

58. ANSOM, AP 3047, Mission Kair, "Rapport no. 45," Mar. 26, 1919.

59. A recent case study of the use of administrative coercion to intensify cocoa cultivation in southeastern Ivory Coast between 1908 and 1920 draws a similar conclusion. The author points out that although the local inhabitants pioneered cocoa cultivation, "market forces . . . were not moving fast enough to suit the French." They intervened to "ensure that this process of diffusion took place at an accelerated pace" (Groff, "Carrots, Sticks and Cocoa Pods," p. 416).

60. "Abusive" was the adjective Kair claimed that Antonetti used in justifying his systematic recourse to coercion. See ANSOM, AP 3047, Mission Kair, "Rapport no. 60," Sept. 8, 1919.

61. ANSOM, AP 3047, Mission Kair, "Rapport no. 61," Feb. 21, 1919.

62. Arrêté "promulguant en AOF le décret du 21 août, 1930," Feb. 18, 1933, *JOAOF*, p. 258. In passing this decree the government stressed "obligatory public labor" rather than "forced labor" in references to French labor policies. The term "forced labor," it was argued, evoked the horrors of the slave trade, whereas "obligatory public labor" underscored progress. It is important to note that although Paris passed this decree in 1930, it was not promulgated in West Africa until three years later.

63. Only in 1926, when the ILO began to look into the question of forced labor, did the French government express an interest in the issue. In that

year, Colonial Minister Léon Perrier sent a circular requesting information on existing labor legislation. ANSOM, AE, Main d'oeuvre 1, circulaire no. 521, Ministre des Colonies to gouverneurs généraux, gouverneurs et commissaires de la République, Nov. 17, 1926. Perrier also asked the Conseil Supérieur des Colonies to recommend labor regulations that could apply throughout the empire. The Conseil studied the question for two years before determining that forced labor remained permissible under certain regulated conditions. For their debates, see ANSOM, AE, Main d'oeuvre 2 and 5. For a more detailed account of the ILO's investigation than what I give here, see Fall, *Le travail forcé*, chap. 8; Van Beusekom, "Colonial Rural Development," pp. 89–96.

64. Several works appeared shortly after the French government decided not to sign the ILO treaty, justifying the French position in Geneva in 1929–1930 on forced labor and discussing the 1930 decree on obligatory public labor. The more balanced of these works are Fayet, *Esclavage et travail obligatoire*, and Folliet, *Le travail forcé aux colonies*; other studies of the question from this period include Mercier, *Le travail obligatoire*, and Lespinasse, *Le travail forcé*. A second account of the French position at Geneva is provided in a series of reports assembled in 1930 by Marius Moutet, a Socialist deputy and future colonial minister under the Popular Front. These reports, while critical of the government's decision not to ratify the treaty, indicate that requisitioning labor for public works was acceptable, provided local authorities guaranteed workers decent salaries and adequate working conditions. See ANSOM, PA 28, Papiers Marius Moutet, 4/127.

65. Statistics on men recruited in these colonies only began to be kept after the war. Research is providing a picture of the scale and the devastating impact recruitments could have upon local economies. Buell recorded a total of 49,000 workers recruited from Upper Volta for railroad construction in Ivory Coast and the Western Sudan between 1921 and 1925 (*Native Problem*, 1: 1043). Between 1920 and 1930 the administration recruited an additional 15,839 Africans, or approximately 1,400 annually, from the colony to work for three separate French enterprises (David, *Les navétanes*, pp. 154–158). The circle of Koudougou in Upper Volta lost an average of 3,117 workers a year, out of a total able-bodied male population of 60,000, to forced wage labor between 1925 and 1931; most of this labor was directed to either the Ivory Coast railroad or European-owned forest or cocoa concessions (Cordell and Gregory "Labour Reservoirs and Population," pp. 222–223). In the Western Sudan, a case study of one of the largest companies has shown an average recruitment of 1,000 to 1,614 workers annually between 1919 and 1942 (Fall, "Une entreprise agricole privée," p. 338). In the Niger Valley, 1,850 workers were requisitioned in 1925, then 2,850 in 1926, and 4,500 in 1925, to work on dam construction (Schreyger, *L'Office du Niger au Mali*, p. 76).

66. Arrêté "promulguant en AOF le décret du 22 octobre, 1925, régle-

mentant le travail indigène en AOF," Mar. 29, 1926, *JOAOF*, pp. 301–304; arrêté "fixant les conditions d'exécution de décret du 22 octobre, 1925," Mar. 29, 1926, *JOAOF*, pp. 304–309. Instructions from Carde followed the two arrêtés. This legislation would not apply to or interfere with the *navétanat* migrant labor patterns between the Western Sudan and Senegal. The federal administration estimated that 54,000 *navétanes* freely left the interior each year to work for six months on coastal peanut farms. Carde, Discours, Conseil de Gouvernement, *JOAOF*, Nov. 22, 1928, pp. 849–850.

67. Interest in Guinea was slower to develop. By the late 1920's, the administration had helped launch a program of banana production for export, but this production would only take off in the 1930's. For a summary of banana exports, see Trentadue, "Mouvements commerciaux."

68. Schreyger, *L'Office du Niger au Mali*, p. 27.

69. French officials estimated that between 20,000 and 25,000 workers from Upper Volta had migrated to Gold Coast in 1928. As was the case with the *navétanes*, these workers were often fleeing French labor requisitions in their home territories. See Touré, "Le refus du travail forcé," pp. 29–33; David, *Les navétanes*, p. 155; Cordell and Gregory, "Labour Reservoirs and Population," p. 222; Asiwaju, "Migrations as Revolt," pp. 577–594.

70. One petition sent to the colonial minister demanded that the administration recruit a minimum of 100 laborers within fifteen days of a request's being made. Companies owning more than one concession were to have the appropriate multiples of 100 workers. Quoted in Oloruntimehin, "Economy of French West Africa," p. 73.

71. ANSOM, AE, Main d'oeuvre 23, Mission Moretti, Soudan, 1923, "Rapport no. 23," Jan. 14, 1923.

72. ANSOM, AP 2808, "Note sur la réglementation de la main d'oeuvre," n.d. [ca. 1920]; ANS, circulaire no. 120 "a. s. de la réglementation du travail en Afrique occidentale française," Gouverneur général to lieutenants gouverneurs, Aug. 7, 1923. These reasons for drawing up a labor code were further developed by Carde before the Council of the Government General in December 1924. ANS, 6 E 48 FM, Conseil de Gouvernement, Procès-verbal, 1924. It is interesting to note that in France, too, there was considerable discontent with "unreliable" foreign workers at this time. Immigrants directed by the Foreign Labor Service into the least lucrative jobs often broke their initial contracts for better work elsewhere—hence, the only legislation concerning immigrants during the 1920's. In August 1926 a law "protecting national labor" required that immigrants stay a full year in the job for which they were admitted to France; employers could not hire them before that year had expired. And identity cards for foreigners now specified whether they were workers. Cross, *Immigrant Workers*, p. 158; Bonnet, *Les pouvoirs publics français*, pp. 145–150.

73. ANS, 6 E 48 FM, Conseil de Gouvernement, Procès-verbal, 1924.

74. Titre I "Régime du travail," in arrêté, Mar. 29, 1926, *JOAOF*, pp. 301–304; Titre II "Conditions des travailleurs," in arrêté, Mar. 29, 1926,

JOAOF, pp. 304–309. The *pécule* was debated while the code was being drafted. One critic suggested that the laborer would not understand; it was nevertheless retained, although its use was made optional. See ANSOM, AE, Main d'oeuvre 23, "Note du Directeur des Affaires Economiques pour la Direction Politique," Mar. 17, 1925.

75. Titre III " Des conseils d'arbitrage," in arrêté, Mar. 29, 1926, *JOAOF*, pp. 301–304.

76. "Instructions à Messieurs les Lieutenants Gouverneurs des Colonies du Groupe au sujet de la réglementation du travail indigène," Mar. 29, 1926, *JOAOF*, p. 313; Titre II "Du contrat de travail," in arrêté, Mar. 29, 1926, *JOAOF*, pp. 301–304; Titre III "Hygiène du travail," in arrêté, Mar. 29, 1926, *JOAOF*, pp. 304–309.

77. See circulaire 279 bis, part b, Aug. 1, 1930, *JOAOF*, pp. 702–706.

78. First instituted during the war, immigrant labor placement offices grew dramatically in the 1920's. The state, employers, and organized French labor used them to direct and restrict foreign labor to the most unskilled jobs available. Although outright coercion was not used, a variety of more subtle constraints limited the mobility of the foreign worker; these included identity cards, work permits that tied workers to specific jobs, and the threat of expulsion. Cross, *Immigrant Workers*, pp. 42–44, 148–159. Carde gave detailed instructions for the *offices de travail* in his local-application arrêté. He hoped they would compile an inventory of all labor resources in a colony, then distribute them in a balanced and rational fashion. None appear to have been created before 1930.

79. ANSOM, AE, Main d'oeuvre 23, Réglementation de la main d'oeuvre. "Note au sujet de la crise de la main d'oeuvre à la Côte d'Ivoire," Direction des Affaires Economiques, Apr. 28, 1925.

80. ANSOM, AE, Main d'oeuvre 23, Mission Picanon, Côte d'Ivoire, 1925, Gouverneur général to ministre des Colonies, no. 2700 A.E., Aug. 20, 1925.

81. ANSOM, AP 31, Papiers Henri Dirat, Gouverneur général de l'Algérie to gouverneur général p.i. de l'Afrique Occidentale Française, July 13, 1931.

82. Kair suggests this connection in his final report. ANSOM, AP 3066, Mission Kair, Côte d'Ivoire, 1930–1931, "Rapport no. 125," May 25, 1931. See also Fréchou, "Les plantations européenes en Côte d'Ivoire." Europeans settled the colony in the greatest numbers between 1925 and 1930. Most farms were small, and their owners arrived with little experience in growing tropical commodities. From the outset, they relied upon the administration for their labor needs. This labor was recruited predominantly from areas to the north of the colony.

83. Conditions in Ivory Coast were unique. In Dahomey rich land, together with high population density, made land scarce; in Upper Volta, poor soil automatically earmarked it as a labor exporter; in Senegal, subjects could defend their rights against the depredations of an imprudent administration and the abuses of employers. See ANSOM, AP 3066, Mission Kair, "Rapport no. 125," May 25, 1931.

84. ANSOM, PA 28, Papiers Moutet, 4/127, contains additional information on labor recruited for European forestry concessions.

85. Kair's findings do not appear exaggerated when compared to other accounts of Africans working for Europeans. Similar abuses prevailed in the Western Sudan for workers on French-owned sisal farms, where mortality rates were sometimes as high as 10 percent. Fall, "Une entreprise agricole privée," pp. 340–348. Conditions were no better on public works projects. Mortality rates between 1925 and 1927 on the Niger Valley dams were between 6 percent and 13 percent. Schreyger, *L'Office du Niger au Mali*, p. 76.

86. ANSOM, AP 3066, Mission Kair, Côte d'Ivoire, 1930–1931, "Rapport no. 143," July 13, 1931. See also "Rapport no. 105," June 20, 1931, and "Rapport no. 110," June 21, 1931. Kair's complaint that excessive coercion was only increasing the African's "natural" antipathy for work reflected a growing African aversion to the kind of wage labor being offered in the colony. What Kair failed to see was that though Africans rejected wage labor, they were going to work for themselves. Faced with the constant threat of recruitment and the undesirable labor conditions on European farms, Africans in Ivory Coast showed less interest in working for the settlers and more in becoming independent cocoa planters. The 1920's thus saw the rise not only of a European settler class but also of an indigenous African farmer class comparable to that already flourishing in Gold Coast. Weiskel, "Labor in the Emergent Periphery."

87. ANSOM, AP 3066, Mission Kair, "Rapport no. 125," May 25, 1931.

88. Ibid.

89. Arrêté "promulguant en AOF le décret du 21 août, 1930," Feb. 18, 1933, *JOAOF*, p. 258.

90. ANSOM, AP 3066, Mission Kair, Côte d'Ivoire, 1930–1931, "Rapport no. 103," June 19, 1931. "Pressure" was in fact exerted until 1946.

91. Carde, Discours, Conseil de Gouvernement, Nov. 25, 1929, *JOAOF*, p. 1027.

92. Carde, Discours, Conseil de Gouvernement, Nov. 22, 1928, *JOAOF*, p. 838.

93. Instruction, Feb. 15, 1926, *JOAOF*, p. 198.

CONCLUSION

1. Colloque "Commémoration du centenaire de la création de l'Afrique occidentale française," Dakar, June 16–23, 1995.

2. This is the view, in particular, of Weber, *Peasants into Frenchmen*, pp. 486–493. How provincial French reacted to this attempt to civilize them remains, of course, in dispute—but there is little doubt that the governing elite of the Third Republic consciously undertook such an effort during these years.

3. Nord, "Welfare State in France," p. 833. See also Mayeur and Rebérioux, *Third Republic*, pp. 352–353.

4. Silverman, *Art Nouveau in Fin-de-Siècle France*, p. 13.

5. See, for example, Elwitt, *Third Republic Defended;* Nye, *Crime, Madness and Politics in Modern France;* and Ewald, *L'état providence.*

6. For more on these trends see, in addition to Schneider, *Quality and Quantity,* and M. L. Roberts, *Civilization without Sexes,* Maier, *Recasting Bourgeois Europe;* Kuisel, *Capitalism and the State;* Becker and Berstein, *Victoire et frustrations.*

7. Wright, *Politics of Design,* p. 306.

8. The essays in Johnson, *Double Impact,* discussing the impact of Africa on French culture confined themselves to metropolitan developments in art, architecture, literature, and ideologies of race. But this influence was equally pervasive in the political and social arenas.

9. Among the exceptions, for example, are Lebovics, *True France;* Meyer et al., *Histoire de la France coloniale,* vol. 1, *Des origines à 1914;* Thobie et al., *Histoire de la France coloniale,* vol. 2, *1914–1990.*

10. For a recent review essay on the state of this field, see Drayton, "Science and the European Empires."

11. Fall, *Le travail forcé,* pp. 219–226.

12. For a good overview of these developments see Cooper, "Conflict and Connection."

13. Cooper, *From Slaves to Squatters,* p. 65.

Bibliography

Primary Sources

ANS   ARCHIVES NATIONALES DE LA RÉPUBLIQUE
DU SÉNÉGAL (DAKAR, SÉNÉGAL)

Archives du gouvernement général de l'AOF

The documents in this archive are classified into two *fonds*, the *fonds ancien* and the *fonds moderne*. The *fonds ancien* contains all documents prior to 1920, while the *fonds moderne* contains all documents after 1920. The entire archive has been divided into series, and each series into numbered dossiers. Published catalogs exist for the *fonds ancien* and the 2-G series (periodic reports), but not for the *fonds moderne*. Documents from the *fonds moderne* are designated FM. The ANS also contain annual bound volumes of all the circulars issued by the governors general to the lieutenant governors of the federation. Although many of these circulars were published in the *Journal Officiel de l'Afrique Occidentale Française*, some were not. Documents from these volumes appear in the notes as ANS, circulaire number and date.

Series 4 D, Personnel militaire
Series 1 E, Généralités: Organisation des assemblées
Series 5 E, Conseil de Gouvernement de l'AOF
Series 6 E, Commission permanente du Conseil de Gouvernement de l'AOF
Series 2 G, Rapports périodiques (politiques, économiques, administratives)
Series 4 G, Missions d'Inspection des colonies
Series 17 G, Affaires politiques, AOF
Series 18 G, Affaires administratives, AOF
Series H, Santé
Series K, Esclavage et travail

Series M, Tribunaux judiciaires
Series Q, Affaires économiques

ANSOM   ARCHIVES NATIONALES, SECTION
OUTRE-MER (AIX-EN-PROVENCE, FRANCE)

AOF VIII

Affaires Politiques (AP)
Affaires Economiques (AE)
Personnel (EE)
Télégrammes (Téls.)
Papiers Marius Moutet (PA 28)
Papiers Henri Dirat (AP 31)
Papiers Léonce Jore (APC 54)
Commission Guernut (ANSOM, CG)

INSTITUT DE FRANCE (PARIS, FRANCE)

Fonds Auguste Terrier

GOVERNMENT SERIALS

Annuaire du gouvernement général de l'Afrique occidentale française.
    Saint-Louis, Sénégal: Imprimerie du gouvernement général, 1904–1922.
Annuaire du Ministère des Colonies. Paris: Imprimerie H. Charles La-
    vauzelle, 1899–1936.
Journal officiel de la République française (JORF) 1895–1905
Journal officiel de l'Afrique occidentale française (JOAOF) 1904–1936
Journal officiel du Sénégal et Dépendances (JOSD) 1895–1905

OTHER PUBLICATIONS

André, Ed.-C. *De l'esclavage à Madagascar.* Paris: A. Rousseau, 1899.
Barot, Dr. *Guide pratique de l'Européen dans l'Afrique Occidentale à
    l'usage des militaires, fonctionnaires, commerçants, colons et touristes.*
    Paris: Flammarion, 1902.
Brévié, Jules. *Islamisme contre "naturisme" au Soudan français: Essai de
    psychologie politique coloniale.* Paris: Leroux, 1923.
Bruno, G. *Le tour de la France par deux enfants: Devoir et patrie.* 388th ed.
    Paris: Belin Frères, 1922.
Buell, Raymond. *The Native Problem in Africa.* 2 vols. London: Macmillan,
    1928.
Calmette, Dr. Albert. "Les missions scientifiques de l'Institut Pasteur et
    l'expansion coloniale de la France." *Revue Scientifique* 50, no. 5 (Feb. 3,
    1912): 129–133.
Cendrieux, J. *François Phuoc, métis.* Paris: Charpentier, 1929.
Chailley-Bert, J. *Dix années de politique coloniale.* Paris: A. Colin, 1902.
Charmeil, Pierre. *Les gouverneurs généraux des colonies françaises: Leurs*

pouvoirs et leurs attributions. Paris: Librairie moderne de droit et de jurisprudence, 1922.

Chivas-Baron, Clothilde. *Confidences de métisse.* Paris: Charpentier et Fasquelle, 1926.

———. *La femme française aux colonies.* Paris: Larose, 1929.

"Circulaire relative à l'application de l'arrêté du 6 mars, 1924." Mar. 15, 1924. Gorée: Imprimerie du gouvernement général, 1924.

"Circulaire relative à l'intensification de la production agricole et pastorale en Afrique occidentale française." Feb. 25, 1930. Gorée: Imprimerie du gouvernement général, 1930.

Clozel, François Joseph. *Dix ans à la Côte d'Ivoire.* Paris: A. Challamel, 1906.

Clozel, François Joseph, and Roger Villamur, eds. *Les coutumes indigènes de la Côte d'Ivoire.* Paris: A. Challamel, 1902.

Conférence Coloniale instituée par M. A. Maginot. Paris: Larose, 1917.

Cosnier, Henri. *L'Ouest africain français: Ses ressources agricoles, son organisation économique.* Paris: Larose, 1921.

Deherme, Georges. *L'Afrique occidentale française: Action politique, action économique, action sociale.* Paris: Librairie Bloud, 1908.

de Kersaint-Gilly, Félix. "Essai sur l'évolution de l'esclavage en Afrique occidentale française: Son dernier stade au Soudan français." *Bulletin du Comité d'Etudes Historiques et Scientifiques de l'Afrique Occidentale Française* 9, no. 3 (1924): 468–478.

Delafosse, Maurice. *L'âme nègre.* Paris: Payot, 1922.

———. *Broussard; ou, les états d'âme d'un colonial, suivis de ses propos et opinions.* Paris: Larose, 1923.

———. *Les civilisations nègro-africaines.* Paris: Stock, 1925.

———. "Clozel, un grand africain disparu." *Bulletin du Comité de l'Afrique Française,* no. 1 (1918): 76–82.

———. *Haut-Sénégal-Niger.* Paris: Larose, 1912. Reprint, 3 vols., Paris: G. P. Maisonneuve et Larose, 1972.

———. *Les nègres.* Paris: Editions Rieder, 1927.

———. *Les noirs de l'Afrique.* Paris: Payot, 1922.

———. "Les points sombres de l'horizon en AOF." *Bulletin du Comité de l'Afrique Française,* no. 8 (1922): 271–284.

———. "Sur l'orientation nouvelle de la politique indigène dans l'Afrique noire." *Bulletin du Comité de l'Afrique Française—Renseignements coloniaux,* no. 6 (1921): 145–153.

Delavignette, Robert. *Les vrais chefs de l'empire.* Paris: Gallimard, 1939.

"Enquête sur les croisements ethniques." *Revue Anthropologique* 22 (Sept.-Oct. 1912): 337–396.

L'enseignement aux indigènes: Documents officiels précédés de notices historiques. 2 vols. Brussels: Institut Colonial International, 1909.

Faure, J. L., ed. *La vie aux colonies: Préparation de la femme à la vie coloniale.* Paris: Larose, 1938.

Favre, Lucienne. *L'orientale* 1930. Paris: B. Grasset, 1930.

Fayet, Charles. *Esclavage et travail obligatoire: La main d'oeuvre non-volontaire en Afrique.* Paris: Librairie générale de droit et de jurisprudence, 1931.

Folliet, Joseph. *Le travail forcé aux colonies.* Paris: Editions du Cerf, 1936.

François, Georges. *L'Afrique occidentale française.* Paris: Larose, 1907.

Froidevaux, Henri. "L'enseignement indigène dans les colonies françaises (valeur, nature, méthode)." In *L'enseignement aux indigènes: Documents officiels précedés de notices historiques,* vol. 1, 469–472. Brussels: Institut Colonial International, 1909.

Gay, P.-H., and O. Mortreux, eds. *French Elementary Schools: Official Courses of Study.* New York: Teachers' College Press, 1926.

Gouvernement Général de l'Afrique Occidentale Française. *Justice indigène: Instructions aux administrateurs sur l'application du décret du 10 novembre, 1903 portant réorganisation du service de la justice.* Gorée: Imprimerie du gouvernement général, 1905.

"Les grands travaux sur fonds d'emprunts dans l'AOF." *Bulletin du Comité de l'Afrique Française—Renseignements coloniaux,* no. 10 (1905): 378–379.

Gueye, Lamine. *De la situation politique des Sénégalais originaires des communes de plein exercice telle qu'elle résulte des lois des 19 octobre, 1915, 29 septembre, 1916 et dans la jurisprudence antérieure, conséquences au point de vue du conflit des lois françaises et musulmanes en matière civile.* Paris: Editions de "La vie universitaire," 1921.

Guy, Camille. *Les colonies françaises: La mise en valeur de notre domaine coloniale.* Paris: A. Challamel, 1900.

Hardy, Georges. *Ergaste ou la vocation coloniale.* Paris: Larose, 1929.

———. *Une conquête morale: L'enseignement en A. O. F.* Paris: A. Colin, 1917.

Henry, Yves. *Le coton dans l'Afrique occidentale française.* Paris: A. Challamel, 1904.

Herbart, P. *Le chancre du Niger.* Paris: Gallimard, 1939.

Humbert, Charles. "L'AOF sous l'administration de M. W. Ponty." *La Grande Revue* (May 1911): 49–70.

Joucla, Edmond, and Gilbert-Desvallons, eds. *Jurisprudence de la Chambre d'Homologation.* Gorée: Imprimerie du gouvernement général, 1910.

Leroy-Beaulieu, Paul. *De la colonisation chez les peuples modernes.* 1st ed. Paris: Librairie Guillaumin, 1874.

———. *De la colonisation chez les peuples modernes.* 3d ed. Paris: Librairie Guillaumin, 1886.

Lespinasse, Jean. *Le travail forcé dans les colonies françaises et la Société des Nations.* Bordeaux: Y. Cadoret, 1933.

"Lettre des Amicales de Fonctionnaires à M. le Gouverneur Général de l'Indochine." *La Revue Indigène* 97 (June 30, 1914): 354–359.

Lévy-Bruhl, Lucien. "L'Institut d'Ethnologie de l'Université de Paris." *Revue d'ethnographie et des traditions populaires*, nos. 23–24 (1925): 233–236.

Marty, Paul. "La politique indigène du Gouverneur Général Ponty en Afrique occidentale française." *Revue du monde musulman* 31 (1915): 1–22.

Maunier, René. *Sociologie coloniale.* Vol. 1, *Introduction à l'étude du contact des races.* Paris: Domat-Montchrestien, 1932.

Mazet, Jacques. *La condition juridique des métis dans les possessions françaises, Indochine, Afrique occidentale française, Madagascar.* Paris: Domat-Montchrestien, 1932.

"Mémorial Maurice Delafosse." *Outre-mer: Revue générale de colonisation* 1 (1929): 263–285.

Meunier, Pierre. *Organisation et fonctionnement de la justice indigène en Afrique occidentale française.* Paris: A. Colin, 1914.

Moiret, Joseph-Marie. *Mémoires sur l'expédition de l'Egypte.* Paris: P. Belford, 1984.

Moreau, Paul. *Les indigènes de l'Afrique occidentale française: Leur condition politique et économique.* Paris: Domat-Montchrestien, 1938.

"L'organisation budgétaire de l'AOF." *Bulletin du Comité de l'Afrique Française* no. 3 (1905): 112–113.

Pelleray, Emmanuel. *L'Afrique occidentale française: Le milieu, l'organisation, la mise en valeur. Le Togo.* Paris: Notre domaine colonial, 1923.

"La pénétration de la Côte d'Ivoire." *Bulletin du Comité de l'Afrique Française—Renseignements coloniaux*, no. 10 (1909): 193–204.

Ponty, William Merlaud. *Justice indigène: Instructions aux Administrateurs sur l'application du décret du 16 août, 1912 portant réorganisation de la justice en AOF.* Gorée: Imprimerie du gouvernement général, 1913.

Randau, Robert. *Le chef des porte-plume: Roman de la vie coloniale.* Paris: Editions du monde nouveau, 1922.

Raynal, Abbé. *A Philosophical History of the Settlements and Trade of the Europeans in the East and West Indies.* Vol. 4, trans. J. O. Justamont, rev. ed. Dublin: J. Exshaw, 1784.

Régismanset, Charles. *Questions coloniales 1900–1912.* Paris: Larose, 1912.

Richet, Charles. *Sélection humaine.* Paris: F. Alcan, 1919.

Robiquet, Paul, ed. *Jules Ferry: Discours et opinions.* Vol. 5. Paris: A. Colin, 1896.

Roustans, Mario. "L'accession à la qualité de citoyen français." *Annales coloniales*, Sept. 17, 1925.

Runner, Jean. *Les droits politiques des indigènes des colonies.* Paris: Larose, 1927.

Sarraut, Albert. *La mise en valeur des colonies françaises.* Paris: Payot, 1923.

———. "La mission civilisatrice de la France." *Panorama*, no. 132 (1925).

Schoelcher, Victor. *L'esclavage au Sénégal en 1880.* Paris: Librairie centrale des publications populaires, 1880.

———. *Polémique coloniale.* 2 vols. Paris: Dentu, 1882–1886.

"La science et les métis." *La Revue Indigène* 94 (Mar. 9, 1914): 143–151.

Sonolet, Louis. *Les aventures de deux négrillons.* Paris: A. Colin, 1924.

———. *Moussa et Gi-gla: Histoire de deux petits noirs.* Paris: A. Colin, 1916.

Sonolet, Louis, and A. Pérès. *Le livre du maître africain à l'usage des écoles de village.* 2d ed. Paris: A. Colin, 1923.

Une âme de chef: Le Gouverneur Général Joost Van Vollenhoven. Paris: Plon, 1920.

Volney, comte de. *Voyage en Egypte et en Syrie.* 3d ed. Paris: Dugour et Durand, 1799. Reprint, Paris: Mouton, 1959.

Wild, Herbert. *L'autre race.* Paris: Albin Michel, 1930.

Secondary Sources

Abrams, L., and D. J. Miller. "Who Were the French Colonialists? A Reassessment of the Parti Colonial, 1890-1914." *Historical Journal* 19, no. 3 (1976): 689–726.

Adas, Michael. *Machines as the Measure of Men: Science, Technology and Ideologies of Western Dominance.* Ithaca: Cornell University Press, 1989.

Ageron, Charles-Robert. "L'Exposition coloniale de 1931: Mythe républicain ou mythe impérial?" In Pierre Nora, ed., *Les lieux de mémoire.* Vol. 1, *La République,* pp. 561–591. Paris: Gallimard, 1984.

———. *France coloniale ou parti colonial?* Paris: Presses universitaires de France, 1978.

Agulhon, Maurice. *Le Cercle dans la France bourgeoise.* Paris: A. Colin, 1977.

———. *1848 ou l'apprentissage de la République, 1848–1852.* Paris: Seuil, 1973.

———. *Histoire vagabonde.* 3 vols. Paris: Hachette, 1988–1996.

———. *La République au village.* Paris: Plon, 1970.

———. *La République: 1880 à nos jours.* Paris: Hachette, 1990.

Aissi, Antoine. "La justice indigène et la vie congolaise, 1886–1936." *Thèse de 3e cycle,* University of Toulouse le Mirail, 1978.

Ajayi, J. F. A., and Michael Crowder, eds. *History of West Africa.* 2 vols. London: Longman, 1974.

Amselle, Jean-Loup. *Logiques métisses: Anthropologie de l'identité en Afrique et ailleurs.* Paris: Payot, 1990.

Andrew, C. M. *Théophile Delcassé and the Making of the Entente Cordiale: A Reappraisal of French Foreign Policy, 1898–1905.* London: Macmillan, 1968.

Andrew, C. M., and A. S. Kanya-Forstner. "French Business and the French Colonialists." *Historical Journal* 19, no. 4 (1976): 981–1000.

———. "The French Colonial Party: Its Composition, Aims and Influence." *Historical Journal* 14, no. 1 (1971): 99–128.

Anignikin, Sylvain Coovi. "Les origines du mouvement national au Dahomey, 1900–1939." *Thèse de 3e cycle,* University of Paris, 1980.

Asiwaju, A. I. "Control through Coercion: A Study of the *Indigénat* Regime in French West Africa, 1887–1946." *Bulletin de l'IFAN* 41, ser. B, no. 1 (1979): 35–71.

———. "Migrations as Revolt: The Example of the Ivory Coast and Upper Volta before 1945." *Journal of African History* 17, no. 4 (1976): 577–594.

August, Thomas G. *The Selling of the Empire: British and French Imperialist Propaganda, 1890–1940.* Westport, Conn.: Greenwood Press, 1985.

Auspitz, Katherine. *The Radical Bourgeoisie: The Ligue de l'Enseignement and the Origins of the Third Republic, 1866–1885.* Cambridge, Eng.: Cambridge University Press, 1982.

Bado, Jean-Paul. "La maladie du sommeil en Afrique de l'Ouest jusqu'en 1914." *Revue française d'histoire d'outre-mer* 82, no. 2 (1995): 149–168.

Ballard, John. "The Porto-Novo Incidents of 1923: Politics in the Colonial Era." *University of Ife Journal of African Studies* 2, no. 1 (1965): 52–75.

Bancel, Nicolas, Pascal Blanchard, and Laurent Gervereau, eds. *Images et colonies: Iconographie et propagande coloniales sur l'Afrique française de 1880 à 1962.* Paris: ACHAC, 1993.

Barry, Boubacar. *La Sénégambie du XVe au XIXe siècle: Traite negrière, Islam, conquête coloniale.* Paris: L'Harmattan, 1988.

Bathily, Abdoulaye. "Aux origines de l'Africanisme: Le rôle de l'oeuvre ethno-historique de Faidherbe dans la conquête française du Sénégal." In Pierre Bourdieu, ed., *Cahiers Jussieu no. 2, Université de Paris VII: Le mal de voir. Ethnologie et orientalisme: Politique et épistémologie, critique et autocritique,* pp. 77–107. Paris: Union générale d'éditions, 1976.

Bazin, Jean. "A chacun son bambara." In Jean-Loup Amselle and Elikia M'Bokolo, eds., *Au coeur de l'ethnie: Ethnies, tribalisme et état en Afrique,* pp. 87–129. Paris: La Découverte, 1985.

Becker, Jean-Jacques and Serge Berstein. *Victoire et frustrations, 1914–1929.* Paris: Seuil, 1990.

Bender, Thomas. "The Development of French Anthropology." *Journal of the Behavioral Sciences* 1, no. 1 (1965): 139–151.

Beneton, Philippe. *Histoire de mots: Culture et civilisation.* Paris: Presses de la Fondation Nationale des Sciences Politiques, 1975.

Benot, Yves. *Diderot, de l'athéisme à l'anti-colonialisme.* Paris: La Découverte, 1970.

———. *La Révolution française et la fin des colonies.* Paris: La Découverte, 1988.

Berge, François. *Le sous-secrétariat et les sous-secrétaires d'état aux colonies: Histoire de l'émancipation de l'administration coloniale.* Paris: Société française d'histoire d'outre-mer, 1962.

Betts, Raymond F. *Assimilation and Association in French Colonial Theory, 1890–1914.* New York: Columbia University Press, 1961.

Bhabha, Homi K. "The Other Question: The Stereotype and Colonial Discourse." *Screen* 24, no. 6 (Nov.-Dec. 1983): 18–36.

Blackburn, Robin. *The Overthrow of Colonial Slavery, 1776–1848.* London: Verso, 1988.

Blakemore, Priscilla. "Assimilation and Association in French Educational Policy and Practice: Senegal, 1903–1939." In Charles Lyons and Vincent Battle, eds., *Essays in the History of African Education*, pp. 85–103. New York: Teachers' College Press, 1970.

Blanchard, Pascal et al. *L'Autre et Nous: "Scènes et Types."* *Anthropologues et historiens devant les représentations des populations colonisées des "ethnies," des "tribus" et des races depuis les conquêtes coloniales.* Paris: Syros, 1995.

Blanning, T. C. W. *The Origins of the French Revolutionary Wars.* London: Longman, 1986.

Bonnet, Jean-Charles. *Les pouvoirs publics français et l'immigration dans l'entre-deux guerres.* Lyon: Centre d'histoire économique et sociale dans la région lyonnaise, 1976.

Bonneuil, Christophe. *Des savants pour l'empire: La structuration des recherces scientifiques coloniales au temps de "la mise en valeur" des colonies françaises.* Paris: Editions de l'ORSTOM, 1991.

Bouche, Denise. *L'enseignement dans les territoires de l'Afrique occidentale de 1817 à 1920: Mission civilisatrice ou formation d'une élite?* 2 vols. Lille: Atelier Reproduction des Thèses, 1975.

———. *Histoire de la colonisation française.* Vol. 2, *Flux et reflux (1815–1962).* Paris: Fayard, 1991.

———. *Les villages de liberté en Afrique noire française, 1887–1910.* The Hague: Mouton, 1968.

Boulègue, Marguerite. "La presse au Sénégal avant 1939: Bibliographie." *Bulletin de l'IFAN* 27, ser. B, nos. 3–4 (1965): 715–754.

Boulle, Pierre. "In Defense of Slavery: Eighteenth-Century Opposition to Abolition and the Origins of Racist Ideology in France." In Frederick Krantz, ed., *History from Below*, pp. 219–246. Oxford: Oxford University Press, 1988.

Boutillier, J. L. "Les captifs en A.O.F. (1903–1905)." *Bulletin de l'IFAN* 30, ser. B, no. 2 (1968): 511–535.

Boyer, Marcel. *Les sociétés indigènes de prévoyance, de secours et de prêts mutuels agricoles en Afrique occidentale française.* Paris: Domat-Montchrestien, 1935.

Braibant, Patrick. "L'administration coloniale et le profit commercial en Côte d'Ivoire pendant la crise de 1929." *Revue française d'histoire d'outre-mer* 63, nos. 3–4 (1976): 555–573.

Brooks, George. "Peanuts and Colonialism: Consequences of the Commercialization of Peanuts in West Africa, 1830–1870." *Journal of African History* 16, no. 1 (1975): 29–54.

Brubaker, Rogers. *Citizenship and Nationhood in France and Germany.* Cambridge, Mass.: Harvard University Press, 1992.

Brunschwig, Henri. *Mythes et réalités de l'impérialisme colonial français, 1871–1914.* Paris: A. Colin, 1960.

———. *Noirs et blancs dans l'Afrique noire française, ou, Comment le colonisé devient colonisateur (1870–1914).* Paris: Flammarion, 1983.

————. "Note sur les technocrates de l'impérialisme français en Afrique noire." *Revue française d'histoire d'outre-mer* 44, no. 1 (1967): 171–187.

Campion-Vincent, Véronique. "L'image du Dahomey dans la presse française 1890–1895: Les sacrifices humains." *Cahiers d'études africaines* 7, no. 1 (1967): 27–58.

Capron, Jean. *Communautés villageoises bwa: Mali, Haute-Volta.* Paris: Institut d'Ethnologie, 1973.

Chanet, Jean-François. *L'école républicaine et les petites patries.* Paris: Aubier, 1996.

Chanock, Martin. *Law, Custom and Social Order: The Colonial Experience in Malawi and Zambia.* Cambridge, Eng.: Cambridge University Press, 1985.

Charles-Roux, F. *Bonaparte, gouverneur d'Egypte.* Paris: Plon, 1936.

————. *France, Egypte et la Mer Rouge, de 1715 à 1798.* Cairo: Cahiers d'histoire égyptienne, 1951.

Chaunu, Pierre. *L'Amérique et les Amériques.* Paris: A. Colin, 1964.

Christelow, Allan. *Muslim Law Courts and the French Colonial State in Algeria.* Princeton: Princeton University Press, 1985.

Clancy-Smith, Julia A. *Rebel and Saint: Muslim Notables, Populist Protest, Colonial Encounters, 1800–1904.* Berkeley: University of California Press, 1994.

Clancy-Smith, Julia A., and Frances Gouda, eds., *Domesticating the Empire: Languages of Gender, Race, and Family Life in French and Dutch Colonialism.* Charlottesville: University Press of Virginia, forthcoming.

Clark, Linda. *Schooling the Daughters of Marianne: Textbooks and the Socialization of Girls in Modern French Primary Schools.* Albany: State University of New York Press, 1984.

Clark, Terry N. *Prophets and Patrons: The French University System and the Emergence of the Social Sciences.* Cambridge, Mass.: Harvard University Press, 1973.

Clifford, James. *The Predicament of Culture: Twentieth-Century Ethnography, Literature and Art.* Cambridge, Mass.: Harvard University Press, 1988.

Codo, Bellarmin Cofi. "La presse dahoméenne face aux aspirations des 'évolués': La Voix du Dahomey (1927–1957)." *Thèse de 3e cycle*, University of Paris, 1978.

Cohen, William B. *The French Encounter with Africans: White Response to Blacks, 1530–1880.* Bloomington: Indiana University Press, 1980.

————. "Gambettists and Colonial Expansion before 1881: The *République française.*" *French Colonial Studies / Etudes Coloniales Françaises* 1 (1977): 54–64.

————. "Health and Colonialism in French West Africa." In Jan Vansina et al., eds., *Etudes africaines offertes à Henri Brunschwig*, pp. 297–307. Paris: Editions de l'Ecole des Hautes Etudes en Sciences Sociales, 1982.

————. "Imperial Mirage: The Western Sudan in French Thought and Action." *Journal of the Historical Society of Nigeria* 7, no. 3 (1974): 417–445.

———. "Malaria and French Imperialism." *Journal of African History* 24, no. 1 (1983): 23–36.

———. *Rulers of Empire: The French Colonial Service in Africa, 1880–1960.* Stanford: Hoover Institution Press, 1971.

Coleman, William. *Death Is a Social Disease: Public Health and Political Economy in Early Industrial France.* Madison: University of Wisconsin Press, 1982.

Conklin, Alice. "Democracy Rediscovered: Civilization through Association in French West Africa, 1914–1930." *Cahiers d'études africaines* 37, no. 1 (1997): 59–84.

———. "A Mission to Civilize: Imperialism and Ideology in French West Africa, 1895–1930." Ph.D. diss., Princeton University, 1989.

———. "Of Titians and Camels: The Intellectual Origins of the *Mission Civilisatrice* in France." Paper presented at the Davis Seminar, Princeton University, Mar. 9, 1991.

———. "Redefining Frenchness: Citizenship, Imperial Motherhood and Race Regeneration in France and West Africa, 1914–1940." In Julia A. Clancy-Smith and Frances Gouda, eds., *Domesticating the Empire: Languages of Gender, Race, and Family Life in French and Dutch Colonialism.* Charlottesville: University Press of Virginia, forthcoming.

Cooper, Frederick. "Conflict and Connection: Rethinking Colonial African History." *American Historical Review* 99, no. 5 (1994): 1516–1545.

———. *From Slaves to Squatters: Plantation Labor and Agriculture in Zanzibar and Coastal Kenya, 1890–1925.* New Haven: Yale University Press, 1980.

Cooper, Frederick, and Ann Stoler. *Tensions of Empire: Colonial Cultures in a Bourgeois World.* Berkeley: University of California Press, 1997.

Copans, Jean. *Critiques et politiques de l'anthropologie.* Paris: F. Maspéro, 1974.

Coquery-Vidrovitch, Catherine. "L'Afrique coloniale française et la crise de 1930: Crise structurelle et genèse du sous-développement." *Revue française d'histoire d'outre-mer* 63, nos. 3–4 (1976): 386–424.

———. "Colonialisme ou impérialisme: La politique africaine de la France entre les deux guerres." *Mouvement Social* 107 (1979): 51–76.

Cordell, Dennis D. and Joel W. Gregory. "Labour Reservoirs and Population: French Colonial Strategies in Koudougou, Upper Volta, 1914 to 1939." *Journal of African History* 23, no. 2 (1982): 205–224.

Cornevin, Robert. "Evolution des chefferies traditionnelles en Afrique noire d'expression française." *Recueil Penant* 71 (1961): 235–250, 539–566.

———. "Joost Van Vollenhoven (1877–1918): Un protestant 'pied noir' au service de la France." *Bulletin de la Société de l'histoire du protestantisme français* 135, no. 2 (1989): 291–297.

Cross, Gary. *Immigrant Workers in Industrial France: The Making of a New Laboring Class.* Philadelphia: Temple University Press, 1983.

Crowder, Michael. "Indirect Rule, French and British Style." *Africa* 34, no. 2 (1964): 197–205.

———. *Senegal: A Study in French Assimilation Policy.* Rev. ed. London: Methuen, 1967.

———. *West Africa Under Colonial Rule.* London: Hutchinson University Library for Africa, 1981.

———. "West African Chiefs." In Michael Crowder, ed., *Colonial West Africa: Collected Essays*, pp. 209–231. London: F. Cass, 1978.

Cruise O'Brien, Rita. *White Society in Black Africa: The French of Senegal.* Evanston, Ill.: Northwestern University Press, 1972.

Curtin, Philip D. *Death by Migration: Europe's Encounter with the Tropical World in the Nineteenth Century.* Cambridge, Eng.: Cambridge University Press, 1989.

Cutter, Charles. "The Genesis of a Nationalist Elite: The Role of the Popular Front in the French Sudan (1936–1939)." In G. Wesley Johnson, ed., *Double Impact: France and Africa in the Age of Imperialism,* pp. 107–141. Westport, Conn.: Greenwood Press, 1985.

Daget, Serge. "Les mots esclave, nègre, Noir, et les jugements de valeur sur la traite negrière dans la littérature abolitionniste française de 1770 à 1845." *Revue française d'histoire d'outre-mer* 60, no. 3 (1973): 511–548.

D'Almeida-Topor, Hélène. "Les populations dahoméenes et le recrutement militaire pendant la première guerre mondiale." *Revue française d'histoire d'outre-mer* 60, no. 2 (1973): 196–241.

David, Philippe. *Les navétanes: Histoire des migrants saisonniers de l'arachide en Sénégambie des origines à nos jours.* Dakar: Nouvelles éditions africaines, 1980.

Davis, Shelby. *Reservoirs of Men: A History of the Black Troops of French West Africa.* Chambéry: Imprimeries réunies, 1934.

Day, C. Rod. "Education for the Industrial World: Technical and Modern Instruction in France Under the Third Republic, 1808–1914." In Robert Fox and George Weisz, eds., *The Organization of Science and Technology in France, 1808–1914,* pp. 127–154. Cambridge, Eng.: Cambridge University Press, 1980.

Debbasch, Yvan. *Couleur et liberté: Le jeu de critère ethnique dans un ordre juridique esclavagiste.* Paris: Dalloz, 1967.

de Benoist, Joseph Roger. *L'Afrique occidentale française de 1944 à 1960.* Dakar: Nouvelles éditions africaines, 1982.

———. "La balkanisation de l'Afrique occidentale française." *Thèse de 3e cycle,* Ecole des Hautes Etudes en Sciences Sociales, Paris, 1976.

———. *Eglise et pouvoir colonial au Soudan français: Les relations entre les administrateurs et les missionnaires catholiques dans la Boucle du Niger de 1885 à 1945.* Paris: Karthala, 1987.

DeGroot, Sylvia. "Joost Van Vollenhoven: L'apprentissage d'un fonctionnaire colonial." *Itinerario* 15, no. 2 (1991): 33–57.

Delafosse, Louise. *Maurice Delafosse: Le berrichon conquis par l'Afrique.* Paris: Société française d'histoire d'outre-mer, 1976.

Derman, William. *Serfs, Peasants and Socialists: A Former Serf Village in the Republic of Guinea.* Berkeley: University of California Press, 1973.

Deschamps, Hubert. "Et maintenant, Lord Lugard?" *Africa* 33, no. 3 (1963): 293–306.

———. *Les méthodes et les doctrines coloniales de la France du XVIe siècle à nos jours.* Paris: A. Colin, 1953.

Dewitte, Philippe. *Les mouvements nègres en France, 1919–1939.* Paris: L'Harmattan, 1985.

Dias, Nélia. "Langues inférieures, langues supérieures." In Claude Blanckaert, ed., *Des sciences contre l'homme.* Vol. 1, *Classer, hiérarchiser, exclure,* pp. 95–110. Paris: Autrement, 1993.

———. *Le Musée ethnographique du Trocadéro (1878–1902): Anthropologie et muséologie en France.* Paris: Presses du CNRS, 1991.

Diouf, Mamadou. *Le Kajoor au XIXe siècle: Pouvoir ceddo et conquête coloniale.* Paris: Karthala, 1990.

Dirks, Nicholas B., ed. *Colonialism and Culture.* Ann Arbor: University of Michigan Press, 1992.

Domergue-Cloarec, Dominique. "Politique coloniale française et realités coloniales: L'exemple de la santé en Côte d'Ivoire 1905–1968." *Thèse pour le doctorat d'Etat,* University of Poitiers, 1984.

Donzelot, Jacques. *The Policing of Families.* Trans. Robert Hurley. New York: Pantheon, 1979.

Dozon, Jacques. "Quand les pastoriens traquaient la maladie du sommeil." *Sciences Sociales et Santé* 3, nos. 3–4 (1985): 27–56.

Drayton, Richard. "Science and the European Empires." *Journal of Imperial and Commonwealth History* 23, no. 3 (1995): 503–510.

Drescher, Seymour. "The Ending of the Slave Trade and the Evolution of European Scientific Racism." *Social Science History* 14, no. 3 (1990): 415–450.

Duchet, Michelle. *Anthropologie et histoire au siècle des lumières: Buffon, Voltaire, Rousseau, Helvétius, Diderot.* Paris: F. Maspéro, 1971.

Echenberg, Myron. "Paying the Blood Tax: Military Conscription in French West Africa, 1914–1929." *Canadian Journal of African Studies / Revue Canadienne des Etudes Africaines* 9, no. 2 (1975): 171–192.

———. "Slaves into Soldiers: Social Origins of the *Tirailleurs Sénégalais.*" In Paul Lovejoy, ed., *Africans in Bondage: Studies in Slavery,* pp. 311–335. Madison: University of Wisconsin Press, 1986.

Echenberg, Myron, and Jean Filipovich. "African Military Labour and the Building of the Office du Niger Installations, 1925–1950." *Journal of African History* 27, no. 3 (1986): 533–551.

Elias, T. Olawale. *The Nature of African Customary Law.* Manchester: Manchester University Press, 1956.

Ellis, Jack D. *The Physician-Legislators of France: Medicine and Politics in the Early Third Republic, 1870–1914.* Cambridge, Eng.: Cambridge University Press, 1990.

Elwitt, Sanford. *The Making of the Third Republic: Class and Politics in France, 1868–1884.* Baton Rouge: Louisiana State University Press, 1975.

———. *The Third Republic Defended: Bourgeois Reform in France, 1880–1914.* Baton Rouge: Louisiana State University Press, 1986.

Emerit, Marcel. *Les Saint-Simoniens en Algérie.* Paris: Société d'édition "Les Belles Lettres," 1941.

Ewald, François. *L'état providence.* Paris: B. Grasset, 1986.

Fall, Babacar. *Le travail forcé en Afrique-Occidentale française, 1900–1946.* Paris: Karthala, 1993.

———. "Une entreprise agricole privée du Soudan français: La société anonyme des cultures de Diakandapé (Kayes), 1919–1942." In Catherine Coquery-Vidrovitch, ed., *Actes du colloque entreprises et entrepreneurs en Afrique, XIXe et XXe siècles,* vol. 1, pp. 335–350. Paris: L'Harmatttan, 1983.

Febvre, Lucien. "Civilisation: Le mot et l'idée." In *Centre international de synthèse, première semaine internationale de synthèse,* pp. 1–55. Paris: La Renaissance du livre, 1930.

Foner, Eric. *Nothing but Freedom: Emancipation and Its Legacy.* Baton Rouge: Louisiana State University Press, 1983.

Ford, Caroline C. "Which Nation? Language, Identity and Republican Politics in Post-revolutionary France." *History of European Ideas* 17, no. 1 (1993): 31–46.

Fraisse, Geneviève. *Reason's Muse: Sexual Difference and the Birth of Democracy.* Trans. Jane Marie Todd. Chicago: University of Chicago Press, 1994.

Fréchou, H. "Les plantations européenes en Côte d'Ivoire." *Cahiers d'Outre-Mer* 8, no. 1 (1955): 56–83.

Frémeaux, Jacques. *Les bureaux arabes dans l'Algérie de la conquête.* Paris: Denoël, 1993.

Fuglestad, Finn. *A History of Niger 1850–1960.* Cambridge, Eng.: Cambridge University Press, 1983.

———. "Les révoltes du Touareg du Niger 1916–1917." *Cahiers d'études africaines* 13, no. 1 (1973): 82–120.

Furet, François. *La Gauche et la révolution au milieu du XIXe siècle: Edgar Quinet et la question du Jacobinisme, 1865–1870.* Paris: Hachette, 1986.

Furet, François, and Mona Ozouf, eds. *Le siècle de l'avènement républicain.* Paris: Gallimard, 1993.

Garcia, Luc. "Les mouvements de résistance au Dahomey, 1914–1917." *Cahiers d'études africaines* 10, no. 1 (1970): 144–178.

———. "L'organisation de l'instruction publique au Dahomey, 1894–1920." *Cahiers d'études africaines* 11, no. 1 (1971): 59–101.

Garner, Reuben. "Watchdogs of Empire: The French Colonial Inspection Service in Action, 1815–1913." Ph.D. diss., University of Rochester, 1970.

Geggus, David. "Haiti and the Abolitionists: Opinion and Propaganda and International Politics in Britain and France, 1804–1938." In David Richardson, ed., *Abolition and Its Aftermath: The Historical Context 1790–1916*, pp. 113–141. London: F. Cass, 1983.

———. "Racial Equality, Slavery, and Colonial Secession during the Constituent Assembly." *American Historical Review* 94, no. 5 (1989): 1290–1308.

Gervais, Raymond. "Contribution à l'étude de l'évolution de la population de l'AOF, 1904–1960." *Les dossiers du CEPED*, no. 23 (July 1993): 1–50.

———. "Creating Hunger: Labor and Agricultural Policies in Southern Mosi, 1919-1940." In Dennis D. Cordell and Joel W. Gregory, eds., *African Population and Capitalism: Historical Perspectives*, pp. 109–121. Boulder: Westview Press, 1987.

Gildea, Robert. *Education in Provincial France, 1800–1914*. Oxford: Clarendon Press, 1983.

Gillispie, Charles C. "Aspects scientifiques de l'Expédition d'Egypte." In Henry Laurens, with Charles C. Gillispie, Jean-Claude Golvin, Claude Traunecker, *L'Expédition d'Egypte: La Révolution française et l'Islam, 1798–1801*, pp. 371–396. Paris: A. Colin, 1989.

Girardet, Raoul. *L'idée coloniale en France de 1871 à 1962*. Paris: Le livre de poche, 1972.

Godechot, Jacques. *La grande nation: L'expansion révolutionnaire de la France dans le monde de 1789 à 1899*. 2 vols. Paris: Aubier, 1956.

Goerg, Odile. *Commerce et colonisation en Guinée, 1850–1913*. Paris: L'Harmattan, 1986.

Groff, David H. "Carrots, Sticks and Cocoa Pods: African and Administrative Initiatives in the Spread of Cocoa Cultivation in Assikasso, Ivory Coast, 1908-1920." *International Journal of African Historical Studies* 20, no. 3 (1987): 401–416.

———. "The Dynamics of Collaboration and the Rule of Law in French West Africa: The Case of Kwame Kangah of Assikasso (Côte d'Ivoire), 1898–1922." In Kristin Mann and Richard Roberts, eds. *Law in Colonial Africa*, pp. 146–166. Portsmouth, N.H.: Heinemann, 1991.

Grosz-Ngaté, Marie. "Power and Knowledge: The Representation of the Mande World in the Works of Park, Caillé, Monteil, and Delafosse." *Cahiers d'études africaines* 28, no. 3 (1988): 485–511.

Gueye, Lamine. *Itinéraire Africain*. Paris: Présence africaine, 1966.

Guillaumin, Colette. *L'idéologie raciste: Genèse et langage actuel*. Paris: Mouton, 1972.

Guiraud, Xavier. *L'arachide sénégalaise: Monographie d'économie coloniale*. Paris: Librairie technique et économique, 1937.

Harding, Léonhard. "Les écoles des Pères Blancs au Soudan français, 1895–1920." *Cahiers d'études africaines* 11, no. 1 (1971): 104–129.

Hargreaves, John D. *West Africa: The Former French States*. Englewood Cliffs: Prentice-Hall, 1967.

———. *West Africa Partitioned.* Vol. 1, *The Loaded Pause.* London: Macmillan, 1974. Vol. 2, *The Elephants and the Grass.* Madison: University of Wisconsin Press, 1985.

Harrison, Christopher. *France and Islam in West Africa, 1860–1960.* Cambridge, Eng.: Cambridge University Press, 1988.

Hause, Stephen. *Women's Suffrage and Social Politics in the French Third Republic.* Princeton: Princeton University Press, 1984.

Headrick, Daniel. *The Tentacles of Progress: Technology Transfer in the Age of Imperialism.* Oxford: Oxford University Press, 1988.

———. *The Tools of Empire: Technology and European Imperialism in the Nineteenth Century.* Oxford: Oxford University Press, 1981.

Heisser, David R. "The Impact of the Great War on French Imperialism, 1914–1924." Ph.D. diss., University of North Carolina, 1972.

Hildreth, Martha. *Doctors, Bureaucrats, and Public Health in France, 1888–1902.* New York: Garland, 1987.

Hobsbawm, Eric. "Introduction: Inventing Traditions." In Eric Hobsbawm and Terence Ranger, eds., *The Invention of Tradition,* pp. 1–14. Cambridge, Eng.: Cambridge University Press, Canto edition, 1995.

Hobsbawm, Eric, and Terence Ranger, eds. *The Invention of Tradition.* Cambridge, Eng.: Cambridge University Press, Canto edition, 1995.

Hopkins, Anthony G. *An Economic History of West Africa.* New York: Columbia University Press, 1973.

Idowu, H. Oludare. "Assimilation in 19th Century Senegal." *Cahiers d'études africaines* 9, no. 2 (1969): 194–218.

Jennings, Lawrence C. *French Reaction to British Slave Emancipation.* Baton Rouge: Louisiana State University Press, 1988.

Johnson, G. Wesley. *The Emergence of Black Politics in Senegal: The Struggle for Power in the Four Communes, 1900–1920.* Stanford: Stanford University Press, 1971.

———. "The Impact of the Senegalese Elite upon the French, 1900–1940." In G. Wesley Johnson, ed., *Double Impact: France and Africa in the Age of Imperialism,* pp. 155–179. Westport, Conn.: Greenwood Press, 1985.

———. "William Ponty and Republican Paternalism in French West Africa, 1866–1915." In L. H. Gann and Peter Duignan, eds., *African Proconsuls: European Governors in Africa,* pp. 127–156. New York: Free Press, 1978.

Johnson, G. Wesley, ed. *Double Impact: France and Africa in the Age of Imperialism.* Westport, Conn.: Greenwood Press, 1985.

Julien, Charles-André. *Histoire de l'Algérie contemporaine.* Vol. 1, *La conquête et les débuts de la colonisation, 1827–1871.* Paris: Presses universitaires de France, 1954.

July, Robert W. *The Origins of Modern African Thought.* New York: Praeger, 1967.

Kanya-Forstner, A. S. *The Conquest of the Western Sudan: A Study in French Military Imperialism.* Cambridge, Eng.: Cambridge University Press, 1969.

Kelly, Gail. "Interwar Schools and the Development of African History in French West Africa." *History in Africa* 10 (1983): 163–185.

———. "The Presentation of Indigenous Society in the Schools of French West Africa and Indochina, 1918–1938." *Comparative Studies in Society and History* 26, no. 3 (1984): 523–542.

Kern, Stephen. *The Culture of Time and Space, 1880–1918.* Cambridge, Mass.: Harvard University Press, 1983.

Klaits, Joseph, and Michael H. Haltzel, eds. *The Global Ramifications of the French Revolution.* Cambridge, Eng.: Woodrow Wilson Center Press and Cambridge University Press, 1994.

Klein, Martin. *Islam and Imperialism in Senegal: Sine-Saloum 1847–1914.* Stanford: Stanford University Press, 1968.

———. "Slave Resistance and Slave Emancipation in Coastal Guinea." In Suzanne Miers and Richard Roberts, eds., *The End of Slavery in Africa,* pp. 203–219. Madison: University of Wisconsin Press, 1988.

———. "Slavery and Emancipation in French West Africa." In Martin Klein, ed., *Breaking the Chains: Slavery, Bondage and Emancipation in Modern Africa and Asia,* pp. 171–196. Madison: University of Wisconsin Press, 1993.

Klein, Martin, ed. *Breaking the Chains: Slavery, Bondage and Emancipation in Modern Africa and Asia.* Madison: University of Wisconsin Press, 1993.

Kloosterboer, W. *Involuntary Labour since the Abolition of Slavery: A Survey of Compulsory Labour throughout the World.* Leiden: Brill, 1960.

Knibiehler, Yvonne. *Cornettes et blouses blanches: Les infirmières dans la société française 1880–1980.* Paris: Hachette, 1984.

Knibiehler, Yvonne, and R. Goutilier. *La femme au temps des colonies.* Paris: Stock, 1985.

Kuisel, Richard F. *Capitalism and the State in Modern France: Renovation and Economic Management in the Twentieth Century.* Cambridge, Eng.: Cambridge University Press, 1981.

———. *Ernest Mercier: French Technocrat.* Berkeley: University of California Press, 1967.

La Berge, Ann. *Mission and Method: The Early Nineteenth-Century French Public Health Movement.* Cambridge, Eng.: Cambridge University Press, 1992.

La Berge, Ann, and Mordechai Feingold, eds. *French Medical Culture in the 19th Century.* Amsterdam: Rodopi, 1994.

Laffey, John. "The Roots of French Imperialism in the Nineteenth Century: The Case of Lyon." *French Historical Studies* 6, no. 1 (1969): 78–92.

Lagana, Marc. *Le parti colonial français: Eléments d'histoire.* Sillery: Presses de l'Université du Québec, 1990.

Lambert, Michael. "From Citizenship to *Négritude*: 'Making a Difference' in Elite Ideologies of Colonized Francophone Africa." *Comparative Studies in Society and History* 35, no. 2 (1993): 239–262.

Landes, Joan. *Women in the Public Sphere in the Age of the French Revolution*. Ithaca: Cornell University Press, 1988.

Langley, J. Ayodele. *Pan-Africanism and Nationalism in West Africa, 1900–1945*. Oxford: Clarendon Press, 1973.

Latour, Bruno. *The Pasteurization of France*. Trans. Alan Sheridan and John Law. Cambridge, Mass.: Harvard University Press, 1988.

Laurens, Henry, with Charles C. Gillispie, Jean-Claude Golvin, Claude Traunecker. *L'Expédition d'Egypte: La Révolution française et l'Islam, 1798–1801*. Paris: A. Colin, 1989.

————. *Les origines intellectuelles de l'expédition d'Egypte: L'orientalisme islamisant en France (1698–1798)*. Istanbul: Editions Isis, 1987.

Lebon, André. *La politique de la France en Afrique, 1896–1898*: Mission Marchand—Niger—Madagascar. Paris: Plon, 1901.

Lebovics, Herman. *True France: The Wars over Cultural Identity 1900–1945*. Ithaca: Cornell University Press, 1992.

Leitch, David Archibald. "The Colonial Ministry and Governments General in the French Empire before 1914." Ph.D. diss., Cambridge University, 1985.

Lejeune, Dominique. *Les sociétés de géographie en France et l'expansion coloniale au XIXe siècle*. Paris: Albin Michel, 1993.

Léonard, Jacques. *Les médecins de l'ouest au XIXe siècle*. 3 vols. Lille: Atelier Reproduction des Thèses, 1978.

Lequin, Yves, ed. *L'histoire des étrangers et de l'immigration en France*. Paris: Larousse, 1992.

Lewis, Martin D. "One Hundred Million Frenchmen: The Assimilationist Theory in French Colonial Policy." *Comparative Studies in Society and History* 4, no. 2 (1962): 129–153.

Liauzu, Claude. *Aux origines des tiers-mondismes: Colonisés et anticolonialistes en France (1919–1939)*. Paris: L'Harmattan, 1982.

Le livre des expositions universelles, 1851–1989. Editions des arts décoratifs. Paris: Herscher, 1983.

Lochore, R. A. *History of the Idea of Civilization in France*. Bonn: L. Röhrscheid, 1935.

Lokke, Ludwig. *France and the Colonial Question: A Study of Contemporary French Opinion, 1763–1801*. New York: Columbia University Press, 1932.

Lombard, Jacques. *Autorités traditionnelles et pouvoirs européens en Afrique noire: Le déclin d'une aristocratie sous le régime colonial*. Paris: A. Colin, 1967.

————. *Structures de type 'féodal' en Afrique noire: Etudes des dynamismes internes et des relations sociales chez les Bariba du Dahomey*. Paris: Mouton, 1965.

Lorcin, Patricia. *Imperial Identities: Stereotyping, Prejudice and Race in Colonial Algeria*. London: I. B. Tauris, 1995.

Lovejoy, Paul, ed. *Africans in Bondage: Studies in Slavery*. Madison: University of Wisconsin Press, 1986.

Lucas, Philippe, and Jean-Claude Vatin. *L'Algérie des anthropologues*. Paris: F. Maspéro, 1975.

Lundgreen, Peter. "The Organization of Science and Technology in France: A German Perspective." In Robert Fox and George Weisz, eds., *The Organization of Science and Technology in France, 1808–1914*, pp. 332–363. Cambridge, Eng.: Cambridge University Press, 1980.

Lunn, Joe Harris. "Memoirs of the Maelstrom: A Senegalese Oral History of the First World War." Ph.D. diss., University of Wisconsin–Madison, 1993.

Lyautey, Maréchal Hubert. "Le sens d'un grand effort." In *L'Illustration, Numéro spécial sur l'Exposition Coloniale et Internationale de Paris*. Paris, May 23, 1931.

Maclane, Margaret. "Railways and 'Development Imperialism' in French West Africa Before 1914." *Proceedings of the Western Society for French History* 18 (1991): 505–514.

Madiéga, Georges. "Esquisse de la conquête et la formation territoriale de la colonie de Haute-Volta." *Bulletin de l'IFAN* 43, ser. B, nos. 3–4 (1981): 217–277.

Magasa, Amidu. *Papa-commandant a jeté un grand filet devant nous: Les exploités des rives du Niger, 1900–1962*. Paris: F. Maspéro, 1978.

Maier, Charles. *Recasting Bourgeois Europe: Stabilization in France, Germany and Italy in the Decade after World War I*. Princeton: Princeton University Press, 1975.

Manchuelle, François. "Assimilés ou patriotes français? Naissance du nationalisme culturel en Afrique française (1853–1930)." *Cahiers d'études africaines* 35, no. 2 (1995): 333–368.

———. "Le rôle des Antillais dans l'apparition du nationalisme culturel en Afrique francophone." *Cahiers d'études africaines* 32, no. 3 (1992): 375–408.

Mandell, Richard D. *Paris 1900: The Great World's Fair*. Toronto: University of Toronto Press, 1967.

Mangeot, Général. *La vie ardente de Van Vollenhoven*. Paris: F. Sorlot, 1943.

Mangolte, Jacques. "Le chemin de fer de Konakry au Niger." *Revue française d'histoire d'outre-mer* 55, no. 1 (1968): 37–105.

Mann, Kristin, and Richard Roberts, eds. *Law in Colonial Africa*. Portsmouth, N.H.: Heinemann, 1991.

Manning, Patrick. *Slavery, Colonialism, and Economic Growth in Dahomey, 1640–1960*. Cambridge, Eng.: Cambridge University Press, 1982.

Marcovich, Anne. "French Colonial Medicine and Colonial Rule: Algeria and Indochina." In Roy Macleod and Milton Lewis, eds., *Disease, Medicine and Empire: Perspectives on Western Medicine and the Experience of European Expansion*, pp. 103–117. London: Routledge, 1988.

Marseille, Jacques. *L'âge d'or de la France coloniale*. Paris: Albin Michel, 1986.

———. *Empire colonial et capitalisme français: Histoire d'un divorce.* Paris: Albin Michel, 1984.

Martin, Gaston. *L'abolition de l'esclavage, 27 avril, 1848.* Paris: Presses universitaires de France, 1948.

Martin, Phyllis H. *Leisure and Society in Colonial Brazzaville.* Cambridge, Eng.: Cambridge University Press, 1995.

Masson, André. "L'opinion française et les problèmes coloniaux à la fin du second Empire." *Revue française d'histoire d'outre-mer* 51, nos. 3–4 (1962): 366–435.

Mayeur, Jean-Marie, and Madeleine Rebérioux. *The Third Republic from Its Origins to the Great War, 1871–1914.* Trans. J. R. Foster. Cambridge, Eng.: Cambridge University Press and Editions de la Maison des Sciences de l'Homme, 1984.

Mbodj, Mohamed. "The Abolition of Slavery in Senegal, 1820–1890: Crisis or the Rise of a New Entrepreneurial Class?" In Martin Klein, ed. *Breaking the Chains: Slavery, Bondage and Emancipation in Modern Africa and Asia*, pp. 197–214. Madison: University of Wisconsin Press, 1993.

M'Bokolo, Elikia. "Du 'commerce licite' au régime colonial: L'agencement de l'idéologie coloniale." In Daniel Nordman and J. P. Raison, eds., *Sciences de l'homme et conquête coloniale: Constitution et usages des sciences humaines en Afrique, XIXe et XXe siècles*, pp. 205–221. Paris: Presses de l'Ecole Normale Supérieure, 1980.

———. "Peste et société urbaine à Dakar: L'épidémie de 1914." *Cahiers d'études africaines* 22, no. 1 (1982): 13–46.

McClellan, James E. *Colonialism and Science: Saint Domingue in the Old Regime.* Baltimore: Johns Hopkins University Press, 1992.

McKay, John. *Tramways and Trolleys: The Rise of Urban Mass Transport in France since 1789.* Princeton: Princeton University Press, 1976.

McMillan, James. *Housewife or Harlot: The Place of Women in French Society, 1870–1940.* New York: St. Martin's Press, 1981.

Meillassoux, Claude, ed. *L'esclavage en Afrique précoloniale.* Paris: F. Maspéro, 1975.

Mercier, René. *Le travail obligatoire dans les colonies africaines.* Paris: Larose, 1933.

Meyer, Jean, Jean Tarrade, Annie Rey-Goldzeiguer, and Jacques Thobie. *Histoire de la France coloniale.* Vol. 1, *Des origines à 1914.* Paris: A. Colin, 1991.

Michel, Marc. *L'appel à l'Afrique: Contributions et réactions à l'effort de guerre en A. O. F. 1914–1919.* Paris: Publications de la Sorbonne, 1982.

———. *Gallieni.* Paris: Fayard, 1989.

Miers, Suzanne, and Richard Roberts, eds. *The End of Slavery in Africa.* Madison: University of Wisconsin Press, 1988.

Miller, Christopher L. "Unfinished Business: Colonialism in Sub-Saharan Africa and the Ideals of the French Revolution." In Joseph Klaits and Michael H. Haltzel, eds., *The Global Ramifications of the French Revo-*

lution, pp. 105–126. Cambridge, Eng.: Woodrow Wilson Center Press and Cambridge University Press, 1994.

Mitchell, Alan. *The Divided Path: The German Influence on Social Reform in France after 1870.* Chapel Hill: University of North Carolina Press, 1991.

Moitt, Bernard. "Slavery and Emancipation in Senegal's Peanut Basin: The Nineteenth and Twentieth Centuries." *International Journal of African Historical Studies* 22, no. 1 (1989): 27–50.

Monéta, Jakob. *La politique du parti communiste français dans la question coloniale, 1920–1963.* Paris: F. Maspéro, 1971.

Moseley, Katheryn Payne. "Indigenous and External Factors in Colonial Politics: Southern Dahomey to 1939." Ph.D. diss., Columbia University, 1975.

Moses, Claire Goldberg. *French Feminism in the Nineteenth Century.* Albany: State University of New York Press, 1984.

Moulin, Anne Marie. "Bacteriological Research and Medical Practice in and out of the Pastorian School." In Ann La Berge and Mordechai Feingold, eds., *French Medical Culture in the 19th Century*, pp. 327–349. Amsterdam: Rodopi, 1994.

———. "Patriarchal Science, the Network of the Overseas Pasteur Institutes." In Patrick Petitjean, Catherine Jami, and Anne Marie Moulin, eds., *Science and Empires: Historical Studies about Scientific Development and European Expansion*, pp. 307–322. Dordrecht: Kluwer Academic Publishers, 1991.

Moulin, Annie. *Peasantry and Society in France since 1789.* Trans. M. C. and M. F. Cleary. Cambridge, Eng.: Cambridge University Press, 1991.

Murard, Lion, and Patrick Zylberman. "De l'hygiène comme introduction à la politique expérimentale (1875–1925)." *Revue de synthèse*, 3d ser., no. 115 (1984): 313–341.

———. "La raison de l'expert ou l'hygiène comme science sociale appliquée." *Archives européenes de sociologie* 26, no. 1 (1985): 58–89.

Murphy, Agnes. *The Ideology of French Imperialism, 1871–1881.* Washington, D.C.: Catholic University Press, 1948.

Newbury, Colin. "The Formation of the Government General of French West Africa." *Journal of African History* 1, no. 1 (1960): 111–128.

———. "The Government General and Political Change in French West Africa." *St. Anthony's Papers* 10, African Affairs, no. 1 (1961): 41–59.

Nicolet, Claude. *L'idée républicaine en France (1898–1924).* Paris: Gallimard, 1982, 1994.

Noiriel, Gérard. *Le creuset français: Histoire de l'immigration, XIXe–XXe siècles.* Paris: Seuil, 1988.

Nord, Philip. *The Republican Moment: Struggles for Democracy in Nineteenth-Century France.* Cambridge, Mass.: Harvard University Press, 1995.

———. "Republican Politics and the Bourgeois Interior in Mid-Nineteenth

Century France." In Suzanne Nash, ed., *The Home and its Dislocations in Nineteenth-Century France*, pp. 193–214. Albany: State University of New York Press, 1993.

———. "The Welfare State in France, 1870–1914." *French Historical Studies* 18, no. 3 (1994): 821–838.

Nordman, Daniel, and J. P. Raison, eds. *Sciences de l'homme et conquête coloniale: Constitution et usages des sciences humaines en Afrique, XIXe et XXe siècles.* Paris: Presses de l'Ecole Normale Supérieure, 1980.

Nye, Robert. *Crime, Madness and Politics in Modern France: The Medical Concept of National Decline.* Princeton: Princeton University Press, 1984.

Oloruntimehin, B. Olatunji. "The Economy of French West Africa between the Two World Wars." *Journal of African Studies* 4, no. 1 (1977): 51–76.

Opoku, Kwame. "Traditional Law under French Colonial Rule." *Verfassung und Recht in Ubersee* 2, no. 1 (1974): 139–155.

Osborne, Michael. "The Medicine of the Hot Countries, Philology, and European Settlement in Algeria, 1830–1870." Paper presented at the Davis Seminar, Princeton University, Apr. 19, 1990.

———. *Nature, the Exotic, and the Science of French Colonialism.* Bloomington: Indiana University Press, 1994.

Pagden, Anthony. *European Encounters with the New World: From Renaissance to Romanticism.* New Haven: Yale University Press, 1993.

Pasquier, Roger. "Les débuts de la presse au Sénégal." *Cahiers d'études africaines* 2, no. 3 (1962): 477–489.

Paul, Harry. *From Knowledge to Power: The Rise of the Science Empire in France, 1860–1939.* Cambridge, Eng.: Cambridge University Press, 1985.

Peabody, Sue. *There Are no Slaves in France: The Political Culture of Race and Slavery in the Ancien Régime.* Oxford: Oxford University Press, 1996.

Pedersen, Susan. *Family, Dependence and the Origins of the Welfare State: Britain and France, 1914–1945.* Cambridge, Eng.: Cambridge University Press, 1993.

Péhaut, Yves. *Les oléagineux dans les pays d'Afrique occidentale associés au marché commun.* Paris: H. Champion, 1976.

Pelissier, Paul. *Les paysans du Sénégal: Les civilisations agraires du Cayor à la Casamance.* Saint Yvieux: Imprimerie Fabrègue, 1966.

Perkins, Kenneth J. *Qaids, Captains, and Colons: French Military Administration in the Colonial Maghrib, 1844–1934.* New York: Africana, 1981.

Persell, Stuart M. *The French Colonial Lobby, 1889–1938.* Stanford: Hoover Institution Press, 1983.

Petitjean, Patrick, Catherine Jami, and Anne Marie Moulin, eds. *Science and Empires: Historical Studies about Scientific Development and European Expansion.* Dordrecht: Kluwer Academic Publishers, 1991.

Pheffer, Paul. "Railroads and Aspects of Social Change in Senegal." Ph.D. diss., University of Pennsylvania, 1975.

Picciola, André. "Quelques aspects de la Côte d'Ivoire en 1919." *Cahiers d'études africaines* 13, no. 2 (1973): 239–274.

Pinkney, David. *Decisive Years in France, 1840–1847.* Princeton: Princeton University Press, 1986.

Pluchon, Pierre. *Nègres et Juifs au XVIIIe siècle: Le racisme au siècle des lumières.* Paris: Tallandier, 1984.

Popkin, Richard H. "The Philosophical Basis of Eighteenth-Century Racism." *Studies in Eighteenth-Century Culture* 3 (1973): 245–442.

Prakash, Gyan, ed. *After Colonialism: Imperial Histories and Postcolonial Displacements.* Princeton: Princeton University Press, 1995.

Prévaudeau, Albert. *Joost Van Vollenhoven, 1877–1918.* Paris: Larose, 1953.

Price, Roger. *The Modernization of Rural France: Communications Networks and Agricultural Market Structures in Nineteenth Century France.* New York: St. Martin's Press, 1983.

Prost, Antoine. *Histoire de l'enseignement en France, 1800–1967.* Paris: A. Colin, 1968.

Pruneddu, Jacky. "La propagande coloniale et l'image du noir sous la Troisième République (1870–1914)." In Daniel Nordman and J. P. Raison, eds., *Sciences de l'homme et conquête coloniale: Constitution et usages des sciences humaines en Afrique, XIXe et XXe siècles,* pp. 223–238. Paris: Presses de l'Ecole Normale Supérieure, 1980.

Pyenson, Lewis. *Civilizing Mission: Exact Sciences and French Overseas Expansion, 1830–1940.* Baltimore: Johns Hopkins University Press, 1993.

———. "Cultural Imperialism and Exact Sciences Revisited." *Isis* 84, no. 1 (1993): 103–108.

Rabinbach, Anson. *The Human Motor: Energy, Fatigue and the Origins of Modernity.* New York: Basic Books, 1990.

Rabinow, Paul. *French Modern: Norms and Forms of the Social Environment.* Cambridge, Mass.: MIT Press, 1989.

Renault, François. "L'abolition de l'esclavage au Sénégal. L'attitude de l'administration française (1848–1905)." *Revue française d'histoire d'outremer* 58, no. 1 (1971): 5–80.

Rey-Goldzeiguer, Annie. *Le royaume arabe: La politique algérienne de Napoléon.* Alger: Société nationale d'édition et de diffusion, 1977.

Richter, Melvin. "Tocqueville on Algeria." *Review of Politics* 25, no. 3 (1963): 362–398.

Robert, André. *L'évolution des coutumes de l'ouest africain et la législation française.* Paris: Librairie autonome, 1955.

Roberts, Mary Louise. *Civilization without Sexes: Reconstructing Gender in Postwar France, 1917–1927.* Chicago: University of Chicago Press, 1994.

Roberts, Richard. "The Case of Faama Mademba Sy and the Ambiguities of Legal Jurisdiction in Early Colonial French Soudan." In Kristin Mann and Richard Roberts, eds., *Law in Colonial Africa,* pp. 185–204. Portsmouth, N.H.: Heinemann, 1991.

———. "The End of Slavery in the French Soudan, 1905–1914." In Suzanne Miers and Richard Roberts, eds., *The End of Slavery*, pp. 282–307. Madison: University of Wisconsin Press, 1988.

———. *Warriors, Merchants, and Slaves: The State and the Economy of the Middle Niger Valley, 1700–1914*. Stanford: Stanford University Press, 1987.

Roberts, Richard, and Martin Klein. "The Banamba Slave Exodus of 1905 and the Decline of Slavery in the Western Sudan." *Journal of African History* 21, no. 3 (1980): 375–394.

Roberts, Stephen. *History of French Colonial Policy, 1870–1925*. 2 vols. London: P. S. King, 1929.

Robinson, David. *Chiefs and Clerics: Abdul Bokar Kan and Futa Toro, 1853–1891*. Oxford: Clarendon Press, 1975.

———. "Ethnography and Customary Law in Senegal." *Cahiers d'études africaines* 32, no. 2 (1992): 221–237.

Rosanvallon, Pierre. *L'état en France de 1789 à nos jours*. Paris: Seuil, 1990.

———. *Le sacre du citoyen: Histoire du suffrage universel en France*. Paris: Gallimard, 1992.

Saar, Dominique. "La Chambre Spéciale d'Homologation de la Cour d'Appel de l'Afrique Occidentale Française et les coutumes pénales 1903–1920." *Annales africaines* 1 (1974): 101–115.

———. "Jurisprudence des tribunaux indigènes du Sénégal: Les causes de rupture du lien matrimonial de 1872 à 1946." *Annales africaines* 2 (1975): 141–178.

Saar, Dominique, and Richard Roberts. "The Jurisdiction of Muslim Tribunals in Colonial Senegal." In Kristin Mann and Richard Roberts, eds., *Law in Colonial Africa*, pp. 131–145. Portsmouth, N.H.: Heinemann, 1991.

Sabatier, Peggy. "Educating a Colonial Elite: The William Ponty School and Its Graduates." Ph.D. diss., University of Chicago, 1977.

———. "'Elite' Education in French West Africa: The Era of Limits, 1903–1945." *International Journal of African Historical Studies* 11, no. 2 (1978): 247–267.

Said, Edward W. *Culture and Imperialism*. New York: Knopf, 1993

———. *Orientalism*. New York: Vintage, 1979.

Sala-Molins, Louis. *Le Code Noir, ou, le calvaire de Canaan*. Paris: Presses universitaires de France, 1987.

Salleras, Bruno. "La peste à Dakar en 1914: Médina ou les enjeux complexes d'une politique sanitaire." *Thèse de 3e cycle*, Ecole des Hautes Etudes en Sciences Sociales, 1984.

Salomon-Bayet, Claire, et al. *Pasteur et la révolution pastorienne*. Paris: Payot, 1986.

Schivelbusch, Wolfgang. *The Railway Journey: The Industrialization of Time and Space in the Nineteenth Century*. Berkeley: University of California Press, 1986.

Schnapper, Bernard. *La politique et le commerce français dans le golfe de la Guinée de 1838 à 1871.* Paris: Mouton, 1961.

———. "Les Tribunaux musulmans et la politique coloniale au Sénégal (1830–1914)." *Revue historique de droit français et étranger* 39, no. 1 (1961): 90–128.

Schneider, William H. *An Empire for the Masses: The Image of West Africa in Popular French Culture, 1870–1900.* Westport, Conn.: Greenwood Press, 1980.

———. *Quality and Quantity: The Quest for Biological Regeneration in Twentieth-Century France.* Cambridge, Eng.: Cambridge University Press, 1990.

Schor, Ralph. *L'opinion française et les étrangers, 1919–1939.* Paris: Publications de la Sorbonne, 1985.

Schreyger, Emil. *L'Office du Niger au Mali: La problématique d'une grande entreprise agricole dans la zone du Sahel.* Wiesbaden: Steiner, 1984.

Searing, James F. "Accommodation and Resistance: Chiefs, Muslim Leaders and Politicians in Colonial Senegal, 1890–1934." 2 vols. Ph.D. diss., Princeton University, 1985.

———. *West African Slavery and Atlantic Commerce: The Senegal River Valley, 1700–1860.* Cambridge, Eng.: Cambridge University Press, 1993.

Seck, Assane. *Dakar, métropole ouest-africaine.* Dakar: IFAN, 1970.

Seeber, Edward D. *Anti-Slavery Opinion in France during the Second Half of the Eighteenth Century.* Baltimore: Johns Hopkins University Press, 1937. Reprint, New York: Greenwood Press, 1969.

Shapiro, Ann-Louise. *Housing the Poor of Paris, 1850–1902.* Madison: University of Wisconsin Press, 1985.

Shinn, Terry. *L'Ecole Polytechnique: Savoir scientifique et pouvoir social, 1794–1914.* Paris: Presses de la Fondation Nationale des Sciences Politiques, 1980.

Sibeud, Emmanuelle. "La naissance de l'ethnographie africaniste en France avant 1914." *Cahiers d'études africaines* 34, no. 4 (1994): 639–658.

Silverman, Deborah. *Art Nouveau in Fin-de-Siècle France: Politics, Psychology, and Style.* Berkeley: University of California Press, 1989.

Skinner, Elliot P. *The Mossi of the Upper Volta: The Political Development of a Sudanese People.* Stanford: Stanford University Press, 1964.

Smith, Bonnie. *Ladies of the Leisure Class: The Bourgeoises of Northern France in the Nineteenth Century.* Princeton: Princeton University Press, 1981.

Snyder, Francis G. *Capitalism and Legal Change: An African Transformation.* New York: Academic Press, 1981.

———. "Colonialism and Legal Form: The Creation of Customary Law in Senegal." *Journal of Legal Pluralism* 19, no. 1 (1981): 49–90.

Spence, Jonathan D. *The Search for Modern China.* New York: Norton, 1990.

Spiegler, J. S. "Aspects of Nationalist Thought Among French-Speaking West Africans, 1921–1939." Ph.D. diss., Oxford University, 1968.

Spivak, Gayatri C. *In Other Worlds: Essays in Cultural Politics.* New York: Methuen, 1987.

Stocking, George W., Jr. *Victorian Anthropology.* New York: Free Press, 1987.

Stoler, Ann. "Making Empire Respectable: The Politics of Race and Sexual Morality in 20th-Century Colonial Cultures." *American Ethnologist* 16, no. 4 (1989): 634–660.

———. "Rethinking Colonial Categories: European Communities and the Boundaries of Rule." *Comparative Studies in Society and History* 31, no. 1 (1989): 134–161.

Stone, Judith. *Sons of the Revolution: Radical Democrats in France, 1862–1914.* Baton Rouge: Louisiana State University Press, 1996.

Stovall, Tyler. "Color-blind France? Colonial Workers During the First World War." *Race and Class* 35, no. 2 (1993): 35–55.

Summer, Anne, and R. W. Johnson. "World War I Conscription and Social Change in Guinea." *Journal of African History* 19, no. 1 (1978): 25–38.

Suret-Canale, Jean. "A propos de Vigné d'Octon: Peut on parler d'anti-colonialisme avant 1914?" *Cahiers d'études africaines* 18, no. 2 (1978): 233–239.

———. *L'Afrique noire: L'ère coloniale 1900–1945.* Paris: Editions sociales, 1962.

———. "La fin de la chefferie en Guinée." *Journal of African History* 7, no. 3 (1966): 459–493.

———. "Un pionnier méconnu du mouvement démocrate et national en Afrique." *Etudes dahoméenes* 3, no. 1 (1964): 5–30.

Swindell, Ken. "SeraWoolies, Tillibunkas and Strange Farmers: The Development of Migrant Groundnut Farming along the Gambia River, 1848–1895." *Journal of African History* 21, no. 1 (1980): 93–104.

Taguieff, Pierre-André. *La force du préjugé: Essai sur le racisme et ses doubles.* Paris: La Découverte, 1987.

Talmy, Robert. *Histoire du mouvement familiale en France, 1896–1939.* 2 vols. Lille: Aubenas, 1962.

Taylor, Maxine. "French Scientific Expeditions in Africa during the July Monarchy." *Proceedings of the Western Society for French History* 16 (1989): 243–252.

Thobie, Jacques, Gilbert Meynier, Catherine Coquery-Vidrovitch, and Charles-Robert Ageron. *Histoire de la France coloniale.* Vol. 2, *1914–1990.* Paris: A. Colin, 1990.

Thomson, Ann. *Barbary and Enlightenment: European Attitudes toward the Maghreb in the 18th Century.* Leiden: Brill, 1987.

Touré, Oussouby. "Le refus du travail forcé au Sénégal oriental." *Cahiers d'études africaines* 24, no. 1 (1984): 25–38.

Trentadue, Michel. "Mouvements commerciaux et évolution économique de la Guinée de 1928 à 1938: L'essor de la spécialisation bananière." *Revue française d'histoire d'outre-mer* 63, nos. 3–4 (1976): 575–587.

————. "La société guinéene dans la crise de 1930: Fiscalité et pouvoir d'achat." *Revue française d'histoire d'outre-mer* 63, nos. 3–4 (1976): 629–639.

Turin, Yvonne. *Affrontements culturels dans l'Algérie coloniale: Ecoles, médecines, religion, 1830–1880.* Paris: F. Maspéro, 1973.

Unesco General History of Africa. Vol. 7, *Africa Under Colonial Domination 1880–1935,* ed. A. Adu Boahen. Paris: Unesco, 1985.

Van Beusekom, Monica. "Colonial Rural Development: French Policy and African Response at the Office du Niger, Soudan Français (Mali), 1920–1960." Ph.D. diss., Johns Hopkins University, 1989.

Van Hoven, Ed. "Representing Social Hierarchy. Administrators-Ethnographers in the French Sudan: Delafosse, Monteil, and Labouret." *Cahiers d'études africaines* 30, no. 2 (1990): 179–198.

Villandre, Jean-Jacques. "Les chefferies traditionnelles en Afrique occidentale française." *Thèse pour le doctorat,* University of Paris, Law Faculty, 1950.

Vodouhe, Capko. "La création de l'Afrique occidentale française, 1895–1904." *Thèse de 3e cycle,* University of Paris, 1974.

Warshaw, Dan. *Paul Leroy-Beaulieu and Established Liberalism in France.* De Kalb: Northern Illinois University Press, 1991.

Weber, Eugen. *France: Fin de Siècle.* Cambridge, Mass.: Harvard University Press, 1986.

————. *Peasants into Frenchmen: The Modernization of Rural France, 1879–1914.* Stanford: Stanford University Press, 1976.

Weiskel, Timothy C. *French Colonial Rule and the Baule Peoples: Resistance and Collaboration, 1889–1911.* Oxford: Clarendon Press, 1980.

————. "Labor in the Emergent Periphery: From Slavery to Migrant Labor Among the Baule Peoples, 1880–1925." In Walter L. Goldfrank, ed., *The World-System of Capitalism: Past and Present,* pp. 209–233. Beverly Hills: Sage, 1979.

Williams, Elizabeth. "Anthropological Institutions in Nineteenth-Century France." *Isis* 76, no. 2 (1985): 331–348.

Williams, Marshall, and Glyndwyr Williams. *The Great Map of Mankind: Perception of New Worlds in the Age of Enlightenment.* Cambridge, Mass.: Harvard University Press, 1982.

Williams, Rosalind. *Dream Worlds: Mass Consumption in Late Nineteenth-Century France.* Berkeley: University of California Press, 1982.

Wooten, Stephen. "Colonial Administration and the Ethnography of the Family in the French Sudan." *Cahiers d'études africaines* 33, no. 3 (1993): 419–446.

Worboys, Michael. "The Emergence of Tropical Medicine: A Study in the Establishment of a Scientific Specialty." In Gérard Lemaine et al., *Perspectives on the Emergence of Scientific Disciplines,* pp. 75–98. The Hague: Mouton, 1976.

Worboys, Michael, and Paulo Palladino. "Science and Imperialism." *Isis* 84, no. 1 (1993): 91–102.

Wright, Gwendolyn. *The Politics of Design in French Colonial Urbanism.* Chicago: University of Chicago Press, 1991.

Zeldin, Theodore. *France 1848–1945: Intellect and Pride.* Oxford: Oxford University Press, 1980.

Index

In this index an "f" after a number indicates a separate reference on the next page, and an "ff" indicates separate references on the next two pages. A continuous discussion over two or more pages is indicated by a span of page numbers, e.g., "57–59." *Passim* is used for a cluster of references in close but not consecutive sequence.

Library of Congress Cataloging-in-Publication Data

Conklin, Alice L.
  A mission to civilize: the republican idea of empire in
  France and West Africa, 1895–1930 / Alice L. Conklin.
    p.   cm.
  Includes bibliographical references and index.
  ISBN 0-8047-2999-9 (cloth: alk. paper)
  ISBN 0-8047-4012-7 (pbk.: alk. paper)
    1. Africa, French-speaking West—Politics and gov-
  ernment—1884-1960.   2. Governors general—Africa-
  French-speaking West—History.   3. France—Colonies—
  Administration—History.   4. France—Politics and
  government—1870-1940.   5. Racism—France—
  History.   6. Republicanism—France—History.
  I. Title
  JQ336-.C69   1997
  325′.344′0966—dc21
                                                          97-9868
                                                             CIP

⊗ This book is printed on acid-free, recycled paper.

Original printing 1997
Last figure below indicates year of this printing:
10   09   08   07   06   05